Losing Control

Losing Control
How and Why People Fail at Self-Regulation

Roy F. Baumeister
Department of Psychology
Case Western Reserve University
Cleveland, Ohio

Todd F. Heatherton
Department of Psychology
Harvard University
Cambridge, Massachusetts

Dianne M. Tice
Department of Psychology
Case Western Reserve University
Cleveland, Ohio

Academic Press
San Diego   New York   Boston   London   Sydney   Tokyo   Toronto

This book is printed on acid-free paper. ∞

Academic Press
A Division of Harcourt Brace & Company
525 B Street, Suite 1900, San Diego, California 92101-4495

United Kingdom Edition published by
Academic Press Limited
24-28 Oval Road, London NW1 7DX

Library of Congress Cataloging-in-Publication Data

Baumeister, Roy F.
    Losing control : how and why people fail at self-regulation / by
  Roy F. Baumeister, Todd F. Heatherton, Dianne M. Tice,
        p.   cm.
    Includes bibliographical references and index.
    ISBN 0-12-083140-6
    1. Self-control.   2. Self-management (Psychology)   I. Heatherton,
  Todd F.   II. Tice, Dianne M.   III. Title.
  BF632.B29   1994
  158'.1--dc20   94-17313
                                                            CIP

PRINTED IN THE UNITED STATES OF AMERICA
              99 QW 9 8 7 6 5 4

Contents

Part I
Basic Issues

1 Introduction: Self-Regulation Failure in Social and Theoretical Context

2 General Patterns and Mechanisms of Self-Regulation Failure

Part II
Controlling Thoughts, Feelings, and Actions

Part III
Controlling Impulses and Appetites

Part IV
Conclusion

Preface

For over two decades, the broad topic of "the self" has been one of the most studied issues in psychology, and indeed in all the social sciences. The focus of psychological research has shifted among multiple aspects of the self, however. Researchers were quick to grasp the importance of studying self-concepts and self-esteem, and the study of self-presentation likewise did not have to wait long to enjoy a great deal of attention.

The aspect of the self as an entity that controls itself, however, has been slower to attract the attention of researchers. Indeed, it was not until the late 1980s that social psychology and personality journals began to feature a large number of articles on self-regulation. Although some thinkers had indeed already begun talking about issues of self-regulation in the 1960s, the larger research community only seemed to awaken to the full importance of the topic in the last half dozen years or so. Several reasons for the delay could be suggested, including the lack of effective methodologies and the higher priority given to studying other areas. Alternatively, one could put the reasons for the delay in a more positive way, based on societal interests. When the baby boom was in adolescence and trying to find itself, issues of forming identity and learning about the self-concept were salient; and when the baby boomers were embarking on career development, they brought attention to issues of making good impressions on others. In the 1980s, a broad set of social problems, from dieting to drug addiction, focused attention on the issues of self-control.

Whatever the reason, it is clear that many psychologists now regard self-regulation as one of the most fascinating and important issues to study under the entire umbrella of research on the self. We share that belief. Some years ago we set out to bring together all the scattered research on self-regulation in the hope of making a broad synthesis. As we read the reports of numerous investigators and attended to our own data, we gradually came to the conclusion that what was most needed, most interesting, and most appropriate given the current state of knowledge was a synthesis of work on self-regulation failure. This book is our effort to provide that synthesis.

This book took much longer to write than we originally planned and hoped. Two main reasons accounted for this delay. First, it was very difficult simply to get the material together: there is an immense amount of research, presented in many different guises and in different jargons and languages, scattered through many different journals and places. Second, we had to keep refining our ideas to enable them to encompass such a broad and diverse range of phenomena.

Ultimately it may be impossible to bring together every bit of empirical evidence available. Probably most experts in the field could think of yet another subtopic or set of studies that could have been included in this work. Our efforts to cover everything gradually receded from the possible. Thus, for example, we had initially planned to have one chapter on impulse control; instead, we now have five. Likewise, our original plan was to have one short chapter on controlling thoughts and feelings, but we ended up with two long chapters with a great deal of material. Although we cannot cover everything, we have managed to cover a wide range of phenomena in considerable detail, and that gives us reason to be confident that our conclusions and general theories are well founded.

We began this work because we believed that self-regulation was an important topic. These several years of work have greatly increased our appreciation of its importance, both for basic theorizing about human self-hood and for practical application to many pressing social problems. We hope that our work will be useful both to those seeking to solve society's troubles and to those seeking to understand human nature.

Acknowledgments

This book is based on our collaborative research from 1989 to 1994, with most of the writing being done in 1993–1994. During that time, we were aided and supported by multiple sources, without which this book might never have emerged.

Roy Baumeister is grateful for grants from the National Institute of Mental Health (United States), the Humboldt Foundation (Germany), and the Cattell Fellowship Fund (United States). He also thanks the Elsie B. Smith family for their endowment of his professorship at Case Western Reserve University during that time. He is indebted to Case Western Reserve University for a leave of absence during 1991 and for a sabbatical during 1993–1994, as well as to the institutions which hosted him during those leaves, the Max-Planck-Institute (1991) and the University of Virginia (1993–1994).

Todd Heatherton gratefully acknowledges the support of the Social Sciences and Humanities Research Council (Canada) for his postdoctoral fellowship and Case Western Reserve University as the host institution for that fellowship. Subsequently, he was supported by Harvard University, and is particularly grateful to the students in several seminars on self-regulation that he taught during that time.

Dianne Tice expresses her thanks to Case Western Reserve University for its support and for both a leave of absence and a sabbatical, to the Max-Planck-Institute in Munich, Germany, for financial support and facilities during the first leave, and to the University of Virginia, which supported her as host institution for the sabbatical.

Part I
Basic Issues

Introduction: Self-Regulation Failure in Social and Theoretical Context

Self-regulation failure is the major social pathology of the present time. As America lurches toward the end of the twentieth century, it finds itself beset by all manner of social problems and discontents. Some of these reflect problems of social structure and have economic and sociological roots, but others are based in the difficulties that individual citizens have in managing their lives. Many of these individual difficulties revolve around the inability to control oneself. All over the country, people are miserable because they cannot control their money, their weight, their emotions, their drinking, their hostility, their craving for drugs, their spending, their own behavior vis-à-vis their family members, their sexual impulses, and more. America is regarded by some observers as a society addicted to addiction: Therapies and support groups proliferate, not just for alcoholics and heroin addicts, but for people who cannot control a craving for Coca-Cola, an impulse to beat their children, an urge to masturbate or sleep with multiple strangers, a debt balance on credit cards, or the daily consumption of coffee or chocolate. Some of these problems are large, while others seem small to all but those who suffer from them; but they share an acutely vexed awareness of failure at self-regulation.

The consequences of these problems go beyond individuals. Self-regulation failure is central to many of the problems that are widely discussed and bemoaned as allegedly hastening the decline and doom of America. Teen pregnancy and single parenthood, which supposedly perpetuate a cycle of poverty and which threaten the cherished images of family life, are often the result of a failure to regulate one's sexual actions—either by abstaining from intercourse or, at least, by taking contraceptive precautions. Heedless, uncontrolled, unsafe sex has also brought epidemics of several major venereal diseases, from AIDS to gonorrhea. Drug abuse, alcoholism, and binge eating all consist of an inability to stop oneself from indulging one's appetites to excess.

Economists note with chagrin that the American economy suffers because our citizens save and invest much less of their money than citizens of other industrialized countries, and one reason for this is an inability to discipline one's private finances. Indeed, the lack of fiscal discipline goes much further than an inability to save; many people find themselves chronically in debt. Many middle-class citizens struggle with huge credit card balances and ballooning mortgage payments and other debts, while some working-class citizens live in constant fear of having their telephone service or electricity shut off or their furniture repossessed because of unpaid bills, and others find themselves still making monthly payments on cars that have already gone to the junkyard.

Americans continue to pledge lifelong fidelity at their weddings, but in fact they are getting divorces in record numbers, and it took a series of major scares about incurable and deadly venereal diseases to slow the rise in extramarital sex. Instead of working out marital problems, Americans head for divorce court, and many people repeat the cycle with a series of stormy marriages and costly divorces. A new willingness to talk about family problems has revealed epidemic levels of domestic violence: One out of eight or nine American husbands admits to physically attacking his wife in the past year, and wives are equally or perhaps even more likely to attack their husbands (although the husbands are less likely to suffer serious injury). Marital rape, once considered to be a contradiction in terms, has now become recognized as a widespread problem. Children are beaten uncontrollably and are sexually abused as well. Elderly parents are beaten by their grown offspring.

Impulsive crimes have risen steadily. Statistics on rape, muggings, murder, robbery, assault, and similar offenses show alarming increases. The increase is not primarily due to any rise of organized crime or planned criminal activity, but rather it mostly indicates a tendency for people to give in to violent impulses. One sign of this is that our prisons are overflowing, not with Mafiosi, but with school dropouts and the offspring of neglecting, absent, alcoholic or addicted, criminal, or abusive parents, who tend to fail worst at instilling self-control in their children.

Meanwhile, even the most law-abiding citizens suffer from problems arising from lack of self-control. Health experts routinely say that many, perhaps even most, causes of American deaths are preventable if only people would regulate their behaviors better: quit smoking, eat right, exercise regularly.

The school achievement of American pupils lags behind the rest of the industrialized world. There are multiple reasons for the problems of our schools, but the lack of self-discipline of our students is among them. Students cut class, fail to complete homework assignments, disrupt classrooms with misbehavior, and drop out altogether. Instead of learning, many students spend their time in school distracted with issues of violence, weapons, drugs, and sex. Even the most talented students often seem to think that the route to success is less a matter of hard work, good study habits, and meeting deadlines, than of doing extra-credit projects, being creative, and circumventing authoritarian rules with clever excuses and well-phrased requests for special treatment.

Currently there seems to be a widespread hope, which is probably no more than an absurd and idle fantasy, that raising self-esteem will solve these problems. If only we loved ourselves more, the assumption is, all our problems would vanish. From the perspective of self-regulation theory, the fascination with self-esteem is a pathetic and self-indulgent wish. People mess up their lives with various forms of irresponsible behavior, such as abusing alcohol or drugs, spending more money than they have, or abusing marital trust. When the destructive consequences of self-regulation failure catch up with them and they contemplate the sorry state of their lives, they feel a loss of self-esteem. As a result, they come to associate the problem with the loss of self-esteem—but conclude, wrongly, that the low self-esteem is the cause rather than the result of their reckless or self-destructive behavior. Solving their problems would in fact require hard work and self-discipline to change their patterns of behavior and deny themselves the instant gratification of their impulses. Instead of accepting that sober reality, however, people wish that they could effect a magical transformation by merely deciding not to feel guilty any more. They wish to forgive themselves (and be forgiven by others) for their misdeeds and to start a new chapter of their lives with a clean slate and a generous dose of self-admiration. Unfortunately, this prescription does not change the core problems of poor self-regulation; in fact, it merely offers the individual a way to avoid learning from his or her mistakes. It seems likely to lead merely to another round of indulgent, irresponsible behavior and another set of problems.

The three authors of this book have spent many years doing research on self-esteem (e.g., Baumeister, 1982, 1993a; Baumeister, Heatherton, & Tice, 1993; Baumeister, Tice, & Hutton, 1989; Heatherton & Polivy, 1992; Tice, 1991, 1993). Normally, researchers like to see the variables they study become a focus of national interest, because it increases the recognition of one's own work. We cannot, however, go along with the national preoccupation with self-esteem. In our view, America is not suffering from low self-esteem. It suffers from a spreading epidemic of self-regulation failure.

The importance of self-regulation failure has not escaped the attention of social scientists. Psychological research on issues of self-control has expanded dramatically since the middle of the 1980s. Unfortunately, there is not much coordination of this research. Researchers in multiple fields have examined many phenomena in isolation from each other.

The purpose of this book is to pull together much of this work on self-regulation failure. The goal is understanding rather than intervention or social critique. We hope to assemble the information about self-regulation failure, now scattered among dozens of journals and seemingly unrelated fields of inquiry, in order to identify some general patterns and principles and to offer a resource for others who may wish to know about self-regulation failure for other purposes, including possibly clinical work, social work, policy analysis, and basic research and theorizing. Regarding the last of these, which is closest to our own work, we note that self-regulation failure is of interest in several ways. First, it is an intriguing problem in its own right. Second, it is part of a broader theoretical question of self-regulation per se. (That is, to understand how people control themselves successfully, it is useful to have a body of knowledge about *failures* of self-regulation, so that one can understand the limits and pitfalls of efforts to regulate the self.)

Third, self-regulation is important for the compelling project of understanding the nature of human selfhood. In our view, a very significant and central part of the self is its activity as a self-regulator. No cognitive, motivational, emotional, or behavioral theory about the self can pretend to be complete without addressing the issue of self-regulation.

WHAT IS SELF-REGULATION?

If life is indeed a miracle, then it is a many-sided one, and one of the most miraculous of these sides is the ability of living things to control themselves. Among most species, the ability to alter oneself is confined to certain limited and innately prepared mechanisms, such as homeostasis, but among human beings the ability to exert control over one's own inner states, processes, and responses is extensive.

Most living things have some set of inner mechanisms that regulate the system. Homeostasis, after all, is not a neutral state or passive outcome but a dynamic state that is the product of frequent adjustments in response to constantly changing circumstances. Food is ingested and digested. Body temperature is adjusted. Cuts, bruises, and other tissue damages are repaired. Opponent processes spring into action to offset unusual states and conditions (see Solomon & Corbit, 1974). Thus, living systems are all self-regulating.

Among human beings, however, the capacity for self-regulation far exceeds what most other living things can do. Part of the reason for this is the involvement of the conscious human mind in the process. Human beings develop a broad variety of techniques for regulating their actions and inner states. They do so with reference to far more than a steady-state outcome; indeed, people regulate themselves with reference to ideals, long-range goals, others' expectations, and other standards that may not correspond to anything they have yet experienced. Some people have elevated control over bodily processes to an extraordinary level, such as the yogis who allow themselves to be buried alive for a week or who melt large blocks of ice with their naked bodies.

Human culture has long recognized people's capacity for regulating themselves. Words such as *self-control* and *self-discipline* embody popular conceptions of self-regulation. We shall favor the term *self-regulation*, but from our perspective *self-control* has a very similar meaning and *self-discipline* is only slightly narrower, and we shall use the latter two terms to connect our discussion with the way people talk about these issues and problems in everyday life.

We use the term *self-regulation* broadly, to refer to any effort by a human being to alter its own responses. These responses may include actions, thoughts, feelings, desires, and performances. In the absence of regulation, the person would respond to the particular situation in a certain way, whether because of learning, habit, inclination, or even innate tendencies. Self-regulation prevents this normal or natural response from occurring and substitutes another response (or lack of response) in its place.

Thus, the essential nature of self-regulation is that of *overriding*. In an important sense, self-regulation theory requires that the person (or other organism) have multiple processes or levels of action. One process interrupts or overrides another. For example, a person may wish to complete a certain project at work. While she works, she may feel a growing thirst, as her body uses up its moisture. Normally the increase in thirst would prompt her to get a drink; the urgency of the work, however, may prompt her to override this typical response and stay at her desk until the project is completed. She has regulated her behavior in a way to make it depart from normal or habitual ways of acting.

The concept of overriding encompasses starting, stopping, or changing a process, as well as substituting one outcome or response for another. The most basic form of override, however, is simply to bring a response sequence to a stop. The original and rudimentary form of self-regulation is therefore what we call *self-stopping*: Intervening in one action or response pattern in order to bring it to a halt. Successful self-regulation may involve stopping oneself from drinking another beer, from eating another helping, from thinking about what might have been, from yelling out one's anger, and the like.

Indeed, most forms of self-regulation can in theory be analyzed as instances of self-stopping, although there are some exceptions (such as getting oneself out of bed in the morning, which requires one to start an action rather than to stop one; although in a sense one stops oneself from indulging in the lazy desire to lie in bed). It is an instructive exercise to try to reduce all self-regulation to self-stopping. Although we do not subscribe to such extremely reductionistic views, one can analyze the vast majority of instances of self-regulation in that way. Addicts stop themselves from indulging their cravings; dieters stop themselves from eating; infantry soldiers stop themselves from running away; decision makers stop themselves from being swayed by improper sources or unwelcome evidence; persevering workers stop themselves from giving in to the pain or fatigue that sends an impulse to quit; angry or distressed people stop themselves from dwelling on what upset them; and so forth.

BASIC INGREDIENTS OF SELF-REGULATION

Although this book is focused on self-regulation failure, some initial comments about self-regulation per se need to be made. In other words, it is useful to have some grasp of what the main processes are, in order to understand how they may fail.

It is necessary to begin with the assumption that there is more than one thing going on inside a human being at any given time. Multiple processes operate in parallel in a complex creature such as a human being. At any moment, the body may be regulating temperature, breathing, and digesting food, the mind may be pondering some problem while also replaying some remembered piece of music, and the emotional system may be reacting to thoughts with various feelings. Self-regulation begins with competition among such multiple processes. Self-regulation is a matter of one process overriding another, and that result emerges from competition among these parallel processes.

To understand self-regulation, it is also necessary to have some concept of a hierarchy among these multiple processes. The competing processes are not equal. Indeed, the hierarchy concept was central to one of the most important works on self-regulation, namely the model advanced by Carver and Scheier (1981, 1982). Higher processes involve longer time spans, more extensive networks of meaningful associations and interpretations, and more distal or abstract goals (see also Baumeister, 1991a, 1991b; Vallacher & Wegner, 1985, 1987). Self-regulation involves higher processes overriding lower processes; when the reverse happens, it is *failure* of self-regulation. The person may be torn between the desire for a cigarette and the resolution to quit, and the latter is higher on the hierarchy. If the person manages to avoid smoking in that situation, then that was an instance of successful self-regulation, because the self's resolve overrode the (lower) desire to smoke. It is not self-regulation, however, if the desire to smoke overrides the resolution to abstain. Rather, if the person gives in and has a cigarette, that is a case of self-regulation failure.

Much of the research and theorizing about self-regulation has emphasized the concept of the feedback loops, borrowed from systems theory (Miller, Galanter, & Pribram, 1960; Powers, 1973; Carver & Scheier, 1981, 1982). Feedback-loop theory was advanced in the 1940s in connection with the development of sophisticated weapons such as ballistic missiles, but the most familiar example from everyday life is the room thermostat, which turns on the furnace or air conditioner whenever the room temperature departs from a preset range. Feedback loops are also commonly called TOTE loops; TOTE is an acronym for test-operate-test-exit, reflecting the sequence of steps in such a loop. The initial *test* phase refers to a comparison of current circumstances (e.g., the room temperature, or a person's current dress) to a standard (the desired temperature, or the desired level of dress). If there is a discrepancy, such that current circumstances fall short of the standard, then there is a phase of *operation*: The thermostat turns on the furnace, or the person changes clothes. Then comes another *test*, to see whether the circumstances have reached the goal or not. If not, the system continues to operate to produce change (more heat; further changes in clothes). Finally, when the circumstances measure up to the standard, the system *exits* the loop, and the cycle ends.

The feedback loop model presupposes three things that are important ingredients for self-regulation. First, there must be *standards*; to pursue the example, the thermostat cannot operate without being set to a particular target temperature. When people seek to exert control over themselves, they invoke various standards, which are abstract concepts of how things should be. These may be social norms, personal goals, the expectations of others, and the like. When standards are unclear, ambiguous, lacking, or conflicting, self-regulation will be less effective.

Second, a feedback loop requires some way of *monitoring* the current circumstances (in the test phase). People can only regulate themselves successfully if they pay attention to what they are doing, or if they have some other way of gaining the knowledge of their responses. People who use their charge cards indiscriminately, without keeping track of how much they are spending, will have a much harder time regulating their finances than people who continue to monitor their expenditures.

Third, people must have some means of operating on themselves in order to bring about the desired changes or responses. As we have said, self-regulation involves overriding responses that might normally, naturally, or habitually occur. If people cannot override these, self-regulation will be unsuccessful.

Understanding self-regulation as an override process portrays the problem as one of competition between responses, and indeed in many instances of self-regulatory challenge people feel as if there is an inner conflict going on, in which they are pulled in opposite directions. The decision to keep to a strict diet conflicts with the urge to gobble down that doughnut that someone has placed on the table in front of you. In some sense, therefore, the stronger response wins. Successful self-regulation therefore requires that the responses high in the hierarchy carry enough strength to override the lower tendencies.

This concept of strength resembles the colloquial concept of *willpower*. In the familiar example, a person uses willpower to resist temptation. Strong people will be able to resist; weak people will not. Although this common-sense model may have some shortcomings (for example, we should not assume that strength is a constant quantity that reflects some good or bad property of the person's character), it is valid in some important ways. We shall return to issues of strength repeatedly throughout this book. In particular, factors that deplete or decrease self-regulatory strength may increase the likelihood of self-regulation failure. By the same token, if the lower impulse becomes stronger and stronger—such as if the temptation becomes more appealing, or the person's deprivation becomes more acute—then it may be able to thwart the person's efforts to override it.

IMPORTANCE OF SELF-REGULATION

The central importance of self-regulation to human life has already been suggested by our opening remarks that linked self-regulation failure to many of the major social problems of our contemporary society. Indeed, the notion that self-regulation is important is far from new. Although ancient philosophers and wise men may have neglected to use the term, they nonetheless recognized its importance. Indeed, the Aristotelian exhortation to pursue moderation in all things can be understood as a recommendation that people regulate their desires and their actions so as to prevent destructive, undesirable extremes.

Traditional conceptions of virtue and vice have often referred to self-regulation patterns. Medieval Christians were frequently warned about the "seven deadly sins," for example. Five of the seven—greed (avarice), lust, gluttony, sloth (laziness), and anger (wrath)—referred to issues of self-regulation failure, ones that we shall cover in the pages of this book. Thus, the majority of major sins referred to selfish impulses and actions, and sinners were defined as people who failed to overcome these impulses. Meanwhile, virtues such as fidelity, temperance, loyalty, chastity, prudence, courage, humility, and steadfastness celebrated people who did manage to keep their own behavior up to high standards by resisting temptations and maintaining consistency.

Likewise, the traditional male and female sex roles embodied idealized conceptions of self-regulation, although these often tended to be expressed in somewhat different spheres. Male ideals often invoked heroic feats of self-control, such as conquering one's fear in battle so as to be able to perform effectively and aggressively despite great personal danger. Self-discipline has also been admired in male work, where great accomplishments often require laboring for long grueling hours at strenuous tasks, such as in farming. Female ideals, meanwhile, have placed even greater emphasis on self-control, usually requiring consistent exercise over long periods of time rather than more isolated, heroic feats. The culture has treated self-denial, chastity, fidelity, self-sacrifice, emotional control, and dutiful submission to the sometimes arbitrary and capricious commands of others as feminine virtues, and self-regulation is central to all of those. Indeed, it is possible to say that self-control has been the quintessential feminine virtue in Western culture. Although resisting temptation has been regarded as an important task in the achievement of virtue by either sex, there has generally been greater tolerance of occasional lapses by males (whose periodic indulgence in intoxication, sexual shenanigans, or aggressive misbehavior has been regarded as inevitable and perhaps appropriate), which implies that females have generally been held to higher standards than males for the capacity to overcome desires and impulses (for a discussion, see Bullough & Brundage, 1982).

Recent research has continued to verify the value and importance of self-regulation in various ways, as several examples will readily show. One significant problem in our society is the high divorce rate. Kelly and Conley (1987) examined a broad host of personality and attitudinal factors in order to see which ones predicted marital breakup. Three variables stood out as especially powerful predictors. Two of these were the neuroticism of the husband and the neuroticism of the wife, indicating that (not surprisingly) grumpy, unhappy, irritable people are more prone to marital dissatisfaction and divorce. The only other variable that ranked with those two obvious factors was the husband's impulse control. Thus, marriages break up in large part when husbands are deficient at self-regulation.

In a possibly related finding, Strube, Turner, Cerro, Stevens, and Hinchey (1984) linked lack of control to hostile aggression and family violence. These authors noted that many researchers had suggested that the Type A, coronary-prone personality tended to be accompanied by higher levels of aggression than other personality types, but the nature of this aggressiveness had not been spelled out. Their own research ruled out the notion that Type A aggression is instrumental; instead, it appears that Type A people's aggression often emerges as a hostile response to frustration and an inability to prevent oneself from violent action when one has been angered.

In one of the most provocative studies to examine long-term effects of self-regulatory capabilities, Mischel, Shoda, and Peake (1988) showed beneficial effects lasting for over a decade. More precisely, children who showed a high capacity to resist immediate temptations and choose delayed gratifications while still preschoolers later became more successful and well-adjusted adolescents. In this study, researchers assessed the children's ability to delay gratification when the children were 4 and 5 years old. About 10 years later, the researchers contacted the parents for reports on how the children were doing. The adolescents who had been the most self-controlled children were superior in school performance, social competence, and coping abilities (i.e., being able to deal with frustration and stress effectively). Another follow-up study found that the children who had been most able to delay gratification at age 4 had higher SAT scores when they applied to college! (Shoda, Mischel, & Peake, 1990).

These findings suggest that self-regulatory capacity is a central, powerful, stable, and beneficial aspect of personality. Research by Funder, Block, and Block (1983) has confirmed its importance in personality. High capacity to delay gratification is linked to being attentive, reasonable, intelligent, resourceful, competent, and cooperative (all of these as perceived by teachers and psychologists). Children who have low ability to delay gratification tend to be aggressive, restless, unable to deal with stress, prone to feelings of victimization, and likely to be regarded as sulky and whiny.

Turning from beneficial to destructive patterns, self-regulation again emerges as a central factor. In an important work synthesizing a great deal of research on many types and patterns of crime, Gottfredson and Hirschi (1990) concluded that the most important generalization about crime and criminality is that they arise from lack of self-control. Most crimes are impulsive actions, and most criminals exhibit broad and multifaceted patterns of lacking self-control. We shall return to this in some detail as we examine specific processes of self-control failure; for now, the important point is that self-regulation failure has been implicated as possibly the single greatest cause of destructive, illegal, and antisocial behavior.

To put things in a broader context, it appears that self-regulation is a vital aspect of human adaptation to life. A classic paper by Rothbaum, Weisz, and Snyder (1982) argued that human adaptation involves two processes, which they termed primary and secondary control. Primary control referred to direct efforts at changing the environment in order to suit the self. Secondary control, in contrast, involved changing the self to fit in to the environment. As a way of operating on the self, secondary control can be understood as a concept that is closely related to self-regulation. Thus, self-regulation accounts for roughly half of the adaptive activities of human beings.

And, in fact, self-regulation may be the more important half. When Rothbaum et al. (1982) wrote their article, they argued that people generally began by trying to exert primary control (hence the term) and only resorted to secondary control if primary control failed, but research has failed to support that sequence. In fact, subsequent work by these authors consistently found that measures of secondary control were the ones most closely related to successful adjustment (F. Rothbaum, 1988, personal communication). In their work, as in the work by Mischel et al. (1988), self-regulation emerged as the most powerful and decisive key to becoming a successful, well-adjusted person.

Thus, self-regulation has been widely and justly recognized as an important aspect of personality and of human behavior. Society benefits when its members have high self-control, because social relations remain more orderly, predictable, and constructive. Individuals benefit from self-control, because over the long run they have a better chance of meeting their goals, fulfilling their plans, and adapting to their environment.

PLAN OF BOOK

In this book we plan to survey the research literature in several major domains where self-regulation failure has been studied. In reading these literatures, our goal has been to understand each phenomenon on its own terms and then to look for common patterns and principles that hold up across different domains. These patterns and principles constitute a general understanding of self-regulation failure, which can then be reapplied to the individual spheres and domains. It would be unrealistic to expect all self-regulation failures to follow a single causal process or to conform to a uniform pattern. Still, there do exist broad similarities across multiple spheres, and these deserve careful attention and emphasis.

Chapter 2 will discuss the general patterns and principles that we found in diverse forms of self-regulation failure. We shall present these in the form of a general theoretical discussion of self-regulation failure, derived largely from an understanding of how successful self-regulation functions.

The subsequent chapters will present the evidence about specific spheres of self-regulation failure. Our goal has been to cover the main findings and conclusions about each type of self-regulation failure, regardless of whether it fits our theoretical scheme or not. We shall of course refer back to the general theoretical discussion from Chapter 2 wherever appropriate, but we have sought to avoid a Procrustean policy of forcing all research findings to conform to our ideas.

The main body of the book, therefore, is organized by phenomenon rather than by conceptual process. Thus, for example, rather than covering all instances of underregulation together and then proceeding to all instances of misregulation, we cover both underregulation and misregulation in each chapter. The chapters cover the major areas of self-regulation failure so as to be accessible to readers who have a specific interest in one sphere. The four chapters of Part II involve self-regulation failure in several of the main spheres studied by social and personality psychologists: task performance, self-management, mental processes, and emotions. Part III covers self-regulation failures with regard to impulses and appetites, including eating, drinking alcohol, gambling, smoking, shopping, and aggressive misbehavior.

Our final chapter, then, will summarize the mass of evidence in relation to the general ideas and patterns explained in Chapter 2. We shall also seek to outline areas where knowledge remains most fragmentary and incomplete, in the hope that researchers will redouble their efforts in these areas.

2

General Patterns and Mechanisms of Self-Regulation Failure

The purpose of this chapter is to outline some broad ideas and theories about how self-regulation fails. These can then be examined, tested, and refined in further chapters, in which we examine what is known about specific spheres of self-regulation failure.

There are two main categories of self-regulation failure: *underregulation* refers to a failure to exert control over oneself, and *misregulation* refers to exerting control in a way that fails to bring about the desired result, or particularly in a way that leads to some alternative result. Underregulation is more studied, although recently some evidence has accumulated about misregulation too. Accordingly we shall emphasize underregulation. In any case, the two are quite different and follow different processes, so it is necessary to analyze them separately.

Logically, one might suppose that something in the nature of *overregulation* would be a possible form of self-regulation failure. But overregulation presumably accomplishes its goal, even if it puts extra energy into the task or does more than is necessary, so it is not a form of failure. The only exception would be if overregulation produces some undesirable results, in which case it is a form of misregulation. For that reason, we will not have a separate treatment of overregulation.

The basic features and ingredients of self-regulation were covered in Chapter 1. These include having some standards, monitoring oneself in relation to these standards, and altering the self's responses so as to make them conform better to the standards. Self-regulation failure can occur with any of those: there can be a problem with knowing the standards, a problem with monitoring the self, or a problem with making the self conform to them.

CONFLICTING STANDARDS

The first sort of problem is one of the standards themselves. There could be a complete lack of standards, in which case one does not have any basis for self-regulation (e.g., Karoly, 1993). More common, though, is the problem in which one has multiple standards that are inconsistent, conflicting, or otherwise incompatible. If the person has several conflicting sets of standards, then it is very difficult to decide which one to use as the basis for self-regulation. Shakespeare's *Hamlet*, for example, depicted a young man torn between conflicting standards. On the one hand, he felt his duty as a prince to be loyal to his king, the man whom his mother had married and who had generally treated him well. On the other hand, he suspected the king to be a usurper who had murdered Hamlet's own father, and if these suspicions were correct it was his duty as a son to avenge his father's death. Caught between these incompatible obligations, Hamlet spent much of the drama paralyzed by indecision, ruminating about the proper course of action, misbehaving in various ways, and even seeming to lapse into madness.

Empirical evidence supports the view that self-regulation is severely hampered by conflicting standards. When people have multiple, conflicting goals, they become unable to manage themselves effectively. Paralysis, confusion, and other dysfunctional patterns result, just as they did for Hamlet. Emmons and King (1988) showed that conflicting goals tend to produce rumination rather than action, and in consequence the person fails to make progress toward any goals. Van Hook and Higgins (1988) showed that discrepant, conflicting self-guides (i.e., internal sets of standards) lead to muddled, indecisive, unsure, rebellious responses, confusion about identity, and emotional distress. They noted that these internal conflicts make self-assessment difficult, which contributes to self-regulatory difficulties.

Maphet and Miller (1982) provided similar evidence in a study with children that was based on the assumption that self-control derives from the internalization of instructions originating with an external, controlling agent. These researchers showed that children could effectively obey instructions that prohibited a certain behavior, even weeks after the prohibition was expressed. If the two authority figures (in this case, two experimenters) disagreed about the rules, however, the child was not likely to conform to their instructions.

REDUCTION OF MONITORING

A second prominent cause of self-regulation failure arises when the person ceases to monitor what he or she is doing. As we saw, effective self-regulation requires that the person frequently evaluates self and actions against the relevant standards, to see how one is measuring up. When the monitoring function breaks down, self-regulation becomes difficult if not impossible. In an authoritative overview of the problems that plague clinical, therapeutic efforts to improve self-regulation, Kirschenbaum (1987) concluded that clients' failure to monitor their behavior is a prominent and central cause of self-regulation failure.

A failure of monitoring may be central to one of the most discussed and controversial issues in all of social psychology, namely that of attitude–behavior consistency. For decades, social psychologists studied attitudes on the assumption that people's behaviors are based on their attitudes. Rather abruptly, however, the value of all that work came into question when researchers found that assumption to be false. Wicker (1969) compiled a large body of evidence to suggest that attitudes have at best a weak and inconsistent relationship to behavior. Over the following two decades, attitude researchers scrambled to establish a more compelling link between attitudes and behavior in order to justify the study of attitudes.

One important explanation for the frequent weakness of attitude–behavior correlations was that people often fail to monitor their behavior in relation to these attitudes. Ajzen and Fishbein (1977) pointed out that researchers often measured general attitudes and then sought links to very situationally specific behaviors; for example, a researcher might measure a general attitude about helping other people and then see if those who held the strongest pro-helping attitudes were also the most willing to give blood in response to a specific request. Studies like that often failed to find much of a relationship, partly because people failed to see the request to give blood as relevant to their broad general attitude about helping others. Instead, they may respond to that request in terms of squeamishness about needles, their own commitments or needs to have all their energy that evening, or other factors. Fazio, Powell, and Herr (1983) demonstrated that general attitudes can predict specific behaviors—but mainly when people think about these general attitudes and interpret the immediate situation with reference to them. When reminded of their broad feelings about helping others, for example, people might be more inclined to think of a request to give blood as a test of their helpfulness, and in such cases—that is, when they monitor their behavior against the relevant standards—their behavior does tend to become consistent with their attitudes.

The paradox of *deindividuation* is also related to issues of monitoring. Deindividuation means losing self-awareness and evaluation apprehension, especially as occurring when the person feels submerged in a group of people (e.g., Diener, 1979; Dipboye, 1977). The paradox was that the loss of individuality was often accompanied by behaviors that seemingly reflected the true feelings and impulses of the inner self. What is lost during deindividuation, however, appears to be very much a matter of the monitoring of self; people cease to attend to what they are doing and evaluate their actions against their own personal standards, with the result that ordinary restraints and inhibitions are suspended. Consequently, behavior may reflect impulses and feelings that would normally be held in check.

A familiar example of deindividuation is the lynch mob, that is, a group of people who take it upon themselves to punish and usually kill someone (usually someone accused of a crime). Mullen (1986) showed that factors conducive to a loss of individual self-awareness were associated with more severe, violent, and deadly behavior by lynch mobs. The implication is that when people stop monitoring their actions individually in relation to their personal standards and ideals, they become capable of performing dangerous and violent acts that lie beyond what they would normally do.

More generally, any loss of self-awareness may contribute to self-regulation failure, because attending to self is the essence of the monitoring function. Alcohol, for example, has been shown to reduce self-awareness (Hull, 1981). People lose the capacity to think about themselves, evaluate themselves, compare themselves to standards, and grasp the implications of current events for their future selves. It has long been known that under the influence of alcohol people will do things that they would not ordinarily do, and even things that they will later regret. One reason, apparently, is that alcohol reduces cognitive processing in relation to the self (Hull, 1981). Self-regulation may therefore be more likely to break down under alcoholic intoxication, allowing the person to perform actions that would normally be inhibited or stifled (e.g., Steele & Southwick, 1985).

Likewise, when the mind is preoccupied with other activities, the capacity to monitor the self may be reduced. And in some cases people want to escape from self-awareness, such as when it is unpleasant to think about the self (e.g., after a distressing failure experience), and the flight from self-awareness will often be accompanied by a reduction or cessation of monitoring and, consequently, by patterns of unusual and disinhibited behavior (e.g., Baumeister, 1991a; Heatherton & Baumeister, 1991).

INADEQUATE STRENGTH

We suggested in Chapter 1 that self-regulation involves a kind of strength, analogous to the common-sense concept of willpower. If that is correct, then self-regulation failure may occur when the person's strength is inadequate to the task. In an important sense, self-regulation involves a contest of strength: the power of the impulse and its resulting tendency to act, against the power of the self-regulatory mechanism to interrupt that response and prevent that action.

Strength failure is relevant to the third ingredient of self-regulation, namely the inability to make the self conform to the relevant standards. The problem is not an absence or disappearance of standards, nor is it a failure to monitor the self; indeed, the person may be quite acutely aware of the relevant standard and of his or her failure to live up to it. But the person feels unable to alter his or her responses to bring them into line with the desired, prescribed ones.

The nature of the "strength" that is needed for successful self-regulation can be illuminated by considering self-stopping, which we noted is probably the first and most basic form of self-regulation. Research suggests that self-stopping involves both mental and physical exertion, as suggested by multiple studies.

The cognitive aspect of self-stopping was studied directly by Gilbert, Krull, and Pelham (1988). These authors showed subjects a videotape of a social interaction, and the videotape contained a sequence of irrelevant and meaningless stimuli at the bottom. Subjects in the control condition simply watched the interaction on the film, and subsequent measures showed that they had processed the social information reasonably well. In the experimental condition, however, subjects were instructed to ignore those irrelevant and meaningless stimuli. This should have been easy enough; after all, the control subjects ignored that gibberish without being instructed to do so. The experimental subjects, however, felt they had to exert control over their gaze in order to prevent themselves from looking at the gibberish at the bottom of the screen, and this effort of self-control consumed some of their attention—with the result that they ended up with a more superficial and incomplete impression of what had happened in the interaction they watched. Self-regulation thus appeared to require some mental effort, to the extent that they were less able to attend fully to what they were watching and hence less able to understand its implications.

The link between self-stopping and physical exertion (usually measured in terms of physical arousal) has been suggested by several studies. Wegner, Shortt, Blake, and Page (1990) showed that suppressing thoughts about sex led to an arousal response that was higher than actually thinking about sex—thus, it is arousing to stop oneself from thinking about sex. Pennebaker and Chew (1985) required subjects to tell one lie mixed in with a series of truthful responses, and they found that the lie was associated with both the inhibition of incidental nonverbal behaviors (presumably as a means of stopping oneself from revealing one's untruthfulness) and increased psychophysiological arousal. Notarius, Wemple, Ingraham, Burns, and Kollar (1982) suggested that the inhibition of facial expression of emotion was marked by increases in physiological arousal. Waid and Orne (1982) found that levels of socialization moderated the tendency of inhibitory response conflict to generate high levels of electrodermal response; the implication is that arousal responses such as anxiety, guilt, and fear may be instrumental in enabling people to inhibit antisocial impulses. Thus, self-stopping often depends on those forms of emotional arousal.

Self-stopping thus appears to involve both mental and physical resources. To override an impulse, a habit, or some other tendency, one often has to exert oneself both mentally and physically. The resource that makes such exertion possible can thus be analyzed as a kind of strength. If a lack of strength makes the person unable to create the necessary cognitive or physical response, self-regulation may fail.

There are three main reasons that someone would have inadequate strength for successful self-regulation: one chronic, one temporary, and one external. The person may lack strength because he or she is a weak person who would probably never be able to override that same impulse. Alternatively, the person may be exhausted or tired, and so he or she is unable on some particular occasion to override a habit or impulse. Lastly, the impulse may be so strong that even someone with well-developed self-regulatory skills would be unable to conquer it. Let us consider each of these causes of weakness in turn.

The first is that of chronic weakness, and this is closest to the common-sense notion of willpower as a character trait. It is almost certainly true that some people have more self-discipline than others, are better able to control their actions and feelings, are more capable of resisting temptation. If self-regulatory capacity is a kind of strength, then like a muscle one should be able to increase its capacity over time (by exercising it frequently). Conversely, it should be vulnerable to becoming weak and incapable if it is not challenged regularly. People who are not accustomed to controlling themselves should find it difficult to do so when it suddenly becomes necessary.

Self-regulatory strength has been studied by Funder and Block (1989) under the rubric of *ego control*. In their view, people differ on the trait of being able to control impulses, desires, and actions. Risk taking and a capacity to resist immediate temptations (in order to garner greater but delayed rewards) are related to this trait. Ego control holds similarities to what nonpsychologists might call the trait of willpower.

The second cause is temporary. Strength is a limited resource that can be depleted by multiple, simultaneous demands. Like a muscle, it may become tired if it is subjected to considerable exertions in a relatively short span of time, and so even if it is chronically strong it may lose its capacity to function effectively. At any given time, a person's strength is limited, and so when that is used up the person should become incapable of further self-regulation.

Hence factors that consume the person's strength should contribute to self-regulation failure. Physical tiredness should be one factor; the strength model will predict that people will be less effective at self-regulation when they are tired, such as late in the evening. Likewise, confronting stressful or other circumstances that are unusually demanding should also impair self-regulation. When going through divorce, or when coping with a busy season at work or final examinations in school, for example, people should be more likely to exhibit breakdowns in self-regulation (such as would be reflected in increases in smoking, drinking, or overeating). Even the demands of a new self-regulatory task, such as in setting out on a very tough diet, might consume so much of one's strength that one's self-regulatory capacity breaks down in other spheres (such as the capacity to prevent oneself from speaking crossly to others).

A particularly interesting implication is that people's capacity for self-regulation needs to be managed like any other limited resource. It will not be possible to regulate everything at once. Some months will be better than others to quit smoking, for example; one will be more successful at a time when other demands on one's self-control are relatively low.

The third factor is the strength of the impulse or other response that has to be controlled. If self-regulation depends on one response overriding another, then the strength of the competing response may prevent the override from occurring even if the person has a great deal of self-discipline. The notions of an "uncontrollable impulse" or an "unstoppable desire" reflect the belief that some responses are too strong to be regulated. Self-regulation failure is to be expected in such cases; in general, the stronger the impulse, habit, or desire (or other response), the greater the likelihood of self-regulation failure.

It is also important to remember that impulses and desires do not always remain at the same strength but may become stronger over time. Self-regulation may be initially successful but may eventually fail simply because the competing motivation becomes too strong to be stifled. A simple example of this is the desire to go to the bathroom. Most adults can resist that urge effectively for a period of time, but eventually the need will be too strong to resist, regardless of the person's resources of self-discipline and strength.

The fact that motivations change in strength over time, thereby making the self-regulatory process harder or easier, brings up the relevance of temporal change. The next section will examine an even more important way in which timing affects self-regulatory failure.

PSYCHOLOGICAL INERTIA

Because we have depicted self-regulation as a matter of one response process overriding another, the issue of timing is crucial. Two responses may compete in such a way that one will have precedence at one time but another will have precedence at another. As an example, consider the school pupil doing homework on a Saturday afternoon while tempted to go outside and play. Self-regulation is a matter of overcoming the impulse to go play, in order to make himself persist at his work. As the afternoon wears on, the competition between the two processes may shift repeatedly. Perhaps he was physically restless after lunch and the urge to play was especially strong, but later in the day that may wear off, making it easier to continue working. Perhaps there was a rainstorm, in which case the urge to go outside was likely to vanish entirely. Meanwhile, his devotion to his homework might fluctuate as a function of his encouraging successes, his fatigue, or his frustration with it.

It is thus difficult to generalize about how timing will affect self-regulation. There is one general pattern, however, that in the absence of other fluctuations may prove decisive. This is the fact that response sequences apparently are easiest to override early in the sequence. There may be many actions that could easily be stopped early on but may become difficult to stop once they have gained a certain momentum.

This principle may be designated as psychological *inertia*. The term *inertia* refers to an obsolete and discredited concept in physics, namely that bodies in motion have a force that impels them to continue moving. Physical motion does not constitute or create any such force. Psychological processes, however, may indeed gain such a force. Thus, the longer someone is doing something, the more difficult it may be to get that person to stop.

The implications for self-regulation are important. Self-regulation will be most effective and will require the least strength when it overrides a response as early as possible. The longer one allows an objectionable response to go on, the harder it will be to stop it, just as a bad habit will be harder to break as it becomes more and more ingrained.

Illustrations of inertia are not difficult to find. Consider the example of self-stopping in terms of the person who is on a diet and gets an impulsive wish to have some ice cream. The diet would suffer a serious setback if the person were to go to the freezer, get out a carton of ice cream, and eat the entire carton. In principle, this outcome could be avoided by self-stopping at any point along the way, before the carton is emptied. In practice, however, we suspect it will be easiest to accomplish this early in the sequence. If the person can avoid getting up to walk over to the refrigerator, the diet is saved, and this might be relatively easy. In contrast, stopping may be much more difficult after the carton has been taken out and opened and the person is sitting at the table with the first spoonful of ice cream already in hand. And once the person has begun seriously eating the ice cream, interrupting the binge in progress may be even more difficult.

A similar argument can probably be made about most other instances of self-stopping. Consider illicit sex, for example. Anyone who has preserved his or her virginity through high school in recent decades probably has an implicit understanding of the principle of inertia. Refraining from sex is undoubtedly much easier if one backs away after (or even before) the first kiss than if one waits to intervene until after an hour of passionate necking and after garments have already been unbuttoned, unclasped, and unzipped. The longer one waits, the greater the effort of will that is required to override the sexual response.

The hypothesis of psychological inertia is hardly new or unique in our analysis. Indeed, versions of this hypothesis date back at least to the 1920s, when the Zeigarnik (1927) effect was first demonstrated. The Zeigarnik effect indicated that it is particularly difficult to interrupt a response sequence in the middle, and that as one approaches the fulfillment or conclusion of a sequence of actions, interruption brings increased rumination about the interrupted activity. Presumably there would be less rumination and less desire to resume if the response could be prevented from starting or, that failing, interrupted right away rather than later on.

Inertia should not be overstated. As already noted, it is not the only way in which timing is relevant to self-regulation. Sometimes things can lose their appeal, making self-regulation easier after some satisfaction has reduced the motivation. People do, after all, generally stop eating before they have consumed all the food in the house. Some grow tired of watching baseball games after seeing a couple hundred of them, and so they cease watching without having to exert themselves to override any desire. Even bulimic eating binges eventually come to an end. In short, there are multiple factors that can cause responses to stop after a period of time. But as one significant factor among several, inertia is important.

The implication of inertia is that self-regulation can be achieved most effectively if instigated as early as possible. Prevention will be easier and more effective than interruption. Self-regulation failure may therefore gradually snowball; the crucial thing is for the failure to get started, and once failure has begun, then regaining and reasserting self-control will become progressively more difficult.

But even the matter of snowballing is not as simple as it may seem. When self-regulation begins to fail, there are often other factors that come into play. These lapse-activated causes may be totally irrelevant to the onset of self-regulation failure, but they are decisive in transforming a minor failure into a major breakdown. The next section will examine these.

LAPSE-ACTIVATED CAUSAL PATTERNS

There has been a great deal of attention—not only in the research literature, but also in the popular press, in works of fiction, and even in everyday gossip—to the factors that conspire to bring a person to break the law, or a resolution, or a diet, or a promise, or some other commitment. That first step that crosses over the imaginary line is of considerable interest as well as drama. This is quite justified: After all, breakdowns in self-control do have to start with some signal failure, and the first step is undoubtedly a central event in that story.

But it is not the whole story. The one step across the line may be the only one, and the person can sometimes step back quickly—that is, reassert self-control. The first violation does not necessarily spell disaster. Sometimes, to be sure, the first step leads to another, and another, and another, until there is a full-blown breakdown of self-regulation, but other times it doesn't. Some researchers have focused their attention on just this issue of what causes some missteps to "snowball" into large-scale breakdowns while others remain minor, exceptional violations. The snowball metaphor is popular because it seems to capture the notion of something growing larger and larger as it continues on its way, just as a real snowball grows by picking up snow when it is rolled across a wintry field.

These lapse-activated snowballing patterns have been documented by some researchers under the rubric of *abstinence violation effects* (e.g., Marlatt, 1985). As the term implies, they have been mainly noted by researchers working with impulse control. When people break their diets or fall off the wagon or indulge in other activities that they have forbidden themselves, they often find that the initial lapse is quickly followed by a large-scale indulgence.

The key point here is that there are two sets of causes involved in self-regulation failure. One set consists of the factors that lead to the first lapse in self-control, that is, the first violation of one's program. The second set consists of factors that transform the initial lapse into a major binge. The second set only comes into play when the first set has finished causing the lapse.

The "snowball" metaphor for self-regulatory breakdowns is thus clearly inadequate, for two reasons. First, it leaves out the extremely important issue of what causes the initial lapse. In terms of the metaphor, it skips the question of where the initial, small snowball comes from. Second, not all lapses do end up snowballing into wholesale self-regulatory breakdowns.

An adequate explanation of self-regulation failure may therefore have to deal with two sets of causes which may be almost entirely separate. The first set of causes produces the initial lapse. The lapse, however, activates a second set of causes, which determine what happens next—in particular, whether there is a snowballing effect in which self-regulation breaks down extensively.

The recognition that two panels of causes may operate to cause failure is not new, even if theoretical models may change. Here is an account from Evagrius of Pontus, born in A.D. 345, whom Russell (1988) called "the greatest of the monastic psychologists." It is an elaboration of themes developed by the great theologian Origen:

> Our souls, having fallen from heaven and now being embedded in the body, are bent, their vision of God blurred. They are dominated by emotional turmoils they cannot shake off. . . . From turmoil arise worldly desires, which open gates for the demons lurking to attack us. Watching us carefully, Satan sees when we are weakened by a particular desire and then sends into the breach demonic troops suited and trained to exploit that particular temptation. Alert to each tiny breach, the demons pour through the hole and enlarge the beachhead. A desire for a woman may quicken in a man's heart, for example; the demons will rush in, flooding the mind with lewd images until his soul is a boiling cauldron. A woman may begin to dwell too much upon the investments she plans for her financial security; the demons will obsess her with money, turning need into greed and enslaving her to avarice. (quoted by Russell, 1988, p. 92)

Evagrius's explanation is especially relevant to a modern psychological approach if one can dismiss the supernatural forces as being merely metaphoric (which Evagrius himself probably would not have done, to be sure). He explains the initial lapse in terms of loss of strength as due to external stress and the mental and emotional overload of coping with the periodic difficulties of life. Amid all that turmoil, the person gives in to some temptation and indulges some impulse. That act of yielding sets in motion other forces (Satan's demons) that enter the picture after the initial breach of proper behavior and help transform the small misstep into a major breakdown.

As we shall find, emotion is often relevant to self-regulation failure—and not necessarily in the way Evagrius suggested, as a cause of the initial weakness, but rather as a factor that contributes to snowballing. In other words, emotions often enter the picture as lapse-activated causes. When a person violates a personal rule or goal or maxim, he or she may have an (often unexpected) emotional response. That emotion may influence subsequent behavior and contribute to the snowballing effect.

A vivid illustration of the role of emotion in lapse-activated causal patterns is provided in research on extramarital sex (see Lawson, 1988). Many people (particularly men, according to Lawson) reportedly commit their first act of infidelity in a desire for sexual novelty and adventure, and they firmly expect that the episode will remain a minor fling that will pose no threat to their marriage. Once they begin, however, some of them find themselves falling in love with the new sex partner. The affair ceases to be casual and can indeed lead to a breakup of the marriage. In short, the unexpected emotional reaction to the initial action helps produce a snowballing involvement that has serious consequences.

More generally, there are multiple ways in which emotional responses to an initial self-regulatory lapse can figure in lapse-activated causation and set the snowball in motion. Emotion involves arousal, and it consumes and manipulates attention; thus, it uses up both physical and mental strength that might otherwise be available for self-stopping. In addition, sometimes the emotion itself becomes a source of further motivations, such as a desire to continue to have sex or a need to escape guilt. Someone who has long abstained from alcohol or drugs, for example, may feel guilty after an initial lapse, and the desire to blot the guilt out of his or her mind may prompt the person to consume more of the forbidden substance.

One of the ironies of this duality of causal patterns is that certain factors that may support self-regulation in the initial phase can turn about and contribute to self-regulatory failure in the second phase. As an example, consider *zero-tolerance* beliefs, similar to the ones recently touted by American officials in response to drug use. The zero-tolerance view is that no misstep, no violation, can be allowed, because it will lead almost inevitably to disaster. There is no gray area, no allowance made for minor indulgences, no sympathy of occasional backsliding. Instead, all the attention and effort are focused on making certain that self-regulation is 100% effective at preventing any lapse at all.

Zero-tolerance beliefs are promoted on the not unreasonable assumption that if no one starts taking drugs, no one will become addicted. There is no danger of snowballing, of minor drugs serving as stepping stones to heavier, more dangerous drugs, of growing disregard for the risks or rising enjoyment of the newly discovered pleasures. As such, these beliefs may well contribute to help people avoid taking that first step across the line.

The problem with zero-tolerance beliefs, however, is that if a lapse does happen these beliefs may contribute to subsequent snowballing. And because people are not perfect and do not live absolutely by the rules 100% of the time, some of these lapses are likely to occur. Zero-tolerance beliefs catastrophize the first step in order to frighten people away from taking it. Once they do take it, however, the catastrophe has already seemingly occurred, so there is no particular reason to stop there. Some people may believe that what really matters, namely absolute compliance, has already failed with that first step (the first drug experience, the first cookie that violates the diet, the first cigarette after quitting, etc.), and so one might as well do some more. Others may notice that no catastrophe occurred after all: One had sex, or smoked pot, or skipped church, and instead of the feared cataclysm life went on just as before. Such discoveries may serve to discredit the authoritative sources that warned one against such indulgences in the first place. The person may then feel some extra urge to explore or indulge further in this hitherto forbidden realm.

Thus, zero-tolerance beliefs can be compared to a military strategy of putting all one's defenses on the front line, with no reserves. The front line is defended maximally well; but if there is a breach, there is no fallback option, and catastrophe ensues.

There are of course other factors that contribute to snowballing effects; we have brought up the zero-tolerance beliefs here merely to illustrate how exactly the same cause, such as a commitment to perfect abstinence, can aid self-regulation and can also undermine and weaken it, depending on the phase of self-regulatory failure. Zero-tolerance beliefs contribute to lapse-activated causes by changing the meaning of an initial lapse. But this is getting ahead of the story. First we must take a more thorough and systematic look at what might cause the initial lapse.

RENEGADE ATTENTION

In reading the research literature on self-regulation, we were repeatedly struck by the central role of attention. In all spheres of self-regulation—controlling emotion, appetites and desires, performances, thought processes, and the rest—the management of attention emerged as a significant factor. Not only was it ubiquitous, but it also seemed widely effective. Managing attention is not only the most common technique of self-regulation, it may well be the most generally effective one (see also Kirschenbaum, 1987).

There are several good reasons for the preeminence of attention in successful self-regulation. In the first place, whatever is not noticed cannot have much in the way of consequences, whereas things that receive extensive attention tend to gain considerable power for producing psychological consequences.

The inertia principle furnishes another reason for the importance of attention. The inertia principle holds that response chains will be harder and harder to interrupt as they go on for longer amounts of time. The implication for self-regulation is that the easiest and most effective approach will be to intervene as early in the response process as possible. Attending to something—noticing it—is inevitably the first step in cognitive processing, and so there is relatively little inertia to overcome. In colloquial terms, attention management is the optimal strategy for nipping something in the bud.

Once the person loses control of attention, self-regulation becomes much more difficult. Any stimulus that manages to capture the person's attention will have a much improved chance of generating psychological reactions, such as impulses and desires, that will require ever greater exertions of self-regulatory strength to overcome. For that reason, the best strategy may be to prevent any dangerous or tempting stimulus to capture one's attention: It is probably easier and more effective to avoid temptation than to resist it. A reformed alcoholic may do quite well in a setting where drinking is neither done nor discussed, because there is little external cause to direct one's attention to the joys of the grape. In contrast, it may be far more difficult to stay on the wagon if the person resumes going to bars with his or her old friends who still drink.

The importance of managing attention leads to a seemingly paradoxical prediction, namely that being preoccupied can have opposite effects on self-regulation. On the one hand, if the person is seriously preoccupied with thinking about certain things, he or she may be less likely to notice tempting or threatening stimuli, and so there will be less difficulty resulting from conflicting impulses that need to be controlled. On the other hand, if such impulses do arise, being preoccupied may make it more difficult for the person to control them. We noted earlier that self-stopping apparently requires some mental resources, and so self-stopping should become more difficult when people are distracted, preoccupied, or operating under some other form of cognitive load.

Attending to the stimulus is not the only important attentional matter, however. One can also think more or less about the standard or goal that self-regulation is supposed to serve. Then, even when confronted with the threatening or tempting stimulus, one may still manage to retain control.

The key to this second attentional trick can be designated as *transcendence*. In essence, it involves seeing beyond the immediate stimulus environment. Other species, such as nonhuman animals, seem to find it very difficult to respond to anything beyond the immediate stimulus environment, but human beings can transcend their surroundings to an almost astonishing degree. Indeed, the history of Christian martyrdom records many examples of individuals acquiescing in their own certain death while singing hymns, which often made a deep impression on their executioners and onlookers. Such responses were possible because the martyrs were able to transcend the death-dealing stimuli in their immediate environment and focus instead on their anticipated rebirth and salvation in heaven.

At a more mundane level, the dieter who passes up the dessert, or the student who continues studying rather than stopping to play or rest, is engaging in transcendence too. One refuses to respond merely to the immediate stimulus and instead responds on the basis of more long-range, more abstract, or more distal goals and standards.

Transcendence too has important implications for self-regulation failure.

Successful self-regulation often requires one to transcend the immediate stimulus environment. When, instead, the immediate stimulus environment floods awareness and the person is unable to look beyond it, self-regulation will be much more difficult. Thus, one important reason for losing control of attention—leading to self-regulation failure—occurs when the person becomes immersed in the immediate present. The transition from a long-term, broadly meaningful state of mind to a here-and-now, concrete focus is likely to accompany and even cause many significant patterns of self-regulatory breakdown.

The most likely mechanism of transcendence failure would involve cognitive shifts that reject broadly meaningful patterns of thought in favor of attending to immediate, concrete stimuli. Vallacher and Wegner (1985, 1987) provided an insightful and influential analysis of how any given act can be conceptualized at multiple levels, ranging from high levels (marked by long-range time spans and broadly meaningful implications) to low levels (marked by short-term immediacy and physical movement rather than meaning). Baumeister (1991b) has applied this idea broadly to explain a variety of patterns by which people seek to escape from self-awareness and unpleasant emotions. Emotion depends on a broadly meaningful understanding, so emotions exist mainly at high levels of thinking (see also Pennebaker, 1989). To escape from emotional distress, people may therefore shift toward more immediate and low-level styles of thinking.

Transcendence is linked to high levels of thinking, of course, so transcendence would fail whenever people escape into immediate, concrete forms of awareness. By the same token, inhibitions typically exist at highly meaningful levels, because inhibitions usually focus on a meaningful action (e.g., murder) rather than low-level acts (e.g., moving a finger in a way that would pull a gun's trigger). Inhibitions (and other forms of self-control) are thus weakened or even removed when awareness shifts down to low levels of meaning.

In general, therefore, we should find that transcendence facilitates self-regulation. When people are able to think beyond the immediate situation and interpret events with reference to long-range meanings and implications, they should be able to exert substantial control over themselves and override many impulses. In contrast, when they become immersed in the here and now and their awareness focuses on mere movements and sensations, self-control will cease to be effective.

ROLLING THE SNOWBALL

Thus far we have considered how self-regulation failures can begin, through loss of control of attention and through failure of strength. These are the things that cause people to step across the line and commit the first offense, first sin, first backslide, and so forth. The major instances of self-regulation failure, however, go far beyond the first step. Indeed, they often seem so extreme that one wonders how the same person could have maintained self-regulation so well up to that point and then lost control to such an extreme. The reason is that the first lapse may set off various reactions that escalate what might otherwise have been a minor lapse into a major breakdown. We turn our attention now to these other factors—in other words, to the lapse-activated causes and the resultant snowballing of self-regulation failure.

We have already mentioned two of the factors that can cause snowballing. First, we noted how zero-tolerance beliefs change their meaning and significance once a violation has occurred. These beliefs may support self-control as long as the person can live up to standards, but once a lapse has occurred, zero-tolerance beliefs tend to imply that the cause is already lost, and so they may foster a tendency to abandon further efforts at self-control. Second, we described the way emotional reactions to the initial lapse can interfere with subsequent self-regulatory efforts.

Another factor that may often contribute to snowballing of self-regulatory failure is a reduction of monitoring. We have already noted that successful self-regulation depends on monitoring oneself so as to compare one's actions and circumstances against the desired standards. Ceasing to monitor oneself can contribute to any phase of self-regulation failure, but there are reasons to think that in many cases it is especially relevant to lapse-activated patterns. More precisely, the person's reaction to the initial lapse may be to stop monitoring. For example, the person may feel guilty about the initial misstep and in order to prevent the feelings of guilt and remorse may make efforts to avoid self-awareness. Once people stop monitoring, it becomes essentially impossible to regulate themselves further.

Reduction of monitoring is actually common to several patterns that may produce snowballing of self-regulation failure. Indeed, zero-tolerance beliefs may even sometimes work by undermining the person's monitoring efforts, because they suggest that there is no longer any point in monitoring oneself.

Some byproducts of self-regulatory lapses may also weaken the tendency to monitor oneself. For example, if one consequence of self-regulatory failure is to drink alcoholic beverages, the person may become unable to monitor. One of the direct effects of alcohol consumption is a reduction in self-awareness (Hull, 1981): People lose the capacity to think about themselves, evaluate themselves, compare themselves to standards, and grasp the implications of current events for their future selves. It has long been known that under the influence of alcohol people will do things that they would not ordinarily do, and even things that they will later regret. One reason, apparently, is that alcohol reduces cognitive processing in relation to the self (Hull, 1981).

Without self-awareness—that is, without being able to reflect on one's actions and think through their implications for one's self—people cannot monitor themselves effectively (see Carver & Scheier, 1981, 1982). Therefore, alcohol use may directly reduce the effectiveness of self-regulation. A person such as a reforming alcoholic, who is trying to avoid drinking, may find that one small violation of being "on the wagon" may quickly snowball into a drunken binge. A reason for this is that the first drink already weakens the capacity to reflect on one's actions, and so the second drink is easier to take than the first, and quickly the person loses count.

Other forms of self-indulgence may also bring an immersion in immediate sensory pleasure that has the same effect, even without the psychophysiological basis, that alcohol has. Thus, the fanatical dieter may find that the first bite of cheesecake after a long period of bland, dull diet food tastes so wonderful that the mind becomes lost in the pleasing sensations and hence stops monitoring what one is doing. Again, the person may quickly lose count of how many bites have been had, until three pieces have been consumed and the person is bloated and suffering from indigestion.

Another, particularly interesting pattern is that of spiraling distress. In some cases, the first lapse of self-regulation may lead, not to pleasure, joy, or relaxation, but to emotional distress. The person may feel guilty, or worried, or disappointed with the self because of having lost self-control, however briefly. (Zero-tolerance beliefs may especially foster such reactions, because they magnify the supposed consequences of any misstep.) This distress is associated with attending to the self, and so it makes it doubly unpleasant to be aware of self. To be sure, some people may respond to this by stepping up their self-monitoring in order to make certain that this does not happen again, but undoubtedly there are many who will be less inclined to monitor themselves when every thought of self brings new distress. In these cases, a vicious cycle develops. Each violation of one's standards brings negative affect, which makes it unpleasant to be self-aware, so the person avoids monitoring his or her own behavior, which makes further violations possible. The longer this goes on, the more unpleasant it is to resume monitoring oneself, because one must recognize that one has severely violated one's desired patterns of behavior.

ACQUIESCENCE: LETTING IT HAPPEN

A theoretically elusive but very important issue is whether people actually acquiesce in their own self-regulation failures. We have analyzed self-regulation failure in terms of depletion of strength and other causes. These make it seem that such failure is something that happens to a person, something that the person is more or less powerless to prevent. On the other hand, some would argue that people allow themselves to fail, that they cooperate in their own failure to exert self-control.

Part of the interest in the issue of acquiescence comes from moral issues. If people cannot help what they are doing, then presumably they cannot be blamed for their self-regulatory failures. On the other hand, if the conscious self actively participates in abandoning self-control, then the person bears some responsibility for the results of his or her actions.

Given the moral (and legal) implications of this debate, there are powerful and outspoken voices in the national media taking sides. Alcoholics and drug addicts wish to be regarded as helpless and relatively innocent victims of genetic predispositions and of external, evil influences, rather than as irresponsible, self-indulgent pleasure seekers. Criminals wish their violent acts to be ascribed to "irresistible impulses" rather than to be regarded as deliberate choices.

Acquiescence is also important for the basic theoretical understanding of self-regulation failure. Thus, the strength model could be taken to imply that acquiescence has nothing to do with it; when the person's strength is gone, self-regulation will inevitably fail. Yet while that may be true, most self-regulation failures probably do not occur when the person's strength is completely gone. The person is merely tired, rather than fully exhausted; and in such circumstances, the person may choose to allow self-regulation to fail, because the tiredness makes the exertion of self-control that much more unappealing. The person does not wish to put forth the effort that would be required for successful self-regulation.

The issue of acquiescence has been in the background of several factors we have discussed. For example, one could object to our analysis of how people stop monitoring their behavior after an initial lapse occurred by saying that the person must be cooperating—acquiescing—in the cessation of monitoring. The dieter *could* count the number of bites, if necessary. The binge drinker is continuing to raise the glass to the lips and to pour or order another drink. The person is thus not a helpless, passive victim of being overwhelmed by forces that make self-regulation impossible; rather, in a sense the person *chooses* to stop keeping track of his or her own behavior and thus actively allows self-regulation to fail (see Peele, 1989).

Although it is very difficult to obtain decisive empirical data regarding the issue of acquiescence, we suspect that acquiescence is the norm, not the exception. It is rare that human behavior is the result of inner forces that the person is entirely helpless to stop or control. Going on a week-long drinking binge is not like the involuntary blinking of the eyes when a blast of hot air hits the face. In explaining self-regulation failure, therefore, the model of human behavior is less one of deterministic cause-and-effect than one of explaining why people allow themselves to lose control.

Often there are powerful factors that contribute to the person's acquiescence. In particular, many circumstances make people want to lose self-awareness, to escape from themselves and forget about the image of self they are projecting to the world (see Baumeister, 1991a). When people have had a bad day, or things have made them lose their sense of being a worthy person, or even when the stress of maintaining an acceptable public image becomes excessive, people may want to "let their hair down" and cease being self-aware. A small sensory indulgence such as a couple of drinks or some tasty dessert may often be part of such a relaxation. But these people will then be extra susceptible to the tendency to cease monitoring after the initial indulgence, because they are precisely wanting to escape from self-awareness.

There may indeed be some cases under which self-regulation is literally impossible and so it fails without any acquiescence by the individual. Undoubtedly there are other cases where people simply allow their self-control to lapse. In the subsequent chapters, we shall examine many forms of self-regulation failure, and these will offer some basis for addressing the question of whether people are to some extent responsible participants in these failures.

MISREGULATION

Our discussion thus far has focused on things that may prevent people from engaging in self-regulation. But this is not the only kind of self-regulation failure. It is also possible for people to engage in active efforts at self-regulation—but to do so in a way that is nonoptimal or counterproductive. In such cases, self-regulation failure may also occur—not because of a lack of trying, but because one used a technique or method that produced some result different from the desired one. In a word, it is *misregulation*, rather than underregulation.

It seems safe to say that the majority of misregulation patterns involve some kind of deficiency in knowledge, especially self-knowledge. The essence of misregulation is that the person tries to engage in self-regulation and knows what effect is wanted, but the regulatory methods produce the wrong effect. The methods must therefore be flawed in some way. If the person knew what the effects of these methods would actually be, he or she would not use them.

The knowledge flaws that lead to self-misregulation can have their origins in multiple places. After all, people are well stocked with beliefs that are simply false (see Gilovich, 1991). Future chapters will examine many ways in which false assumptions can originate, leading to misregulation of self. Let us just briefly review some of them here.

First, there is the problem of *overgeneralization*. People may assume that what works for one problem in one setting will work elsewhere. Thus, for example, many people feel better after consuming a small amount of alcohol, but in fact alcohol narrows attention, and so under some circumstances alcohol can simply focus the mind even more strongly on one's troubles (Steele & Josephs, 1990). When depressed people self-medicate by drinking heavily, they may end up feeling even more depressed (e.g., Doweiko, 1990).

Another factor may be the desire to believe that one can exert control even when one cannot, and so one intervenes with occasionally disruptive consequences. A good analogy is much of premodern medicine. Lacking valid techniques for curing illness, but feeling pressure to do something, premodern physicians resorted to various techniques (such as bleeding the patient or even cutting holes into the skull) that often did more harm than good. As we shall see, some major patterns of failure at task performance result from just such an attempt to control the uncontrollable.

A third source of distortion in self-knowledge is motivated. People want to have particular beliefs about themselves, and these may influence people's efforts to regulate themselves. In particular, people tend to exaggerate their abilities and other good points, and these exaggerations may lead to patterns of overcommitment.

Lastly, the culture may support various beliefs that can hamper optimal self-regulation. For example, American culture fosters the belief that persistence will eventually lead to success. Although persistence undoubtedly increases one's chances of success in many cases, it can also increase the danger of costly setbacks in others, because persistence in a failing or losing endeavor may compound a person's losses.

Misregulation also occurs in some cases because people focus their self-regulatory efforts on the wrong aspect of their behavior. There are two major patterns of this. First, people may sometimes try to control things that are not inherently controllable. Seligman (1994) has argued that people's efforts to control their lives and make themselves better are often thwarted by focusing on things that they cannot control. For example, nearly all researchers agree that most adult women cannot make themselves be as thin as the fashion models that appear on magazine covers. Indeed, the models themselves may often be unable to be that thin; some publications use computer image alteration techniques to stretch the pictures of models, thereby making the women seem thinner. Despite the impossibility of these ideals, and despite evidence that most men do not really want their wives and girlfriends to be so extremely thin, many women diet for years and do other things to try to make themselves conform to those ideals.

The second pattern involves focusing particularly on controlling one's emotions rather than on controlling whatever is the primary concern. Alcohol and drug problems may arise, for example, because people consume these substances as a way of making themselves feel better. Even though they know that excessive consumption may be bad for them, they focus their self-regulatory efforts on their emotional distress rather than on their substance abuse. In a similar vein, people may withdraw effort from a task in order to protect their feelings from the danger of failure, even though they would be better off in the long run to focus their self-regulatory efforts on making themselves persist in order to perform better.

SUMMARY AND CONCLUSION

In this chapter we presented some central concepts for understanding self-regulation failure. There are two main forms. Underregulation consists of a failure to control oneself. Misregulation consists of controlling oneself in a fashion that produces an undesirable or counterproductive outcome.

We began our analysis of underregulation with the three basic ingredients of self-regulation, as suggested in Chapter 1, namely standards, monitoring, and the capacity to alter behavior so as to bring it into line with the standards. A deficiency with any of those will tend to bring about self-regulation failure.

Standards are the conceptions of how one ought to act or be. When people lack standards, or when they have multiple and conflicting standards, self-regulation becomes difficult or even impossible.

Effective self-regulation also depends on monitoring oneself and one's behavior with respect to the standards. Accordingly, self-regulation failure will become more likely when people cease or fail to monitor themselves. When people stop keeping track of what they are doing or become unable (or unwilling) to pay attention to themselves, self-regulation will be impaired.

The most important aspect of the ability to alter one's behavior—the implementation aspect of self-regulation—is a form of strength. Even despite having clear standards and effective monitoring, people may fail at self-regulation because they lack the strength to alter their behavior in the desired fashion. Self-regulatory strength is akin to the colloquial concept of willpower, although it is necessary to remain cautious and skeptical about incorporating such concepts into psychological theory.

There are several main reasons that strength may be inadequate for effective self-regulation. There may be a chronic lack of strength, such as if the person is weak. This notion is closest to the conventional concept of willpower, and it suggests that certain people who lack self-discipline will tend to be vulnerable to many different forms of self-regulation failure at many times. In principle, however, people could build up their strength over time by practicing self-control or learning to regulate themselves effectively.

Alternatively, strength may be temporarily low, either because they are simply tired or because their strength has been depleted by recent exertions. Self-regulation failure may therefore occur when people are exhausted, such as late in the evening, or during times of stress, when there are many competing demands on one's self-regulatory capacity.

Lastly, strength may be inadequate simply because the impulse or behavior is itself too strong to overcome. Most people can control their appetites to some degree, for example, but if they are deprived of food for long enough the desire to eat may become overwhelming.

Several additional concepts are relevant to underregulation. *Inertia* refers to the principle that behaviors in progress are more difficult to override and overcome than behaviors that have not yet begun. Partly because of inertia, the management of attention is generally a crucial aspect of effective self-regulation, because it is the first step in information processing. Self-regulation failure will therefore tend to be marked by a loss of control over attention.

Effective self-regulation often requires adopting a long-range perspective that invokes distal outcomes and higher values—in other words, transcending the immediate situation. One particular form of loss of control of attention is therefore *transcendence failure*, in which the person loses the capacity to see beyond the immediate situation and begins responding mainly to immediate, salient environmental cues.

Unlike underregulation, misregulation occurs despite the fact that the person is successfully controlling his or her own behavior. The person is simply doing this in a counterproductive fashion. Misregulation often arises from faulty assumptions about the self, the world, or the consequences of certain actions. It also arises when people try to control things that cannot be effectively controlled or when they devote their self-regulatory efforts toward protecting their emotions and feelings instead of focusing on the task or problem itself.

Many serious instances of self-regulation failure involve two groups of causes. The first set of causes consists of what leads the person to begin the behavior. The second set, which may only become apparent after that point, transforms the initial behavior into a large-scale breakdown. We have chosen to designate this second set as *lapse-activated causes*, in order to indicate both the switching from one set of contingencies to another and the subsequent escalation (snowballing) of the self-regulatory failure. One example of a lapse-activated causal pattern would be that an initial misdeed creates an emotional reaction that leads to another misdeed, in a vicious cycle. Some causes can even facilitate self-regulation at one stage but hamper it in the other. For example, highly moralistic or absolutist beliefs that catastrophize any misdeed at all may help the person resist the temptation to commit the first misdeed, but if the first misdeed does nonetheless occur, such beliefs then imply that there is nothing left to lose and the person is a hopeless failure, which may then undermine any effort to stop the self-regulation failure from snowballing into a major breakdown.

Part II

Controlling Thoughts, Feelings, and Actions

3

Task Performance and Self-Regulation Failure: Blowing It

One of the most dramatic stories from the 1976 Olympic games occurred during the men's gymnastics team competition, which featured a showdown between the co-favorite teams of Japan and Russia. The rules of the team competition stipulated that six men could compete and the top five scores would count, so one athlete (only) could afford to have a bad performance on each event. Unfortunately for Japan, one of their team members was injured and had to withdraw during the competition, and as a result their team had to go the rest of the way with only five men—which meant that every performance had to count. There was no margin for error left.

As was later revealed, misfortune continued to plague the Japanese team. In the next to last event of the competition, Shun Fujimoto broke his leg slightly near the knee. That would leave them with only four athletes, and their chances to win the gold medal would be destroyed. Fujimoto, however, elected to make his final performance despite the broken leg. The final event was the rings, in which the athlete performs a series of spins and tosses while supporting himself by holding a pair of rings. In principle, one could get away with a serious leg injury if one could keep the leg straight (judges would detract points if the leg moved). The major problem was the dismount: At the end of the routine, the athlete had to spin himself around to build up momentum, let go of the rings, perform a somersault or two while flying through the air, and then land in a standing position. Normally Olympic athletes can execute that dismount maneuver reasonably well, but to spin through the air and land on a broken leg would certainly bring excruciating pain. Undoubtedly Fujimoto knew all through his routine that the dismount would bring intense agony as his spinning, hurtling body landed on the fractured leg.

In a remarkable exercise of willpower, however, Fujimoto performed his exercise very well, never showing any sign of his leg injury until the very end. When it came time to perform his dismount, he showed no hesitation. He launched himself into the air and came down precisely and sharply on his two legs. The only sign of his injury and the resulting pain was the way his leg flinched right after he landed on it, recoiling from the impact, but even then he maintained his balance and put the leg back into position. His performance was so credible that the judges and spectators did not even realize that he was injured, much less that his leg was broken, and when the story broke his routine was replayed over and over on television (and in later years as well). Japan won the team gold medal by the slimmest margin ever, and thus his performance on the rings had proven decisive. Years later, when interviewed, he said he did not know if he could do it again, knowing what it would feel like to land on that broken leg, but he had done it on the crucial occasion and, by doing so, brought his team the gold.

Fujimoto's story reveals an extreme of the self-regulation of performance. While seriously injured and while knowing that an intensely painful and possibly harmful experience (if the injury were further aggravated) is awaiting one at the end of one's performance, one must still execute a strenuous and demanding routine with world-class skill. Any gold medal performance in such a skilled sport requires self-regulation to a high degree, but to maintain one's self-control and concentration in the face of such a distracting prospect—of somersaulting through the air to land on a broken leg—attests to an extraordinary level of self-control.

Fortunately, most performances do not require such heroic exertions, and few people have to have the level of self-regulatory capacity that Fujimoto showed on that memorable occasion. Still, self-regulation is a vital and central ingredient in the successful performance of many tasks, and self-regulation failure can lead to all manner of failure and disappointment.

This chapter will examine self-regulatory failures in the performance realm. (Performance is understood here in the sense of task performance, that is, doing one's best in an achievement or competition or occupational situation.) Performance is vitally important in business, education, sports, warfare, and elsewhere, and anything that impairs effective self-regulation can be costly in many ways.

UNDERREGULATION

Both underregulation and misregulation can lead to performance failures. We begin with underregulation. The essence is that the person performs poorly because the person does not self-regulate enough.

Quitting

To give up and withdraw one's effort from a task is probably the most familiar among the varieties of self-regulation failure that impair performance. Success often depends on trying hard, and so when people withdraw effort, their likelihood of failure is increased. Continued exertion may require self-regulation, because it is strenuous and aversive. You have to make yourself try and try harder. Giving up because you neglect to make yourself keep trying is an important form of underregulation.

In persistence, the role of strength may often be clearer than in some other forms of self-regulation. Persisting at a difficult task may often feel like a strenuous exertion. When strength is depleted, the likelihood of quitting increases. Performers grow tired after a period of exertion, and to keep putting forth effort requires a great deal of willpower—which is to say, it requires effective self-regulation.

It may seem at first that self-stopping is irrelevant, because persisting is the opposite of stopping, but this is misleading. As the mind or body grows tired, the person will feel a natural urge to slow down and rest. It is precisely this urge to relax that becomes the focus of self-stopping, because that is what must be overridden. In effect, one has to stop oneself from quitting.

This sort of conflict can be vividly seen among marathon runners. Every four years, the final event of the Summer Olympics is the men's marathon race. The runners set a furious pace—what would amount to almost a sprint for the average person—and must maintain it for over two hours. Running is not inherently difficult, insofar as nearly everyone knows how to run, and the running techniques of champions are not much different from those of beginners (unlike, say, fencing or Ping-Pong or skiing, where skill increments are long and elaborate). There is no mystery about *how* to win the marathon. The problem is in doing it. The marathon boils down, in an important sense, to a contest of self-regulation. As the miles go by, each runner's body begins ever more insistently to demand a rest, but each runner must continually override that insistent impulse and force the body to continue exerting itself.

What are the factors that make some people give up easily, while others resist the impulse and continue striving? Strength is undoubtedly one factor—not just physical strength, as is obviously needed to run a marathon, but self-regulatory strength in the sense of willpower. Training for a marathon undoubtedly involves the cultivation of self-discipline as well as physical strengthening; we should all be very surprised to learn that a champion marathoner led a private life resembling that of a rock star.

In Chapter 2, we pointed out that self-regulatory strength may have both trait and state effects; that is, self-regulation may fail either because the person is chronically weak, or because the person is temporarily exhausted and depleted. Thus far we have emphasized stable, long-term strength, but there is also evidence that persistence can be affected by short-term demands. Our strength model of self-regulatory capacity suggests that when people's strength is depleted by stress or external demands, the likelihood of self-regulatory failure should increase.

One compelling demonstration of the depletion of self-regulatory strength by stressful demands, with a resulting decrease in task persistence, was provided by Glass, Singer, and Friedman (1969). Subjects in their experiment were initially required to perform a simple task under one of three conditions, one of which involved exposure to stressful, unpredictable noise. Later, in a quiet room, subjects were tested on their capacity to persist at a difficult, frustrating task (which involved repeated attempts to solve unsolvable anagrams). The main outcome measure was how well subjects persisted at this task.

The results were consistent with the strength analysis. People who had had to endure the most stress (i.e., the unpredictable noise) showed a strong tendency to quit earlier than other subjects, who had either not been put through any noise or who had listened to regular, predictable noise patterns (which are much less stressful than unpredictable noise). The authors concluded that there is a "psychic cost" of adapting to stress, such that this cost is reflected in diminished capacity to persist afterward. In plain terms, coping with stress takes something out of you, making you more prone to give up easily during your next task. For present purposes, it appears that some self-regulatory capacity can be depleted by coping with stress.

What else, beyond strength, can contribute to quitting? We proposed in the preceding chapter that attentional control is a vital ingredient of effective self-regulation, and this certainly holds true with performance. Or, more to the point, loss of control of attention is often a key factor in producing self-regulatory failure. Effective persistence despite rising fatigue may depend very heavily on controlling attention. The more one attends to the feelings of pain and weariness, the more difficult it is to resist the urge to relax and quit.

The power of attention was demonstrated in a clever investigation by Pennebaker and Lightner (1980). In a first study, subjects performed on a treadmill, where speed, duration, and other factors were held constant. Subjects who were exposed to distracting sounds reported less fatigue than subjects who were not thus distracted. This pattern suggests that the latter subjects attended to internal sensations and hence felt more tired.

In a second and even more dramatic study, subjects were asked to jog a prescribed distance. Half jogged cross-country, while the other half were assigned to run the same distance on an indoor lap track. The results showed that the joggers were able to run significantly faster outdoors without being any more tired than the indoor joggers. From a purely physical standpoint, the two should have been nearly equal, or if anything it should be more tiring to run outdoors, because the ground is uneven and so there is extra stress on the body. But from a psychological perspective there is one important advantage to the outdoor setting, which is that it is full of appealing distractors. Sky, trees, other people, and plenty of other stimuli are available to keep the outdoor runner's attention away from the feelings of muscular pain and exhaustion. The stimulus-rich outdoor setting contrasts with the stimulus-poor indoor track, where there is nothing to look at except the same few walls and floor. Indoors, one's attention returns all too easily to the inner sensations that are constantly signaling that it would be nice to stop and rest.

Although Pennebaker and Lightner (1980) did not measure persistence per se (indeed, they required everyone to run the same distance), their findings are directly relevant and can easily be extrapolated to persistence. People quit sooner when they are tired, sore, and otherwise fatigued, and so the fact that attentional focus determines subjective feelings of fatigue strongly suggests that attentional focus should be a crucial mediator of persistence.

Indeed, one of the authors of this book had a personal experience that confirmed that attentional manipulations can determine persistence by affecting the self-perception of fatigue in the way Pennebaker and Lightner (1980) showed. While on leave at the Max-Planck Institute in Munich, Germany, he tried to maintain his familiar pattern of jogging, transplanting it from the relatively isolated suburban parks of Cleveland, Ohio, to the large English Gardens in the center of urban Munich. During the winter months, these gardens—actually a sprawling park with meadows, small groups of trees, rapid streams, and hidden beer gardens—were relatively devoid of people except for the most indomitable walkers and occasional bicyclists. He jogged in near solitude, across the snowy meadows and by the icy streams.

As spring began, he suffered a badly sprained ankle, which took a long time to heal because he had no car and therefore had to walk everywhere, and when it began to heal there were several trips to take, and so he did not jog for several months. Finally, as summer was in full bloom, he felt good enough to go out to jog again. Mindful of the still tender ankle, he planned a shorter route than the one he had frequented during the winter. As he began to traverse the park, however, he noticed that it was quite changed. The empty expanses of snow and ice were gone, the fields were full of lush green grass and were packed with sunbathers. Moreover, he was surprised to discover that the European women were in the habit of sunbathing topless and not infrequently bottomless, unlike their counterparts in the American Midwest. Under the influence of these distractions, he forgot about his tender ankle and about his plans to cut short his jogging route—thus persisting longer than he had intended. Only when at last he reached the final group of trees near the end of his run, having left behind the last of these attractive summer scenes, did he notice any painful soreness in the injured ankle!

Self-distraction is not the only attentional or cognitive strategy in self-regulation, of course. Later in this work, when we discuss impulse control, we shall point out that people can either distract themselves from stimuli or, in other cases, can rationalize certain activities in order to keep themselves from worrying about potentially undesirable effects. Performance regulation has a parallel distinction. As we have just seen, persistence is affected by distracting oneself from inner states (such as fatigue) that might lead to quitting.

Using cognitive strategies to reframe stimuli and activities can also be useful, however.

Such reframing is perhaps most important when the task is a boring one. Boredom is an important factor in persistence; it is common knowledge that people find it harder to make themselves persist at a boring task than at an interesting one (e.g., Berlyne, 1960). How, then, can one succeed in making oneself persist at a boring task? One answer is to make it interesting.

Sansone, Weir, Harpster, and Morgan (1992) studied persistence at boring tasks. They found that when people were committed to continuing at a seemingly boring task, they developed cognitive strategies for making it seem more interesting to them. They noted several varieties of such strategies that have emerged from their and others' research. People sometimes enhance the salience of personal challenge posed by some activity, in a sense to make it more difficult for them. Others may focus on issues of personal competence, acting on the principle that even boring tasks are more fun if you feel you are good at them. Still others may seek to inject variety into a task, on the principle that boredom reflects repetition and so any novelty at all will help reduce boredom. Lastly, people try to make the most out of any potentially interesting aspect of the situation, such as by focusing on peripheral or previously overlooked aspects of the surroundings or the activity.

As an example of the latter, Sansone et al. (1992) cited a recent news story about the painfully boring job of inspecting potato chips for uniformity of appearance. One person livened up this job by trying to discover intriguing and seemingly meaningful images in the nonuniform chips. This person gradually developed a collection of special chips, such as one that bore an alleged resemblance to Elvis Presley. Clearly, such an attitude would enhance one's enjoyment (and probably performance) at what would otherwise be an extremely monotonous task.

These studies by Sansone and colleagues have focused on what makes self-regulation more effective, but one can simply look at the converse in order to learn about self-regulatory failure. The clear implication of these findings is that people will be less able to make themselves persist at tedious jobs when they fail to develop cognitive strategies that enhance their interest and involvement (see also Erber & Tesser, 1992; Sansone & Harackiewicz, in press).

Such failures may be part of what we have identified as problems of transcendence. Transcendence involves the capacity to see (and think) beyond the immediate stimuli, and overcoming boredom is precisely such a matter of transcendence. The more one's attention is confined to the immediate activity, the more boring it is likely to be, whereas one transcends the task by thinking about it in the context of some more challenging or engaging activity. When the task is monotonous, a mental attitude that emphasizes here-and-now, narrow awareness is a recipe for boredom, and this will make persistence less likely.

Undoubtedly one of the most studied patterns of quitting is that of learned helplessness (see Seligman, 1975). To be sure, the original evidence for learned helplessness was based on studies with animals (Overmier & Seligman, 1967) and it seems a doubtful stretch to interpret them in terms of self-regulation failure. Among human beings, however, it quickly became apparent that the relevant responses were subject to many different and more complex influences than operated with animals (cf. Roth & Bootzin, 1974; Roth & Kubal, 1975), and it does seem fair to consider self-regulation as one of these.

The essence of learned helplessness is that powerful or multiple experiences of lack of control, particularly associated with failure or trauma, cause a person to give up trying to exert control. The person becomes passive, ceases to try, and becomes unable to learn how to exert control over the environment even when control is available. In the original animal studies, the subjects were exposed to inescapable electric shocks and then put into some situation where they could learn to exert control (such as by escaping further shocks). Normally, animals learn such contingencies rather easily and soon become quite adept at escaping from shocks. "Helpless" animals, however, who had been exposed to the uncontrollable situation, failed to learn the contingencies. Indeed, efforts by researchers to force the animals to learn (such as by demonstrating to them how to escape) often proved fruitless, and the subjects remained helpless victims over many trials, thereby enduring a great deal of avoidable suffering.

Among human beings, it proved necessary to be quite thorough and intense in order to create helpless reactions, presumably because people are accustomed to being in control and so they resist learning that they are helpless. Indeed, in one of the first experiments to test the theory of learned helplessness on people, the researchers were at first pleased to see that they obtained strongly significant results, but then they found out that the results were precisely the opposite of what they had predicted (Roth & Bootzin, 1974)! Apparently, when subjects had been exposed to a situation where they lacked control, they approached their next situation with all the more determination to reassert control, and so they were more aggressive and controlling than subjects who had not received the so-called helplessness training.

In subsequent work, however, it was possible to make people respond like the helpless animals. Roth and Kubal (1975) gave subjects a series of problems to work on, while in fact the problems were unsolvable. Although even this was not enough to make subjects helpless, the researchers did finally succeed with an additional manipulation, which was to tell subjects that the problems were arranged in order of decreasing difficulty. Hence each time the subject failed to find a solution, he or she could be confident that he or she would succeed on the next, presumably easier problem—only to be disappointed and frustrated again. The likely result was a series of experiences of failure and presumably an escalating sense of frustration and helplessness. Following this procedure, subjects were more prone to give up easily and fail to find solutions on another set of (this time solvable) problems.

Attentional control is an important part of learned helplessness patterns in humans. Mikulincer (1989) found that performance was impaired as a function of cognitive interference. These off-task cognitions were particularly concerned with thinking about the self and how the self was inept or incapable of doing well. In Mikulincer's words, "the habitual tendency to turn attention inward makes people more susceptible to the debilitating effects of unsolvable problems" (p. 133). These results suggest that quitting is mediated by thinking that one will fail, consistent with the learned helplessness theory. If one can keep one's mind on the task, one may be better able to maintain effort and perform well, but thinking about the self leads to quitting and failure.

There is a seeming contradiction here. Following Carver and Scheier (1981, 1982), we have suggested that self-awareness generally improves self-regulation, partly because it facilitates the monitoring process. Yet Mikulincer (1989) concluded that attending to self leads to helplessness and thus increases the tendency to give up. Which is correct?

To resolve this contradiction, it is useful to consider what Mikulincer's subjects may have felt when they attended to themselves. Presumably they monitored their performance and concluded that they were not making progress and were not likely to succeed. The more they thought about themselves, the more discouraged and upset they may have felt about their lack of progress. Emotional distress would follow from such self-perceptions, and to avoid further distress people may have become inclined to avoid the task.

These results suggest an important extension of the notion that self-awareness is beneficial for self-regulation. To be sure, people can only be fully effective at regulating their behavior if they monitor it. On the other hand, there are certain circumstances when monitoring oneself will reveal that one is doing very poorly, and the result may be emotional distress that can impair further self-regulation. In particular, emotional distress may make people want to escape the entire situation and the activity they are doing. Under such circumstances, monitoring can accentuate a tendency to give up and abandon an activity.

Indeed, if we combine Mikulincer's results with those of Pennebaker and Lightner (1980), as described earlier in this chapter, it is hard to avoid the conclusion that directing attention away from self is often most effective for self-regulation when persistence at a difficult task is the issue. The reason for this seeming difference is that the source of the impulses that need to be stopped is inside the person in these cases; inner feelings of distress or fatigue can lead to an impulse to quit and escape. In order to self-regulate effectively—that is, to persist—one has to direct attention away from these feelings, in order to resist the temptation to give up. Attending to self is likely to make these feelings all the more salient and thus enhance the impulse to quit. Hence, it may be most effective to direct attention outwardly, toward the task at hand or toward distracting stimuli.

Several theorists have challenged the nature and scope of learned helplessness. The findings themselves are beyond dispute: It is clear that people will sometimes withdraw effort, give up, and fail after receiving discouraging feedback. The mechanisms that lead to this effect, however, have been questioned.

Most likely there are multiple causal pathways. The controversy itself does not concern us here, but one of these challenges indicates another relevant mechanism for why people may quit.

This research was done by Frankel and Snyder (1978). They proposed that people may quit after initial failure, not because they feel passive and helpless and are unable to even try, but because they want to preserve their self-esteem from further blows. They proposed that quitting is thus strategic: People withdraw effort from spheres where failure is likely and threatening. In Frankel and Snyder's study, subjects showed the standard pattern of performing poorly after initial failure feedback. In a crucial condition, however, some subjects were told that the next set of anagrams would be especially difficult. If subjects felt helpless and incompetent, they should have performed especially poorly in this condition, but in fact these subjects performed relatively well. The implication was that the threat to their self-esteem was removed when they were told that the next test would be especially difficult, because it is no disgrace to perform poorly at such a test. Other subjects withdrew effort to protect their self-esteem from further damage, but when the experimenter said that the next test would be so hard that to fail would not endanger one's self-esteem, subjects *were* willing to exert themselves, and as a result they performed well.

Lastly, it is instructive to consider the issue of acquiescence in quitting. To be sure, when the person's resources are fully exhausted, quitting is inevitable. To return to the example of Olympic marathon runners, there are indeed periodic cases in which athletes use up every bit of their strength and need to be carried away on a stretcher to recuperate from exhaustion. These are the exceptions, however. Most quitting appears to involve a rather deliberate decision. Over time, the performer grows increasingly tired or discouraged or bored, and so further persistence demands ever greater exertions of willpower. At some point the person ceases to be willing to put forth that effort and therefore gives up. The role of external factors and events in contributing to fatigue or discouragement is undeniable; still, the person does at some point capitulate and abandon the project. In an important sense, then, self-regulation failure occurs when the person does acquiesce and cooperate with external causes.

Thus, task persistence is an important realm of self-regulation. When people give up or quit prematurely, self-regulation failure is evident. The causes of such failure reflect many of the principles we have emphasized: Loss or lack of strength (such as due to stress or exhaustion), loss of control over attention, inability to transcend the immediate stimuli, threats to self-esteem and the accompanying emotional turmoil, and problems with monitoring and self-awareness. The only one of these that failed to fit the general patterns described in Chapter 2 was the last one, namely monitoring and self-awareness. For persistence at a difficult or boring task, it is often best to reduce attention to self, because impulses to quit may arise from inside the person. When the source of the problematic impulse is inside the person, self-regulation is facilitated by shifting attention to external distractions.

Inablility to Concentrate

Effective performance often requires the ability to concentrate. Solving an equation, writing an essay, or evaluating someone else's work can only be done well if the person pays close attention. An inability to concentrate is thus a potentially powerful cause of poor performance. Moreover, because attention is subject to a variety of automatic, uncontrollable, and external causes, there may be much less acquiescence in concentration problems than in other forms of self-regulation failure.

In a sense, having concentration problems is one of the crucial mechanisms for self-regulation failure that we have emphasized, namely, the inability to control one's attention. In some tasks, however, it ceases to be merely a mechanism and becomes the problem itself.

Some of the findings we have already presented are relevant. Thus, Mikulincer's (1989) evidence that thinking about the self is associated with learned helplessness patterns is very relevant; people become distracted and discouraged by thinking about how bad they are, and these thoughts interfere with performing well. Ruminating and worrying about the self prevented the person from concentrating on the task sufficiently.

Worrying about the self has been identified as a troublesome factor in other spheres of performance failure. Test anxiety, in particular, has been linked to such problems. Test-anxiety is a well-known species of educational failure. The test anxious person is one who presumably knows the material well but is unable to write it down during the examination. A poor grade results, not because the person has failed to learn the material, but because the person becomes paralyzed by anxiety and is unable to perform effectively during the task.

Many theories have been applied to test anxiety, with uneven success. Psychologists have tested hypotheses derived from Freudian theories about castration anxiety, about "fear of success," and about many other issues. Over time, what emerged as the correct interpretation had to do with self-focused attention (see Wine, 1971). Test anxiety involves becoming caught up in thinking about oneself, including worries about one's looming failure and the emotional distress that ensues. Often there appears to be a vicious cycle: When the person starts the exam, he or she soon reaches a question for which he or she does not know the answer, and attention then becomes focused on the inability to produce the answer. As a result, the person sits there obsessed with being unable to come up with the answer and with the associated worry that one will not be able to do well on the test. Soon the person is doing nothing precisely because he or she is so very worried about the fact that he or she is doing nothing.

Thus, once again attention to self has been shown to be destructive for effective self-regulation in task performance. In fact, when people who suffer from test anxiety are guided to shift attention away from themselves (and especially back on to the task), they often find themselves able to perform perfectly well (Sarason, 1981).

Other research suggests that the strength model is relevant to concentration. We already mentioned the stress research by Glass et al. (1969). These authors also included a measure of proofreading effectiveness. Proofreading is a good task for measuring concentration, because the person has to attend carefully to the text in order to spot errors. Glass et al. found that subjects who had to cope with the most stressful (i.e., loud and unpredictable) noise in the first phase of the experiment were the ones who were least effective at proofreading in the second phase, even after the noise was turned off. Once again, the implication was that coping with stress involved a "psychic cost" that depleted some form of self-regulatory strength. This depletion impaired subjects' capacity for making themselves concentrate effectively on the proofreading task.

Research by Keinan (1987) is likewise relevant to the strength model. Keinan showed that stress affected the way people dealt with problems. Under normal, nonstressful conditions, people tended to consider all the alternatives and then select the best one. Under stress, however, they tended to choose the first viable option that they found, even if they had not seen all the options yet. Keinan's results must be regarded as an important first step rather than the definitive answer to all possible questions, but they do suggest very helpful insights into self-regulation. Under stress, people may be unable to make themselves compare and contrast many different alternatives, because their attentional capacity is depleted. Therefore, they evaluate each option they confront on its own merits and take the first good one they find—hence losing out on the possibility that a later one may be even better.

Keinan's results can be regarded as a form of speed–accuracy trade-off. Under stress, people may feel an impulse to seize any acceptable solution to their task or problem rather than making themselves wait for the best. This approach will increase speed but will sacrifice accuracy. If this is indeed the correct interpretation, then it brings up a pattern of self-regulation failure that we shall cover later in this chapter. We have chosen to cover speed–accuracy tradeoffs under misregulation, because in many cases they clearly are that, but it is plausible that in some instances maladaptive speed–accuracy tradeoffs involve underregulation. These cases would be the ones in which people have impulses to favor speed that must be kept under control. Stress apparently decreases people's ability to check the impulse toward speed. Let us now turn to issues of misregulation and speed–accuracy tradeoffs.

MISREGULATION

Self-regulatory failure in task performance does not always involve a breakdown in regulation. Sometimes, people may be quite able and willing to exert themselves at self-regulation, yet they may still fail. These cases involve misregulation. There are several crucial patterns of misregulation in task performance.

Speed versus Accuracy

We begin with the pattern mentioned at the end of our discussion of underregulation, namely speed–accuracy tradeoffs. Many tasks involve a continuum between speed and accuracy: People may work slowly and carefully, trying to do everything correctly, or they may increase speed at the cost of lower quality work and more mistakes. These tradeoffs can be found everywhere, from painting walls to painting portraits, from plumbing to college aptitude exams, from filling out forms to writing novels. It is not an either-or choice but rather a matter of finding some balance along the continuum.

If speed and accuracy had equal, linear effects on performance quality, it would not matter where one struck the balance, because any decrease in the one would be offset by the increase in the other. More often, however, the relationship may be nonlinear, and so one may increase speed up to a point without dramatically reducing accuracy, whereas beyond that point accuracy drops off substantially. Optimal self-regulation requires finding just such a point on the continuum, in order to maximize performance.

It is also important to realize that the optimal point may depend on the situation, particularly on the contingencies associated with speed and accuracy. Sometimes speed may be more important, and other times accuracy may, because of external factors. For example, when working on a bomb squad or on a jury in a capital case, accuracy is at a premium, because the costs of a single error can be so high. Accordingly, defusing a bomb tends to be associated with very slow work in order to maximize accuracy, as do jury trials. At the opposite extreme, assault weapons tend to face a technological version of the same tradeoff, because the faster a weapon fires, the less accurate it is. With assault weapons, manufacturers and generals have generally agreed that speed is more important. Soldiers who are charging an enemy position generally do not have the time, opportunity, or (indeed) presence of mind to aim carefully at concealed defenders, and so they are best served by firing a rapid hail of bullets toward the enemy position rather than a series of single, well-placed shots (e.g., Keegan, 1976). Indeed, some military historians have concluded that the term "precision bombing" was an oxymoron, at least prior to the 1991 Gulf War, and so "saturation bombing"—emphasizing speed (and thus quantity) over accuracy—was generally most effective (Fussell, 1989). In a similar vein, Hackworth and Sherman (1989) described how during the Korean War Hackworth effectively discouraged the enemy's nighttime and sneak attacks by randomly ordering a "mad minute," during which his soldiers would fire all their weapons and artillery at maximum speed aimlessly into no man's land in front of their position. In the dark, they had no chance to be accurate at all in hitting possible targets, but the rapid and abrupt firing of all those weapons made it too hazardous for the enemy even to send reconnaissance patrols into the area between the two armies.

In sum, speed and accuracy are to some extent mutually exclusive, and so people must find an optimal point along the continuum, that is, an optimal mixture of the two. The optimum point may depend on objective circumstances as well as on nonlinear relationships between the two. Researchers have not yet managed consistently to identify what these optimal points are and what causes subjects to fail to reach them, but evidence is accumulating about the factors that alter speed–accuracy tradeoffs, and this evidence suggests what some of the decisive factors will be.

One factor, apparently, is anxiety. Leon and Revelle (1985) found that highly anxious subjects performed generally poorer than nonanxious subjects, consistent with many other findings of performance decrements under anxiety. When high stress was added, however, in the form of increasing evaluation apprehension (by telling the subject that the task was related to intelligence) and placing a time limit on the test, highly anxious subjects increased their speed while decreasing accuracy, whereas nonanxious subjects favored accuracy over speed. These results suggest that highly anxious subjects cope with external pressures and stresses by increasing their speed and quantity of responses.

Why do highly anxious subjects lean toward speed over accuracy? One reason suggested by Leon and Revelle was that the increased activity gives them the sense that they are at least doing something. In addition, the increased activity helps prevent these subjects from ruminating about what is taking place, and such ruminations might otherwise increase their anxiety even further. Results in our own laboratory have produced similar results, in which anxious subjects made more decisions and actions in a fixed amount of time in response to external pressure.

It is worth noting that this function of anxiety seems opposite to the effects of anxiety in the animal world, where anxiety causes animals to freeze. Indeed, our own investigation was attempting to replicate this "freezing" effect, in order to show that anxiety caused people to postpone or evade decisions, but we repeatedly found the opposite effect. Apparently, anxiety inclines people to step up their efforts on the more controllable dimension (of speed), even if the less controllable dimension of accuracy suffers.[1]

On the assumption that impulsive subjects are deficient in self-regulation, several studies have examined trait impulsivity in relation to speed–accuracy tradeoffs. Using a card-sorting task, Dickman (1985) showed that impulsive

---

[1]The only apparent exception to this is test anxiety, in which subjects appear to freeze. In such cases, however, the option of increasing speed may be unavailable to them, because they cannot come up with anything to say on the examination. As described earlier in this chapter, test anxiety tends to involve a vicious cycle in which attention is directed toward one's own inability to respond, and it is conceivable that test-anxious people are often engaged in a frantic mental search even though physically they appear to be immobile. Still, this apparent exception to the general pattern may merit further research.

subjects tend to favor speed over accuracy, whereas non-impulsive subjects show the opposite preference. More precisely, impulsive subjects seem inclined to try to make quick responses and correct them later if necessary, whereas low-impulsive subjects prefer to get it right the first time.

A further study on impulsiveness by Dickman and Meyer (1988) suggested that the difference between impulsive and nonimpulsive subjects lies chiefly in their cognitive strategies. In that study, the execution of motor responses was found to occur at roughly the same speed in both groups of subjects, but the mental judgments showed the differences in speed–accuracy tradeoffs. Thus, it is a matter of information-processing strategies that make impulsive subjects faster and less accurate than other subjects. Dickman and Meyer noted that this helps explain a common finding in the therapy literature, namely that efforts to change the response style of impulsives can usually succeed in making them slower but typically fail to increase accuracy. They suggest that such therapeutic efforts probably end up changing the overt execution of the response to make it slower, rather than operating on the information processing that precedes the response—and it is the information processing where the problem lies.

Extraversion is related to the trait of impulsivity, and it has also been examined in connection with speed–accuracy tradeoffs. Nichols and Newman (1986) undertook to explain the familiar phenomenon that psychopaths, who score high on extraversion, tend to be unfazed by punishment. Nichols and Newman examined how extraverts would change their response styles in response to previous rewards and punishments. They found that differences emerged only when feedback mixed rewards and punishments; when feedback consisted of only rewards or only punishments, extraverts and introverts responded roughly the same. In the mixed-feedback condition, they found that on the trials after a punishment (failure) had been administered, extraverts sped up while introverts slowed down.

Thus, it appears that extraverts tend to be affected by the presence and availability of rewards, and they adopt a certain response style that favors speed over accuracy. When they receive failure feedback, this response style is intensified, and so they respond faster, presumably as a way of trying to get more rewards. They are not insensitive to failure or punishment, as some researchers have suggested. Rather, failure facilitates their reward-seeking behavior. Introverts, in contrast, respond to failure by slowing down a bit, perhaps as a way of increasing accuracy and/or benefiting from the lesson inherent in the failure feedback. By speeding up, extraverts seem to fail to learn from punishment, which is probably what previous researchers have noticed.

One of the most important and ambitious studies of speed–accuracy tradeoffs was conducted by Heckhausen and Strang (1988) with semiprofessional basketball players in Europe. These subjects had to perform a task in which they dribbled the ball (i.e., bounced it in a controlled fashion from their hand) around a course, including one section where they had to dribble it for a stretch below a railing (thus requiring skilled control), and then shoot a basket.

After shooting, they returned to the starting point and got another ball, repeating the process as often as they could within the time limit. In the control condition, they simply performed the task; in the "record" condition, they were exhorted to try to set a personal record for their best performance.

The athletes in this study did indeed modify their performance process depending on their goal level. When trying for a record, subjects increased their speed, taking more total shots as a result. Meanwhile, there was a marginally significant decrease in accuracy and a substantial increase (actually double) in dribbling errors. Thus, when trying for a record, subjects improved on speed measures but got worse on accuracy measures.

Ironically, the athletes in Heckhausen and Strang's study refused to believe the results even after they participated. The researchers noted that subjects continued to believe that "an increase in effort leads in linear fashion to improved performance" (1988, p. 496). This may reflect an adaptive belief that one should maximize the controllable parts of one's performance, namely one's effort, and that it will pay off in terms of a better outcome. Some subjects, of course, did do better under pressure, and these appeared to be the ones who did not suffer anxiety or other bad moods in response to the pressure to do one's best. Thus, affect regulation may prove to be important for producing effective task performance.

What, then, has research in personality and social psychology contributed to the understanding of speed–accuracy tradeoffs as a means of self-regulation of performance? It appears that personality differences emerge most strongly in response to external stresses or pressures, such as evaluative threat or the contingency of both rewards and punishments. Under such circumstances, some people respond by slowing down and taking more care, presumably in the hope of increasing accuracy, whereas others speed up. Increased speed tends to be accompanied by a decrease in accuracy, so it is often unproductive and sometimes counterproductive, but people may still do it because it helps distract them from inner turmoil such as anxiety.

Another pattern that is relevant to self-regulation is that sometimes speed–accuracy tradeoffs are decided by the wrong reasons. That is, factors such as a wish to escape from anxiety or other unpleasant emotions may cause people to increase speed at the expense of accuracy. Such responses are not likely to be good for performance; after all, the way to perform best is to adapt one's performance strategy to the task (and its contingencies), rather than setting it on the basis of one's own emotional turmoil. Poor performance under those circumstances would be another example in which emotional distress interfered with effective self-regulation.

Choking under Pressure

We turn now to another pattern of misregulation. This is the paradox of "choking under pressure." Choking is paradoxical because subjects are typically trying to improve performance and to do their best, but the way they go about this backfires and produces the opposite effect. It is thus a classic example of misregulation of performance.

To understand the misregulation that causes choking, it is necessary to appreciate the nature of skilled performance. Typically, when people first learn a skill, they pay careful attention to the *process* of what they are doing. Their performances tend to be slow and awkward and to require a great deal of their attention. Learning, however, is a process of gradual automatization, and as the person continues to practice he or she may find that the performance seems to come more and more naturally—that is, without requiring deliberate, conscious attention. Highly skilled people may find that they can perform best while scarcely paying attention to their own performance processes, focusing instead on the results of what they are doing, on the environment and its pitfalls and opportunities, or indeed on their opponent. To pay attention to their own internal processes—to *how* they are executing their performance—is often in fact disruptive to highly skilled people (see Kimble & Perlmuter, 1970). Thus, effective skilled performance requires keeping attention carefully focused on the task but not on one's own internal responses and processes.

Pressure can be understood simply in terms of the importance of doing well. Pressure consists of incentives or contingencies that call for good performance. People may feel pressure when there are large rewards and punishments (such as money or grades) riding on their performance, when many other people are watching, when they are burdened with high expectations, or even just when this is their last or only chance to succeed (see Baumeister, 1984; Baumeister & Showers, 1986). Pressure thus increases people's motivation to do well.

Unfortunately, a common response to pressure is to pay extra careful attention to one's internal processes, and this (as we have seen) is counterproductive. One wants to make sure that one performs well, and so one focuses on how one is performing. This attention undermines the automatic quality of performance and hence disrupts the smooth execution of skills.

There is thus a cruel irony about choking under pressure. The person directs his or her conscious attention to the process of performance, in order to help run the show and make certain that everything is done right. But the conscious mind does not hold the knowledge of how to execute the performance properly. The increased conscious attention merely interferes with the automatic quality of the well-learned response. The result might be compared to the company president who returns to the factory and tries to operate the machines, only to find that he no longer knows how they work, and the result is a costly failure.

When people choke under pressure, they sometimes say that they might have been "trying too hard." At first blush, their explanation makes no sense; how can one try too hard? And indeed if performance depended entirely on how hard one tried, there would be no such thing. In a 100-yard dash, for example, or even in a marathon, there would be no such thing as trying too hard.

When performance depends mainly on skill, however, trying hard may not benefit performance. Moreover, there is an important sense in which one *can* try too hard. Trying to control one's performance, to make certain that one does everything exactly right, can indeed backfire and impair performance. It is not the effort one puts into the task that is the problem—it is the effort one puts into self-regulation that is too much and hence is counterproductive.

Evidence about choking under pressure was provided by Baumeister (1984). Subjects in one study were told to perform a manual dexterity task (a roll-up task). In one condition, they were told to attend to their hands while performing the task; these subjects performed worse than no-instruction subjects and worse than subjects who were given other attention instructions. Thus, paying attention to one's own limb and muscle movements impaired the execution of a skill task. In other studies, subjects who were put under pressure (through implicit competition, audience presence, or offering a cash reward for good performance) showed similar decrements in performance. Moreover, the effects of choking were mainly found for people who were not accustomed to paying attention to themselves, consistent with the notion that it is an unfamiliar increase in self-awareness that mediates choking.

Other studies have confirmed that increased attention to self leads to choking. Being the focus of others' expectations for performing well—the proverbial "burden of expectations"—causes people to perform worse in many cases (Baumeister, Hamilton, & Tice, 1985). Even professional athletes tend to choke when playing for a major championship in front of their home fans, who watch them closely and expect them to win (Baumeister & Steinhilber, 1984; Baumeister, 1985).

For understanding self-regulation failure, it is particularly important to note that choking under pressure appears to be limited to skill tasks. When performance depends mainly on effort, choking does not occur, and in fact many of the same factors that hamper skilled performance lead to improvements in effortful performance. A series of studies by Baumeister, Pelham, Krull, and Swinkels (1987) showed opposite effects of situational variables on effort versus skill tasks. Effort tasks were characterized as those for which trying harder can lead to improved performance, learning is nearly absent, and fatigue or loss of motivation can reduce performance. Squeezing a handgrip, holding one's hand in ice water, sorting cards into order as rapidly as possible, and hanging from a horizontal bar are examples of such tasks. On skill tasks such as shooting or archery, in contrast, a person cannot usually improve by simply wanting or trying to do better. Instead, they show evidence of gradual learning (improvement) over time, with practice.

In the studies by Baumeister et al. (1987), offering people a cash reward for improving their performance caused them to perform better on effort tasks but worse on skill tasks. Setting somewhat high versus unrealistically high goals had opposite effects also: High goals caused people to choke on skill tasks, whereas unrealistically high goals created no pressure and so had no effect on performance (because one could not expect to meet them). In contrast, high goals improved performance on the effort-based tasks, whereas the unrealistically high goals impaired performance (because people quickly gave up).

Praise was also shown to have opposite effects on skilled as opposed to effortful performance (Baumeister, Hutton, & Cairns, 1990). Praise makes people self-conscious, and so it impaired people's performance on a skilled task—indeed, even totally irrelevant praise such as "That's a nice shirt you're wearing" lowered performance scores. But the same forms of praise on an effort task led to improved performance.

The key difference between effort and skill tasks is in the degree of conscious controllability. The conscious mind can determine how much effort to put forth, but it cannot execute skills, to the extent that these involve automatic processes. When it is particularly important to perform well, the conscious mind tends to respond to this pressure by taking over the internal process of performance. For effort tasks, this conscious intervention is often beneficial, because the person can make certain to put forth maximum effort. For skill tasks, on the other hand, conscious intervention is counterproductive. Unable to regulate skilled performance, the conscious mind ends up simply interfering with the normal flow, and performance gets worse instead of better. As an example of counterproductive intervention, this is a prototypical example of misregulation.

Before concluding our discussion of choking, it is worth noting that there may be lapse-activated causal patterns, although these have not yet been clearly shown in laboratory studies. Still, any sports spectator can probably recite examples of contests between seemingly well-matched competitors that remained close for a certain time and then, after an initial mistake or setback by one, evolved into one-sided affairs. Indeed, two of the authors of this book both attended a meeting in New York on the weekend of the 1993 Super Bowl between the veteran Buffalo Bills and the talented upstart Dallas Cowboys. Analysts considered the teams reasonably evenly matched and many expected a close game. It remained close for the first few drives, but then a quick pair of Buffalo mistakes gave Dallas the lead, and from then on things got worse and worse for the hapless Bills. In the end, it was one of the most embarrassing defeats in Super Bowl history. The Bills had turned the ball over (i.e., make a bad mistake such as dropping the ball that resulted in losing their chance to score) nine times. Few experts believed that the difference in score (52 to 17) represented the true difference in the quality of the two teams, and indeed one could argue that the outcome might have been different had those initial mistakes not put the Bills into a situation of desperation and despair. Once they started to lose, however, the snowball began. Part of the explanation was a vicious cycle: They needed to score quickly to recoup any chance of winning, and so they had to try increasingly risky plays, which repeatedly backfired and put them even further behind.

Although this evidence is merely anecdotal, further work may well find vicious-cycle patterns in choking under pressure, consistent with the notion of lapse-activated causation. The initial mistake may in itself be minor, but the performer's reaction to it may produce an escalating series of mistakes that prove decisive.

Misguided Persistence

Earlier in this chapter we paid considerable attention to quitting as a form of self-regulation failure. Clearly, when people fail to persist, they reduce their chances of success. American culture is saturated with the belief that persistence is a supreme virtue. From children's stories such as "The Little Engine That Could," to the hagiographic summaries of heroic athletic feats, to the countless novels and movies that celebrate how unrequited lovers can win the hearts of their beloved ones in the end (see Baumeister & Wotman, 1992), to the rags-to-riches success literature (Huber, 1987), our culture bombards people with the promising message that persistence will be rewarded in the end. Persistence does improve one's chances of success, and so the inability to make oneself persist is one costly form of self-regulation failure.

On the other hand, persistence does not always pay off, despite the cultural messages and myths. Many aspiring suitors who persist at trying to win the heart of a rejecting beloved person simply compound their own humiliation and extend the ordeal, without getting any closer to success in the end. Scientists who persist at trying to prove incorrect theories or to use flawed methods may end up wasting their careers. Investors who cling to losing stocks may end up losing far more money than they would have if they simply cut their losses and looked elsewhere for a more profitable and promising investment.

In short, it is useful to know when to quit. Although quitting too early is one route to failure, persisting past the optimal point is a less celebrated but often equally pernicious pathway to costly failure.

We covered quitting as a form of underregulation: The person fails to make himself or herself keep trying. Excessive persistence does not seem to involve underregulation, because the person may be engaged in self-regulation in order to make himself or herself keep at it. Excessive persistence is thus better understood as a form of misregulation. The person self-regulates, but not in an optimal or effective fashion, and so the regulatory efforts produce an unwelcome, undesirable outcome.

Misguided persistence appears to be due in part to the errors in judgment or faulty knowledge that we cited as a common cause of misregulation. When people are encouraged to make careful and accurate calculation of probabilities and contingencies, they are less likely to persist excessively (Conlon & Wolf, 1980). Thus, counterproductive persistence appears to be linked to not paying enough attention to the contingencies—not analyzing the situation to determine one's best interests.

Sunk costs represents another important factor that contributes to counterproductive persistence. When people have already invested a substantial amount of time, energy, or money into some endeavor, and these initial invest-ments will be lost if the individuals choose to pull out, then people tend to become reluctant to quit. The unwillingness to abandon all one has invested may be a factor in keeping people in relationships that they might otherwise be terminated (e.g., Johnson & Rusbult, 1989), indeed even unsatisfying or abu-sive relationships. After one has struggled and suffered a great deal, one is reluctant to cut those losses and start over with someone new. Military and business ventures show similar patterns: Having suffered or lost a great deal already, one is reluctant to abandon the venture, which would entail that all those efforts or losses were for nothing.

These patterns suggest that persistence can acquire a kind of psychological inertia. Earlier, we proposed that inertia is often a source of obstacles to self-regulation, but self-regulatory efforts may themselves in turn acquire an inertia, making it that much harder for the person to override them. The role of inertia is especially confirmed by evidence that counterproductive persistence arises when it is the passive option. Brockner, Shaw, and Rubin (1979) studied people in either of two contrasting versions of a persistence situation. In one, the per-son kept going unless he or she made an active move to stop, and so the passive option (i.e., the one that occurred in the absence of any move by the subject) was to continue. In the other condition, the person would automatically stop unless he or she made an active move to go on, and so the passive option in this case was to stop. In both cases, the passive option was the one more commonly used, consistent with inertia. Counterproductive persistence was thus especially likely when it required active intervention for the person to stop.

Counterproductive persistence is a form of self-defeating behavior (see Baumeister & Scher, 1988), and as with many of those patterns, egotism can often be a substantial cause. Concern over one's self-esteem has already been implicated in several patterns of self-regulatory failure, and it plays a role in excessive persistence too. Several studies have shown that when people feel individually responsible for the initial decision, they are much more likely to persist past the optimal point. Staw (1976) showed that people persisted more when the initial decision had been their own rather than someone else's, which suggests that they persisted because they felt personally responsible for what was happening. Bazerman, Giuliano, and Appelman (1984) found that when people feel personally responsible for bad oucomes, they paradoxically increase their feelings of commitment to continuing with that course of action and their confidence that further efforts will eventually bring success.

The role of egotism is further confirmed by some evidence that opposition can cement one's commitment. Fox and Staw (1979) found that people were especially likely to persist if the initial decision had been met with resistance or controversy. Logically, the voicing of alternative or dissenting views should make it easier for people to notice that their chosen course of action is leading toward failure, but instead it appears that such opposition makes people that much less willing to see the circumstances objectively. The reason, presumably, is that to cancel a course of action that one has initiated oneself is to admit failure or defeat, and people are very reluctant to do that. When others had opposed the decision, the loss of face by admitting defeat is intensified. One hates to hear others say "We told you so," and so one ignores the signals and forges ahead, sometimes with disastrous results.

SUMMARY AND CONCLUSION

Managing task performance is an important dimension of self-regulation. Both underregulation and misregulation patterns have been found to lead to poor performance.

The most common and familiar form of underregulation involves quitting. People give up and withdraw effort for several reasons. Consistent with the strength model, they give up more readily when their strength has been depleted by recent stressful experiences. Managing attention is a powerful tool for concentration, and as attention escapes control it may focus on things that increase the desire to give up. Meanwhile, persisting on boring tasks often requires the ability to transcend the immediate situation such as by inventing new, more interesting ways to think about what one is doing, and so transcendence failure is often a factor when boredom leads to quitting.

Important work on quitting in the sense of giving up and withdrawing effort has been conducted in connection with the concept of learned helplessness. Findings from that line of work implicate several familiar aspects of self-regulation failure, including control of attention and depletion of strength by stressful experiences. In addition, focusing on thoughts of the self as bad or incompetent seem to lead to giving up, possibly in connection with the emotional distress that they cause. There is also evidence that people may sometimes withdraw effort as a way of protecting their feelings and their self-esteem from further failure.

Many tasks require the person to concentrate in order to perform effectively, and so on these tasks losing control of attention is a direct cause of failure. Studies of test anxiety have shown that allowing one's thoughts to become preoccupied with one's own shortcomings and inadequacies furnish a powerful distraction that undermines the ability to concentrate on the task at hand. Stress research has also furnished findings that stress—which presumably or apparently depletes self-regulatory strength—leads to decreases in the person's ability to manage attention properly and concentrate effectively on the task.

Several patterns of failing to regulate performance involved misregulation. Some tasks involve tradeoffs between speed and accuracy, and people perform poorly when they fail to find the optimal balance between the two. Anxiety and emotional distress is one factor that moves people toward greater (and excessive) speed. Another is situational pressures for good performance.

Some people (with the trait of impulsiveness) are especially prone to emphasize speed over accuracy, and their responses tend to be mediated by focusing attention on possible rewards and on certain superficial styles of processing information.

Choking under pressure is another common form of misregulation. Under pressure to perform well, people direct attention to the self and try to exert control over well-learned, habitual, skilled aspects of performance, with the result that they disrupt the smooth execution of skills. Choking thus involves a failure to manage attention effectively, often driven by pervasive concern with how one is doing.

Persistence can also involve misregulation, especially when people force themselves to persist in a losing endeavor. Faulty assumptions about the self and about contingencies, failure to attend carefully to possible responses and contingent outcomes, and threats to self-esteem play central roles in these failures.

There is not a great deal of evidence about lapse-activated causal patterns and snowballing effects in performance failures, but it is likely that some such patterns apply. Initial failures may bring emotional distress and may increase the subjective pressure to perform well—or the wish to quit and distance oneself from a frustrating, distressing, losing endeavor. Such reactions may interfere with subsequent efforts at self-regulation.

The survey of performance-regulation failures yielded mixed results regarding the issue of acquiescence. Some patterns of failure, such as quitting, excessive persistence, and speed–accuracy tradeoffs, clearly involve conscious decisions, and so it is necessary to conclude that people do acquiesce in them. Others, however, such as choking under pressure and loss of concentration, may often occur contrary to the person's best efforts and conscious intentions, and so it would not be fair to implicate the person as actively participating in his or her self-regulation failure.

4

Self-Management: Taking Care of Yourself

When the singer-composer Madonna had her first hit single, "Material Girl," she was not taken very seriously by the music industry or the general public. Most critics and experts agreed that she did not have the voice, the musical talent, nor the physical attractiveness to be a major success. People were surprised when she had a second hit, and then a third. Over a decade later, she reigned as one of the most famous and richest women in the world, having sold millions of records and videos, made multiple movies, and been the center of a series of highly publicized adventures. Early in her career *Playboy* dug into its files and published some nude photographs of her, revealing a nice-looking but unspectacular body, and again the veteran observers predicted a speedy decline for her career, this time because she presumably had lost her mystery and would not have much else to reveal. They were wrong again; she was only beginning her rise as an international sex symbol, it turned out, one that would culminate many years later in millions of dollars of sales of a book of nude photos of her.

Observed from an objective distance, the remarkable aspect of the Madonna phenomenon was not her initial rise to success but rather how she managed to stay on top in several separate spheres of the entertainment industry without apparently having an overpowering talent in any of them. Put another way, it was not her success per se, but the ratio of her success to her apparent talent, that was exceptional. Her success was sometimes compared in scope, longevity, and riches to that of her contemporary Michael Jordan. But Jordan was often referred to as the greatest basketball player of all time, and his physical talent left most observers in awe. Nothing about Madonna could elicit such effusive and consensual praise. Nothing, that is, except her amazing facility for parlaying a modest collection of gifts into one of the most successful careers anywhere, in any field.

In terms of our analysis, where Madonna excelled was in self-management. (To be sure, she may have had some expert advice.) If her natural gifts were not all that extraordinary, she used them to maximum effectiveness. She stayed on top as a sex symbol not by keeping her body hidden but by continuing to reveal more and more: first the nude pictures, then various stories and songs and performance pieces involving sexual escapades that became progressively wilder, including masturbation, lesbianism, transvestism, and sadomasochism, none of which had been systematically exploited by the sex symbols of previous decades. Moreover, when she recorded songs with attention-getting lyrics, such as dealing with teen pregnancy or erotic spanking, she did not content herself with the sales that the verbal message alone would have gotten, as many performers would have done; instead, she worked hard to make the songs musically competent and interesting too, so that they could be enjoyed even by those who paid no attention to the words.

Madonna is thus a remarkable example of self-regulatory success. Her story sheds a harsh light on the careers of so many other, more talented people who reach an early pinnacle of success and then disappear from the scene. Undoubtedly a substantial measure of ability is one factor in creating success, and another is having a series of "breaks" or opportunities. Yet even the majority of people who have both of these advantages fail to achieve any lasting success.

Although Madonna may be perceived as a special case, there are many less flamboyant examples. University students provide plenty of examples of the importance of effective self-management. Probably every professor who has taught in a Ph.D. program for any length of time can cite cases of exceptionally talented and intelligent students who never seemed to produce work that fit their potential; indeed, probably every professor can cite cases of exceptionally intelligent students who seemed unable to complete their doctoral dissertations! And although people who are not intelligent do not normally finish their Ph.D.'s, there are many cases of students with only intermediate intellectual gifts who perform exceptionally well, both in graduate school and afterward. These academic Madonnas are typically well organized, highly motivated, and hard-working, and they seem able to set realistic goals and meet them on schedule.

Why do many gifted people become underachievers after they first reach the top? What sets the Madonnas apart from them?

The other chapters of this book examine self-regulation (and self-regulation failure) in the common and well-defined spheres of self-control issues, such as in issues of controlling one's appetites or performing a task effectively. In this chapter, we turn to examine a more global, complex form of self-regulation, which is sometimes called self-management. Self-management typically involves coordinating multiple self-regulation processes, such as when one must both set appropriate goals and then live up to them.

The importance of effective self-management was shown by Wagner and Sternberg (1985). They showed that self-management depends on effective self-knowledge plus applying that knowledge appropriately. That is, you have to know the conditions under which you work best, and then you need to find or create those conditions, in order to maximize your performance. Many tests measure intelligence and knowledge, but hardly any of them measure the ability to motivate oneself—yet being able to motivate yourself may be one of the most decisive factors in determining occupational sucess. In their findings, self-management skills (measured in terms of knowledge about self, peers, and career contingencies) were associated with enhanced success in various spheres of life. For example, business managers who scored high on self-management skills received bigger salary raises than those who scored low in a given year; across their careers, the good self-managers ended up reaching higher levels in the company hierarchy and earning higher salaries. Self-management thus does seem to be an important ingredient for career success.

To be sure, there are substantial obstacles to effective self-management. Self-knowledge is not fully accurate and realistic in general. Taylor and Brown (1988) have documented a broad tendency for people to overestimate how good they are at many things. Vallone, Griffin, Lin, and Ross (1990) found that people's predictions about themselves showed a broad, persistent pattern of overconfidence. If people routinely overestimate themselves, they will most likely end up overcommitted or aiming for overly difficult goals, which in turn will lead to failure.

And yet there may be hope. In a provocative study, Gollwitzer and Kinney (1989) found that people seemed able to turn off these illusions when they needed to make a decision. After all, confidence is often helpful when you are actually performing; it is merely during the decision-making stage that accuracy is rewarded. Gollwitzer and Kinney found that when people were in the frame of mind that accompanies making personal decisions, they did not show the usual patterns that exaggerate one's perceived efficacy. When people were in the frame of mind that accompanies performing a task, then these self-enhancing illusions resumed. If this pattern is indeed generally true, then it suggests that people can often manage themselves quite well while also maintaining favorable, even inflated views of themselves most of the time. Only when they need to make a decision do they suddenly become sober, realistic, and objective about themselves.

Although researchers such as Wagner and Sternberg (1985) have begun to examine self-management, there exists far less empirical evidence about it than about the other spheres of self-regulation covered in this book. There are studies on goal setting and on the more complex forms of self-regulation that co-ordinate multiple kinds of regulating activities (which is what self-management often consists of), but often it will be necessary to rely mainly on laboratory analogue studies without being able to consult nonlaboratory evidence for confirmation. We shall present relevant studies where they are available, including some of our own, but often it will be necessary to be more speculative in this chapter than in the rest of the book.

AIMLESSNESS: NOT SETTING GOALS

Setting the right goals for oneself is an important first step in effective self-management. People who fail to set goals, or who set inappropriate goals, impair their chances to fulfill their potential. Goals (or other standards) are a prerequisite for effective self-regulation, and so a lack of goals will make self-regulation ineffective or even impossible.

Both long-range and short-term goals are valuable for effective self-management. Having long-term goals is important for orienting oneself and providing continuity across one's efforts. Thus, a study by De Volder and Lens (1982) showed that having long-range goals was associated with doing better in school. Students who had goals in the distant future, and who also interpreted their present efforts as working hard to reach those distal goals, had higher grade point averages than other students. Long-range goals may help one transcend the immediate situation and its unpleasant demands or distracting temptations.

Long-range goals alone can be daunting, however, and so they may even backfire. If your goal were to become president of a major corporation, you would not have much sense that you were making progress toward this goal from day to day or probably even from year to year. The goal would seem hopelessly far off, and you might easily become discouraged. It is therefore valuable and effective to elaborate a set of short-term goals that lead to the long-range goals.

Bandura and Schunk (1981) showed the benefits of having proximal (i.e., short-term) as well as distal goals. People who pursued a set of proximal goals gained a sense of self-efficacy by the fact that they were frequently approaching and reaching these goals. In that way, they avoided the discouragement that comes from seeing how remote one's ultimate, long-range goals are and how little apparent progress one is making from day to day.

Thus, it is most helpful to have both proximal and distal goals. Manderlink and Harackiewicz (1984) found that distal goal setting increased people's intrinsic motivation, whereas proximal goal setting led to more positive expectations for success. People who have both types of goals will tend to enjoy the benefits of having a long-term plan that structures their activities and provides a continuous source of motivation, as well as receiving the encouraging feedback of making progress toward these goals.

The implications for self-regulatory failure are straightforward. People who lack long-term goals will tend to find that their lives wander haphazardly from one undertaking to another, or that they seem to be at the mercy of external demands. Even if they have plenty of short-term goals, these may not lead anywhere. The person may respond to each crisis or challenge that arises, yet after several years these have not amounted to anything, and the person may find himself or herself being no further along than he or she was initially. Moreover, it becomes difficult to resist temptations or to avoid being swamped by each problem that arises. If you don't know where you are going, there is no reason not to take every promising turn in the road, and although you may have some pleasant sights you may end up going in circles.

Long-range goals are particularly important for transcendence, because such goals allow one to see beyond the immediate situation, short-term outcomes, and pressing stimuli. Without long-term goals, transcendence is very difficult. A person without long-term goals will tend to become immersed in the present. He or she may even work very hard at meeting external demands and handling short-range challenges, but over the long run these do not lead anywhere. It is impossible to structure the present in terms of its long-range significance if one does not have the distal goals.

On the other hand, people who have *only* long-term goals may end up never approaching them. These people may transcend the present too much. Nothing in the immediate present involves satisfying the distal goal, and so it is difficult to motivate oneself to perform one's tasks and duties in the present. The difficulty is compounded by the discouraging sense that one is not reaching one's distal goals. One knows where one wants to be, but one is not there, and this does not seem to change.

Thus, we have two forms of self-management failure that are linked to not setting goals. First, one fails to set distal goals, and second, one fails to set proximal goals based on the distal goal. Either of these can impair effective self-management.

OVERLY RIGID GOALS AND PLANS

In the preceding section we argued that a lack of goals can lead to self-regulation failure. The opposite is also true, however: an excess of goals, particularly ones that are held in a rigid fashion, can also impair effective self-management. Apparently it is best both to have some goals and to leave some room for choice, spontaneity, and modification along the way.

This conclusion emerged somewhat by accident. Kirschenbaum, Humphrey, and Malett (1981) undertook to study people's planning and the role it would have, beyond mere goal setting, in producing beneficial, desirable outcomes in life. Subjects in their study were college students enrolled in a study skills improvement course. They were randomly assigned among conditions that asked them to make up either detailed, daily plans for their studying, or general monthly plans, or no plans. The researchers hypothesized that the most detailed and specific plans (i.e., the daily plans) would produce the best results, but to their surprise they found that subjects who made the monthly plans did the best. (Inspection of their data suggest, however, that among those subjects who already had reasonably good grades, the daily plans led to bigger improvements in grades than did the monthly plans.) Not only did the monthly plans produce bigger increments in study time than the daily plans; these increments also proved more durable. In short, planning helps, but perhaps overly specific and detailed planning may backfire and interfere with effective work. Lasting improvements in grade point average, as established by a one-year follow-up (Kirschenbaum, Malett, Humphrey, & Tomarken, 1982), were best among people with the moderately specific plans—as opposed to no plans *or* highly detailed, specific plans.

Why? A subsequent investigation by Kirschenbaum, Tomarken, and Ordman (1982) examined possible explanations for the apparently counterproductive effects of daily planning. These researchers concluded that detailed, specific plans have several drawbacks. In the first place, of course, it takes more time to draw up a daily plan than to draw up a monthly plan, and so the planning activity itself may take time and energy away from performing the task. Second, and related to that, detailed planning may be sufficiently arduous that people stop making plans fairly soon, thereby thwarting the effort to teach them self-regulatory skills by having them make plans. Indeed, in the earlier study by Kirschenbaum et al. (1981), monthly planners made plans for several months, whereas most daily planners stopped making plans after the first month.

Third, and most important, daily plans restrict the room for choice and discretion, and this rigidity may become oppressive. Kirschenbaum, Tomarken, and Ordman (1982) concluded that having some scope for continuing to make choices along the way is a powerful and important component of a good long-term self-regulation strategy. Monthly plans left it up to the person what exactly should be done from day to day, whereas daily plans did not allow for such ongoing choices. As one continues to work over time, one may come to see new ways of improving or performing efficiently, and these can be effectively implemented within a general, long-term plan—but they would violate a detailed and specific plan. The ridigity would therefore become counterproductive, hindering further creativity.

The authors also found that people seem to *enjoy* making choices along the way, consistent with a great deal of other research on the benefits of making choices (e.g., Brehm, 1966; Linder, Cooper, & Jones, 1967), and so finding oneself bound to a rigid and detailed plan could prove aversive simply because one feels deprived of freedom. Indeed, Kirschenbaum, Tomarken, and Ordman (1982) included several conditions in which subjects were explicitly deprived of some potential options, and these "lost-choice" subjects performed consistently worse than other subjects even with the same kind of overall plan.

Lastly, Kirschenbaum, Tomarken, and Ordman (1982) pointed out that overly specific plans will tend to breed more experiences of failure and frustration. Within the context of monthly goals and plans, there is ample room for the person to reallocate small blocks of time and to deal with unforeseen delays and problems that may arise. For example, a three-day virus may cause the person to make no progress at all, but the monthly plan can still be fulfilled by working harder on other days. When goals are set on a daily basis, however, any disruption or deviation becomes a failure experience. A three-day virus may cause two weeks of failure experiences, because it may take that long to get back on the original schedule. Thus, even if the daily planner and the monthly planner have both recovered from the virus and caught up with their work by the end of the month—and thus have accomplished the same amount—the daily planner had to suffer through two weeks of failure experiences, while the monthly planner did not, and so the monthly planner is likely to start off the next month with a much more positive attitude than the daily planner.

Although the results of these several investigations are not fully consistent, they do make it clear that planning can backfire. Overly detailed and specific plans can end up being oppressively rigid. Self-management may be most effective when it consists of broad, long-range plans that are only moderately specific and that therefore leave the person scope for adjustment, adaptation, and improvisation along the way. We have emphasized that self-management is beneficial for optimum performance, achievement, and happiness, but too much planning can be almost as deleterious as too little.

UNREALISTIC GOALS, FOOLISH COMMITMENTS

Perhaps one of the most common forms of self-regulation failure in the area of self-management involves setting inappropriate goals. Several studies have shown that people undermine their chances for success by setting improper goals, either too high or too low.

One sign of this was provided by Ward and Eisler (1987). They showed that Type A (coronary-prone) subjects mismanaged themselves by tending to set goals that were too high. Because of these lofty goals, their actual performance tended to fall short, and so they evaluated themselves badly. These poor self-evaluations then produced emotional distress. In short, they made themselves miserable because they aimed too high.

Personality traits may operate through emotional states. Type A subjects have been characterized as hostile and irritable (Spence, Helmreich, & Pred, 1987), and these unpleasant emotional states could conceivably have something to do with their inappropriate goal setting. Although Ward and Eisler (1987) showed that the emotional distress was a *result* of setting excessive goals (and then falling short), emotional distress may also *cause* people to set goals inappropriately. This was suggested by Wright and Mischel (1982), who manipulated subjects' emotional states, provided subjects with either success or failure feedback, and then saw how they set goals. Subjects who experienced both negative affect and initial failure tended to set extremely high goals. Indeed, Wright and Mischel characterized these subjects' goal setting as self-destructive, because they set goals above their expectations. If you are shooting for a goal that is higher than what you expect to be able to achieve, you are likely to fail.

A series of studies by the authors of this book examined both goal setting and outcome, in order to examine the full scope of self-management. That is, we had people both set goals and perform. After all, studies like Wright and Mischel's, important as they are, do not establish that the goals subjects set were in fact self-destructive. Possibly people could perform up to the high goals. Setting high goals is only self-defeating if one cannot live up to them.

In our studies (Baumeister, Heatherton, & Tice, 1993), subjects spent time learning a task—we used a video game as a standard skill task —and then performed it for a series of trials. Subjects then received an ego threat just prior to the final trial. In different experiments, the ego threat was manipulated either by saying derogatory things to the subject (i.e., hinting that the subject was the sort of person who might choke under pressure) or giving the subject bogus failure feedback on a creativity test. Subjects were then allowed to set the cash incentives for their final performance. In two studies, subjects were told that they had already won some money, and they were allowed to bet any or all of it, triple or nothing, on their final trial. (In the other study, they were allowed to select a goal, with more difficult goals worth more money.) We also measured subjects' trait self-esteem. After the goal or bet was set, the subject performed the final trial and was paid whatever he or she had earned.

The purpose of these studies was to learn about what circumstances might lead to self-regulatory failure. Self-regulatory failure meant losing all one's money. In the betting studies, one could do well either by making a low bet and hence keeping one's previous earnings regardless of how one performed, or by making a high bet and then performing well. In reading the literature on self-regulation while preparing to write this book, we found over and over that ego threats and self-esteem are important factors in self-regulation failure, and we wanted to learn whether they would also make a substantial difference in self-management.

The experiment thus corresponded to common life situations in which people must know approximately how well they can do and then must select a situation that offers them the chance to maximize their outcomes based on their level of ability. One can always play it safe, but to earn the maximum amount one must take some chances—chances that can be kept to a reasonable amount of risk as long as one keeps one's capabilities in mind.

Under good (nonthreatening) conditions, we found that people with high self-esteem performed better at self-management than people with low self-esteem. The measure of self-management, again, was how much money people had left at the end of the experiment. People with high self-esteem were very effective at placing high bets or setting high goals if they were going to perform well and making low bets or setting low goals if they were not going to do well.

This advantage may well reflect the superior self-knowledge of people with high self-esteem (see Baumgardner, 1990; Campbell, 1990; Campbell & Lavallee, 1993).

Following the ego threat, however, people with high self-esteem abruptly became poor at self-management. They tended to set unrealistically high goals and then to perform worse, thereby losing all their money. People with low self-esteem did relatively well after the ego threat, but people with high self-esteem seemed to lose all their self-regulatory skills.

It is well known that people with high self-esteem respond in extreme ways to ego threat. Normally they do not expect to fail or to be rejected or to have their worth questioned in other ways. When ego threats do materialize, people with high self-esteem become very distressed and agitated and frequently are determined to counter the threat immediately (see especially McFarlin & Blascovich, 1981; also Baumeister, 1993a; Blaine & Crocker, 1993). That appears to be what they did in our studies. Confronted with an ego threat, they immediately set high goals for themselves or placed heavy bets that they would succeed the next time, and often this rash self-confidence was misplaced and costly.

These studies suggest that self-management depends heavily on self-esteem. People who think well of themselves and who, along with their high self-esteem, typically tend to have thorough and detailed self-knowledge, normally seem quite proficient at self-management. They set appropriate goals and then manage their performances to live up to them. Indeed, their skill at self-management may be one factor that keeps their self-esteem high. Just because two people have equal levels of ability, this does not guarantee that they will enjoy equal amounts of success in life. People who know their strengths and weaknesses and can choose effectively what they should undertake and where they should perform will enjoy the most successes. A person with low self-esteem may be just as smart as someone with higher self-esteem but because of choosing tasks that are too easy or too difficult will never have the meaningful, important successes that the other will.

Yet the superior self-management of people with high self-esteem appears to break down in the face of ego threat. These people respond to such threats by ceasing to set goals and choose situations in a rational, optimal way. Instead, they seem to become determined to prove themselves at all costs, and so they rashly undertake projects that may be beyond their ability. The emotional distress and defensive, boastful response to ego threat apparently prevent them from managing themselves effectively, and the result can be costly.

These findings have important implications for the discussion of self-knowledge in self-management that we had at the beginning of the chapter. We noted evidence that people can maintain pleasantly inflated views of themselves most of the time while becoming rational and objective when they need to make an important decision (Gollwitzer & Kinney, 1989). Ego threats appear to disrupt this smooth reversion to objective accuracy about oneself, however. Ego threats apparently mobilize defensive responses that make people cling to these inflated views of self. Accordingly, their decision-making processes are biased and impaired, leading to self-management failure.

FAILING TO DELAY GRATIFICATION

The previous section examined how self-management can fail because people set goals inappropriately. We turn now to the complementary problem: failing to pursue one's goals sufficiently. Two major patterns of such failure have been studied in the experimental literature. The first is delay of gratification, which we shall cover in this section. The other, self-handicapping, will be covered in the next.

Delay of gratification is an important pattern of self-management. Many spheres of endeavor in life offer only distant payoffs and require immediate sacrifice or exertion. The person must therefore overcome impulses to enjoy the present in order to work toward the more rewarding but deferred rewards. The eventual rewards may be far greater than the immediate ones, but the immediate ones may often seem more tempting simply because they are immediate. For example, it is well established that finishing high school and earning a college degree both cause large increases in the amount of money the person is likely to earn in one's lifetime—but in the short run the person will earn significantly less by staying in school than by quitting to get a job. The choice is thus between having a moderate amount of money right away or a much larger amount of money in the distant future.

Funder et al. (1983) confirmed the relevance of delay of gratification to self-regulation by showing what personality traits are linked to high and low capacities for delaying gratification. That is, people who showed a low capacity to delay gratification showed other self-regulatory deficiencies as well. Among males, these included being irritable, fidgety, aggressive, and having a broad lack of self-control. Females who were low in the ability to delay gratification were also prone to go to pieces under stress, and tended to be sulky and whiny. In contrast, people who were effective at delaying gratification were able to control their impulses, were resourceful, competent, and reasonable, as well as having various other traits indicative of self-regulatory strength.

Delay of gratification is another instance in which self-regulation failure clearly seems to involve the person's conscious acquiescence. Indeed, the usual laboratory paradigms for studying it require the person to express a deliberate choice between the immediate and the delayed reward, or to make an active effort to procure the immediate reward for oneself. The conscious acquiescence is similar to quitting on tasks (or yielding to impulsive temptations, as will be covered in our chapters on impulse control), because the person abandons the disciplined pursuit of long-range goals in order to follow a course of action that will be more immediately pleasant.

A great deal of research has been conducted to examine the strategies that people use to delay gratification. As usual, the first line of defense for effective self-regulation is managing attention. Whether the person attends to the immediate reward or is able to avoid the immediate reward is often a decisive factor. For instance, Mischel (1974) described spontaneous behaviors observed during the delay process and found that the most common (and successful) strategy used by children was self-distraction; some sang to themselves, some invented games with their hands and feet, some covered their eyes so that they could not see the rewards, and some even tried to put themselves to sleep.

The importance of managing attention in order to succeed at delaying gratification was suggested by the data of Funder et al. (1983), insofar as they showed that the capacity to delay gratification was positively correlated with several attentional skills, such as being able to concentrate. Rodriguez, Mischel, and Shoda (1989) showed that attention deployment was vitally important for delaying gratification: Specifically, people had to direct their attention away from the immediate reward. The more one thinks about the immediate pleasure, the harder it becomes to resist it in favor of the delayed reward.

By extension, an important cause of self-regulation failure is the salient presence of the immediate temptation. As we have suggested, it is easier to avoid temptation if one can avoid the cues that trigger impulses to engage in a behavior. When faced with the object of desire, the children in the work of Mischel, Shoda, and Rodriguez (1989) apparently were trying their own form of stimulus control: They sought to distract their attention away from the object.

If that is true, then we should find—as we have in other spheres—that attentional breakdown is associated with self-regulatory failure. Sure enough, research by Karniol and Miller (1983) showed that giving up on a delay of gratification exercise was preceded by thinking about the rewards. Specifically, subjects would reassess the rewards and tell themselves that the delayed reward was not so great as they had previously thought and hence was not worth waiting for, so they might as well take the short-term option. The reassessment may well be a rationalization of one's inability to resist the proximal temptation.

As children grow up, they become better able to use effective strategies, including self-instructions, focusing on the better reward, using abstract reasoning, and learning to distract themselves with other thoughts or behaviors (Mischel et al., 1989; Mischel & Mischel, 1983; Rodriguez et al., 1989). These strategies all tend to use the form of attention control that we have labeled as *transcendence*: seeing beyond the immediate stimuli and understanding the immediate situation in relation to long-range concerns. Indeed, the problem of delaying gratification is a prototype for transcendence, because it emphasizes a choice between an immediate, salient, stimulating reward and a remote but more valuable one.

Hence, if a person were unable to transcend the immediate situation, he or she would most likely be unable to resist the temptation to take the short-term reward and hence would never be able to hold out for the greater, but delayed, reward. Evidence for the last point is provided in studies with children. When children focus on the sensory properties of the reward (such as thinking about how delicious that candy bar will be), they lose the ability to delay gratification (Mischel et al., 1989). Thus, once again, immersion in immediate sensory stimuli—the opposite of transcendence—leads to self-regulation failure.

Attention deployment is not the only factor that determines the capacity to delay gratification, of course. The capacity to delay gratification may well be an important indicator of general self-regulatory strength. Accordingly, it can well be used as a test of character that may indicate how well the person will be able to manage himself or herself and to have self-control over impulses. As we noted in Chapter 1, Mischel et al. (1988) found that the capacity to delay gratification early in life correlated with several major adjustment measures in adolescence, including social competence and stress tolerance. The potency of this variable for predicting significant and conceptually distant outcomes over a decade later is a powerful sign that one is dealing with a central aspect of personality.

In general, then, life often confronts people with endeavors which will require long, hard, preparatory effort. Success in life may often require foregoing immediate pleasure and relaxation in order to make oneself work hard to prepare for some possible future challenge and the rewards it may bring. Effective self-management thus involves the ability to make oneself put forth those exertions, and anything that undermines the willingness to practice (or study, or prepare oneself in whatever fashion is relevant) should be linked to self-regulatory failure.

SELF-HANDICAPPING

The preceding discussion of delay of gratification emphasized the point that success in life often requires hard work to prepare oneself for an important achievement or performance. Indeed, motivating oneself to study or practice or prepare in other ways is a central feature of self-management (see Wagner & Sternberg, 1985). We have already seen that problems with strength or attention can detract from people's likelihood of preparing well enough. There is, however, another, more troubling and sinister set of causes for failure to prepare. Sometimes people seem to want to avoid preparing. Such motivations are self-destructive almost by definition, because they limit the person's eventual capacity to perform well. What might cause people to shoot themselves in the foot in this way?

One important line of work has shown that an important reason people fail to prepare sufficiently may be due to *self-handicapping*. The phenomenon of self-handicapping was suggested in 1978 by Jones and Berglas (also Berglas & Jones, 1978) and has been widely noted and discussed. Originally applied to explain patterns of alcohol abuse and drug addiction, it has since been used in other spheres, and it is one of those later applications that concerns us now.

Self-handicapping is a matter of putting obstacles in the way of one's own performance. It is thus a self-defeating pattern of behavior: You make things harder for yourself. The paradoxical, self-destructive aspect makes self-handicapping at first seem absurd and improbable, until one grasps that having obstacles to one's performance confers important advantages. If one fails, the failure can be blamed on the obstacle. If one succeeds, one gets "extra credit" for overcoming the obstacle (Jones & Berglas, 1978). Thus, many people would prefer to have their failures attributed to drunkenness than to lack of intelligence, and if they do succeed despite being drunk it seemingly testifies to extra high intelligence.

Tice and Baumeister (1990) applied the logic of self-handicapping to preparatory effort. Specifically, people were given the opportunity to practice as long as they wanted for an upcoming test. In the public condition, the experimenter kept careful records of how long they practiced, whereas in the private condition it would supposedly remain known only to the subject (i.e., duration of practice was monitored unobtrusively). Tice and Baumeister found that subjects with high self-esteem practiced so as to maximize the public credit they would get for their performance. When their practice time was known only to them, they practiced for a long time so as presumably to maximize their ability and hence make the best possible impression by doing well. When their practice time was being recorded by the experimenter, however, they practiced significantly less, as a form of self-handicapping. By minimizing the amount of time they practiced, they could increase the credit to their ability that would accompany a success, while also reducing the degree to which they would look bad if they did fail.

Was this poor self-management? Naturally, if one could indeed succeed with minimal practice, then minimum practice would be the most efficient strategy. But Tice and Baumeister found that duration of practice was significantly correlated with performance quality (as is usually the case in life, no doubt). Thus, subjects who practiced less performed worse. In that context, reducing one's practice time in the service of impression management was foolish and self-destructive.

A further series of studies by Tice (1991) clarified the motives that cause people to reduce their preparatory effort for the sake of self-handicapping. These motives appear to differ by level of trait self-esteem. That is, people with both high and low self-esteem will engage in self-handicapping (by reducing preparatory effort), but under different circumstances that reflect different reasons. People with high self-esteem will self-handicap mainly in order to increase their credit for success. Their high level of self-confidence leads them to downplay the likelihood of failure, and they want to maximize how good they look when they succeed, and so they may practice as little as is necessary (in their view) for success. Meanwhile, people with low self-esteem self-handicap primarily to afford themselves a protective excuse for possible failure. Being low in self-esteem, they do not expect to succeed so often and do not spend a great deal of time thinking about how to maximize the credit they may get for success, but they do worry about failure and are concerned to minimize its damaging implications. Accordingly, they will withdraw preparatory effort in order that if they fail it will not be taken as proof of stupidity or incompetence.

Self-handicapping is thus an important form of *misregulation* of self. It is not that the person is unable to control impulses to seek enjoyment or relaxation or pleasure and hence fails to prepare oneself adequately. Rather, the person chooses a self-defeating course of action in order to serve goals of managing one's image. Self-handicapping confers a double benefit, namely reducing the disgrace for failure and increasing the credit for success, but it does so at the cost of increasing the likelihood of failure. Underachievers—an important category of self-handicappers (see Jones & Berglas, 1978)—withhold effort in order to enhance success and provide an excuse for failure, but they do so at the cost of never performing up to their true capability. In the long run, therefore, self-handicapping mismanages the self and squanders its resources.

PROCRASTINATION

If people were immortal, there would always be plenty of time to accomplish any task, and so procrastination would not be a problem. Because life is short and time is limited, however, people are constantly confronted with the necessity of getting things done on certain schedules and meeting various deadlines. When someone confronts a deadline, there is often an adequate amount of time available if the person were to use it in a rational fashion. Unfortunately, many people seem utterly incapable of using time effectively. They wait until almost the last minute and then try to accomplish everything in a rush. As a result, they suffer from considerable stress and they often perform far below their capabilities (e.g., Lay & Shouwenburg, 1993; Solomon & Rothblum, 1984). Procrastination is thus a classic example of self-destructive failure at self-management (e.g., Ferrari, 1992; Ferrari & Olivette, 1994; Lay, 1990). Why do people do it?

Consider an example. Sara is a college sophomore with a paper due at the end of the semester. Because the paper is fairly extensive, she knows that she should pick a topic early in the semester, and that she should start working on it by about a third of the way through the semester. However, as she sits down in front of her computer to start working on the paper, she starts to feel bad. She has a great deal of difficulty writing the first paragraph. When she picked her topic it seemed like an important topic about which she had a lot to say, but as she sits in front of the blank computer screen she is unable to put her thoughts into words. Her goal in writing this paper is to write an outstanding composition that will take the breath away from her instructor as he reads it because of its profound insights and extreme lucidity (which will also demonstrate her superior intellect). The first sentences she writes, however, are awkward and stilted, and even Sara can recognize them for the cliches they are. This makes her feel bad. She is depressed and disappointed in herself that she cannot communicate her intelligence when she has the chance, as she believes she does in writing this paper. She is anxious about how her instructor will perceive her, and about what grade she will get on the paper. When she was not actually working on the paper but merely thinking about writing it, she was sure that the paper would be so outstanding that she would, of course, be assigned a high grade. Now that she is in the process of actually writing the paper, it is clear to her that she is not accomplishing her goals, which makes her anxious and depressed.

Sara now has two problems: the problem of writing her paper and the problem of her negative emotions. She does not like to feel anxious and depressed and to doubt herself and her intelligence. If the paper is not due for some time, then she may try to regulate her negative emotions at the expense of getting her paper done, and procrastinate. If she stops working on her paper now, she will not have to confront the reality that her paper is not going to win a Pulitzer Prize and she can resume her idealistic daydreams about its success. Because working on the paper makes her feel bad, she may stop working on the paper and instead do something that makes her feel in a better mood, such as going shopping with her friends, or alphabetizing her books (an easy project that gives her a sense of accomplishment about completing tasks but that does not help her at all with any of her papers or exams). Shopping with friends or alphabetizing her books may successfully regulate the negative emotions she was experiencing—but at the expense of long-term self-management.

The above example illustrates several of the misregulation strategies that lead to procrastination. First, an overemphasis on regulating bad moods at the expense of pursing other goals is a common feature of procrastination (see Ferrari, 1991; Solomon & Rothblum, 1984). Because working on the project makes procrastinators feel bad (e.g., they may feel anxious about performance evaluation, depressed because of not meeting their ideals, or just plain bored by the task; see Hamilton, Aldarondo, Moss, & Clark, 1994), they may concentrate on eliminating the negative emotions and avoid the project altogether (see Wertheim & Schwartz, 1983).

Another feature of procrastination demonstrated by the above example is the failure to set short-term or proximal goals. As discussed above, both proximal and distal goals are essential for optimal self-management. In the example, Sara set a distal goal of writing an extremely high-quality paper, but she did not set proximal goals such as having an outline of the paper by a certain date, having a first draft of the introduction by one week later, and so forth. Because Sara was unable to make measurable progress toward her distal, long-term goal, she experienced negative affect. Withdrawing from the project was generally the easiest way to escape from those distressed feelings.

A third factor that can contribute to procrastination is having unrealistically high goals (e.g., Ferrari, 1992). Sara's goal of astounding her instructor with her brilliance is less likely to be obtained than a more realistic goal of writing an adequate, B-or-better paper that makes sound arguments and is grammatically correct. If one's goals are too high (in particular, if one's goals far exceed one's abilities), then a failure to meet these unattainable goals is likely to lead to negative affect. In a desire to escape the negative emotional state, one is likely to withdraw from the task. Having unrealistic goals is not just common in academic tasks; people frequently are unable to meet their unrealistic goal of finding the "perfect" job or birthday gift or having a conflict-free marriage, so they put off gift buying or job hunting or marriage so they do not have to confront their inability to meet their excessive goals.

Thus, having unrealistically high goals and having only distal and no proximal, short-term, attainable goals is likely to lead to a negative emotional state because of a failure to meet one's standards. People may desire to escape from this bad mood by escaping from the situation causing the bad mood, and thus they may procrastinate. An overemphasis on controlling bad moods even at the expense of completing one's required tasks may result in procrastination.

Hamilton et al. (1994) suggest that their are two types of tasks that people procrastinate on: anxiety-producing, evaluative tasks and boring, non-self-relevant tasks. They suggest that the reasons for procrastination differ for the two types of tasks. For evaluative tasks, people procrastinate for the reasons similar to those described above: They experience negative affect in the form of evaluation apprehension when they begin to work on the task, so they regulate the negative emotion by withdrawing from the task. This pattern fits one we have already seen in several parts of this chapter, namely that self-management breaks down because of ego threats. Meanwhile, for boring, non-self-relevant tasks such as mowing the lawn, writing thank-you notes, or changing the oil in the car, the boredom itself may serve as a negative mood, so people escape the bad mood by withdrawing from (or never engaging in) the task (see also Milgram, Batori, & Mowrer, 1993).

WHEN SUCCESS BREEDS FAILURE

We have emphasized how ego threats arising from actual or possible failure experiences can cause self-regulatory failure, but in some cases success can also cause problems. Indeed, the career trajectories of many people and groups show a rise to prominence and success followed by a decline, and one suspects that there are good reasons for both the rise and the fall. Somehow, success causes them to cease doing what brought the success in the first place, and these alterations bring about the decline.

A significant factor may be that success seems to confirm that one is doing things right and properly, and so one becomes reluctant to change. Whatever the person focuses on as the cause of success may therefore become permanent. Moreover, success may encourage egotism, particularly if the person concludes that the cause of success is innate, superior ability. One begins then to feel that one does not have to try as hard anymore, because one's work is inevitably good. When one is on the make, one may exert oneself maximally without expecting others to appreciate it, but once one has made it one may relax and coast. And coasting can lead one to lose one's competitive edge, especially if one's rivals continue to improve.

We have not found any compelling evidence for this in laboratory studies, and indeed it may be hard to show such effects in laboratory studies because they tend to occur over a long period of time and involve slow, gradual changes in self-perceptions. We have, however, found some historical evidence that lends itself to interpretation in these terms. The history of military innovation shows many examples of cases in which success led one country and its military establishment to conclude simply that they and their methods were innately superior to the opposition, and so they did not need to pursue innovations or new techniques (see, for example, McNeill, 1982).

To illustrate these patterns, let us consider the relations between two of the major military rivals of European history, namely France and Prussia (Koch, 1978; McNeill, 1982; Parker, 1987). The Prussian state was built up into a serious power after the Thirty Years' War, partly because during that war Prussia had suffered so much from foreign armies passing through it that its rulers felt it had to be able to defend itself better in the future. They designed a variety of social institutions and military reforms to create a serviceable army despite the small size and relative poverty of their country. Prussia tried out new weapons and experimented with various forms of military drill, which up to this point had not been widely practiced. Meanwhile, France enjoyed the envy and admiration of Europe as the supreme military power. If any winner could be identified for the Thirty Years' War, it was France, and the French forces had been the decisive factor in the last decade of the war. The French high command certainly saw no need to experiment with new tactics or practices, because they were clearly the best land force in Europe.

The next major conflict was the Seven Years' War, initiated by Frederick the Great of Prussia. He took on not only France but also Russia and the giant Austrian empire. Although egregiously outnumbered, he prevailed, aided greatly by the efficient army his predecessors had built up and by his own remarkable tactical innovations. It would have been considered a shock for France fighting alone to lose to Prussia; for France to lose even despite the aid of Austria and Russia was regarded as a disgrace and a humiliation. The Prussian army became the model whose tactics, drills, organizational systems, and weapons were envied and copied by the rest of Europe. It was their turn to rest on their laurels and remain content with the systems that had succeeded so well for them.

France, on the other hand, was deeply affected by their defeat and disgrace. The status quo could no longer be defended, because it had been proven inadequate. When the French Revolution instituted sweeping reforms of the military, the old guard could not insist on keeping to the old ways. Extraordinary reforms were instituted, including promoting officers from the ranks based on merit (instead of selling commissions to aristocrats, as was the usual custom), coordinating the marches of multiple columns so as to concentrate great forces at the same place and time, and developing new, lighter cannons that could be pulled by horses to a battlefield.

Although their pride was still smarting, France's armed forces quietly moved to a level of superiority over the rest of Europe by virtue of these new practices. It is fortunate for them that they did, because the crowned heads of the rest of Europe were determined not to allow the regicide French republic to survive. The French revolutionary government was soon attacked by all the major continental powers. Although the issue of monarchy became moot when the new dictator, Napoleon, had himself crowned emperor, the conflicts continued. As is well known, Napoleon enjoyed a tremendous success and conquered most of the continent, including Prussia.

The Prussians responded to their defeat at Napoleon's hands by taking steps to reform their army and match his tactics. Their war of liberation from France was partly aided by what they learned, although it also benefited from the depletion of French manpower through the many wars (particularly the destruction of the French cavalry during the retreat from Russia, a blow from which Napoleon never recovered and which played a decisive role in thwarting his comeback). Although Wellington's British troops are rightly credited with the final defeat of Napoleon at Waterloo, the decisive moment in the battle was the arrival of the Prussian forces on the battlefield late in the day, when both sides were badly mauled and desperately hoping for reinforcements. Arrival on the battlefield may sound like a trivial or accidental matter, but in fact it reflects planning, military intelligence, and troop mobility, all of which were the focus of the military advances of the time that the Prussians had emphasized.

Although Napoleon had been defeated, it was clear that his methods and armies had been the best in Europe. The French defeat had been due more to overreaching (e.g., invading Russia) and being outnumbered than to shortcomings of forces or tactics. Accordingly, it was now France's turn to stand pat as the best army in Europe, while Prussia and others scrambled to copy France's methods and to experiment with other innovations. For example, the Prussians developed staff work, in which officers would do calculations and paperwork to aid the planning of troop movements. This sort of work was pooh-poohed by old-line military officers (including the French) as sissy work, but it proved to have advantages (as already suggested by the decisive arrival of the Prussians at Waterloo).

Half a century after Napoleon, the Franco-Prussian War pitted these two rivals against each other again. France's armies were larger, but the Prussians were better disciplined, and the superior planning and coordination (due partly to the staff work) gave the Prussians a decisive victory once more. The prestige that the Napoleonic Wars had brought to the French military system was badly tarnished.

The story could be continued, but the point is clear. This long-standing military rivalry was marked by a pattern in which each victory in a war confirmed the winner's sense that its military system was superior, and so innovation slowed or ceased. Would-be innovators had difficulty convincing the top generals to change the tactics that were the envy of the world and that had brought such resounding success. Meanwhile, the loser of each war was stimulated to overhaul its system, borrowing techniques from the victors and adding new ones. The two rivals therefore tended to alternate victorious wars, because each victory contained the seeds of a subsequent defeat.

It is undoubtedly difficult to initiate radical changes in the wake of major success. The basic principles of learning dictate that success will reinforce the tendency to continue doing things in the same way, and innovations involve taking chances that may have unknown results. Career and political pressures within an organization may intensify this pattern. After all, if a manager were to abandon a system that had brought success and initiate a new system, and the new system failed, the manager's career would undoubtedly suffer a severe blow; it is difficult to imagine how one can make oneself look more stupid than by replacing effective methods with ineffective ones.

Yet circumstances do continue to change, and competition produces strong tendencies for successful methods to be copied, and so continued success requires that one make innovations. There have been ample illustrations of this pattern in our own times and society, even though nothing has quite the history of the Franco-Prussian rivalry. The computer company IBM, for example, made its name and fortune dealing in large mainframe computers and was therefore slow to create products for the new market in small, personal computers. As a result, in the early 1990s IBM's profits dwindled and the price of their stock—long regarded as the ultimate reliable, blue-chip stock—dropped substantially.

By the same token, in sports, many observers have noted the remarkably frequent turnover of coaches. Very few men remain head coaches for a decade or more, even ones who achieve great successes. One reason may well be that even a brilliant coach generates his innovations early in his career, achieves success with them, but then loses the competitive edge when his successful practices are copied and embellished by his competitors while he stands pat. The careers of the very few who hold long-term coaching success, such as Don Shula of Miami, Dean Smith of the University of North Carolina, and Bobby Knight of Indiana University, reflect continued innovation and adaptation. Smith, for example, achieved early success pioneering the "four corners" stall in which players would pass the ball around without attempting to score or advance, but he also abandoned that technique (even before the rules changed to put time limits on keeping the ball) when his opponents adapted to it, and indeed his first national championship was won without using that tactic that had made him famous.

MISMANAGING MONEY

Before concluding, let us examine one other important sphere in which people suffer from poor self-management: money. Although there is ample advice available on how to manage one's money, and indeed common sense seemingly would often be sufficient to enable people to keep their financial affairs in order, people repeatedly find themselves suffering from money problems. A recent survey in *Money* magazine found that Americans think about money more than they think about sex (Belsky, 1993), but despite this thought many find themselves in difficulties; indeed, the difficulties may be a major reason that so many think so much about money.

Most people both earn money and spend money. Common sense says that one must earn more than one spends, or else one will find oneself in trouble. Many people find themselves unable to live by this simple guideline, however. Although some working-class people may have effective money-managment stragegies, many working-class people find themselves in a chronic cycle of debt. Rubin (1976) observed that when she asked people what they would do if they suddenly came into a large sum of money, such as by winning a state lottery, nearly all her working-class respondents said that the first thing they would do would be to pay off their debts. This answer was relatively infrequent from middle-class individuals.

Of course, Rubin's data were collected before the extraordinary expansion of credit cards, which have to some extent burdened middle-class households with substantial debts as well. Indeed, credit cards may be regarded as one of the major hidden problems of self-regulation—at least, hidden from research psychologists. Accountants are quite familiar with stories of people who, for example, have $13,000 of credit card debt in a year when their gross income is $30,000!

The self-destructive nature of credit card mismanagement is clear. Credit cards encourage people to make purchases without paying for them. Instead, one only pays a minimum payment and keeps the rest of the cost as part of a debt owed to the credit card company. These debts typically have exorbitant interest rates. Depending on the interest rate and the schedule of paying it off, the person may pay as much as double the actual price of the item. It is thus a foolish and costly way to buy something.

Indeed, people would often do better to borrow money from a bank (even a second mortgage) rather than run up credit card bills, because the interest payments would be less. Some financial advisors, such as Jane Bryant Quinn in *Newsweek*, counsel people to do just that: take out a major loan from a bank and pay off all the credit card balances, thereby reducing the size and amount of interest payments one must make. Quinn cautions, however, that there is a major self-regulation fallacy in this approach. If people then run up new credit card bills, they will be worse off, because they still have the old debt (simply relocated to owing the bank rather than owing the credit card company) plus the new ones on top of it.

It is not surprising that some people come to perceive credit cards as dangerous and evil. One of the authors recalls watching, as a child, as mother and father cut their credit cards into pieces with scissors, as if conducting a ritual exorcism. Month after month the credit cards had produced shockingly high bills and had as a result burdened the family with an oppressive and expensive debt.

Undoubtedly a significant aspect of credit card mismanagement involves a failure of self-monitoring, just as we have seen in other spheres of self-regulation failure. (More precisely, this is a form of underregulation rather than misregulation.) If people kept careful track of their credit card expenditures, they could predict very accurately how much the bill will be at the end of the month, and they could keep it within acceptable limits. The mystery often seems to be how a series of seemingly trifling purchases, in the range of thirty or forty dollars each, could result in a bill of several hundred dollars at the end of the month. Each purchase seems small and reasonable and scarcely worth concerning oneself over. Yet to people's surprise and chagrin, very big bills can result from small expenditures. The surprise reflects the failure to monitor one's expenditures accurately while they are made.

There are several common approaches to using credit cards, and these may be linked to people's self-regulatory style and effectiveness. There are people who pay their bills in full each month, either because they keep track of their purchases or because they manage to prevent themselves from spending too much. These people are the successful self-regulators in this sphere. Another approach is to refuse to have or use credit cards at all. This manipulates the environment, removing the opportunity for one to lose control, and it must be considered also to be an effective form of self-regulation, even though it is based on the premise that one cannot self-regulate past the first line of defense. In contrast, there are many people who spend themselves into debt and anguish by overusing their credit. They find that credit cards lead them to spend more money than they have, leaving them with an ill-advised and costly debt. This pattern is the main one of self-regulatory failure.

Credit card mismanagement is often part of a broader pattern of fiscal mismanagement, in which people fail to save money. Once again, common sense dictates the logical and prudent course, which is to spend significantly less than one's income and put the rest into savings or investments. (Under some circumstances, such as hyperinflation, this strategy ceases to be prudent, but these circumstances are unusual and in the United States they have not arisen.) Keeping expenditures approximately equal to one's income is not an ideal model of self-regulation, although it is of course far superior to spending more than one's income. Having no savings leaves one vulnerable to catastrophe if any unforeseen expense arises or if one's income is interrupted for whatever reason. To be sure, many people find it is necessary to live in this hand-to-mouth fashion for a period of time, such as during one's student years. But when one settles into normal adult life, it is highly advisable to save money on a regular basis, and people who fail to do this qualify as having problems in fiscal self-regulation.

Saving requires self-regulation, however. If one has the money and wants something, there is the natural temptation or urge to spend it. Saving money is a form of delay of gratification (or is similar if not precisely the same thing). Success requires transcending the immediate stimulus environment and acting in accordance with long-term, maximal benefits.

Many people find themselves unable to save. Working-class people in particular often pursue a lifestyle in which they cash their paychecks and immediately start spending the money. The days before the next paycheck comes may be fraught with worry and enforced frugality, because they literally have no money left. Often they cultivate networks of friends who borrow from each other to tide themselves over until the next paycheck comes. The unfortunate result is that when the next check comes, much of it is already effectively spent and must be repaid to the friend.

It is of course possible to live on a very tight budget, but careful self-regulation is necessary. With higher incomes, self-regulation seemingly ought to be easier, but many people increase their expenditures in step with their rising incomes, and so one periodically encounters instances of people who find themselves in desperate financial straits despite high salaries. Such cases highlight the fact that hardly anyone is immune from the catastrophic dangers of self-regulation failure.

SUMMARY AND CONCLUSION

Self-management is a relatively high-level form of self-regulation. The basic principles of effective self-management are to know one's strengths and weaknesses and to make plans and commitments accordingly (i.e., so as to maximize one's strengths and work around or minimize one's weaknesses), as well as to maintain steady progress toward realistic, acceptable long-range goals.

Self-management fails for a variety of reasons. Improper, incomplete, or unrealistic goal setting practices can all undermine effective self-management. Some people fail to set long-term goals, in which case their lives meander rather aimlessly from one temporary pursuit to another. Others set only long-term goals, which are daunting and discouraging because one so rarely reaches them. (In other words, both long-term and short-term goals are necessary for optimal self-management.) Others set overly rigid goals, which increase frustration and discouragement when changing circumstances make it impossible to meet them, and which also remove any scope for spontaneity or choice along the way, thereby diminishing the enjoyment of one's work. Still others set unrealistically high goals, which increase the likelihood of depressing and sometimes costly failure.

Egotism—particularly concern with possible loss of face in response to failure or other ego threats—paradoxically emerged repeatedly as a cause of poor self-management. Inflated views of oneself hamper self-management by distorting self-knowledge. People with high self-esteem respond to ego threats by making unrealistic predictions and commitments about future performances. People procrastinate because they fear they will not be able to produce work that is up to the absurdly high level of quality they expect of themselves. People engage in self-handicapping, such as by failing to prepare adequately for an important performance, because they are concerned with having an excuse for possible failure or with creating the image of someone who is so gifted that he or she does not need to prepare extensively. And people who achieve some measure of success may become complacent and conceited, neglecting to improve further or to question their practices that have seemingly been proven correct, and so they fall behind in subsequent competitions.

All these phenomena reflect the pattern of focusing one's self-regulatory efforts on the wrong aspect. People focus on their emotions and on their self-esteem and as a result they neglect to do things that would actually promote the best outcome. The preoccupation with emotions and self-esteem thus becomes paradoxically self-defeating, because in the long run these practices undermine what would actually produce the best emotions and the largest boost to self-esteem, namely success. The procrastinator, for example, may postpone working on the task because of concerns with self-esteem and anxiety, but in the long run the final product is likely to suffer because of procrastination.

Another pervasive obstacle to effective self-management is failure of transcendence. When people lose their capacity to see beyond the immediate situation, they cease to regulate their lives in accordance with optimal long-range goals. Money problems, failures to delay gratification, and procrastination all have elements of transcendence failure.

These appear to be the major and common causes of self-management failure, but a number of other factors have occasionally been implicated too. Relatively little evidence pertains to the issue of strength, but the personality differences (such as differences in likelihood of proscrastinating and self-hand-icapping) and long-term consequences associated with successful delaying of gratification suggest that they are related to some form of chronic strength. Also, failure to monitor oneself may be central to a variety of money problems, particularly when people do not keep close track of how much they spend.

5

Thoughts Out of Control

For many people, the decline of religious faith is both a societal and a personal tragedy. For thousands of years, religion has served important purposes in helping people make sense of their world, cope with misfortune, and maintain hope for a better life. Religion also provides a compelling foundation for morality and in that way may contribute to keeping society orderly and forestalling a decline into violence, antisocial behavior, and other forms of moral chaos. Viewed in that light, a loss of religious faith is far more than a change in personal opinions about abstract metaphysical circumstances: It is the loss of a trusted friend and an erosion of an important foundation of a decent, orderly society.

The crisis of faith was perhaps most acutely felt in the American and British middle class during the late nineteenth century (see Houghton, 1957; Meyer, 1976). These men and, to a lesser extent, women tended to discover one day that they could no longer profess sincere belief in the Christian doctrines they had been taught since childhood. For present purposes, the important aspect of many of these cases was that the individuals still *wanted* to believe. They felt that both the society in general and their own personal lives would be better off if they could sustain their religious faith. But they found themselves unable to make themselves believe. Ironically, many of them concluded that the most socially beneficial and ethically appropriate thing for them to do would be to continue to support the Church. They kept their doubts to themselves, went on attending church, and acted as if they still believed in the fundamental truth of Christian dogma. This way, they thought, they were at least setting a good example and refraining from weakening others' faith. This made them vulnerable to the sensitive charge of hypocrisy, but this seemed better than contributing to the moral decay of society by openly defying religion. Still, it was an unhappy compromise; they would have much preferred to continue believing in religion (Houghton, 1957).

The inability to make oneself believe in certain religious doctrines is just one example of a failed effort to control one's thoughts. More generally, it is well known that people seek in multiple ways to regulate their mental processes, and this chapter will take a close look at some of the ways in which these efforts fail.

The notion that people should be able to control their thoughts is well established. Indeed, the belief that students can learn "critical thinking" in universities is based on the assumption that people can develop skills for intervening in their thought processes to exert some control and guidance. Critical thinking means that people can stop and question their preliminary conclusions and can if necessary replace one set of thoughts with another. It also implies that they can learn rules or algorithms for guiding the way they think.

When people cannot control their thoughts, they are surprised and dismayed, like the Victorians who found themselves unable to sustain their religious belief by force of will. Another phenomenon that often forces people to the surprising realization of how little control they have over their stream of thought is meditation. Beginning meditators are often very put out to discover that simple concentration tasks are nearly impossible. The internal monologue runs on by itself despite all sorts of efforts to stop it. It can be something of a shock to recognize how little control one actually may have over one's cognitive processes. Today, American citizens may generally accept the idea that impulses, appetites, performance patterns, and emotions may elude one's control, but people still expect to control their own thoughts. For that reason, thinking may be the most unexpected and (in that sense) most disturbing sphere of self-regulation failure.

OBSESSIONS AND COMPULSIONS

We begin by examining obsessions and compulsions. These are perhaps the most familiar and dramatic examples of the inability to control one's thoughts. Our discussion will be brief, because their value for the present discussion is limited by two factors. First, the causes of obsessions and compulsions are not well understood. Second, they constitute a form of mental illness (obsessive–compulsive disorder, or OCD), and as such lie outside the scope of this work. Still, they do serve as a valuable point of departure.

Obsessions are unwanted ideas or thoughts that plague an individual. During an obsession, a particular set of ideas keeps popping into a person's mind, try as he or she might to banish them. For example, thoughts about death or about sex may keep arising. Religious obsessions are also common, such as when a person keeps reflecting on some phrase from Scripture.

Compulsions refer to behavioral patterns that are similar to obsessions in that they keep happening despite the person's lack of volition for them or even despite the person's wish to stop doing them. Obviously, compulsions have a strong mental component (because the compulsive actions are prompted by recurring thoughts), and so it is not feasible to make firm and definitive distinctions between obsessions and compulsions; most theorists and researchers seem to treat the two as interrelated phenomena.

One standard example of OCD is compulsive hand washing. People become obsessed with the notion that their hands are dirty or vulnerable to germs, and they end up spending an inordinate amount of time scrubbing themselves. Reed (1985) offered a pair of typical cases. Both of the women spent most of their waking hours engaged in washing their hands. One of them would wash her hands forty or fifty times per day, spending about fifteen minutes each time. The other would wash her hands only about five times a day, but each time took three or four hours.

What lies behind this inability to stop oneself from dwelling on these repeated, instrusive ideas? The traditional view is that these thoughts and actions ward off anxiety in some way; in this view, anxiety reappears whenever the person fails to complete the ritual. Rachman and Hodgson (1980) noted, however, that the empirical evidence has not been fully consistent with that view, such as the fact that some compulsive rituals fail to decrease anxiety. Several years later, Reed (1985) argued that the evidence was now much stronger against the anxiety-prevention theory. Reed concluded that the anxiety is often a byproduct of the obsessive–compulsive experience, particularly arising from the sense of helplessness that accompanies it. If anything, he thought, obsessions and compulsions contribute to anxiety rather than alleviating it.

In terms of self-regulation failure, OCD involves a deficit at self-stopping. Rachman and Hodgson (1980) provided some useful insights about this deficit. First, obsessional people are usually able control other thoughts; their problem is not a generalized inability to control any of their thoughts. In other words, they can stop themselves from thinking about neutral or alternate topics, even though they seem unable to stop themselves from thinking about the topic of their obsession. Second, they do form obsessions more easily and effectively than other subjects, when instructed to do so in a research setting. In a sense, then, certain people seem prone or predisposed to the experience of being unable to control their thoughts, even though normally they can shut off many thoughts that do not become a particular problem or concern to them.

Reed (1985) carried Rachman and Hodgson's analysis a step further to address the specific question of whether the problem is the strength of the thought or the weakness of the person's capacity to suppress it. Reed noted that popular conceptions and some early theories about compulsions have emphasized the view that the central problem is a powerful impulse that overwhelms any efforts to control it. Self-reports by compulsives, however, rarely attest to any overwhelming power of the impulse; rather, they describe the impulse as fairly ordinary, and instead they emphasize their own lack of strength to control it. In other words, compulsives describe their subjective experience in terms of a lack of willpower. Over two-thirds of Reed's own research sample made explicit references to weakness of will, lack of self-control, or the like. Thus, they portray the problem in terms of their inability to shut off what seems a normal impulse. References to the overwhelming power of the impulse were quite rare (4%), in contrast. Reed concluded, therefore, that theorizing about obsessions and compulsions should emphasize the failure of the inhibitory apparatus rather than the strength of the impulse.

Recent analyses by Seligman (1994) have pointed out that obsessions and compulsions tend to focus on actions that are highly adaptive. Checking and cleaning are the two most common forms of compulsions, and for the most part checking and cleaning are good for you. After all, people who are careless about checking important things and who disdain personal cleanliness will be more prone to accidents, diseases, and other misfortunes than people who are reasonably scrupulous about checking and cleaning. In a sense, then, checking and cleaning compulsions might reflect patterns that are ingrained for positive, beneficial reasons but that somehow become carried to excess in certain cases. Seligman cited recent evidence about biological factors in OCD in support of his argument. Thus, evolution would select in favor of people who were prone to check and clean. In other words, the impulse to do such things may be part of everyone's normal biological makeup; compulsives either have an excess of such promptings or lack the usual capacity to shut down those impulses once the person has already carried out the behavior.

The view that emerges from these findings is that OCD centrally involves some self-regulatory deficit. In Reed's (1985) view, there is some shortcoming in the person's inhibitory capacity—that is, the person is unable to turn off the system once it has begun. The first behaviors are normal, but then the person is unable to stop himself or herself from continuing, even though the functional need for the behavior has been satisfied. In other terms, the person is unable to "exit" from the feedback loop or to override the impulse to repeat the behavior.

Another version of this theory is that obsessions and compulsions are attempts to compensate for some self-regulatory deficit. Certainly some of the secondary traits associated with OCD can be understood as consequences of the self-regulatory failure. Reed (1985) says that the central problem experienced by obsessives and compulsives has to do with setting limits and fixing boundaries (such as to limit the need to wash one's hands). The obsessional has difficulty in the normal, spontaneous structuring of experience, and therefore tries to compensate by imposing extra structure in the form of boundaries, limits, time markers, and the like. Lack of tolerance for ambiguity, overstructuring of performance, determining endpoints and time limits, complying with prescriptions and rules, maintaining prescribed structures, and similar traits have been linked with the obsessive–compulsive individual. These traits seem to reflect this preoccupation with structure. The quest for such structure and the excessive adherence to structure, which have been commonly observed among these individuals, may be a response to the inner sense that they cannot control themselves without those external aids.

We have emphasized throughout this work that self-regulatory capacity is a kind of strength, and so self-regulation failure tends to occur when there is a lack or loss of strength. Some evidence about OCD is consistent with this view. Obsessions begin under times of high stress, when the person is feeling bad, and further episodes of stress and dysphoria make obsessions worse (Rachman & Hodgson, 1980). Thus, when strength is depleted, which as we have said makes self-regulation that much more difficult, these obsessive–compulsive patterns increase.

To conclude, OCD seems to consist of a failure of self-stopping. Most obsessions and compulsions involve things that are sensible and even adaptive, such as checking for safety or cleaning oneself, and the impulse to do such things is not inherently bad or wrong or abnormal in any way. The problem seems to be that the person cannot stop doing those things. Washing hands, for example, is healthy (indeed, health experts now suggest that if everyone were to wash his or her hands with soap once an hour, most of the major flu virus epidemics would be prevented), but the hands are clean after a minute or two, and continuing to wash for another three hours is absurd.

The lack of willpower to shut these obsessions and compulsions down is felt by the individuals as a lack of strength. Some blame themselves for having weakness or lack of character, although theorists think that there may be biological or other causes for this deficit. In any case, the strength aspect is further confirmed by the fact that obsessions and compulsions seem to increase during periods of stress and emotional distress.

UNWANTED THOUGHTS

Although people with OCD may be the most familiar and vivid image of the difficulty of controlling one's thoughts, there are plenty of cases in which healthy, normal people have similar difficulties. Indeed, the problem of not being able to stop one's mind from having certain thoughts is a common one. For example, Karen finds it hard not to think about food when she is on a diet; Jimmy finds his mind keeps returning to thoughts of a sexually attractive newcomer even though he is happily married and does not want to think about cheating on his wife; Doug can't stop thinking about how he embarrassed himself when he met with the dean last week. In all these examples, the unwanted thoughts can be hard to suppress.

Dan Wegner (e.g., 1989, 1992; see Wegner & Erber, 1992; Wegner, Schneider, Carter, & White, 1987; Wegner et al., 1990; Wenzlaff, Wegner, & Klein, 1991; Wenzlaff, Wegner, & Roper, 1988) developed a research paradigm to study thought suppression in the laboratory. Wegner borrowed the initial idea for the paradigm from an episode described by Tolstoy. Tolstoy described being challenged by his older brother to stand in a corner until he could stop thinking about a white bear. Although he had not been not thinking of a white bear before the challenge, knowing that he was not supposed to think about the white bear resulted in intrusive thoughts of a white bear, keeping him in the corner and out of his brother's hair for some time.

Wegner et al. (1987) tried to demonstrate the same effect in the laboratory with college students. Students were asked to speak aloud every single thought that came into their minds for 5 min but not to think about a white bear during that time. They were told to ring a bell every time a white bear thought intruded. It proved quite difficult for them to suppress thoughts of the white bear—on average people had more that six white bear intrusions over the 5-min time span. People did get better with practice; most of the white bear thoughts came at the beginning of the time period. People who were asked not to think about white bears were eventually able to think about them less than people who had been asked to try to think about white bears. However, thought suppression led to a *rebound effect*. When the prohibition against thinking about white bears was subsequently removed, people in the suppression condition showed a rebound effect and thought about white bears even more than people who were asked to think about white bears. In other words, over time people who had tried to suppress thoughts ended up thinking those thoughts more than people who had tried to think those thoughts all along!

One decisive determinant of the effectiveness of efforts at thought suppression is the availability of powerful distractors. For example, when people were instructed to think about a red Volkswagen instead of a white bear, they were able to keep thoughts of the white bear at bay much more effectively than in other conditions. These findings indicate that effective management of attention via self-distraction is an important means of regulating thought processes.

Thus, Wegner et al. (1987) demonstrated that efforts to suppress a thought are normally only partly effective. Although one can learn to distract oneself from a thought one is trying not to think, as soon as the inhibition against the thought is removed, the previously suppressed thought floods the mind (i.e., the rebound effect). Not only do people find it difficult to suppress thoughts, the attempt to do so makes them especially likely to become absorbed with the suppressed thought later. Thus, trying not to think about something may cause people to continue to think about it.

Although early notions of obsessions suggested that they arise as a product of traumatic experiences, Wegner (1989) suggested that *synthetic obsessions* can be created by trying to suppress thoughts. If a person has an unwanted thought, he or she may try not to think about it. Small initial efforts to suppress the thought may fail at first, or the thought may become more frequent during a rebound period when the person is not actively trying to suppress it (perhaps when the person is trying to monitor whether the thought has been properly suppressed). This failure of suppression may cause the person to escalate to more and more urgent suppression tactics. Thus, Wegner (1989) suggested that one may develop something similar to obsessions because one tried to suppress the thought even before it became an obsession, when it was merely an unwanted thought.

Of particular interest for self-regulation failure is the ironic process in which efforts to suppress thoughts can backfire. Wegner and Erber (1992; Wegner, 1994) have suggested that any attempt at mental control brings with it the *ironic* operation of mental monitoring processes that are likely to undermine that control. When a person tries to suppress a thought, the intention to suppress may introduce an automatic, unconscious mental process that searches for that very thought in an effort to monitor whether the suppression has been successful. In other words, the mechanism for avoiding a thought requires monitoring or attending to it or to signs of it. Cognitive load interferes with the conscious mechanism of suppressing the thought, but it does not interfere with the automatic mechanism of monitoring for instances of the unwanted thought. Because the suppression is interfered with but the monitoring is left intact, the likelihood of noticing that one is having the unwanted thought is increased when one is busy or distracted.

Wegner (1994) has also proposed that ironic processes may contribute to a broad variety of self-regulation failures. Indeed, in his view, ironic processes will cause people to do the worst possible thing or whatever is precisely the opposite of what they want. This extremely counterproductive outcome ensues because the monitoring system is engaged in searching out signals of the forbidden or unwanted event, and when the conscious operating system is prevented from counteracting those signals, the operating system will draw the person like a magnet to think, feel, or do the forbidden thing. For example, a recovering alcoholic may form a conscious intention of avoiding alcohol, and to aid this process he develops an automatic monitoring system that watches for danger signals of drinking or wanting to drink. Most of the time, whenever the monitoring system spots such a danger signal the person can respond consciously and avoid the problem. When the conscious mind is burdened and distracted by other issues, however, such as relationship conflicts or problems at work, the monitoring system will still continue to search out cues pertaining to alcohol consumption. The man may then find himself thinking frequently about having a drink.

The findings regarding thought suppression are relevant to OCD, covered earlier, where problems get worse over time. Anxiety results from the continual failure in the struggle to stop oneself from thinking about the forbidden thought. This anxiety may create a cognitive load, which makes all self-control more difficult, including controlling thoughts. In fact, Wegner (1992) suggested that an undesired thought that one is attempting to suppress is likely to become more accessible under conditions of cognitive load, because this load will disrupt the controlled, conscious search for distractors more than it will the automatic scanning for the undesired thought. Thus, anxiety about one's inability to suppress a thought may make it even more difficult for one to control one's thoughts subsequently.

The increase in intrusions of the thought one is trying to suppress when one is under cognitive load is consistent with the strength model we have described in Chapter 2. According to the strength model, anything that overtaxes the operating system will impair self-regulation, while leaving the monitoring system intact. If the control is decreased but the monitoring is unaffected, then more instances of the unwanted thought are likely to be detected.

So far we have been discussing mainly neutral thoughts, such as white bears, which are being suppressed. Although Wegner's research makes it clear that one can create the underpinnings for an obsession from any thought if one tries to suppress it enough, in actuality people are likely to try to suppress some thoughts more than others. Wegner and Erber (1993) have concluded that thoughts that are socially unaceptable are most likely to be the object of suppression attempts. Violence, sexuality, personal shortcomings and self-doubts, fears, concerns about personal hygiene failures, and so forth are thoughts that are not socially approved, and so they are the most likely candidates for suppression. Indeed, obsessive thinking does tend to center on these private or taboo topics (e.g., Rachman & Hodgson, 1980; Stekel, 1949). Other common unwanted thoughts that people frequently report trying to suppress include memories of their past victimizations and desirous thoughts of substances to which they are addicted (Wegner, 1989).

There is considerable evidence suggesting that attempts to suppress these socially inappropriate topics may backfire at least as much as the attempts to suppress neutral topics. Lindemann (1944) found that people who try not to think about their grief over a lost loved one can take the longest to get over their loss. Likewise, incest survivors who try to block out thoughts of their trauma can become particularly obsessed by their tormented memories of the event (Silver, Boon, & Stones, 1983), and people who attempt to control their eating while on a diet by trying not to think about food can become obsessed with food thoughts and even resort to binge eating (Polivy & Herman, 1985). Nolen-Hoeksema (1990) found that people who continually try to control their unwanted thoughts reported greater rates of depression. Thus, research findings in a number of different areas have suggested that trying to suppress thoughts frequently backfires, resulting in even more frequent occurrences of the undesired thought.

Some thoughts may be even more difficult to suppress than others. Exciting, arousing thoughts, such as thoughts about sex, may pose special problems for thought suppression. Wegner et al. (1990) found that subjects who were trying not to think about sex showed elevated skin conductance levels as high or higher than subjects who were instructed to think about sex. In other words, trying to suppress thoughts about sex was as arousing as thinking sexual thoughts. Subjects in this set of studies were also asked to report their thoughts aloud when they were trying to think or not think the requested thoughts.

A minute-by-minute examination of the thoughts was correlated with skin conductance level, and the results suggested that trying not to think about something that is exciting (like sex) produces renewed excitement whenever the thought intrudes. Thus, when one is trying to suppress exciting thoughts, one gets more excited every time the automatic monitoring process finds an intrusion, resulting in a state of excitement as high or higher than if one were engaging in sexual imagery.

In summary, work by Wegner and colleagues suggests that trying to suppress thoughts or avoid thinking unwanted thoughts is difficult to accomplish and can frequently backfire. Individuals who attempt to suppress an unwanted thought may end up thinking the undesired thought more than individuals who had never tried to suppress it. Banishing unwanted thoughts from the mind is thus a difficult self-regulation task, and failures are to be expected. Such failures may of course have consequences beyond thought suppression itself. It seems likely that many failures of impulse control and affect regulation may be linked to the inability to keep one's mind off of a particular stimulus.

DECISIONS AND INFERENCES

Both obsessions and thought suppression deal with the problem of stopping a particular thought or idea from recurring in one's mind. Self-regulation can also concern itself with more complex processes, however, such as reasoning, drawing conclusions, making decisions, and making inferences. In this section we will deal with just such efforts to steer the train of thought and with people's self-regulation failures in connection with such efforts.

Despite a huge amount of research on cognitive processes, relatively little attention has been paid to self-regulation of them. A recent review article by Baumeister and Newman (1994) on the self-regulation of inference and decision processes elicited comments from journal editors and reviewers that such an approach was radically different from anything currently available in the research literature. The work reviewed in that paper dealt in a preliminary way with how people try to direct and override cognitive processes. If the study of self-regulation of cognitive processes is currently in its infancy, the evidence about self-regulation failures in that sphere is even more sparse. Accordingly, our comments will have to be limited and tentative.

Baumeister and Newman (1994) said that there are two main reasons that people will try to regulate their cognitive processes. One is the desire to be especially careful and thorough in order to reach an accurate, correct, or optimal conclusion (e.g., to form an accurate judgment of someone, or to reach the best decision). The other is the desire to reach a particular, preferred conclusion (see also Kruglanski, 1989, 1990; Kunda, 1990). The first of these may be compared to the familiar image of the *intuitive scientist*, which is the term used by psychologists to refer to the way people process information similar to the scientific method: People may assemble and weigh evidence, test hypotheses, rule out alternatives, and so forth. The second reason was dubbed the "intuitive lawyer" by Baumeister and Newman, because it resembles the task to which lawyers are often assigned, namely to try to make the best possible case for a predetermined conclusion. Thus, for example, a lawyer may have to try to show that the evidence is consistent with his client's innocence, even if the lawyer secretly knows that the client is guilty.

The intuitive lawyer shades into issues of self-deception, because the person is trying to reach a conclusion that may not be correct or optimal. Self-deception presents special problems for self-regulation theory and will be covered in the next section. This section will focus on the intuitive scientist— that is, it will examine how people try (and fail) to regulate their mental processes so as to reach correct or optimal conclusions.

One source of failure to control cognitive processes is a classic instance of underregulation: failure to try. Decision and reasoning processes are subject to a variety of biases, errors, distortions, and other problems, and it takes effort to overcome them. The failure to exert oneself hard enough to ensure an optimal and unbiased decision can thus lead to errors.

As evidence for self-regulation failure due to lack of exertion, one can cite a number of studies that show that people can make more correct or otherwise better decisions and inferences when they try extra hard. Thus, Neuberg (1989) showed that people could reach correct conclusions about interaction partners by paying more attention to them, spending more time listening to them, asking more questions, and the like, but they did not do so in the control condition (where they were not given special instructions to emphasize the importance of being especially accurate). Neuberg's study involves several themes that are familiar with regard to self-regulation failure. One is strength, in that the person must exert himself or herself to reach the correct conclusion. Another is attention: Better management of attention is, as usual, an important factor in effective self-regulation. When people do not exert themselves to pay close attention to other people—to *listen* to them carefully, for example—they do not end up with as thorough and accurate an impression of those other people.

Issues of strength and attention management were even more dramatically implicated in a study by Keinan (1987) on how information processing changes under stress. Keinan studied how people dealt with the various alternatives in a decision process. The complexity of having to decide among multiple options (a common feature of decisions) was modeled in the experiment by using a multiple-choice format. Normally, when people take multiple-choice tests or try to choose among multiple-decision options, they review all the alternatives and choose the best one. Under stress, however, people seem to pick the first alternative they encounter that seems correct. Thus, they ignore some of the possible options. These findings suggest that when strength is depleted by having to cope with stress, people pay less attention to all the various possibilities and instead try to zero in quickly on one that seems correct. As a result, their processing of the available information remains somewhat incomplete and hence subject to possible errors. For present purposes, the point is that people may underregulate their cognitive processes when their strength is depleted. They take shortcuts, which increase the danger of error.

Another variable that increases the importance of making the right decision is *accountability*, which refers to any pressure on the person to defend his or her decision or to personally accept bad consequences for making a wrong choice. When people know they will be held accountable, they respond by taking into account more of the available information (e.g., Tetlock, 1985). Other research has shown that when people expect to have to justify their judgments, or even if they merely think that their decisions will be made public, they try harder to be thorough and hence seem able to resist certain biasing factors (such as ethnic stereotypes or even mere primacy effects) when they are judging the quality of someone's work (Kruglanski & Freund, 1983; Freund, Kruglanski, & Shpitzajzen, 1985). Thus, various forms of accountability make people pay more attention, process information more thoroughly, and hence reach more informed decisions and resist bias. The implication is that when people do not try extra hard, they do not process the information as thoroughly, and they are less likely to reach sound and optimal conclusions.

Factors other than accountability can motivate people to be extra careful and thorough in processing information, of course. One factor is simply the expectation that one will meet and interact with other people; after all, it is more important to form a correct impression about someone you will meet than about an anonymous stranger. When people do not care about someone, because they do not expect to meet him or her, they do a more superficial and shallow job of processing information about that person, and they are less prone to make informed, accurate judgments from the information they have (Devine, Sedikides, & Fuhrman, 1989; Monson, Keel, Stephens, & Genung, 1982).

Thus, some bad judgments and wrong decisions arise because of underregulation. Others are due to misregulation, however. That is, sometimes people override their inference and decision processes in ways that fail to increase accuracy and even may reduce accuracy. There are several types of misregulation.

One type of misregulation involves simply paying extra attention to the wrong information and hence being biased by it. Tetlock and Boettger (1989) showed that although accountability may increase effort and improve accuracy under some conditions, it can also increase the *dilution effect*, in which irrelevant information is given extra weight and ends up having more influence on the final decision. Extra effort makes people more thorough but does not necessarily make them more able to judge the relevance and importance of various bits of information, and so sometimes spending more time can simply mislead the person (see also Wilson, Dunn, Bybee, Hyman, & Rotonda 1984).

Misregulation is also apparent in *overcorrection* effects. Sometimes people discover that their preliminary conclusions were distorted by some bias or misleading factor, and they attempt to alter this judgment to compensate for the bias. Unfortunately, they may not know how much their conclusion was affected by the biasing information, and so whatever adjustment they tack on after the fact may be far from correct. Several studies have shown that people sometimes overestimate how much they have been biased, with the result that when they attempt to adjust to compensate for this bias, they end up with a conclusion that is distorted in the opposite direction.

Two studies have shown overcorrection effects in jury simulation contexts. Hatvany and Strack (1980) examined the issue of how jurors respond to inadmissible evidence. That is, the experimental subjects heard a fair amount of testimony, and afterward they were instructed to disregard certain information because it had been ruled inadmissible. The result was directly opposite to the usual assumption that jurors continue to be swayed by evidence that has been ruled admissible: Indeed, subjects in this study adjusted their decisions excessively. Although the controversial evidence suggested that the defendant was guilty, subjects who heard it ended up with a greater likelihood of supporting a not-guilty verdict (as compared with subjects who had not heard this evidence). Presumably they overestimated how much they had been swayed by the inadmissible evidence, and in attempting to erase its influence on their conclusion, they made too large an adjustment.

A similar finding was obtained by Shaffer and Case (1982). Their subjects were drawn from the general, predominantly heterosexual population, which normally has a bias against homosexuals. In a jury simulation procedure, subjects in one condition learned that the defendant was homosexual. The danger, therefore, was that their anti-homosexual bias would influence them to be more harsh toward the defendant. Ironically, however, these subjects ended up being more lenient toward the defendant (as compared with jurors who were not told that the defendant was homosexual). Thus, they assumed that they would be biased against this defendant, and they sought to correct for that bias—but they overestimated how much they had been biased and so they made too large an adjustment. The net result was that their prejudice against this defendant caused them to end up treating him more favorably.

These self-regulation failures occur because people do not know enough about their inner processes to regulate them effectively. Inadequacies of self-knowledge and introspection (see Nisbett & Wilson, 1977) are not limited to overcorrection effects; indeed, they are implicated in a broad range of self-regulation failures. For example, people may regulate the wrong thing, such as when they act on the assumption that they have corrected the bias when they have not. In a well-known study, Darley and Gross (1983) showed that prejudice can influence judgments of individuals even when they think they are carefully avoiding such bias. Subjects in their study were able to refrain from showing any bias (against a schoolgirl from a lower-class background) when they had to judge her solely on her background. However, when they were also able to observe her performance during an oral exam, they ended up forming a more negative assessment of her (than if the same performance had been paired with information depicting her as coming from a privileged, advantageous background). In short, they knew enough to stop themselves from leaping to a conclusion about her abilities directly from her background—but they were unaware that their perception of her performance was biased by knowledge of her background. They were thus unable to prevent the second, indirect, more subtle form of bias.

A related effect arises because the mind is often swayed by memory traces of its own activity, often without realizing such effects. The classic work on theory perseverance, begun by Anderson, Lepper, and Ross (1980) showed that people cannot seem to undo all the effects of some misleading information. In that study, subjects were given false information and then asked to elaborate on it. Later, when told that the initial information was false, they were still biased by it. Even though people could eliminate the initial (and now proven false) information from their final decision, they could not undue its effect on their subsequent mental activity. Subsequent work by Anderson and colleagues (e.g., Anderson et al., 1980; Anderson, New, & Speer, 1985) has concluded that causal thinking, in particular, leads to perseverance of such biases. When you spend time and effort thinking about why something may be true, you have difficulty undoing all your conclusions even if you learn that that "something" is not true at all.

Subsequent work has pointed to a similar conclusion about the difficulty of undoing one's own thinking. Wyer and Unverzagt (1985) had subjects form an impression based on a list of behaviors that someone had allegedly performed. Later, subjects were told to ignore some of those behaviors. They were unable to undo all the effects on their impressions, however, presumably because thinking about those behaviors had led to other conclusions and inferences that were not canceled when the person retroactively tried to ignore the behaviors themselves. Gilbert and Osborne (1989) showed that subjects could retroactively correct a biased trait inference, but in the mean time that inference had colored interpretations of other ambiguous or neutral information, so once again that initial inference continued to have a demonstrable effect on their conclusion even though they had explicitly canceled the inference itself.

These limitations on self-regulation of cognitive processes can be somewhat illustrated by considering recent issues concerning how courts (judges and juries) deal with the danger of racial prejudice. Opponents of capital punishment thought that evidence of racial bias would be a good argument against the death penalty, and so several studies have carefully investigated such effects. To the surprise of many researchers, the evidence indicated that black defendants now receive slightly more lenient treatment on average than their white counterparts (Baldus, Woodworth, & Pulaski, 1990). Apparently, judges and jurors can successfully self-regulate their decision processes so as to prevent anti-black bias from affecting their decisions (see Devine, 1989). However, racial prejudice re-emerged in studies that focused on the race of the homicide *victim*:

There is a tendency for killers of blacks to be treated more leniently than killers of whites.

For present purposes, the crucial implication is that of the limitations on self-regulation of cognitive processes. People may be aware of the danger of bias based on the race of the defendant, and so they can overcome it—possibly even overcorrecting for it, which would explain the currently more lenient treatment of black than of white defendants. On the other hand, people may not be aware of bias based on the victim's race, and so they may fail to correct or adjust for it. Thus, while they eliminate antiblack bias based on the defendant, a similar bias remains in force with regard to victims.

Thus, people may fail to reach optimal or correct conclusions because of several kinds of self-regulation failure. Underregulation is apparent in failing to try hard enough to process all relevant information, failing to search for all pertinent evidence, and failing to watch out for biases and distortions. Misregulation is apparent when people make themselves pay attention to irrelevant information, make adjustments or corrections that are out of proportion to what is being corrected for, or focus their self-regulatory efforts on the wrong aspect of the decision process.

THE STRANGE CASE OF SELF-DECEPTION

Self-deception involves convincing oneself of something that one prefers to believe, presumably something that is not really true (see Sartre, 1953; also Baumeister, 1993b; Haight, 1980). In particular, people deceive themselves with respect to important aspects of their own personal lives, typically convincing themselves that they have more good qualities, more control over life, and more favorable prospects than they actually have (Taylor, 1989; Taylor & Brown, 1988).

With self-deception, there are two competing processes. On the one hand, the person wants to believe some particular thing. On the other, the person wants to know the truth; after all, it is no good simply to believe something pleasant if it is false. The search for truth and the search for a particular answer thus operate against each other, and whichever overrides the other will emerge as the winner. In that sense, self-deception is an anomalous or marginal example of self-regulation. There is no true hierarchy; the person wants to believe something and wants to know the truth, but the person wants that something to be true, and so what the person wants is impossible. Whether to accept miserable truth or pleasant illusion is thus the issue.

For our present focus on self-regulation failure, therefore, we could in principle consider both successful and unsuccessful self-deception. Successful self-deception is in a sense a failure of the mind's efforts to learn and know the truth. Unsuccessful self-deception is the inability to sustain a cherished belief or to confirm a preferred conclusion. Because we have already spent some time considering the inability to make oneself overcome bias and reach correct conclusions (earlier in this chapter), however, and because a full treatment of self-deception would take this discussion far afield, this section will focus on what makes self-deception fail.

In a sense, reality constraints are the most obvious and important cause of failure of self-deception. As Kunda (1990) has pointed out, people cannot simply believe anything they like; they are constrained by their ability to make a plausible, convincing case for what they want to believe. A young man may wish to believe himself to be a genius, but as he accumulates a record of mediocre grades, failed tests, and unspectacular career accomplishments, it may become increasingly obvious that he is no genius. One can generally convince oneself that one is a *little* smarter than objective reality might warrant, but it is difficult to stretch the truth very far.

An important factor that keeps people tied to reality is the social feedback they receive from other people. In isolation, one might perhaps convince oneself of all sorts of things, but such excesses will often be quickly and bluntly curbed when one starts talking about them to other people. Your friends will often tell you if your illusions start to become delusions. Sullivan (1953) suggested that one's "chum" (that is, one's best friend in preadolescence) served an important function by helping one to correct one's inflated self-evaluations from childhood.

Indeed, it may not even be necessary for other people to burst your bubble, because self-deception may be curtailed simply by anticipating how other people might think about things. A study by Baumeister and Cairns (1992) explored a fairly elementary form of self-deception, namely ignoring bad news (or, in self-regulatory terms, managing attention so as to avoid threatening stimuli). People were confronted with unflattering evaluations of their personalities. When these were confidential, people spent a minimum amount of time reading them, presumably because they preferred not to be exposed to such threatening information. When they believed other people would see those evaluations, however, they spent significantly more time reading them carefully and thoroughly. Thus, contact with other people prevented these individuals from simply ignoring and dismissing some threatening information about themselves.

Another self-deceptive strategy is to devise self-serving explanations that remove any undesirable implications from threatening events. Romantic rejection, for example, might threaten one's conception of oneself as an attractive, desirable lover, but such threats are defused if one can ascribe rejection to irrationality or to other external factors (such as the notion that the person who rejected you is not interested in anyone of your gender).

In such cases, one's ability to sustain the pleasant illusion depends on the validity of the explanation one devised; if something undermines that view, the threat resurfaces in a potentially unpleasant fashion. If you dismissed your recent romantic rejection as due to the fact that the person who rejected you is simply unable to appreciate your athletic prowess, you may be especially upset when you learn that the person is now dating the captain of your own sports team (Salovey, 1994).

The vulnerability of such strategies has been implicated in several problems involving racial prejudice. Crocker and Major (1989) noted that, contrary to countless theories about how belonging to a stigmatized or disadvantaged group will lead to low self-esteem, American blacks and women do not seem to suffer any deficit in self-esteem. How do people manage to maintain high self-esteem despite societal messages that convey inferiority? One strategy, apparently, is to ascribe one's failures as due to prejudice and bias. Identical failure experiences may therefore lower the self-esteem of a white man but leave a black man's self-esteem intact, because the black man can assume that the failure reflects prejudice and discrimination instead of any shortcoming on his part. In laboratory studies reviewed by Crocker and Major, black subjects showed no loss of self-esteem in response to failure experiences and bad evaluations—except when they learned that the evaluation was given by someone who did not know their race.

The strategy of ascribing one's failures to prejudice is jeopardized by anything that implies that prejudice is not a powerful, omnipresent force. Steele (1992) has analyzed some of the tragic side effects of this dilemma for upwardly mobile black citizens, who often find themselves subjected to emotional pressures from other blacks and so eventually feel that they cannot identify themselves with their successes. Likewise, during racially motivated riots in Los Angeles, the news media noted with surprise the apparent hostility between poor blacks and Korean immigrant citizens, such that black rioters seemed to single out shops and businesses owned by Koreans as targets. But the successes of upwardly mobile blacks and Koreans may be very threatening to people who maintain self-esteem by explaining all their failures as due to a racist system, because it suggests that their basic assumptions are not valid.

Another strategy for defending the self against threatening implications of events is *temporal bracketing*: drawing a boundary in time and saying that what occurred prior to that boundary is irrelevant. Many people find that they have done things they consider immoral, improper, or regrettable in other ways. To protect their current self-esteem, however, they prefer to insist that those events are so far in the past that they are irrelevant to their present selves and so should not be considered in judging them. Indeed, society has institutionalized some forms of temporal bracketing. Religious experiences of being "born again," or the legal policy of sealing court records of juvenile offenders, both imply that misdeeds occurring before a certain date do not count any more.

A less formal version of temporal bracketing is commonly used by people in discussing all sorts of failures and misdeeds (see Baumeister, Stillwell, & Wotman, 1990; also Baumeister & Ilko, 1994). Transgressors describe their misdeeds as being isolated episodes that are now over and done, with no lasting or continuing consequences. Likewise, people (particularly those with low self-esteem) tend to describe their failures in the past tense and as having no continuing consequences in the present. The present self is thus not implicated.

This strategy, however, can fail if something manages to link the prior event with the present. Victims, in particular, tend to adopt a long-term context for their traumas and to see them as continuing to be relevant to the present (Baumeister, Stillwell, & Wotman, 1990). Seeing one's former victim may therefore be especially threatening to a perpetrator, however, because victims tend to insist on linking the past to the present, whereas the perpetrator wants to bury the past. Likewise, any other attention paid to those events may be disturbing to perpetrators, who wish to see them as ancient history. For example, children of Nazi war criminals and perpetrators often reported that whenever some reference to the Nazi era and its atrocities would come on television or radio, their parents would invariably say something to the effect of, "That old business, why are they are bringing that up again?" or "That was so long ago, who cares about it now?" (Bar-On, 1989; Sichrovsky, 1988).

Such cases bring up the idea of collective self-deception: Sometimes an entire group or entire society attempts self-deception. One cannot assume that people simply believe whatever society tells them to believe, however. Collective self-deception has been known to fail too.

A pair of large-scale efforts at self-deception—one successful and one unsuccessful—was contrasted by Baumeister (1991b). To summarize briefly: Due to social change, the Industrial Revolution, modern science, and other factors, Western society began to move Christian religious faith to the periphery of life around the seventeenth century. This is not to say that people ceased to believe in the Christian God; they merely began to live their daily lives with less and less reference to religious teachings. One result of this was that the notion of the good, happy, fulfilled life, which Christianity had provided for so long, became less relevant, and so people began to look for happiness and fulfillment in secular terms.

Accordingly, in fairly short order, Western culture produced a pair of powerful new ideas about what made for happiness and fulfillment. One of these was the work ethic, which held that devoting oneself to one's work would make one a better person and lead to happiness (particularly in the form of material success). The other was that parenthood would have the same effects (not necessarily through material success, however). Both of these required some considerable stretching of the truth: Most work provides neither spiritual (or psychological) edification nor huge leaps of upward mobility, and parents are less happy than childless couples (see Baumeister, 1991b, for a review). The consensus among modern scholars is that the work ethic has largely failed (e.g., Rodgers, 1978), whereas the parenthood ethic is alive and well. Why?

Several reasons can be suggested. In the first place, again, reality constraints were much more troublesome for the work ethic than for the parenthood ethic. Not only current conditions, but also the direction of changes (e.g., the emergence of assembly line work), made it obvious that work brought neither joy nor riches, whereas children undeniably do bring considerable joy (setting aside, for a moment, the stresses and problems) to many parents. Second, society needs the belief in parenthood more than it needs the belief in work, and the greater motivation may have resulted in more consistent efforts to sustain the illusion. Lastly, parenthood is more compatible than work with Western culture's basic assumptions about fulfillment, in several ways. In particular, at the end of life (when one typically assesses what one has attained), work often recedes into a seemingly trivial progression of paperwork and long-forgotten transactions; meanwhile, parenthood is often best enjoyed at this stage in life, because the worries, stresses, and conflicts are largely forgotten, whereas the relationship with the adult offspring can be an important source of joy and pride.

In short, a variety of external events and factors can challenge self-deception strategies. People do try and do succeed at regulating their thought processes so as to support preferred beliefs, but reality constraints, feedback from other people, and disconfirming events can undermine these efforts.

SUMMARY AND CONCLUSION

Self-regulation of mental processes invokes several special issues and problems that do not seem to be central to other spheres of self-regulation. Moreover, research on controlling mental processes has not progressed far (with a few major exceptions), and so a great deal of further work is needed before a comprehensive understanding is possible.

There appear to be many inherent constraints and limitations on the control of thought, and so efforts at self-regulation are doomed to fail beyond a certain point. Thus, people are unable to adjust or correct for biases of which they are unaware. Efforts to suppress unwanted thoughts are at best partly successful and often backfire. People cannot believe anything they want but are constrained by plausibility. Self-deceptive efforts are thwarted by events that disconfirm preferred theories and by social feedback from other people.

Strength appears to be relevant to the self-regulation of cognitive processes. Some people appear to be prone to lose control of their thoughts, and they often describe or experience this tendency as a matter of weakness. Indeed, obsessions and compulsions appear to reflect an inadequate strength for inhibiting these thoughts (as opposed to the thoughts having great force or power), and considerable research suggests a biological mechanism for this failure. Cognitive processes often seem to be vulnerable to bias and error because of lack of effort, as indicated by the fact that people can reach more thorough and accurate conclusions when they are highly motivated to do so. Under stress, also, when strength is depleted, people process information in a more superficial fashion and hence become prone to some errors.

Failures to regulate cognitive processes also arise due to poor management of attention. In inference and decision processes, people who do not search and find all the relevant evidence or who do not pay enough attention to it when they find it are prone to biases and errors. The suppression of unwanted thoughts is far more effective when people find effective distractors.

Some recent work on ironic processes suggests an important convergence between the strength and attention processes. When people seek to control their behavior, automatic processes begin searching for cues that warn of what they want to avoid, and these processes enable the conscious self to override and prevent that behavior or response. However, when people are distracted (which may be analogous to depletion of strength), the automatic processes continue to monitor cues for the forbidden response, and they may as a result direct attention to precisely what the person wishes to avoid. The person notices it but fails to suppress it.

Some misregulation patterns are also apparent. In particular, when people seek to overcome possible bias, they may overcorrect or undercorrect, because they simply add on an adjustment to their preliminary conclusion rather than going through the entire analysis or reasoning process again. As usual, misregulation arises from faulty or inadequate assumptions about the self—in this case, about how the self has been affected by external information.

6

Failure to Control Emotions and Moods

One of the most successful and controversial movies of 1993 was *Falling Down*. Its success went beyond praise from critics and box-office sales; indeed, it was featured on the cover of *Newsweek*, which is a rare distinction for a film. Although the movie touched on several of the major social issues of contemporary America, there was at least one theme that ran throughout the movie: failure to control emotions.

The film begins by showing the mounting bad mood of the main character. He has been fired from his job because his knowledge and skills have become obsolete. His wife has left him and taken his child. Because of his economic situation, he is unable to make child support payments and therefore is not allowed to see his little girl on her birthday. He is stuck in an interminable traffic jam caused, he believes, by make-work projects invented by the highway crews to justify their outrageous budgets. He swelters in his car, but the air conditioning is broken, and he cannot even open the window because the handle is defective.

He tries to distract himself from his mounting anger over the traffic problem, but as he shifts his attention in various directions he is repeatedly reminded of his multiple dissatisfactions with the world. Finally he tries to escape the anger-producing situation by abandoning his car and heading off on foot. But in a convenience store he gets into a disagreement with the proprietor and ends up madder than ever. Seeking to recover his peace of mind by sitting alone and thinking through his situation, he is accosted by some teenagers who try to rob him, and so again he is unable to feel better. He tries at one point to stop the escalating hostility between him and the teenagers and to speak in a friendly and rational fashion, but this too is to no avail, and again violence is the outcome. Throughout the film, his efforts at emotional control meet with frustration and failure, and it is only through violent and aggressive outbursts that he ever gets what he wants.

Like the protagonist of this movie, many people find themselves unable to escape from aversive emotional states and bad moods. The topic of controlling moods and emotions (*affect regulation*) has emerged in recent years as an important focus of research efforts. This chapter will examine one part of that literature, specifically that of failure at affect regulation. How, when, and why do people fail to regulate their emotional states?

Given the state of knowledge in the field, it will be necessary to narrow the focus of this chapter even further. We shall emphasize the failure to escape from a bad or unpleasant emotional state. In principle, there are at least six main types of emotion control tasks: A person could be trying to get into, get out of, or prolong either a good or a bad mood (Parrott, 1993; Tice, Muraven, & Baumeister, 1994; see also Clark & Isen, 1982; Wegner & Erber, 1993; Morris & Reilly, 1987). At first glance, one might ask when would someone ever desire to get into a bad mood, but such cases do arise and are important. For example, a politician might seek to work up a state of anger in preparation for giving a speech about injustice, a physician might need to put herself into a somber mood when it is necessary to tell a patient that he is dying, and a parent might have to get into a disappointed or outraged mood when discussing failing grades with a child.

Still, the most common attempt to control moods involves getting out of various bad moods (Tice & Baumeister, 1993; Tice et al., 1994), and so research interest has understandably emphasized those attempts. Accordingly, the evidence about self-regulation failure is also concentrated on that topic, and that is the one that will receive most attention here. Like the other self-regulation failures discussed in previous chapters, failure to control one's moods and emotions can result either from underregulation (i.e., not managing to exert sufficient control over these states) or from misregulation (i.e., using ineffective or inappropriate techniques for regulating affect).

Some writers distinguish between mood, affect, and emotion, whereas others use them interchangeably. Although we recognize that greater specificity is often useful, the distinctions are not important for our purposes, and so we shall follow the latter practice.

UNDERREGULATION AND THE MYTH OF VENTING

Although we shall turn shortly to the central problem of unrestrained emotional expression or venting, it is necessary to begin with a more fundamental reason for lack of emotional control: a belief that one should never control emotions. Some people simply believe that they should never try to control their moods.

In a series of surveys about emotion and mood control, Tice and Baumeister (1993) found that up to 4% of adults report that they never consciously attempt to alter their affective states. They typically explain this on the basis of some belief that it is morally wrong or psychologically damaging to alter emotions. Thus, one respondent wrote that "it might be bad for me/for my health to stifle or control my emotions," and another responded that "emotions are a natural part of life and should be experienced naturally." Steinmetz (1977) found that most adults in his sample believed that stifling anger is both harmful and futile. They believed that instead of controlling one's anger, one should express it for cathartic reasons. Tavris (1989) likewise suggested that it is common for people to view the expression of anger as healthful and to believe that it is wrong, useless, and harmful to try to control anger. In Tavris's opinion, this popular misconception has multiple sources, including a bastardized popular version of Freudian theory, which characterized repression as both harmful and ultimately futile, as well as a cultural quest for excuses to enable people to indulge themselves irresponsibly.

Likewise, Averill (1980, 1982) has argued that the cultural construction of emotion as passive (hence the related term "passion") is a deliberately fostered illusion that is designed to allow people to behave in wild or aggressive ways without accepting responsibility. As a prominent example of his approach, Averill cited evidence that juries give lighter sentences for crimes committed in the heat of passion (especially anger) because they believe that people are unable to control their emotions and that strong emotions make people unable to control their actions (Averill, 1979, 1982).

It is worth noting that people may sometimes fail at *not* controlling their emotions. In other words, despite their beliefs that they should allow emotions to proceed without regulation, many people end up using automatic or semi-automatic processes that regulate their moods, even if the people are not conscious of doing so or even if they think that they are unable to exert such control. For example, Gelles (1979) described a man who beat his wife and justified his actions on the basis of the alleged uncontrollability of anger when he was drinking. Yet the man refrained from shooting or stabbing her, and when this control of his behavior was pointed out to him by the therapist he began to realize that his "uncontrollable" angry aggression might indeed be controllable. Likewise, the Malay people long sustained the practice of *running amok*, in which individuals completely lost control of their actions and became wildly destructive. However, when social changes instituted severe punishments for running amok, the Malay discovered suddenly that they could control it after all, and the practice decreased dramatically (Carr & Tan, 1976). Thus, many people do in fact control their emotions and emotional actions even if they seem to insist and believe that such control is not possible for them.

Venting as Underregulation

Venting may be defined as the unrestrained expression of emotions, ranging from mere disclosure of emotional states to outrageous or wildly inappropriate behavior stimulated by emotions. If an entire society were to adopt the minority view mentioned in the previous section, namely that it is wrong and harmful to control emotions and so people should freely vent all emotions that they experience, human social life would be radically different from what it is now: Almost every human encounter would be marked by laughing, weeping, screaming, hitting, or other emotional outbursts. Some would argue that such a society would be more natural and authentic in its behavior. In our view, however, a widespread failure to control emotions (especially anger) would greatly increase the problems, stresses, and hazards of human interaction.

Modern adherents of venting often cite a *hydraulic view* of emotion. Such views depict the human psyche as similar to a container of water, and in that view emotions resemble increases in water pressure—which need to be allowed to discharge periodically, or else the system will explode and be destroyed. The most famous hydraulic model was proposed by Breuer and Freud (1982) (drawing heavily on Helmholtz's principle of the conservation of energy), who used the term *catharsis* to describe the discharge of emotional impulses. In their view, emotional impulses do not go away until they are discharged, and indeed preventing their discharge may actually increase their pressure. They developed the notion of catharsis as a therapy technique: Patients with allegedly "pent up" emotions could vent these feelings in the safety of the therapist's office. However, Freud did not find therapeutic catharsis to be effective, and so he and his colleagues moved on to focus their therapeutic efforts on thoughts and on talking rather than on emotional expressions such as crying.

Although Freud may have gradually discarded catharsis as a major therapeutic technique, the public at large did not. Freud's discourses on the supposedly harmful effects of repressed feelings have influenced several generations of people to think that failing to express one's feelings must invariably be dangerous and unhealthy. The idea that people need to "vent" their emotions has remained ingrained in the public and therapeutic literature (see Tavris, 1989, for a discussion of the harmful consequences of such societal beliefs).

A great deal of research has demonstrated that venting is ineffective at decreasing or eliminating the mood state. In fact, venting is often shown to *prolong* the negative affect, mood, or emotion, rather than reduce it. For example, Gondolf (1985), in his book on spouse abuse, disputed the hypothesis that venting (or "letting it all out short of violence") is a good way to defuse angry hostility. Rather, he cited evidence that "physical abuse by the man is shown to be marked by escalating verbal and physical aggression between the partners" (p. 31). In other words, domestic violence often follows from the venting of anger between spouses.

Gondolf interviewed a number of men who had admitted to battering their wives. These men frequently claimed that the venting of negative feelings was instrumental in beginning the cycle the violence. According to one of the men interviewed, "the anger leads to violence before you know it. . . . It just takes over and you become a different person."

Straus (1974), Straus, Gelles, and Steinmetz (1980), and Steinmetz (1977) likewise provided evidence that venting is likely to lead to more angry aggression, not less. When one member of a couple angrily "vents" his or her negative feelings to the partner, the partner frequently responds in an angry fashion, leading to an escalation of angry exchanges that frequently ends in physical aggression.

To understand why venting is ineffective, it is important to consider some of the details about what venting does. Venting may often fail to reduce anger or other emotions because the components of venting are directly incompatible with other self-regulatory responses. For example, venting involves focusing on one's feelings of anger or sadness in order to express them in detail—but research has demonstrated that focusing on one's negative feelings is ineffective for escaping from the negative mood (e.g., Carver, Scheier, & Weintraub, 1989; Lyubomirsky & Nolen-Hoeksema, 1993; Morrow & Nolen-Hoeksema, 1990). In contrast, *distracting oneself* from the negative thoughts or emotions is an effective way of getting out of a mood (e.g., Miller, 1987; Nolen-Hoeksema, 1990, 1993; Wegner, 1989; Wenzlaff et al., 1988), but venting prevents people from distracting themselves. Indeed, we have seen throughout this work that distraction is often a powerful and effective means of managing attention. Venting directs attention to precisely the wrong place, namely to one's distress and to what is causing it.

Emotional Expressivity

Many researchers have demonstrated that when one expresses an emotion, one is likely to experience that emotion; this effect is known as the *emotional expressivity effect*. James, (1890/1950), Allport (1924), and Jacobson (1929) all described early scientific theories of controlling emotions through the self-control of expressive facial behavior. Izard (1990) claimed that the idea that naturally occurring emotion feelings can be influenced by self-managed expressive behavior "may be at least as old as written records," (p. 489), and he quoted Shakespeare's Henry V's beliefs that altering the outward expression of emotion can alter the inward experience of that emotion:

> Then imitate the action of the tiger;
> Stiffen the sinews, summon up the blood,
> Disguise fair nature with hard-favour'd rage.
> Then lend the eye a terrible aspect;
> Let it pry through the portage of the head,
> Like the brass cannon; let the brow o'erwhelm it,

As fearfully, as doth a galled rock
O'erhand and jutty his confounded base,
Swill'd with the wild and wasteful ocean.
Now set the teeth, and stretch the nostril wide;
Hold hard the breath, and bend up every spirit
To his full height!
—Act III, Scene 1

Multiple studies have provided evidence of the emotional expressivity effect, by demonstrating that facial feedback is an important determinant of how people experience emotion and that such feedback plays an important role in regulating emotions (e.g., Cacioppo, Petty, Losch, & Kim, 1986; Cupchick & Leventhal, 1974; Gellhorn, 1964; Kleinke & Walton, 1982; Kraut, 1982; Leventhal & Mace, 1970). Arranging someone's face to conform to an emotional expression seems to cause the person to begin to feel that emotion (e.g., Lanzetta, Cartwright-Smith, & Kleck, 1976; Laird, 1974, 1984; Strack, Martin, & Stepper, 1988). By the same token, putting someone's face into an inexpressive pattern that might conceal emotion seems to cause that person to feel less emotion. Izard's (1990) review of the facial feedback literature concluded that "patterns of expressive behavior can be effectively used in the management of emotion experience" (p. 496), and that *self*-management or spontaneous use of the technique (of controlling facial expression to regulate emotion) is even more effective than experimentally manipulated use of the technique. Other researchers have demonstrated that not just facial expressiveness, but other bodily expressive cues such as posture, can also affect mood and emotion (Riskind, 1984; Riskind & Gotay, 1982; see also Weisfeld & Beresford, 1982).

These studies suggest one mechanism by which venting will fail. Expressing an emotion tends to make that emotion stronger, not weaker. Hence, if people seek to reduce their anger by expressing it, their expressions are likely to increase the anger, which is the opposite of the desired effect.

Relaxation and Physiological Reactivity

Another reason venting may be ineffective in reducing some emotions is that it strengthens or increases arousal—whereas escaping from distress may often be best served by getting rid of arousal. Relaxation and meditation have been shown to be effective techniques for reducing the high-arousal states associated with negative emotions and moods like fear and anger (e.g., Feindler, 1989; Feindler & Ecton, 1986; Novaco, 1975). Giving vent to one's fear and anger will most likely produce the opposite result. A large number of researchers have found that venting, or outwardly expressing one's anger, has been positively associated with greater heart rate and blood pressure reactivity (e.g., Dembroski, MacDougall, Shields, Petitto, & Lushene, 1978; Diamond et al., 1984; VanEgern, Abelson, & Thornton, 1978), which constitute a physiological component of emotion. If venting leads to greater physiological reactions, which most researchers consider an important or even necessary component of emotion and mood (e.g., Schachter & Singer, 1962; Thayer, 1989), then venting (which leads to an increase in physiological states) should be incompatible with a reduction in the mood one is trying to control. This physiological reactivity associated with venting can be so pervasive that venting is found to be positively associated with coronary heart disease (e.g., Hecker, Chesney, Black, & Frautschi, 1988; Mathews, Glass, Rosenman, & Bortner, 1977) and hypertension (e.g., Harburg et al., 1973).

Silent Seething

It must be acknowledged that some researchers have found what seems at first to be an opposite result, namely that *refraining* from expressing one's anger produces harmful effects. In particular, holding one's anger in (as opposed to venting it) is positively associated with greater heart rate and blood pressure reactivity, coronary heart disease, and hypertension (Funkenstein, King, & Drolette, 1954; Harburg et al., 1973; Haynes, Feinleib, & Kannel, 1980; Holroyd & Gorkin, 1983; MacDougall, Dembroski, Dimsdale, & Hackett, 1985; MacDougall, Dembroski, & Krantz, 1981; Schalling, 1985).

Thus we have seemingly contradictory sets of findings. On the one hand, venting anger ("anger-out," as it is sometimes called) appears to have harmful effects. On the other hand, similarly harmful consequences have been linked to *not* venting, in the sense of keeping one's anger inside ("anger-in"). Which is correct?

One attempt to resolve this controversy was undertaken by Engebretson, Mathews, and Scheier (1989), who proposed that it is simply a matter of individual differences. Perhaps some people are better off expressing their anger, while others are better off keeping it inside. In their study, some subjects were allowed to express their anger at a confederate in their preferred or habitual manner (either anger-in or anger-out), whereas others were required to deal with the anger in the manner opposite to their preferred one. These researchers hypothesized that subjects who were allowed to express their anger at a confederate in their preferred manner would have less cardiovascular reactivity than subjects who were forced to deal with their anger in the opposite mode. Some of their results fit that hypothesis, but they also reported that "individuals who characteristically express their anger outwardly exhibited elevated heart rate during harassment and elevated systolic blood pressure, which persisted even after being harassed and writing a negative story about the confederate" (i.e., aggressing against the harasser; p. 519). In other words, the arousal did not subside after venting, even among people who preferred to vent their anger.

Thus, Engebretson et al. (1989) have shown that individual differences are an important factor in deciding whether anger-in or anger-out is worse. The fact that people who prefer to vent remain aroused after venting complicates the issue, however, and so their findings are not a complete resolution of the inconsistency in previous findings.

What is destructive may be *staying angry*, regardless of whether it is associated with anger-in or anger-out (see Tice, 1994). In this view, venting is bad because it rekindles and strengthens the angry state, leading to increased arousal and increased attention to the problem that caused the anger. Keeping one's anger from being expressed is also bad, however, if it means that the person seethes with anger in silence. Thus, what is common about anger-in and anger-out is that the anger persists; and it is the continued anger that has the destructive effects.

This conclusion fits with several comments made by Engebretson et al. (1989) regarding their unpredicted finding about the persistence of high arousal among the subjects who vented their anger. These authors speculated that the continued arousal levels may have been due to continued rumination about the negative experience with the confederate. Continuing to ruminate typically means that one remains angry—and as long as one remains angry, it is hardly surprising that one's heart rate and other signs of arousal remain high.

More generally, we think that the inconsistent findings in the literature regarding anger-in and anger-out reflect the destructive consequences of staying angry, in part because measures have sometimes confounded anger-in with simply not expressing anger (Tice, 1994). Measures of anger-in may thus combine two kinds of people: those who refuse to show anger while continuing to seethe inwardly, and those who simply manage to exert self-control until the anger goes away.

Thus, the seeming contradictions among past findings may not properly bear on the issue of whether it is a good idea to express one's anger or not; rather, the decisive issue is whether the person stays angry or not. Venting one's anger is likely to lead to staying angry, because of the emotional expressivity effect, attending to the provocation, maintaining arousal, and the like. Refusing to vent one's anger, however, may lead to two quite different outcomes. Some people may stop feeling angry when they hold their tongues (possibly aided by relaxation or self-distraction techniques), and they may end up feeling better; but other people will simply continue to seethe with anger inwardly, which is not likely to be much better than venting.

When Does Expressing Feelings Help?

If venting negative affect is an ineffective strategy for controlling moods as well as being bad for health, how should people communicate their dissatisfaction or unhappiness when someone has wronged them? Without venting one's anger, how can someone prevent the anger-producing event from recurring?

Most current anger therapies (e.g. Feindler, 1989; Feindler & Ecton, 1986; Goldstein & Glick, 1987; Lochman, 1984; Novaco, 1975, 1979) recommend avoiding venting, but they also recommend considering the possibility of discussion after the anger of all parties involved has subsided. An emotion-laden confrontational debate is likely to escalate into an argument and therefore is unlikely to yield constructive resolutions to conflict (e.g., Wilson, 1982; Zillman, 1993). If an individual becomes angry and vents the anger at another, the person listening to the angry individual is likely to become angry as well, and the anger of the dyad or group is highly likely to escalate (e.g., Gondolf, 1985; Straus, 1974; Straus et al., 1980; Steinmetz, 1977).

However, if you wait until the anger has subsided and then attempt to make your feelings known to the others involved, you are less likely to say things that you do not mean or will be sorry for later (which constitutes a very unfortunate case of lapse-activated causation!). Averill (1982) refers to a "cooling time" in which confrontational debate is avoided, which can be followed by rational discussion if the previously angry individual still feels that the issue is worthy of discussion after he or she has "cooled off." This waiting period will only work to help avoid angry confrontation if the parties actually try to control their anger (perhaps through pleasant distraction) during the cooling time. If the parties use the period between the anger-provoking event and the confrontation to rehearse their grievances and brood over their perception of events, then the likelihood of angry aggression and argument is just as strong as if no waiting period had taken place (e.g., Zillman, 1993). In addition, stating one's feelings, such as saying, "I am feeling . . ." is a much more effective means of discussing the emotion-producing event without escalating the anger than is making statements blaming the other, such as saying, "You always . . ." (e.g., Lochman, 1984; Tavris, 1989).

This advice applies to a variety of bad moods and emotions in addition to anger. Many researchers have suggested that one highly effective means of regulating negative affect is to directly confront the problem and make instrumental progress at trying to change the state of affairs that led to the negative feelings (e.g., Billings & Moos, 1984; Morrow & Nolen-Hoeksema, 1990; Parker & Brown, 1982; Rippere, 1976, 1977; Rohde, Lewinsohn, Tilson, & Seeley, 1990). However, waiting until the negative mood has lifted (which one can induce by using effective mood control techniques such as distraction) before attempting to confront the emotion-inducing event or person may be much more effective than venting.

Venting Other Emotions

In the Freudian conception, catharsis technically applied to any negative emotion that was pent up, and Freud in fact was interested in pent-up anxiety, fear, and sadness, as well as anger. Most of the popular interpretation of venting, as well as the scientific research, has focused on the venting of anger. Any conclusions about the efficacy of venting other emotions must remain primarily speculative.

As we have seen, the evidence is quite clear that venting anger is not an effective mood control strategy. The data on venting sadness are not as straightforward, however, perhaps because venting sadness (e.g., through crying, talking about the sadness) has not been as well researched as venting anger. Some researchers think that crying may help to alleviate sad moods, because as tears leave the body they carry with them some of the neurotransmitters that increase feelings of sadness and depression. These findings are far from conclusive, however, and it may be that crying actually increases the total quantity of those transmitters in the brain; it is possible that those neurotransmitters are actually produced in response to crying (see, for instance, Kraemer & Hastrup, 1988, for evidence that crying does not have a cathartic effect and does not reduce sadness).

Meanwhile, there is a fair amount of evidence that continuing to focus attention on one's sadness can lead to depressive episodes, and one effective way to avoid depressed moods is to distract oneself from sad thoughts (e.g., Billings & Moos, 1984; Morrow & Nolen-Hoeksema, 1990; Nolen-Hoeksema, 1990, 1993; Wenzlaff et al., 1988). These findings suggest that self-distraction may be much more effective than venting for escaping from sadness.

Ultimately, it may well be that the conclusion about venting sadness and other aversive mood states parallels the one we have proposed for anger, namely that it is the persistence of the bad mood that is the crucial issue. Venting may typically fail to alleviate the bad mood, but continuing to ruminate silently about the problem may be just as bad. Merely stifling outward expression of distress is inadequate. Instead, people need to use techniques that actually work to remove themselves from persisting in bad moods.

MISREGULATION

In the previous section, we saw that people may fail to control their emotions because they simply do not try to control them. Alternatively, however, people may fail because they resort to methods that backfire or are simply ineffective. As with the misregulation patterns shown in other chapters, a central cause of affect misregulation is people's misconceptions about what will be effective. Inadequate understanding of self, of the nature of emotion, or of the consequences of certain techniques can cause people to exert control over their moods and emotions in a destructive or counterproductive fashion.

Indeed, venting may sometimes be an example of misregulation deriving from faulty knowledge. We covered venting as a form of underregulation, but in some cases people may deliberately vent their emotions because of the mistaken belief that venting is an effective means of bringing these feelings under control or bringing them to an end. Tavris (1989) has described how debased versions of Freudian concepts and misreported research findings have created a popular belief that trying to exert self-control over anger is wrong, useless, and ultimately harmful to one's health. The prevalence of that view, despite the plethora of information contradicting it, may reflect a cultural self-indulgence with finding excuses to behave in a self-gratifying manner, even if it is harmful to others (e.g., Tavris, 1989).

Thus, although some people may engage in the ineffective mood control strategy of venting emotion because they do not want to bother exerting control over their moods, others may engage in the same strategy because of the mistaken belief that venting is an effective form of mood control (based on their very limited and distorted knowledge of the scientific findings). For whichever reason one engages in venting, it is still unlikely to be effective.

Cognitive Suppression

Many people try to regulate their negative feelings by avoiding or suppressing the thoughts that cause them to feel bad (e.g., Billings & Moos, 1984; Morrow & Nolen-Hoeksema, 1990; Rachman & de Silva, 1978; Rohde et al., 1990; Wegner, 1992). In fact, there is even a form of psychological therapy that advocates suppressing thoughts as a means of achieving mental health. Most empirical studies, however, have found that suppressing or avoiding unwanted thoughts or feelings (or suppressing thoughts about the problems that cause these unwanted feelings) is an ineffective method of reducing the unwanted feelings (e.g., Billings & Moos, 1984; Morrow & Nolen-Hoeksema, 1990; Rachman & de Silva, 1978; Rohde et al., 1990; Wegner, 1992).

The preceding chapter covered the inefficacy of simple thought suppression, and that same inefficacy applies to attempts at affect regulation that rely on thought suppression. Wegner's (1989; see also Wegner et al., 1987) work has provided a rather thorough explanation of why thought suppression might be an ineffective manner of controlling moods. When subjects in those studies were asked not to think about something, they were eventually with practice able to suppress thoughts about the forbidden item. However, these subjects later showed a rebound effect in which they thought about the forbidden item even more than people who had not been trying to suppress the thought earlier (or even more than people who had been focusing on the thought earlier!). Thus, ironically, people who try to suppress thoughts often end up actually obsessing about the things they are trying to suppress.

People are less able to suppress the thought under cognitive load (Wegner, 1994; Wegner, Erber, & Zanakos, 1993), so when people are under stress (such as from being tired or from attempting to do several things at once) they are more likely to show the intrusions of the thoughts they are trying to suppress. This is similar to the idea of *strength failure* discussed elsewhere in this book. Under conditions of fatigue, weakness, or competing demands on strength, people are less likely to be able to suppress their mood-relevant thoughts.

Several studies have been directly concerned with the affective implications of thought suppression. Wegner et al. (1990) showed that trying to suppress thoughts about an exciting or arousing topic (like sex) can even lead to greater physiological arousal than trying to think about the topic! In another study, a different version of misregulation through thought suppression was shown. Wenzlaff et al. (1988) found that depressed subjects undertook self-distraction to escape from a sad, distressed mood. Normally, self-distraction is a fairly effective technique, but in this case depressed subjects chose distractors that were themselves unpleasant and sad. Hence, although they may have succeeded in taking their minds off of the initial cause of their distress, they continued to feel bad.

Rumination and Perseveration

If the attempted suppression of unhappy thoughts is ineffective for overcoming a bad mood, it is not surprising that some people will try the opposite technique, namely focusing their thoughts on precisely what is bothering them. It is quite clear that many people spend a great deal of time ruminating about things that have upset them. Many individuals report that they try to control their moods by focusing on their feelings or ruminating about the events or issues that caused the negative moods, although they do not for the most part rate this as a highly effective means of changing their mood (Tice & Baumeister, 1993). Sometimes obsessing over feelings can be inadvertent, such as when one is trying to suppress a thought and the rebound occurs, with numerous and frequent intrusions of the previously suppressed thought (Wegner, 1989).

Ruminating about a bad mood or brooding about what caused a bad mood is not likely to result in mood change (e.g., Billings & Moos, 1984; Lyubomirsky & Nolen-Hoeksema, 1993; Morrow & Nolen-Hoeksema, 1990; Nolen-Hoeksema, 1990, 1993). Indeed, it may be just as ineffective as trying to suppress the thoughts.

There are several reasons that rumination fails to improve affect. When people engage in ruminative, emotion-focused thoughts and behaviors, they are less likely to engage in active problem-solving thoughts and behaviors (Carver et al., 1989; Klinger, 1993; Nolen-Hoeksema, 1993). In other words, one reason brooding about one's emotional state or problems is an ineffective mood control strategy is because it seems to interfere with active problem solving. Rumination may also thwart mood regulation by interfering with instrumental behavior, such as work-related tasks (e.g., Carver et al., 1989). Instrumental tasks are an opportunity for positive reinforcement, so interfering with instrumental behavior reduces one's chances of positive outcomes. In addition, instrumental behavior is a good source of pleasant distraction, so reducing instrumental behavior reduces the set of possible valuable distractors (Nolen-Hoeksema, 1993). Rumination decreases the likelihood of engaging in pleasant behaviors, and engaging in pleasant activities is likely to improve mood (Cialdini, Darby, & Vincent, 1973; Morris & Reilly, 1987; Underwood, Moore, & Rosenhan, 1973). A third reason rumination is ineffective at reducing bad moods is because it may increase the impact of moods on information processing. Nolen-Hoeksema cited a study by Needles and Abramson (1990, in Nolen-Hoeksema, 1993) that suggests that rumination increases the accessibility of negative cognitions, making further negative thoughts more likely.

Rumination fits one pattern we have repeatedly seen in self-regulation problems that are associated with serious, even clinical disturbances, namely the inability to stop oneself from perseverating in a distressful matter. In the preceding chapter, we saw that the core of obsessive–compulsive disorder appears to be an inability to stop the thought (as opposed to being troubled by an exceptionally powerful thought). Several other clinical patterns are marked by the inability to stop ruminating. For example, incest victims continue to think about and ruminate about their trauma even decades after the event (Silver et al., 1983). No practical or beneficial purpose is served by this quixotic quest for meaning, but the rumination does appear to be linked to increased and prolonged distress.

Depression may involve yet another failure at self-stopping, according to Pyszczynski and Greenberg (1987). Sooner or later, everyone suffers failure, rejection, or other losses that threaten one's self-esteem. Most people become self-focused at this time; indeed, self-awareness may arise precisely because falling short of standards is an occasion for self-assessment in order to appraise one's projects and progress (Carver & Scheier, 1981). Moreover, this self-focused state will tend to be an unpleasant one when it follows a serious failure or rejection experience, because it draws attention to something bad about the self.

Most people, however, pull themselves out of this self-focused state in a fairly short time. In particular, if the failure or rejection or other loss is something that cannot be rectified, then there is no point in continuing to dwell on it. Depressed people, however, seem to be unable to let go. Their attention remains focused on themselves and their shortcomings, and when there is no chance to make the situation better they end up dwelling on this tragedy and its implications. Perseverating in this state amplifies their emotional distress and their tendencies to derogate themselves. Subsequent failures or losses are then magnified, because they seem to confirm the unhappy thoughts about the self.

Distractors That Backfire

Although trying to merely suppress thoughts can be difficult, especially in the long run, the use of distractions to take one's mind off of the distressing problems does appear to be be a useful means of regulating cognitions and emotions (e.g., Billings & Moos, 1984; Miller, 1987; Morrow & Nolen-Hoeksema, 1990; Nolen-Hoeksema, 1993; Wegner, 1989; Wenzlaff et al., 1988; Zillman, 1988, 1993).

Distraction is not infallible, however. In particular, if the distractors are themselves distressing, then the person may end up merely exchanging one source of distress for another. As already noted, Wenzlaff et al. (1988) found that depressed individuals were more likely than nondepressed individuals to try to use other negative thoughts to distract themselves from a depressing thought. Depressed individuals were less effective at regulating their bad moods because of their use of this ineffective form of distraction. Similarly, in the example cited at the beginning of this chapter, the main character in *Falling Down* tried to distract himself from the irritating traffic jam by looking around at his surroundings, but the objects that caught his attention when he was trying to distract himself were other things that made him angry, and so he was unable to get out of the bad mood that way.

Zillman and colleagues (e.g., Bryant & Zillman, 1984; Zillman, Hezel, & Medoff, 1980) have examined the use of entertainments and communications media for controlling bad moods. They found that characteristics of the entertainment, such as its pleasantness, its ability to produce arousal or calm, and its tendency to absorb attention, were critical for mood management. Angry individuals, for example, were most likely to reduce their anger if they watched highly absorbing, highly pleasant, but very nonarousing, even calming, movies. Unfortunately, sometimes people choose movies that will be distressing, upsetting, or arousing, and these tend to be very ineffective means of escaping from bad moods (see Zillman, 1988, for a review of this literature).

Another ineffective use of distraction involves using reckless, violent, or dangerous activities to distract oneself from a bad mood. Nolen-Hoeksema (1993; also Nolen-Hoeksema & Morrow, 1991) has shown that people who brood and ruminate about their mood and problems are likely to engage in reckless, dangerous or violent activities, perhaps in a desperate attempt to disengage from the bad mood. Rohde et al. (1990) suggested that subjects who endorse reckless and dangerous coping strategies, such as "Do something reckless (like drive a car fast)" or "Do something rather dangerous" were more likely to be depressed both at the time of assessment and in the future than were subjects who did not endorse these items (see also Parker & Brown, 1979). In other words, using risk-taking or dangerous distractors to distract oneself from one's problems seems to cause or at least increase the chances of depression.

Some current studies in our own laboratories have shed preliminary light on how emotional distress leads to risky behavior. Apparently, bad moods increase a preference for high-risk, high-payoff options. Baumeister and Stillwell (1992) offered subjects a choice between two lotteries. One was a fairly safe bet with a small reward: Subjects had a 60% chance of winning $2. The other lottery was a long shot, offering a 5% chance of winning $20. In both cases, losing the lottery meant that one received no money and would have to undergo an unpleasant experience involving exposure to noise stress (i.e., an amplified recording of the sound of fingernails scratching on a blackboard). Statistical rationality would predict that the safe bet lottery is the better choice, because it yields a higher expected value (calculated by multiplying the chances of winning times the amount one would win).

We found that subjects who were in a bad mood (which was stimulated by an embarrassing experience) were more prone to choosing the long shot. Subjects in good or neutral moods tended to be about evenly divided in their preferences.

Thus, being in a bad mood tended to cause a preference for a long-shot lottery. In a sense, this preference is understandable, because winning a mere $2 might be inadequate to cure the person's bad mood, whereas winning $20 could be sufficient to accomplish that. The bad mood thus increases the attractiveness of the big score. However, consider what would be most likely to happen under such circumstances. The person feels bad and so chooses the high-risk option. Unfortunately, 95% of the time, the outcome will be bad, and so the person will end up with one more reason to feel bad. In that way, the bad mood can be self-perpetuating, even though the person chose the long shot with the hope of escaping from those feelings.

The use of emotionally similar distractors or dangerous distractors when trying to escape from a bad mood is likely to result in what we have called *psychological inertia*. The mood state itself may create conditions that make it more difficult to escape from the mood. Depression may make it more likely that distraction attempts will employ negatively valanced distractors, perpetuating the depressed mood. Anger may make irritating distractors more salient, perpetuating the angry mood. Anxiety may make fearful distractors more accessible, thus perpetuating the anxious mood. In all these cases, there appears to be a loss of control of attention. Angry people do not seem to control their attention toward nonirritating distractors. Wenzlaff et al. (1988) demonstrated that if researchers give depressed individuals pleasant distractors, they are able to make use of them and decrease their depressed mood. However, the normal attentional path of depressed individuals is toward negative distractors, which perpetuate the depression.

Thus, although distraction is normally a highly effective means of controlling bad moods, distractors have to be of a certain type in order to work well. Nolen-Hoeksema (1993) has proposed that in order to be successful at reducing a bad mood, distractors must be engrossing and must have a high probability of positive reinforcement. Doing things with friends, working on an enjoyable hobby, or concentrating on work are examples of distractors recommended by Nolen-Hoeksema (1993) for escaping from depression. Zillman (1993) recommends highly engaging and pleasant stimuli to reduce bad moods. Using distractors that are emotionally similar to the bad mood one is in (such as distracting oneself with different sad thoughts when one is depressed, or arousing media events when one is angry) and use of dangerous, reckless, or risky distractors are not effective at reducing bad moods. If anything, they may be counterproductive.

Consumptive Behaviors

A very different class of affect regulation strategies involves consumptive behaviors: eating, drinking, taking drugs, and the like. Undoubtedly these behaviors have mood-altering effects, and sometimes they may even help people to feel better. In other circumstances, however, they tend to backfire, thereby qualifying as forms of affective misregulation.

Many people, especially women, report eating favorite foods to control their moods, and they report that this strategy is fairly effective for reducing sad moods if they do not overuse it (Tice & Baumeister, 1993). Food may serve to improve a minor sad mood because it serves as a pleasant distractor. Eating may also backfire, however, especially when one considers that most women in modern America are chronic dieters. When people are in a bad mood and want to eat something to make themselves feel better, they may focus on the pleasures of tasting and swallowing or on the feeling of satiety. After having eaten, however—especially if the food was high in fat and calories, like most of the treats people choose to cheer themselves up—people may focus instead on the caloric threat or the violation of one's diet, particularly if they are concerned about weight and body image, and this focus may bring back (or regenerate) a bad mood (Larsen, 1993).

A number of researchers have examined whether eating helps control moods (e.g., Billings & Moos, 1981, 1984; Frost, Goolkasian, Ely, & Blanchard, 1982; Larsen, 1993; Morris & Reilly, 1987; Thayer, 1987, 1989; Tice & Baumeister, 1993). Most of the findings have suggested that eating favorite foods is not an effective way to reduce negative moods (e.g., Billings & Moos, 1984; Larsen, 1993), but a more detailed examination of the data suggests that there may be certain conditions under which mood is improved after eating. Although Thayer (1987) found that a sugary snack could improve mood and energy level in the short run, he found that brief exercise (a brisk 10-min walk) was more effective in the longer run, such as one or two hours later. Tice and Baumeister (1993) suggested that eating does serve to temporarily reduce sad moods, but it does not have an effect on reducing anger. Likewise, although they found that it reduced sad moods produced by minor daily events, other evidence suggests that eating does little to improve long-term, clinical depression, and it may serve to worsen the depressed mood (Billings & Moos, 1984).

Thus, eating may serve to improve mood only in very specific, limited conditions. If the bad mood is sadness, not anger or clinical depression, if the person is not overly concerned with weight or body image (and the loss of control that the eating to improve mood signifies), if the food eaten is consumed in reasonable quantities, and if the strategy is not used too frequently, eating may improve mood.

Similar patterns of misregulation can be found with alcohol consumption. Many people, especially men, report drinking alcohol to reduce bad moods (Larsen, 1993; Morris & Reilly, 1987; Parker & Brown, 1982; Pearlin &

Radabaugh, 1976; Rippere, 1977; Tice & Baumeister, 1993; see also Marlatt, Kosturn, & Lang, 1975). Like the data reported above for eating to control bad moods, drinking alcohol may work only if it is an infrequent strategy used in moderation. Otherwise it may backfire.

Alcohol is often associated with parties, celebrations, and other good times, and so people may unfortunately think that getting drunk will be a generally effective way of feeling better. As a result, people may use alcohol in ways that will end up making them feel worse. Billings and Moos (1984) showed that drinking alcohol is an ineffective strategy for combating clinical depression—in fact, alcohol tends to intensify depressive symptoms. The unfortunate consequence of this pattern may be a vicious cycle, in which a person feels depressed, tries to "self-medicate" by consuming alcohol, ends up feeling worse, and therefore consumes even more alcohol.

Attentional factors may be one reason for the ineffectiveness of alcohol as an affect regulation strategy. As described elsewhere in this book, Steele and Josephs (1990) portrayed the effects of alcohol intoxication as a kind of "myopia": a narrowing of attention. The drunk person can only focus on one or two things at a time. If alcohol use is combined with compelling distractors, such as watching a ball game or engaging in conversation at a cocktail party, it may indeed improve one's mood. But if a depressed person simply consumes alcohol and then thinks about his or her problems, the narrowed focus will make the problems seem even more pervasive than they did before getting drunk. Attention will thus end up being riveted to the distressing issues, and the mood will get worse instead of better.

In a sense, alcoholic myopia contributes to transcendence failure. Transcendence—seeing beyond the immediate situation—is often effective for regulating affect. One can say that one's problems may seem small in a broad context or that things may not be as bad as they seem at the moment. The narrowed focus of alcoholic intoxication makes it harder, however, to take the broad view. One's attention remains immersed in the immediate situation, and so the source of one's distress looms large.

Similar processes apply to people who turn to drink to regulate anger. Angry and irritated men sometimes report choosing to drink in order to "calm down." However, alcohol-intoxicated individuals respond more aggressively to the same provocation than sober people (Taylor & Leonard, 1983; Zillman, 1993), perhaps because they are less sensitive to their opponents' desire to stop fighting (Leonard, 1989). Thus, in the presence of continued irritating stimuli, angry people who drink alcohol are likely to respond more aggressively and therefore remain angrier than angry people who do not drink. Given the tendency of alcohol intoxication to narrow attention to immediate stimuli and to intensify aggressive responses to provocations, it is hardly surprising that many violent crimes are committed by intoxicated people (e.g., Gottfredson & Hirschi, 1990). The alcoholic myopia makes it harder to see beyond the immediate situation—such as thinking that one's pride and honor will not really be tarnished by the disrespectful remarks of another bar patron, or by reflecting that avenging some insult is not worth risking arrest and imprisonment. Without such transcendence, the drunk person's consciousness becomes saturated with the immediate provocation, and violent responses become more likely. (Indeed, according to Gottfredson and Hirschi [1990], many perpetrators of homicide are scarcely able to recall the next day what made them angry enough to kill.) Drink is a poor cure for anger, unless one is surrounded by peaceful and pleasant distractors that are quite compelling.

Other drugs are also implicated in patterns of affect misregulation. People report smoking cigarettes, using tranquilizers, and using illicit drugs in an effort to improve their moods (Tice & Baumeister, 1993), although even self-reported success with these methods is not very high. Billings and Moos (1984) found that smoking and drug use are often associated with intensified depression.

Thus, although there is quite a bit of folk wisdom suggesting that eating favorite foods to be nice to oneself, drinking alcohol, or smoking a cigarette will help one to calm down or to cheer up, there is little empirical support for these beliefs. In fact, as detailed above, there is even considerable evidence suggesting that these efforts at cheering oneself up or calming oneself down will actually serve to worsen one's bad mood. To be sure, they can be effective under very limited and specific circumstances, but for the most part consumptive strategies are not to be recommended as ways of regulating affect.

OVERGENERALIZATION: MISMATCHING MOODS AND STRATEGIES

Not all mood regulation strategies work equally well for all moods. Although a strategy such as socializing with others (e.g., calling family members on the phone, visiting friends, engaging in pleasant activities with companions) might work well for one kind of bad mood like sadness, it might backfire when used to control other kinds of bad moods such as anger (Tice & Baumeister, 1993). Thus, mood control might fail because people have used a strategy successfully in the past to control one bad mood and so are likely to use it again when they feel bad, even if they are experiencing a different unpleasant emotion. This form of misregulation may be especially confusing to people, because a strategy that worked many times in the past suddenly is not effective.

Like socializing with others, social isolation can effectively reduce some bad moods, but it makes other worse. Many angry people report that social isolation, particularly if combined with a pleasant activity, helps to reduce feelings of anger (Tice & Baumeister, 1993). However, sad or depressed people are likely to worsen their sad or depressed mood if they choose to withdraw from others (e.g., Rohde et al., 1990). Even if people are aware that it is effective to be alone when one is angry and be with people when one is sad, they may still misregulate and worsen their bad mood if they spend their solitary time brooding. Social isolation helps to alleviate anger if one engages in a pleasant and distracting activity, but not if one uses the time alone to rehearse one's grievances (e.g., Zillman, 1993; Tice & Baumeister, 1993; Tice, 1994). Likewise, interacting with friends or others helps to reduce sadness only if one engages in pleasant conversation or activities with friends—not if one monopolizes the conversation with discussions of one's problems. Although it may be useful to consult a trusted friend or relative occasionally about one's problems in order to get a fresh approach or even just some sympathy, this backfires if the technique is overused.

One of the reasons that interacting with others can fail to improve a bad mood is that the other people may end up sharing the bad mood after listening to the person's problems. The sad person may hope that after talking with a happy person both people will be happy, but sometimes the outcome may be bilateral sadness (e.g., Pennebaker, 1993).[1] For example, Strack and Coyne (1983) demonstrated that people who talked with a depressed person for only 15 min subsequently reported feeling depressed, anxious, and hostile themselves, and talking to an angry person about one's angry feeling can create anger in the listener (e.g., Tavris, 1989). Living with a depressed person leads to greater depression (Coyne et al., 1987), perhaps because the depressed person communicates his or her sad thoughts and feelings to the roommate.

Another fact that raises problems for some affect regulation efforts is that being together with other people is arousing. Social psychologists have long acknowledged that the presence of members of one's own species tends to produce arousal, dating back at least to Zajonc's (1965) social facilitation theory. This arousal may contribute to a variety of emotional reactions, including excitement, nervousness, anxiety, sexual attraction, and many others. At bottom, many of these reactions are simply due to the fact that people are more readily, easily, and strongly aroused when they are with others.

Because people tend to become aroused when others are there, seeking out other people may often help to overcome feelings of dejection, sadness, or apathy, or indeed any unpleasant mood that is characterized by a lack of arousal. People may overgeneralize the benefits of being with others, however, and so may try to use the same strategy to cure bad moods that are marked by high arousal or agitation. This can easily backfire.

Anger, in particular, is typically marked by high levels of arousal. In order to escape from an angry state, it is generally necessary to calm down. Being together with other people may create further arousal, however, and as a result it becomes that much harder to calm down. There may be exceptions, of course; certain companions may have a strongly calming influence on others, and so

---

[1]Although normally people should not communicate everyday problems and bad moods to others in order to improve their moods, Pennebaker (1990, 1993) has demonstrated that people may be healthier and happier if they can confide their deepest traumas to another person. Pennebaker does not suggest that it is helpful to discuss these traumas continually with friends or with everyone one meets; rather, his point is that the process of organizing one's thoughts, and the reactions of the confidant, may be beneficial enough to justify a one-time, full, detailed confession.

being together with them could be helpful. But in general the presence of other people has an arousing effect and is thus counterproductive for overcoming anger.

Being with others can be counterproductive for escaping anger for other reasons too. An angry person will tend to be irritable. In the normal give and take of social interaction, an angry person may therefore be prone to respond irritably, such as to say something sarcastic or nasty. A stray nasty remark can easily elicit an angry response from someone else, leading to a disagreement or argument, and the result may be that the angry person now has yet another reason to feel angry. The escape from anger has thus gotten even more remote.

The same goes for someone who is feeling upset because of stress. Repetti (1989) found that people in stressful occupations tended to find that a brief period of social withdrawal improved their relationships with their families. If they went straight from a stressful workday to interacting with their families, they were prone to get into arguments and disputes. But spending part of an hour by themselves enabled them to calm down, and subsequent family interactions were therefore much more pleasant for everyone.

Thus, social interaction may produce failure to regulate anger because it is arousing. Other arousing activities have the same pitfall. People may do things that they normally enjoy but find that they fail to overcome an angry state. In a recent summary of research on using the media to control moods, Zillman (1988) reviewed work done by him and his colleagues (Bryant & Zillman, 1984; Zillman et al., 1980) that suggests that arousing stimuli, even if they are absorbing and pleasant, are not as effective at reducing anger as are calming or at least nonarousing stimuli. A fan of exciting action movies may find, for example, that watching such a movie will fail to cure an angry mood. Although most of Zillman's work was done with media distractors such as films and books, other distractors such as games and discussions should operate by the same principles. Even though a rousing game of checkers made you feel better when you were depressed, it may not help at all and may even make you feel worse when you are angry.

Shopping may be another form of mood control that is prone to backfire when overgeneralized. Many people report going shopping when they are sad, but they report that this strategy is not very effective for overcoming anger or irritation (Tice & Baumeister, 1993). It may be that imagining oneself owning the pleasingly displayed items offered for sale, having a successful experience getting a good bargain, finding just the right item for oneself or for a gift, and interacting with others all help to cheer up a sad person, but these positive experiences may not make up for the frequently irritating aspects of the shopping experience: having to wait in line, not being able to find what one came for, dealing with preoccupied or uncooperative salespeople, or having another driver take the parking spot one wanted.

Another similar misregulation of mood control strategies is to use relaxation strategies when one is feeling depressed. Seligman (1994) states that a major misregulation of depression occurs when sad or depressed people try to use relaxation strategies and make themselves even sadder. Popular wisdom, friends and family members, talk show hosts and guests, and others teach people how to relax and calm down when they are feeling "uptight." The problem for people is that they sometimes misapply these strategies to times when they are feeling depressed rather than anxious. Because depression and anxiety tend to co-occur at high rates (e.g., Polivy, 1981), sufferers may focus on one component of the emotion-complex and ignore other components. If a person is suffering primarily from depression but is more aware of or concerned about the concomitant anxiety, then he or she may attempt to use relaxation strategies that worsen the depression. One reason relaxation strategies may not work well for depression is that they frequently require social isolation, and the isolation might interfere with effective coping with the depression.

The problem of dealing with both depression and anxiety brings up one additional, broader problem for affect regulation. Most mood states are not single, discrete moods, but rather a combination of multiple moods (e.g., Izard, 1972, 1977; Polivy, 1981). Thus, even a person who had careful and thorough knowledge of which techniques cure which moods might become perplexed at how to deal with certain mixtures of bad moods. For example, most researchers are familiar with the mixture of depressed sadness, nervous anxiety, and anger that often accompanies having one's work rejected by scientific journals. Few affect regulation strategies seem likely to succeed at ending such a mix of distress. Trying to calm down may help overcome the anger—but may intensify the sadness. Meanwhile, doing something exciting may help overcome the sadness but intensify the anger. The persistence of that particular form of distress—indeed, at any scientific conference one can hear researchers still telling bitter stories about their most upsetting rejections many months and even years after the fact—may be due to the difficulty of finding any strategy that can address all parts of such a blend of bad moods.

Thus, many mood control strategies are best suited to particular moods. When people try to use them to escape from other bad moods, they may backfire. The evidence currently available suggests that overgeneralization problems are mainly associated with the arousal dimension: Exciting activities (even pleasant ones) may fail to cure bad moods marked by high arousal, and calming activities may be counterproductive for overcoming bad moods marked by low arousal.

OVERGENERALIZATION ACROSS CIRCUMSTANCES

A second route into self-regulation failure by way of overgeneralization consists of neglecting the fact that circumstances may thwart techniques that work at other times. If a person discovers that a certain method cures a certain bad mood once, he or she may (not surprisingly) use that technique again, even under conditions that undermine its effectiveness.

Going for an automobile drive is a good example of this. A number of people report that going for a drive is an effective way to reduce anger (Tice & Baumeister, 1993). Driving not only gets the angry person away from friends and family members before he or she says something regrettable; it can also provide a pleasant "flow experience" (Csikszentmihalyi, 1990) that may improve a bad mood. Not all driving experiences are the same, however. Taking a peaceful, unhindered drive down a lonesome country road may help calm one down and allow anger to dissipate. But driving through heavy city traffic, especially where one may get caught in an annoying traffic jam or be subjected to the frustrations of being cut off by rude fellow motorists, is not likely to allow anger to dissipate.

Indeed, we suspect that some of the hostilities currently seen between motorists on American highways (ranging from obscene gestures to gunplay) may derive from just such failed efforts at affect regulation. An angry person may storm out of the house after a dispute and go for a drive, consistent with self-reports that people go driving in order to control their anger. If such a driver objects to the driving practices by another motorist, however, a resort to hostility would not be surprising.

Exercise is another form of mood control that can backfire under some circumstances. Exercise has been proven highly beneficial in reducing both sad moods and long-term, even severe depression (e.g., Bahrke & Morgan, 1978; Doyne, Chambless, & Beutler, 1983; Greist et al., 1979; McCann & Holmes, 1984), and a number of people even report that it is effective in reducing anger (Tice & Baumeister, 1993). Because sadness and depression are states associated with lower than optimal arousal (e.g., Thayer, 1989), it makes sense that getting oneself aroused through exercise would help overcome such moods. Ironically, however, some people report using exercise to overcome anger, which is an aroused emotion. They say that exercise works sometimes but not other times. The discrepancy may be the result of overgeneralization. Whether exercise helps overcome anger may depend on the circumstances.

To understand why exercise may sometimes fail, it is necessary to appreciate how it can affect an angry state. Unfortunately, at present there are several competing hypotheses about the effects of exercise. One view is that exercise makes the person tired, which thus removes arousal and hence precludes a continuation of the angry state (Tice & Baumeister, 1993; see also Thayer, 1989). In that view, the initial, arousing stage of exercise might even magnify the anger. The eventual fatigue would be effective at reducing anger, but it is of course necessary for the person to continue the exercise until that point is reached. If the person interrupts the exercise before becoming tired, the added arousal may leave him or her more angry than ever.

A second hypothesis is that exercise may serve as a misattribution for the arousal caused by anger. If angry people exercise, they may attribute their subsequent arousal to the exercise and not perceive themselves to be as angry as people who had not exercised (see Zillman's work on excitation transfer, e.g., Zillman, 1978, 1979; Zillman, Johnson, & Day, 1974; Zillman, Katcher, & Milavsky, 1972). The danger with such a misattribution strategy is that it could just as well work in the opposite direction. For anger to be misattributed to exercise, the person would presumably have to have not yet labeled the arousal as anger. This may be unlikely; most people seem to know soon enough when they are angry. In contrast, the excitation from the exercise could easily be misattributed to the anger, leading the person again to think that he or she is angrier than ever.

The third hypothesis is that exercise serves as a distraction (e.g., Morgan, 1985; Morrow & Nolen-Hoeksema, 1990). We have repeatedly emphasized the potential effectiveness of self-distraction strategies for self-regulation in general. Still, under some circumstances exercise may fail or even backfire as a distraction. Some forms of exercise are less distracting than others. Jogging, for example, makes few demands on the mind, and so the person may find himself or herself ruminating about what caused the anger, with the result that the exercise session turns into a period of concentrated brooding (leading to increased anger). Moreover, we have already noted the fallacy of using aversive distractors to overcome bad moods, and there is no denying that sport activities can produce frustration, annoyance, discomfort, and other sources of distress. An angry person may resort to a cognitively demanding sport such as tennis or racquetball in order to distract himself or herself, only to find that new irritations such as having to wait for the court, an opponent's self-serving bad calls, or the failure of one's own seemingly unlucky shots, end up producing more anger.

In short, there are many affect regulation strategies whose effectiveness is limited to certain emotions *and* to certain types of circumstances. Self-regulation may fail when people overgeneralize and use these strategies when they are not effective.

IGNORING LONG-TERM CONCERNS

A final set of mood misregulation strategies involves focusing on short-term rather than long-term concerns, with the result that short-term improvements may effectively be obtained but the distress soon returns. Overconcern with immediate concerns has been treated throughout this work under the rubric of *transcendence failure*, and this final set of affect misregulation patterns is related to transcendence failure. Some of them also invoke the kind of counterproductive self-management patterns that we covered in Chapter 4 on self-management.

There are a number of strategies that people use to control their moods that work in the short term but do not seem to have long-term effects, including eating favorite foods, interacting with friends or family members, listening to music, and use of drugs or alcohol (e.g., Aneshensel & Huba, 1983; Larsen, 1993; Morris & Reilly, 1987; see also Thayer, 1987, 1989). Indeed, some of these can produce worse problems in the long run.

If people are in a bad mood because of something that is not able to be changed and is not likely to recur, than focusing on the short term may be helpful. For instance, if one is in a bad mood because a stranger cut ahead in line at the supermarket, doing something that would be a pleasant distraction from the event is likely to make one feel better in the present. (This assumes that the problem is an isolated case of stranger rudeness rather than a reflection of chronic lack of assertiveness.) Because this event is unlikely to recur, just getting out the bad mood temporarily is enough: once out of the bad mood one is likely to continue feeling good.

However, if focusing on the short-term mood change prevents long-term coping with the event causing the bad mood, then the bad mood is likely to come back. For example, if a person with money problems is sad because he is receiving disconnection notices from the utilities because he has neglected to pay his bills, then trying to cheer himself up by going out drinking with his buddies is not likely to make him feel much better tomorrow. Likewise, if a dieter feels bad because her clothes no longer fit since she gained weight, then cheering herself up by eating a sundae is not likely to create lasting mood improvement.

Seeking out social companionship may be another strategy that may sometimes be counterproductive in the long run because it fails to address the basic causes of the bad moods. We have already noted that being with friends is effective for bringing about an immediate improvement in many moods (e.g., Billings & Moos, 1984; Rohde et al., 1990; Tice & Baumeister, 1993; Zillman, 1993). Yet Larsen (1993) found that the affective benefits of social interaction tended to be temporary at best. One reason may be that using social interaction as an escape from one's problems leaves one vulnerable to future distress when the problem returns. For example, if a student feels bad because he received a D in chemistry, and he attempts to make himself feel better by hanging out with his friends at the student center rather than doing chemistry homework and readings, then he is not working at solving the problem that caused the bad mood in the first place. He may feel better on that particular day, but it seems likely that more Ds, and more bad moods, lie ahead.

Not all problems can be solved, and so some bad moods can be improved by interacting with others. For instance, if in the example above the student had felt bad about not getting selected by the fraternity of his choice, then interacting with his friends might have proved to be an effective mood control strategy, because his friends provide reassurance that he is a likable fellow, and besides there is nothing he can do now to reverse the fraternity's rejection. But when social interaction interferes with effective problem solving, then it may result in continued bad mood in the long term.

Thus, if the mood arises from a temporary event that could not be solved by focusing on the problem, then focusing on the short term may be the best one can do. If getting out of the bad mood temporarily is likely to result in our staying in a neutral or positive mood, then escaping from the bad mood by using temporary mood improvement strategies is likely to be effective. On the other hand, if coping with the short-term effects prevents active problem solving so that the problem causing the bad mood is likely to recur, then a short-term focus is problematic.

The self-regulation problem of procrastination (which we covered in the chapter on self-management) may often be traced to a similar overconcern with short-term affective improvement at the expense of long-term self-management. One of the several reasons that people procrastinate is that they wish to avoid the anxiety or other emotional distress that the work gives them. For example, as the would-be novelist sits down at the typewriter to work on her first novel, anxiety about producing a mediocre product and about unclear standards for success may create negative affect that impels her to put off working on the manuscript and avoid the anxious mood. In the short run, she is better off, because the anxiety is in fact prevented. In the long run, however, postponing important work tasks is a recipe for career failure.

INDIVIDUAL DIFFERENCES IN SKILL

A number of researchers have investigated the possibility that some people just have more skill than others at regulating their emotions. Salovey and Mayer (1990) identified the concept of *emotional intelligence*, which they defined as "the ability to monitor one's own and others' feelings and emotions, to discriminate among them, and to use this information to guide one's thinking and actions (Salovey & Mayer, 1990, p. 189; see also Salovey, Hsee, & Mayer, 1993), and they suggested that people with higher emotional intelligence would be better able to regulate their own emotions as well as produce desired emotional responses in others. Mayer and Gaschke (1988; see also Mayer, Salovey, Gomberg-Kaufman, & Blainy, 1991) have developed a scale to discriminate among people's experience and meta-experience of mood, including the ability to regulate emotions. Catanzaro and Mearns (1990; see also Kirsch, Mearns, & Catanzaro, 1990; Mearns, 1991) have focused on individual differences in expectancies for regulating negative moods, whereas Campos, Campos, and Barrett (1989) and Kopp (1989) have examined the developmental aspects that affect one's ability to regulate emotion. Larsen and Ketelaar (1989, 1991) have examined the effects that neuroticism and extraversion have on susceptibility to positive and negative emotional states. Larsen has also demonstrated that some individuals are likely to experience their emotional life much more intensely than others (Larsen, 1984; Larsen, Diener, & Emmons, 1986), and those individuals may have more need to regulate and more difficulty regulating their emotions than people who experience their moods less intensely. Together, these findings suggest that because of differences in background, prior experiences, intelligence, personality, and other individual differences, some people are better able to understand and regulate their emotional experiences than others.

SUMMARY AND CONCLUSION

Self-regulation of mood and emotion is often unnecessary and often unsuccessful. In many cases, emotions serve valuable functions such as to motivate adaptive actions, and suppressing the emotion might therefore prevent helpful actions. Also, as we have noted in many other chapters, a broad variety of self-regulation failures arise when people focus on controlling their feelings and leave the more fundamental and serious problems unresolved.

Emotions contain many automatic components, and therefore they are especially difficult to control directly. Affect regulation is thus limited in what it can accomplish. Many failures are therefore simply attributable to the fact that the person was trying to control something that could not be controlled.

Still, people do have some effective ways of controlling their moods and emotions. Although in theory there are many different types of affect regulation tasks, by far the most common is the attempt to escape from a bad mood or aversive emotional state, and so we have emphasized that one.

Some affects fail to be regulated because of simple underregulation patterns. Two reasons for underregulation are important. First, people sometimes believe that they should not try to control their emotions. Second, many people believe that it is best to vent all their feelings whenever they arise, and so they act out all emotional reactions (particularly anger) rather than trying to exert self-control. The evidence suggests that venting is not helpful and may be counterproductive for reducing anger. (On the other hand, keeping one's anger in can also be harmful; the only beneficial response is to try to bring one's anger to an end.) These beliefs may encourage people to acquiesce in not controlling their emotions.

Misregulation of moods and emotional states occurs for a variety of reasons. Overgeneralization is particularly common as a source of misregulation: People apply strategies that work for one mood to another mood, such as when they seek out companionship of others (which does alleviate sadness and fear) when angry but then make themselves angrier as they tell these other people all their grievances. They also may seek out arousing entertainments when they are already too aroused by some emotional reaction. Others keep using strategies that may have worked once, even though circumstances have now changed and those strategies are no longer advisable or effective.

Misregulation also occurs when people try strategies that simply do not work. They may try to suppress thoughts that are linked to the bad mood, but often people cannot simply block an upsetting matter out of their minds. They also may use distractors that compound the problem by generating other bad moods, such as when people may go to a depressing or upsetting movie in order to take their mind off their own troubles.

Transcendence failure is also a frequent source of failure to regulate affect. The more the person becomes immersed in the immediate situation, the harder it is to escape from the emotional reactions that it engenders. Emotions appear to engender a short-term focus, which may be one reason that moods and emotions acquire inertia and are difficult to overcome.

Many emotions are automatic reactions to circumstances, so the emotions cannot be prevented from arising. On the other hand, when people do things that prolong their exposure to those same circumstances or (indeed) that make things worse, they may be accused of acquiescing in their failure to control emotions. The social context of emotion must always be considered, however, because it often imposes severe limits on the person's ability to control his or her emotional state. The social context also encompasses the reactions of other people to how one deals with one's emotions. Lapse-induced causes may even be invoked, such as when an angry person says something that provokes an angry response from another person, thereby creating a new reason to continue being angry.

Part III

Controlling Impulses and Appetites

7

Impulses and Appetites

The public has now grown accustomed to the spectacle of millionaire celebrities seeing their careers damaged and lives ruined or even ended as a result of alcoholism, drug abuse, and other failures to control their dangerous appetites. As we began to work on this chapter, the news media were featuring the latest such stories. Michael Jackson, who has been one of the most celebrated and successful entertainers over the past two decades, recently confessed an addiction to pain control medications. Such medications may not be the only impulses he has trouble with; indeed, he has said that his overuse of those drugs got worse in response to the stress of his impending trial for sexual misconduct with children. In another occurrence, the promising young actor River Phoenix was found dead at age 23 from an apparent overdose of cocaine and heroin.

These cases are merely the latest in a long list. Elvis Presley is still mourned, decades after his pathetic death, which found him bloated and addicted from an inability to control his prodigious intake of sweets, junk food, and drugs. Comedian and movie star John Belushi died during one of his legendary drug binges. Drugs and alcohol led to the premature deaths of musicians Janis Joplin and Jimi Hendrix.

Meanwhile, other stars have survived their problems but have still had their health and their careers threatened by them. Senator Robert Packwood has been accused by two dozen women of groping and feeling and kissing them against their will, and while his peers call for his resignation he has "defended" himself by claiming that his alcoholism made him unable to control his sexual impulses. Talk-show host Oprah Winfrey, movie star Elizabeth Taylor, and television actress Delta Burke have all recently been in the news for their compulsive eating problems. When such prominent women overeat, their figures balloon up seemingly in front of the cameras, and their weight gains, eating binges, and dietary failures become the focus of national gossip.

Such problems are hardly unique to celebrities. Millions of ordinary citizens struggle with similar ones. They find themselves seemingly unable to resist their impulses and control their appetites. The only difference is that they face their problems in relative obscurity, away from the bright lights and intrusive cameras of the mass media.

Probably every thoughtful American has asked himself or herself at some point in recent years what lies behind all these problems. Why do so many people—especially so many highly successful people whose immense talents and years of hard work have led them at last to the top, where riches and fame await them—allow themselves to be undone by their own excesses and desires? It defies logic that people will sacrifice their careers, their families, and sometimes even their lives in the pursuit of what must often seem banal and fleeting pleasures: the sluggish buzz of drunkenness, the brief euphoria of cocaine, or the cheap and dirty thrills of off-limits sex.

In this part of the book we shall examine how people lose control over their appetites and impulses. This chapter will present some general and basic issues regarding impulse control, and the following chapters will take a close look at self-regulation failure in connection with specific kinds of impulses.

WHAT ARE IMPULSES AND ADDICTIONS?

The term *impulse* is unfortunately used in several different (although related) ways, and because it is necessary for us to preserve those concepts and meanings, they must be made explicit. The most precise meaning of *impulse* is a specific motivation or desire to perform a particular action, as opposed to a general or latent desire or a trait. Being a highly sexed person is not the same as having an impulse, because it denotes a broad, chronic, ongoing interest in a variety of sexual activities. Having sexual desire (being "horny") is also not the same, because it is nonspecific. Rather, a sexual impulse consists of the wish to perform a specific sex act with a particular partner on a particular occasion. By the same token, hunger is not an impulse, but a feeling of wanting to grab that doughnut off the shelf and devour it *is* an impulse. More generally, impulses arise during a brief period of time and appear in consciousness as urges, cravings, or longings to do particular things, such as smoking or drinking or gambling.

The here-and-now property of impulses is also implicit in the notion of "impulsive" behaviors, although researchers have not been fully consistent in that usage. An impulsive behavior is based on sudden whims or desires rather than (for example) arising from careful and deliberate thought. Many researchers have used the term "impulsive" to refer to all behavior that is guided by appetites. Others have used the term to refer to a lack of self-regulation, the way people might contrast an "impulsive" action with an action that was planned or premeditated.

Although the term *impulse* is sometimes restricted to extremely spontaneous behavior, we find it necessary to broaden its usage slightly, in order to encompass desires that arise and persist until appropriate (or inappropriate) action is taken. In some cases, a person may struggle with a recurrent impulse for days or even weeks. Still, it is only the same impulse if it is essentially the same desire to perform the same action on the same occasion. Once it has been acted upon and satisfied, for example, it is gone, and a desire to do the same thing on the following day is a different impulse.

The issue of recurrent desires to perform similar actions, which are then actually performed, raises the further complication of patterns of similar (or even seemingly identical) impulses. Such groups of impulses may be understood as *compulsions*. A compulsion thus refers to a pattern in which some impulsive behavior is repeated over and over, perhaps even against the person's will. It is no accident that many of the impulses we shall cover have been discussed as capable of evolving into compulsions, such as in compulsive shopping, eating, gambling, exercising, or drinking.

Many of the behaviors we shall examine have been labeled *appetitive* behaviors (see Orford, 1985). The term "appetite" is most commonly associated with eating, but people can develop an appetite for many forms of activity and satisfaction, such as a sexual appetite or an appetite for work. In ordinary speech people often use the terms appetite and hunger interchangeably, although some researchers do maintain a careful distinction: Hunger refers to the sensations arising from a specific physiological deprivation, whereas appetite can mean a desire for certain kinds of foods. When referring to an appetite for sex or work, however, people usually mean a desire for any of a variety of activities, although perhaps not all conceivably relevant ones. In a sense, then, impulse is the most specific term and hunger is the most general, whereas appetite is in between.

There are additional terms that laypersons and researchers have used, such as urges, cravings, and longings. Although some experts have called for careful, consistent, and circumspect uses of these terms (see Kozlowski & Wilkinson, 1987), others have followed ordinary speech in using them almost interchangeably. For our purposes, the only important distinction is between the most specific and particular desire (the impulse) and the more general, undifferentiated motivation.

Another widely used yet controversial term is *addiction*, and indeed many of the behaviors we shall discuss—including shopping and sex, as well as drug use—are sometimes labeled as "addictive behaviors." We agree with Peele's (1989) conclusion that the term *addiction* is poorly understood and often misused. The concept of addiction should be confined to physiological and psychological dependency on a given substance that involves some loss of control and that leads to various aversive reactions ("withdrawal") when the substance is absent. Although television talk shows are regularly spiced up with people claiming to be victims of addiction to such things as ice cream, neckties, love, pornography, and video games, these probably do not qualify as addictions in the true sense. Probably such people mean only that they feel strong and frequent impulses to seek those sources of pleasure and that they feel, rightly or wrongly, that their indulgence in such impulses is out of control.

The central theoretical problem in using a broad view of addiction is determining whether the person is in fact uncontrollably dependent on that particular action, substance, or source of satisfaction. As we noted in Chapter 2, this is part of a more general theoretical problem, because often it is obvious that people are actively acquiescing in the behaviors that they wish to regard as out of control. Someone may claim that his drinking is out of control, but is he really incapable of preventing his hands from opening a bottle of beer and raising it to his lips, and unable to prevent his mouth from opening and swallowing? Someone may claim that she cannot control her eating, but do her jaws really move up and down to chew the food against her will? Is the video game addict really unable to stop inserting quarters into the machine and moving the controls? The question, moreover, is not whether such a complete and paradoxical loss of control is possible, but whether everyone who claims to be addicted is so thoroughly powerless over his or her arms, legs, mouth, and the rest. In particular, there is no basis for regarding a love of ice cream or video games or pornography as an addiction in the physiological sense; and so if people constantly yield to their craving for such things, the level of acquiescence must be assumed to be rather high. This is not to deny that people may experience strong and persistent cravings to eat ice cream or play video games or watch pornographic films. But if those indulgences are out of control, it is very likely because the person gives himself or herself permission to indulge them.

A final point is that impulses are not necessarily bad, even if our discussion will highlight many of the problems and misfortunes that arise from indulging one's impulses. Nearly everyone is prone to engage in impulsive behavior on some occasions and in some circumstances. Indeed, when impulses are viewed as spontaneous behaviors they are often viewed as pleasant indulgences that make life worthwhile: last-minute vacations, a surprise bouquet of flowers, unplanned or impromptu sex, ordering pizza. How dreary life would be if everything were planned and all behavior occurred at the correct time and in the right place! Impulses direct people to perform actions that interrupt ongoing plans and behavior, and that very spontaneous and disruptive quality is responsible for some of their best and their worst consequences. Impulsive behaviors can dispel the monotony of life, just as they can hinder the attainment of desired goals and outcomes. Impulses and impulsive behaviors are thus important parts of life—for better or worse. Before we proceed to examine how people fail to control their impulsive behaviors, it is useful to understand impulses more fully.

HOW IMPULSES ARISE

We have defined impulses as highly specific desires to perform particular actions. As such, they are linked to particular people in particular situations. The impulse is an important form of motivation, but it differs from other motivational concepts that often reflect long-term or nonspecific wants and needs. An impulse often consists of a transformation of a long-term motivation: That is, it articulates a general and ongoing interest into a wish to perform a particular action.

Impulses thus exist at the intersection of ongoing motivations and immediate situations or stimuli. A young man may be generally interested in sex, but the impulse to kiss a particular young woman may only arise when he is alone with her and she smiles at him.

Three concepts are necessary to understand impulses. The first of these is the concept of *latent motivation*. People have many motivations in the sense of general, ongoing wants and needs and interests. Any given one of these motivations is not likely to be guiding behavior most of the time. Thus, although interest in sex may be a common motivator for many people, it does frequently recede from awareness and become irrelevant to current behavior, such as when the person is playing soccer, balancing a checkbook, or solving math problems. It is there inside the psyche and ready to be activated, but most of the time it is merely latent.

The second concept is therefore the *activating stimulus*. This is something in the immediate situation that is relevant to the latent motivation and therefore summons that motivation up from its seeming hibernation into awareness. In the absence of an activating stimulus, the motivation is less likely to become active. To pursue the sex example: Medieval Christian monasteries regarded the sex drive as an obstacle to spiritual salvation and sought to prevent it from influencing behavior. It is no accident that they settled on environments where few stimuli would remind the monks or nuns of sex. The individual was typically surrounded with unwashed and drearily clad members of the same sex, and of course the available books and pictures offered little in the way of titillating stimuli. Under such barren surroundings the sex drive was easier to control than it would be if, for example, the person was constantly confronted with seminude and attractive members of the opposite sex or with erotic art.

The impulse itself is therefore the third concept. The impulse typically arises when a latent motivation encounters an activating stimulus. Often the activating stimulus represents one way of satisfying the latent motivation. The impulse, in any case, consists of a specific desire to perform a specific action—to do the sort of thing that the latent motivation generally wants to do, only in the specific way or form suggested by the activating stimulus.

The familiar concept of temptation can be used to illustrate the interplay of these factors. The external stimulus can be regarded as the temptation, because it is what one wants. Yet the want had to be there all along inside the individual (in the form of the latent motivation), or else the tempting stimulus would not be tempting. The impulse is thus the product of the activating stimulus and the latent motivation. Resisting temptation means refusing to carry out the impulse—in other words, succeeding at self-regulation.

Several clarifications need to be made explicit. First, latent motivations are not constant. They may increase or decrease over time, depending on such factors as deprivation, satisfaction, health and vigor, and frequency of external reminders. Most people have a variety of motivations regarding food, and these may be latent much of the time although they are activated several times a day at least; yet the motivation to eat is certainly not constant and will in fact fluctuate steadily throughout the day.

Second, a single cue may activate multiple and even conflicting motivations. The would-be self-regulator then has to manage to integrate these various impulses into a coherent plan of action. Seeing a beer logo in the window of bar, for example, may activate several motivations, creating a thirsty wish for liquid refreshment, a yearning for the pleasure of intoxication, and a fear of what one's spouse will say if one arrives home late and drunk again.

Third, activating stimuli can be either internal or external to the individual. Thus far we have emphasized external, environmental cues, and in fact those may be the most common ones. There is in fact great variety in the ways that things people encounter in the world will activate various motivations. Seeing a police car may activate a desire to avoid getting a traffic ticket, causing an impulse to slow one's vehicle down to reach the speed limit. An angry look from a parent may remind the child to act more appropriately. Seeing one's own reflection in the mirror may prompt one to comb one's hair. Such external signals may bring forth a strong impulse from a motivation that would otherwise have remained completely dormant and unnoticed.

But there are also internal cues. In particular, when motivations become strong enough, they seem able to prompt the person to search his or her memory for cues that can allow an impulse to form even in the absence of external reminders. For example, a habitual smoker's body is accustomed to having a certain minimal level of nicotine in it, and as time goes by without smoking the level of nicotine may drop below that level. The motivation to smoke may become strong enough that the person begins to think about having a cigarette even if no external cue reminds him or her of smoking. In a similar way, a thirsty person may begin to think about having a cold beer, or a hungry person may begin to remember and imagine eating certain foods. There are a number of physiological explanations for the onset of these appetites, and although this book is not concerned with the specific means by which physiological deprivation gives rise to appetite, it is important to acknowledge that many behavioral tendencies are triggered by internal, physiologically stimulated cues.

A general model of appetitive behavior proposed by Kozlowski and Herman (1984) has differentiated between physiological drives and external influences. Kozlowski and Herman proposed that behavior is controlled by physiological drives only at the extremes of depletion or satiety. For instance, the reason that people typically eat is because of social cues, environmental cues, or learned habits (e.g., eating at noon). Similarly, the reason people quit eating is because of palatability or social norms. Less frequently do individuals from our culture eat solely based on hunger sensations or quit eating based solely on the physiological sensations of satiety. Most of the time people operate within what Kozlowski and Herman referred to as a *zone of biological indifference*. From this standpoint, visual cues, social influences, and other external triggers are often more important in determining behavior than is physiological state.

Faulty self-regulation may occur as a result of habitual attempts to ignore internal states. For example, dieting often involves learning to ignore sensations of hunger, and so chronic dieters may often rely on nonphysiological cues to control their eating. Over time, cognitive cues (such as dietary quotas) may take on greater importance than physiological cues, and the eating of dieters may be especially vulnerable to external and cognitive influences (Knight & Boland, 1989).

Heatherton, Polivy, and Herman (1989) reasoned that if chronic dieters are predominantly responsive to cognitive eating cues, they should be strongly affected by cognitive manipulations of hunger state. Chronic dieters and non-dieters were given a "vitamin" (placebo) prior to an ad lib taste test, in which subjects could eat as much delicious ice cream as they desired. When dieters were told that these vitamins had made previous participants in the study feel hungry, they themselves ate more ice cream than other dieters who had been told that previous participants had felt full after consuming the vitamins. Thus, the amount that the dieters ate depended mainly on a false information about how they might feel rather than on their actual internal state. More generally, it appears that learning to ignore internal sensations can lead to misregulation.

THE PROBLEM OF IMPULSE CONTROL

We have presented impulses as arising when some cue activates a latent motivation (including those rarer cases when the motivation becomes so strong that it prompts the person to search the memory for cues and hence generates an impulse even in the absence of external factors). People do not decide consciously or deliberately to have impulses: Impulses arise automatically and without effort.

One important implication is that impulses themselves cannot be controlled. In that sense, the common term "impulse control" is a misnomer. Given the motivation and the cue or opportunity, the impulse cannot be prevented from arising. The person may control what he or she does, and in some cases by managing the environment carefully and controlling one's attention one may prevent an impulse from arising, but the impulse itself is typically an automatic response that defies control.

To illustrate, consider the case of a professional gardener who has been working out in the hot sun for several hours. He comes into the house briefly to report that he has finished and sees on the dining table a tall cool glass of lemonade that the house's owner has poured for herself. It is highly unlikely that he could prevent himself from having an impulse to pick up that glass and drink the lemonade. Of course, he can and probably would prevent himself from acting out that impulse; perhaps he might ask the owner if she would give him something to drink. But in such cases it is the behavior that he is controlling, not the impulse itself.

We proposed that self-regulation can only succeed at overriding certain responses, namely the controllable ones. The formation of an impulse from the encounter between an activating cue and a latent motivation is usually an automatic process, however, in the most narrow and literal sense of the term automatic, and so impulses themselves are decidedly unpromising targets for self-regulatory efforts.

In general, therefore, self-regulation efforts may have to accept the fact that impulses will continue to arise. For many people, such impulses may include cravings for forbidden pleasures, such as drugs or drink or fattening foods or illicit sex. Certain utopian ideals hold that one should learn to want only specific, approved things, but these ideals may be unrealistic and destructive in practice. People should strive to control their actions and other controllable aspects of their inner lives rather than striving, quixotically, to be free of the impulses themselves. Rather than reproach themselves or their relationship partners for having these impulses, people might do better to learn to accept them and even to be proud of their capacity to prevent themselves from enacting them.

ATTENTION, RATIONALIZATION, AND TEMPTATION

Attentional processes are extremely important in impulse control failures (just as they were with other forms of self-regulation failure). The more people attend to the forbidden stimuli, the less likely they are to be able to resist. Indeed, if attention could be prevented from noticing the activating stimulus in the first place, there would be no temptation and no problem of self-regulation.

In Chapter 4 we covered delay of gratification. The problem of delay of gratification is often quite relevant to impulse control, because what opposes the tendency to accept delayed gratification is the temptation to accept an immediate reward. Giving in to temptation can be viewed as the flip side of delay of gratification. Just as it is instructive to examine the strategies that people use to resist temptation, it is instructive to examine the strategies that people use to allow their resolve to fail. In the delay of gratification literature it was found that avoiding thinking about immediate rewards, the use of abstraction, and focusing on long-term outcomes increased the ability to delay. Thus, we might expect that individuals who wish to engage in impulsive behaviors somehow manage to avoid thinking of the long-term consequences, avoid using abstraction for the long-term goals, and focus on the immediate payoffs.

A variety of research has provided general support for these propositions (Sarafino, 1990). For instance, smokers face the choice of obtaining immediate gratification of their addiction or living for a longer period of time. To do this, smokers must ignore or rationalize the long-term consequences of smoking. Thus, for instance, they claim that the evidence is weak linking smoking to cancer, or they fall prey to thoughts that they are personally invulnerable and that it will always be somebody else who develops cancer, heart disease, or lung disease.

Similarly, individuals who may need to lose weight for health reasons often find themselves in tempting situations, in which their self-resolve is threatened by social pressure or appetizing food. Such individuals are known to engage in irrational thought processes during such events ("Well, one cookie won't harm me," "I'll start the diet another day," "People would not like me if I didn't eat their food"). Thus, giving in to temptation also involves a number of cognitive strategies that are used to negate the perceived long-term consequences associated with indulgence. These rationalizations interfere with self-regulation because successful self-regulation necessitates setting goals and adjusting behavior based upon reasonable and accurate knowledge. By selectively ignoring or distorting the negative consequences of behavior, individuals are handicapping their abilities to control their impulses.

Consider the following example. You are incredibly thirsty and when you see a water fountain there is a sign that says "Do Not Use." While you are standing there, another individual walks up and takes a drink. Do you think that you would continue to be inhibited about drinking? Carver, Ganellen, Froming, and Chambers (1983) discuss such a scenario in terms of category accessibility. Essentially, they argue that seeing another person do something activates a schema for a certain behavior.

We earlier discussed Hull's (1981) theory that alcohol acts on inhibitions by lowering the level of self-awareness. Other theories posit that alcohol affects people by impairing cognitive processing. Steele and Josephs' (1990) attention-allocation model proposes that alcohol has a limiting effect on cognitive processes such that it restricts attention to immediate cues and reduces the ability to think abstractly. Thus, behavior is overly reliant on situational cues, which may lead to impulsive and undesirable behaviors. A similar theory has recently been proposed by Sayette (1993). He argues that the pharmacological effects of alcohol disrupt the appraisal of threat cues by impairing the link between ongoing actions and information previously stored in long-term memory. Thus, the factors that usually hold behavior in check (i.e., fear of the consequences of actions) are not encoded or processed normally. Thus, any factors that diminish cognitive resources may impair the ability to resist impulses.

SELF-AWARENESS

Because self-awareness has long been understood in terms of the comparison of self against standards (Carver & Scheier, 1981; Duval & Wicklund, 1972), it follows that self-awareness should intensify inhibitions. An important corollary holds that a reduction in self-awareness is an important component of disinhibition (Diener, 1979; Diener & Wallbom, 1976).

The view that self-awareness promotes inhibitions is supported by a variety of evidence. Diener and Wallbom (1976) showed that mirrors and other self-focusing cues reduced substantially the likelihood of cheating. Whereas 70% of college students normally cheated on an exam (worked beyond the time limit), only 7% cheated when they were confronted with their mirror image. Likewise, Beaman, Klentz, Diener, and Svanum (1979) found that the presence of a mirror reduced the stealing of Halloween candy by over 70% among children aged twelve and over. Some sexual dysfunctions have been linked to anxieties arising from an "internal spectator" (Masters & Johnson, 1970), suggesting that self-focus heightens sexual inhibitions.

Conversely, reductions in self-awareness have been linked to disinhibition (Diener, 1979; Wicklund, 1982). For example, the effects of alcohol include both a reduction in self-awareness (Hull, 1981) and the removal of certain inhibitions, leading to behavioral excess (Steele & Southwick, 1985). Indeed, alcohol is considered the classic disinhibitor and many illegal behaviors are justified on the basis that the person was too drunk to know what they were doing. When there are multiple groups, an increase in the relative size of one group is associated with a decrease in self-awareness (Mullen, 1987) as well as disinhibited aggressive behavior such as lynch mob atrocity (Mullen, 1986). Escape from self-awareness through sexual masochism or presuicidal activities is associated with the removal of various inhibitions (Baumeister, 1989, 1990). The cognitive processes that link escape from self-awareness with disinhibition will be discussed in greater detail in the next section.

It is important to acknowledge that removal of self-awareness does not simply produce a broad spectrum of uninhibited behavior. Rather, specific internal constraints appear to be undermined. For example, alcohol consumption reduces self-awareness but its effects on inhibited behavior are limited and specific. Steele and Southwick (1985) noted that alcohol consumption has disinhibiting effects only when there is an inhibitory response conflict, that is, when the person has both a desire for and an inhibition against a particular activity. When such a conflict exists, a reduction of self-awareness removes the tendency to compare oneself or one's acts against norms and standards, so the inhibiting anxiety or guilt is not felt.

In short, inhibitions depend on comparing oneself or one's possible acts against certain standards, which is the essence of self-awareness. Furthermore, low levels of self-awareness are linked to behavioral disinhibition. One may therefore hypothesize that the strength of various inhibitions will vary in direct proportion to the individual's degree of self-awareness.

Sometimes people want to escape from self-awareness, and under such circumstances a reduction of inhibitions—and loss of self-regulation—may be a by-product. Baumeister (1991a) has elaborated how the effort to escape from self-awareness is behind a variety of behaviors, including sexual masochism, meditation and spirituality, and suicide. As we shall see in Chapters 8 and 9, it is also quite relevant to several major failures of impulse control, including alcohol abuse and binge eating.

A central aspect for the disinhibiting effect of escaping from self-awareness is that people tend to escape by shifting their awareness toward relatively meaningless, concrete, mechanistic forms of thought (see Vallacher & Wegner, 1985, 1987; also Carver & Scheier, 1981). Instead of thinking in long-term, abstract, or meaningful ways, they focus on immediate sensations, movements, and events. This shift favors giving in to temptation. After all, impulses exist at that level (as concrete possibilities in the here and now), whereas inhibitions exist at the highly meaningful level of long-range resolutions and important evaluations.

SNOWBALLING

One last general comment about impulse control is that, contrary to a great deal of rhetoric, a single lapse is rarely a catastrophe. Genuine self-regulation problems are associated with the large binges. Although they do have to start somewhere, it is necessary always to attend to the factors that convert an initial indulgence into a large-scale breakdown. Lapse-activated causes are therefore of central concern.

Marlatt's *abstinence violation effect* is one important type of lapse-activated causal pattern that causes an initial indulgence to escalate into a serious binge. Marlatt (1985) proposed a two-stage model to account for complete loss of control. The first stage consists of a small lapse or slip. Because abstinence is nearly impossible, the person occasionally fails to regulate behavior. Whether the person relapses completely will depend upon the attributions that are made regarding the lapse. The second stage varies according to the specific attributions that are made. If the person attributes the lapse to internal, stable, and global factors that are perceived to be uncontrollable (e.g., there is a lack of willpower or the person has a disease), then the probability of relapse is heightened. The person perceives that there is little reason to continue trying to control what is uncontrollable, or the person concludes that he does not have the necessary skills to control behavior. However, if the lapse is attributed to temporary, external, and specific factors (such as momentary indulgence in a specific high-risk situation), then the lapse will not necessarily lead to relapse. Thus, the subjective perception of the likelihood of future control plays a large role in the abstinence-violation effect model.

Like Marlatt, we suggest that there are two separate stages in the snowball process. The first stage involves the failure to live up to the standards of perfect abstinence. Indeed, one could argue that the problem begins with a matter of misregulation, namely setting unrealistically high standards such as zero-tolerance expectations. Abstinence is extremely difficult and most individuals will experience occasional failures. People give in to temptation or fail to cope with high-risk situations. For instance, very few dieters can resist overindulgence at Thanksgiving or during the holiday season. These momentary indulgences are likely associated with increased positive affect and are likely to be perceived as rewarding, at least in the short term. However, the effect on future self-regulatory effort may be profound if the person relinquishes self-control.

The potentially disastrous consequences associated with relapse intensify the desire to maintain complete abstinence, which in turn leads to further catastrophizing when small lapses occur. The efforts to maintain complete abstinence drain self-regulatory capacities so that the individual may not be willing to face potential challenges or high-risk situations. Thus, an alcoholic in recovery may believe that it is only safe to leave the house to attend AA meetings. The dieter may refuse to attend parties or other social events. The gambler may refuse to enter stores that sell lottery tickets. In some ways, these strategies do form the first line of defense, in that avoiding the cues that trigger the behavior may aid self-regulation. However, when considering complex self-regulation (i.e., regulating all aspects of life), the overemphasis on avoiding potential threats may interfere with other enjoyable life tasks. Self-control may be easier when you lock yourself away, but it is a sad and lonely life, completely dominated by the singular effort to avoid minor transgressions and lapses.

More generally, self-regulatory breakdowns that lead to major indulgences nearly always show a gradual pattern. This principle was conveyed in a humorous fashion by Michael Sangiacomo (1990), a journalist who wrote an article on the 900 numbers that the telephone company offers. He made many calls to a number called "True Confessions" and listened to what people said. Although he was amazed at the variety of things people confessed in this anonymous setting, he was able to ascertain one general pattern, which was the widespread use of the phrase "One thing led to another." As an example, he offered the case of a woman's confession that began with the standard insistence that she had never made such a confession before but wanted to discuss this experience. "One day I met these two guys on the beach. Well, I had a blanket and one guy had a rope, you know? One thing led to another and well, I just enjoyed every second of it." It is of course difficult to assume that the presence of two men with a rope was very compelling as an activating stimulus, and the "one thing led to another" suggests that indeed the shedding of inhibitions (details of which were omitted) was a gradual process.

8

Alcohol Consumption and Abuse

Americans have a love-hate relationship with alcohol. Alcohol is an important aspect of normal social interaction, and having one or two drinks is as commonplace a behavior as eating, working, or watching television. *Cheers*, one of the most popular television programs of the 1980s, featured a lovable cast who spent the vast majority of their time in a bar. The show conveyed the implicit message that moderate consumption of alcohol is viewed as a pleasurable social activity. The character on the show who drank the most heavily (Norm) was seldom if ever inebriated. Even some apparently alcoholic individuals are regarded as amusing characters (e.g., Dean Martin, Foster Brooks) and drunken escapades are an amusing source of entertainment in movies, songs, poems, and popular literature.

Meanwhile, however, alcohol is considered to be at the root of many of our societal problems, such as spousal abuse and other forms of violence. Alcohol is also considered to be a primary determinant of homelessness: The staggering, intoxicated homeless person is a sadly familiar sight in most cities.

Most individuals who drink do so in moderation, although the average American over age fourteen consumes almost 2.5 gallons of pure alcohol per year (United States Department of Health and Human Services, 1993), which corresponds to nearly 600 12-ounce cans of beer. Of course, this includes nondrinkers, social drinkers, and heavy drinkers. It has been estimated that 10% of drinkers consume more than 50% of the total amount of alcohol consumed (American Psychiatric Association [APA], 1987), and some 15 million Americans meet the *Diagnostic and Statistical Manual of Mental Disorders* (3rd ed.—Revised) (*DSM–III–R*) criteria for alcohol dependence (Grant et al., 1991).

Alcohol dependence (colloquially referred to as alcoholism) is defined as abnormal alcohol seeking with some loss of control over drinking accompanied by physiological effects known as tolerance and withdrawal. Although estimates of the prevalence of alcoholism vary widely, it is clear that a great many Americans suffer from it.

People begin drinking early in life. Although high school students are too young to purchase alcohol legally, some 90% of high school seniors have tried alcohol, and in one recent survey almost one-third of seniors had reported a bout of heavy drinking (five or more drinks) within the preceding two weeks (Johnston, O'Malley, & Bachman, 1991).

America's affinity for alcohol is not without consequence. In 1989, alcohol was a factor in over half of all fatal car accidents, killing over 20,000 (United States Department of Health and Human Services, 1993). Indeed, more Americans are killed by drunk drivers every two years than were killed in the entire Vietnam War (Koshland, 1989). One study found that over 24% of suicide victims, 34% of homicide victims, and 38% of unintentional injury victims had blood levels of alcohol that meet legal criteria for impairment (Goodman, Istre, Jordan, Herndon, & Kelaghan, 1991). A recent study by Leigh and Schafer (1993) found that approximately one-third of their 800 subjects reported having sex during a recent heavy drinking occasion, and the heaviest drinkers were likely to have sex with a new or casual partner. Leigh and Schafer note that this places heavy drinkers at great risk for exposure to the AIDS virus. The overall cost of problem drinking, ranging from employee absence to health problems, is estimated to be more than $100 billion (National Council on Alcoholism, 1986).

The historical view on alcohol and impairment has gone through a number of fascinating trends (Orford, 1985). Stanton Peele's (1989) examination of the disease model showed that alcoholism has been alternatively viewed as a moral weakness or as a disease for the past few centuries. For instance, in the seventeenth and eighteenth centuries, alcohol was widely consumed, but only a few "town drunks" were unable to control their intake. As Levine (1978) wrote, "liquor was food, medicine, and social lubricant; even such a Puritan divine as Cotton Mather called it the 'good' creature of God" (p. 145). It was not until the nineteenth century that alcohol took on the "demon rum" label, and the American Temperance Society described alcohol as inherently addictive, much the same way that heroin is viewed today (Levine, 1978). The Temperance Society was dedicated to eliminating consumption of alcohol, which they viewed as the root cause of societal ills (Peele, 1989).

The ambivalence toward alcoholism has continued into this century. In 1951 the World Health Organization (WHO) decreed that alcoholism is a disease process, but three years later McGoldrick wrote "Alcoholism is no more a disease than thieving or lynching. Like these, it is the product of a distortion of outlook, a way of life bred of ignorance and frustration" (cited in Vaillant, 1983, p. 3).

Our society continues to have surprisingly diverse views on alcoholism. On the one hand, many Americans view alcoholism as a disease that a person has no control over. Just as diabetics cannot control the functioning of their kidneys, the alcoholic is seen as unable to control his or her drinking. However, many of the people who believe that alcoholism is a disease also view alcoholics as being morally weak and personally responsible for their illness (Cunningham, Sobell, & Chow, 1992; Miller, 1993; Peele, 1989). Thus, although it is often argued that a disease model is kinder to those who have troubles with alcohol (i.e., it is more humanitarian), most people still believe that only certain (morally corrupt) individuals will develop drinking problems.

The culture's ambivalent attitude about self-regulation failure with regard to drunkenness is reflected in the courts. In a recent case in Massachusetts, a jury awarded $7 million to the family of a victim of a drunk driver—to be paid by the owner of the bar where the driver got drunk. The jury ruled that the bar owner was responsible for not controlling the amount of alcohol consumed by the driver. Such so-called dram shop rules transfer the responsibility from the person to the environment, acknowledging that people may not be able to regulate drinking behavior. Thus, our society views alcoholics as weak and personally responsible for their behaviors, but at the same time many people assume that alcoholism is a disease over which many people do not have control.

In short, the desire for alcohol is one of the most common and pervasive appetites in the United States, and failures to regulate that appetite are both common and destructive. In this chapter we consider the role of self-control, particularly *failures* of self-control, in normal and abnormal drinking.

Alcohol is an important yet sensitive topic to cover in relation to the issue of acquiescence in self-regulation failure. As we shall cover, there are important arguments to the effect that alcoholics cannot control their drinking. On the other hand, it is almost impossible to force someone to drink against his or her will. When people are opening bottles, pouring drinks, raising them to their lips, and swallowing the liquid, it is clear that the person is deliberately and consciously cooperating in the drinking process. On the other hand, the craving for alcohol may be largely beyond conscious control.

Of all the forms of self-regulation failure covered in this book, alcohol is perhaps the most striking and dramatic illustration of lapse-activated causal patterns. That is, one set of factors causes people to start drinking, and then a large additional set of factors enters into the picture to cause the person to continue drinking to the point of excess. It is of course important to examine what causes people to start drinking, but having a drink or two is not normally a problem and does not constitute self-regulation failure. Indeed, some evidence suggests that occasional and moderate doses of alcohol have beneficial effects on health. It is the heavy drinking, whether chronically or in isolated binges, that is harmful and destructive. This chapter is therefore organized in two main sections. The first will examine why people start drinking; the second looks at what leads people into heavy drinking.

HAVING THAT FIRST DRINK

To understand why people fail to control their drinking, it is first necessary to appreciate why they drink at all. As we have acknowledged, consuming alcohol per se is neither harmful nor destructive. Our initial discussion will not emphasize issues of underregulation and misregulation as much as in other chapters, because having an initial drink or two does not necessarily constitute self-regulation failure. Still, self-regulation failures do begin with a single drink, and so it is helpful to understand why people start.

Why Do People Drink Alcohol?

There are two major categories of psychological reasons for consuming alcohol. First, people consume alcohol for social reasons, such as at parties or during celebrations. Consuming a small amount of alcohol in these situations is normative, and refusing to drink may strike others as antisocial or prudish. Second, people drink for individual reasons, such as because of personal enjoyment of the effects of alcohol, or because they are using alcohol to escape from unpleasant circumstances or to cope with stress and anxiety. A recent large study found that the most common reason given for drinking was relaxation, followed by loosening up in social situations, drinking to cheer yourself up, to reward yourself for hard work, and from a belief that during difficult times you deserve a drink (Golding, Burnam, Benjamin, & Wells, 1992).

Moreover, the more people drink, the more possibilities they endorse as reasons to drink; this suggests that as one drinks more and more, alcohol gradually becomes an important ingredient of daily life (Golding et al., 1992). Alternatively, some researchers have interpreted this to mean that the more reasons people have to drink and the less constraining the social situation, the more likely people are to drink heavily (Orford, 1985). This latter suggestion has been supported in surveys of adolescents: Greater consumption is associated with more reasons to drink and fewer contextual constraints (e.g., having parents who encourage drinking) (Kouzis & Labouvie, 1992).

Similarly, a study by Wegner, Vallacher, and Dizadji (1989) had alcoholics and college students assess the possible meanings of drinking alcoholic beverages. Whereas light social drinkers tended to rate the meaning of drinking alcohol at a very low level of meaning (e.g., lifting a glass, swallowing liquid), heavy drinkers and alcoholics tended to identify multiple meanings for drinking alcohol (including such things as "hurting myself," "relieving tension," "overcoming boredom," "getting drunk," and "rewarding myself"). Because identifications may serve as templates for actions (Vallacher & Wegner, 1985), it may be that a greater number of identifications promotes increased drinking for some individuals.

One recent study of college students found that heavy, moderate, and light drinkers differed in the situations that they say lead them to drink (Carey, 1993). Surprisingly, when asked what situations would lead them to engage in excessive drinking, light and moderate drinkers were more likely to report negative affect and because of urges or temptations. Heavy drinkers reported being more likely to drink excessively when there is social pressure to drink or when they are experiencing pleasant emotions. Men and women may also have different motives for drinking heavily. A recent study by Thombs, Beck, and Mahoney (1993) found that heavy drinking among women was associated with the alleviation of negative distress, whereas for men heavy drinking was associated with social situations and rebellion. Thus, there are multiple motives to consume alcohol that may change as a function of drinking experience and may depend upon gender.

Alcohol and Reinforcement

For most people, the consumption of moderate amounts of alcohol is a pleasurable experience. As a psychomotor stimulant, alcohol belongs to a class of drugs that are perceived as highly rewarding (Pihl & Peterson, 1992; Wise & Bozarth, 1987). Alcohol may also trigger action of endogenous opiates, which are typically associated with positive emotional states (Pihl & Peterson, 1992). Thus, in small to moderate doses, alcohol makes people feel good (Hull & Bond, 1986). From a learning perspective, then, alcohol is a positive reinforcer (at least for humans).

Alcohol can also be negatively reinforcing. Because alcohol can dampen anxiety in some situations (Conger, 1956; Sayette, 1993), its use can be reinforced by the removal or dampening of unpleasant emotional experiences. Thus, many people report drinking alcohol in order to relax or to cope with negative circumstances. For the alcoholic, failure to consume alcohol not only denies them the positive rewards, but after a sufficient period of time they begin to experience withdrawal sensations. Subsequent intake of alcohol eliminates withdrawal sensations and thereby reinforces future intake.

It is probably the unique combination of stimulating and anxiolytic effects of alcohol that make it so appealing (or difficult to resist), which is related to the influential opponent-process theory of addiction (Solomon, 1980; Solomon & Corbit, 1974). The opponent-process model starts with the assumption that for every action there is an opposite reaction. Whereas alcohol may initially reduce feelings of anxiety, the removal of alcohol subsequently leads to increased anxiety and other unpleasant sensations. Thus, negative sensations (such as those related to withdrawal) motivate individuals to once again consume alcohol. Over time, Solomon argues, the opponent process becomes more efficient, and therefore you need more and more alcohol to achieve the feelings of euphoria and relaxation (known as tolerance).

The Importance of Expectancies

One of the reasons that people consume alcohol is because of the expected or anticipated effects that alcohol will have on their emotions and behaviors

(Critchlow, 1986; Marlatt & Rohsenow, 1980). Marlatt (1987) described alcohol as the "magic elixir," capable of increasing social skills, sexual pleasure, confidence, power, and aggression. Expectancies about the effects of alcohol are learned very early in life; even young children believe that alcohol has a number of positive functions. Children see that people who are drinking have a lot of fun and that drinking is an important aspect of many celebrations. Teenagers may view drinkers as sociable and grown-up, two things that they are desperately trying to be (Sarafino, 1990). Thus, children learn to expect that the consumption of alcohol will have a number of positive effects.

Indeed, the initial interest in consuming alcohol derives from beliefs that alcohol intoxication will be an important source of innocent, harmless pleasure. People's expectations about the positive effects of alcohol have been shown to predict excessive alcohol intake (Brown, Goldman, & Christiansen, 1985). Children who have very positive expectations are more likely to start drinking and more likely to be heavy drinkers (Christiansen, Smith, Roehling, & Goldman, 1989) than children who do not share those expectations.

Expectations develop through media influences and parental influences (Miller & Brown, 1991), and so media and parental communications likewise play a role in eventual abuse of alcohol. Children whose parents have alcohol control problems expect more positive outcomes from drinking alcohol (Brown, Creamer, & Stetson, 1987). Thus, to the extent that media influences and problem drinkers may overemphasize the positive aspects of alcohol intake, children may develop a belief that alcohol is a useful substance for dealing with problems or for all celebrations. Unfortunately, the existing data suggest that there are both positive and negative consequences associated with alcohol intake, and therefore those who choose to drink alcohol for its positive effects may get more than they bargained for. We have noted that misregulation effects are often linked to erroneous beliefs about the self and about the world; unrealistically positive beliefs about alcohol are probably one factor that starts people on the road to problem drinking.

Research has indeed shown that beliefs about the effects of alcohol are linked to the amount of alcohol consumed. Children with more positive expectancies are likely to start drinking at earlier ages and are likely to drink larger amounts (Christiansen et al., 1989). Positive expectancies are also linked to heavier intake among adults (Brown et al., 1985). Moreover, people also develop expectations for how alcohol will affect other behaviors. Indeed, one appeal of drinking is that it allows people to loosen up and engage in behaviors that they might otherwise restrain. Wilson (1988) remarked that "The superego has been defined as that part of the psyche that is soluble in alcohol" (p. 369).

Marlatt and Rohsenow (1980) pointed out that the *belief* that one has consumed alcohol may have effects on behavior that are independent of whether one has actually consumed alcohol. In a major review of these studies, Hull and Bond (1986) found that expectancies do have profound effects on certain categories of behaviors. Specifically, by using a balanced-placebo design (in which subjects are given either alcohol or placebo under the instructions that the drink contains alcohol or not), research has demonstrated that the alcohol truly does impair (independent of whether people believe they have consumed alcohol or not) motor processes, information processing, and mood. However, the expectancy of consuming alcohol (whether the person actually does or not) leads to disinhibition of a variety of social behaviors, such as sexual arousal and aggression.

Disinhibition is of course especially relevant to the issue of self-regulation failure. Hull and Bond (1986) concluded that it is the belief that one has consumed alcohol (independent of whether one actually did or not) that leads to increased alcohol consumption. As will be discussed later, this finding provides a substantial challenge to the notion that alcohol leads to a loss of control over drinking (cf. Jellinek, 1960).

Still, the actual physiological effects of consuming alcohol may interact with expectancies. For instance, alcohol tends to disinhibit sexual arousal, but it interferes with performance. Studies of alcohol's effects on sexual responding confirm Shakespeare's observation that "Lechery, sir, it provokes, and unprovokes: it provokes the desire, but it takes away the performance" (*Macbeth*, Act II, Scene 3).

Indeed, one way to combat problems with drinking and alcohol abuse may be to challenge the widely held assumptions about the positive aspects of drinking. A recent study has found that by challenging people's expectancies about the effects of alcohol on social and sexual behavior, it was possible to induce people to reduce their consumption of alcohol (Darkes & Goldman, 1993). Thus, from a variety of perspectives, people's beliefs about the putative effects of alcohol are important determinants of the self-regulation of alcohol intake.

False Consensus: Assuming Everybody Else Drinks

One way that people control drinking is by the standards that they believe are appropriate for people in general. Hence people may drink more if they believe that it is normative to drink a lot. A well-known social psychological phenomenon is called the false consensus effect, in which people overestimate the extent to which others share their beliefs, values, and behaviors (Ross, Greene, & House, 1977).

In terms of alcohol, heavy drinkers may believe that other people drink as much as they do. As pointed out by Miller and Brown (1991) heavy drinkers may associate with other heavy drinkers (i.e., they may choose to socialize only with those who share their heavy drinking behaviors, possibly because they avoid the implicit or explicit disapproval of light drinkers), and therefore their reference group for what is normative may become quite biased.

Thus, people may start drinking because they perceive or believe that nearly everyone else is drinking. Perceptions of other people may become self-fulfilling; groups of young adults may progress in step into increasingly heavy alcohol consumption because they all think what they are doing is normal and appropriate, based on observing each other drink more and more. Television commercials and other depictions in the mass media probably encourage that perception.

Conflicting Standards

We noted that conflicting standards or wishes are often implicated in self-regulation failure, and alcohol (like other appetites) offers many vivid examples of such conflicts. Probably almost everyone could avoid drinking if he or she were only certain of wanting to avoid it. Problem drinking arises in part, however, because people like to drink.

Miller and Rollnick (1991) noted that one of the central challenges facing treatment of excessive drinking is that heavy drinkers and alcoholics experience a great deal of ambivalence. Alcoholics typically want to quit drinking, but they have also become attached to their drinking behavior and may resist giving it up. Moreover, they may admit that their drinking is causing them problems, but they want to describe the situation as not being very serious and they might try to minimize the actual costs in order to justify their behavior. Indeed, the greater the extent that the alcoholics believe that drinking brings positive rewards, the more likely they are to fail at their efforts to control their drinking (Brown, 1985). Orford (1985) noted that addictions are classic approach–avoidance conflicts, in which drinkers have reasons both to consume and not to consume alcohol. Alcoholics often perceive periods of heavy drinking as fun and exciting, and alcoholics may look forward to occasional drinking binges (they may even set up the binges; Allsop & Saunders, 1991).

One problem for heavy drinkers is that they want to control their drinking—but they also want to be the life of the party. Carey (1993) found that heavy drinkers were more likely to report excessive drinking in pleasant social situations, in which drinking was part of celebration. This is especially true for men (Thombs et al., 1993). A variety of studies have shown that heavy drinkers and alcoholics develop a myriad of reasons for drinking. Sometimes their reasons even seem to contradict each other (e.g., drinking to celebrate and drinking to escape) (Golding et al., 1992).

We already mentioned the study by Wegner et al. (1989) that examined the ways people identify the action of drinking. Other findings of that study underscore the notion that conflicting goals (i.e., ambivalence) are related to self-regulation failure. In that study, heavy drinkers and alcoholics identified drinking alcohol at much higher levels of meaning than light or moderate drinkers. Thus, the people prone to self-regulation failure identified drinking as something that reduces boredom and anxiety, and also as something that is used for self-reward. However, heavy drinkers also identified drinking as causing potential shame and health consequences, and they made the link between drinking and getting drunk or drinking too much. Wegner et al. speculated that these multiple-action identifications are prepotent templates for behavior. Thus, heavy drinkers and alcoholics view drinking alcohol in multiple and complex ways. As the researchers observed, "The person who looks on drinking as 're-lieving tension' or 'overcoming boredom,' for instance, may believe that 'hurt-ing myself' is merely a necessary evil on the way to a pleasurable experience" (p. 209).

Thus, people who drink a great deal have multiple and conflicting motives for drinking and for not drinking. On one hand, they want to drink because they find it relaxing and because it helps them deal with negative emotions. On the other hand, they want to refrain from drinking because they experience occasional (or not so occasional) negative consequences, such as feeling ashamed of themselves or being hungover. Situational challenges and cues may make some meanings or motives more salient than others, and therefore heavy drinking will be more likely to occur when drinkers focus on the positive fea-tures of drinking.

Strength and Exhaustion

From a strength model perspective, underregulation becomes more likely when people become fatigued or when situational demands overwhelm per-sonal resources. In fact, there is substantial evidence that loss of control over alcohol intake is linked to ineffective coping and lack of personal strength. For instance, people often engage in excessive drinking at the end of day; it is only the most severe alcoholics who lose control of their drinking early in the morn-ing. Not only are people more likely to drink in the evening, but evening drink-ing is more likely to lead to accidents and fatal injuries (Goodman et al., 1991, Smith et al., 1989). Indeed, the majority of traumatic injury deaths between 9:00 P.M. and 3:00 A.M. are likely to involve alcohol (United States Department of Health and Human Services, 1993). Thus, evening is a high-risk situation for excessive alcohol consumption.

Perhaps the most important risk factor for excessive drinking is emotional distress. Marlatt (1985) noted that negative emotional states were related to relapse for a number of addictive behaviors, such as alcoholism, gambling, and heroin addiction. Several studies have examined the impact of distressing ex-periences on craving for alcohol and on alcohol consumption. Litt, Cooney, Kadden, and Gaupp (1990) induced negative moods in male alcoholics by means of hypnotic mood induction. They found that negative mood states in-creased desires for alcohol whether alcohol cues were present or not. That is, negative mood states alone were sufficient to elicit cravings for alcohol. Other studies have demonstrated that individuals will translate cravings into action. In one of the earliest studies, Higgins and Marlatt (1973) told subjects that they would be rated for physical attractiveness by a panel of members of the opposite sex. This distress was associated with increased drinking for college students.

Similarly, the stress associated with having to speak in public led to greater rate and amount of drinking compared to a control condition (Strickler, Tomaszewski, Maxwell, & Suib, 1979). Drinking in response to stress has been shown to be more likely for heavy drinkers (Miller, Hersen, Eisler, & Hilsman, 1974), and for those who are high in the trait of public self-consciousness (Hull & Young, 1983).

Thus, situational demands might overwhelm self-regulatory capacities under times of stress. Indeed, excessive consumption of alcohol has been linked to ineffective coping by a number of researchers. For instance, Cooper, Russell, Skinner, Frone, and Mudar (1992) found that alcohol use and drinking problems were common among males who relied on avoidant forms of emotion coping. This was especially true for those males who had positive expectations regarding the effects of alcohol. Interestingly, women may derive fewer benefits from the stress-reducing effects of alcohol, partially because they find consumption of alcohol distressing in itself (Abrams & Wilson, 1979; Wilson, 1988) and also because women do not have the same expectations as do men about the anxiety-reducing properties of alcohol (Rohsenow, 1983). Similarly, Frank, Jacobson, and Tuer (1990) found that inadequate conflict resolution skills predicted drinking for men, whereas problems with intimacy were more predictive of drinking for women. Thus, men may be more likely to have problems with drinking because they are more likely to use it as a coping mechanism. A recent study demonstrated that teaching at-risk young adults effective coping strategies and teaching them to self-monitor alcohol intake apparently led to a 40% reduction in drinking behavior that was maintained over two years (Baer et al., 1992). Thus, an important aspect of teaching self-control over drinking behavior is to be certain that people learn other effective means of coping with stress.

Findings from alcohol research are relevant to another prediction of the strength model of self-regulation, namely that being able to give up one addictive behavior may in the future increase one's ability to stop oneself from another addictive behavior (just as muscles become stronger with successful exercise). Sobell, Sobell, and Toneatto (1991) conducted a large-scale study of the natural recovery from alcohol problems. They found a substantial number of subjects who had quit smoking subsequently managed to resolve their problems with alcohol (by returning to moderate drinking or by abstaining from alcohol). Sobell et al. (1991) noted "it might be hypothesized that quitting smoking by active alcohol abusers will be predictive of a future successful drinking problem resolution" (p. 227). It is possible that these former smokers increased their self-regulatory strength through smoking cessation, which later assisted them in quitting alcohol.

Controlling Emotion

In the previous section, we noted that emotional distress is associated with a tendency to drink more. Part of this may indeed be due to the reduction in self-regulatory strength that comes from emotional turmoil. There is also, however, the simple fact that people sometimes turn to drink in the hope of forgetting their worries and improving their mood.

Alcohol is viewed by both light and heavy drinkers as having specific anxiety-reducing properties (Sayette, 1993; Stockwell, 1985). Thus, people drink in order to control mood. Unfortunately, the available evidence does not support this belief (Cappell & Greeley, 1987; Cappell & Herman, 1972), and drinking to control mood may even be self-defeating. Although moderate doses of alcohol are associated with increased positive mood, larger doses (as from continued drinking) are associated with worsening of mood (Stockwell, 1985). For instance, Nathan, Titler, Lowenstein, Solomon, and Rossi (1970) found that alcoholics had very positive expectancies regarding the effects of alcohol, such that alcohol would always lead to positive mood and reduced anxiety. However, they found that increasing doses of alcohol actually led to a worsening of mood.

The implication is that drinking to control mood may often reflect misregulation. This stands in contrast to the underregulation patterns noted in the previous section, which arise when the person's strength is depleted because of stress, emotional turmoil, tiredness, or other factors. People use alcohol as an affect regulation strategy. We saw in Chapter 6 on affect regulation that alcohol is often a poor and ineffective means of controlling emotions and moods. For present purposes, it needs to be pointed out that this approach also leads to misregulation of alcohol intake.

Many of these problems of abusing alcohol to alter mood seem to reflect overgeneralization effects. Alcohol works once, and so people think it will always work. A recent review of the literature by Sayette (1993) suggests that alcohol is effective in reducing anxiety only in some circumstances and that people may drink to reduce anxiety because of mistaken interpretations about the effects of alcohol. Wilson (1988) noted that people may show a confirmatory bias such that the one or two occasions in which alcohol was associated with decreased stress might enhance the belief that alcohol is effective in doing so in all situations. Moreover, people may believe that alcohol is effective at reducing anxiety because they imagine that things would be even worse if they had not been drinking (Hodgson, Stockwell, & Rankin, 1979).

Another possibility is that the impairment in memory that accompanies alcohol prevents heavy drinkers from recognizing the possible negative consequences of drinking. They remember the drinking episode as if it were fun and enjoyable, and unless their memory is jogged by angry friends, relatives, or spouses, they may continue to hold this belief and drink more in the future. A person who in a drunken rage calls his boss a jerk, smashes up his car, and tells his spouse to take a hike may wake up the next morning and imagine that he had a wonderful time —perhaps even contemplating starting all over again the next night!

A variety of studies have shown that many people consume alcohol because they lack coping skills necessary to deal with anxiety, distress, and other dysphoric moods. For instance, Miller and Sanchez (1987, cited in Miller & Brown, 1991) found that individuals who reported using alcohol for coping purposes (e.g., to deal with loneliness or to forget their problems) had much higher rates of alcohol use than those with more adequate coping skills. Similarly, Frank et al. (1990) found that males who drank heavily had selective deficits in conflict resolution skills. Thus, inabilities to cope with negative emotions may promote excessive consumption of alcohol.

A concept related to the tension-reducing effects of alcohol has been referred to as "stress-response dampening" (Levenson, Sher, Grossman, Newman, & Newlin, 1980). This theory suggests that alcohol selectively interferes with the processing of threat cues, such that environmental stressors no longer pack the same punch when someone has been drinking. In a major review of this literature, Sayette (1993) noted a number of important findings that indicate drinking in order to reduce stress may be a form of misregulation. Thus, research has demonstrated that alcohol is more likely to dampen stress responses when it is consumed before the stressor than when consumed after the stressor (Farha & Sher, 1989). Sayette proposes that consuming alcohol following the stressor may even increase stress responses. This implies that one needs to be drunk before the distressing experience if alcohol is to help. However, most people who use alcohol to influence mood have a few drinks following the distressing experience. Thus, again, the use of alcohol to combat stress is often a form of misregulation.

Another implication of stress–response dampening for misregulation is that alcohol essentially makes people fearless. Since alcohol interferes with processing of threat cues, intoxicated individuals fail to pick up on danger cues or other indications of appropriate behavior. For example, they may fail to notice their spouse is ready to leave them, their boss is ready to fire them, or the police officer is ready to haul them off to jail. Moreover, they may engage in life-threatening behaviors (such as drinking and driving) because they fail to see the personal threat to safety.

Threats to Self-Esteem

Although the use of alcohol for relaxation and tension reduction is well known, the relation between consumption of alcohol and self-esteem is less understood. Specifically, it appears that one motive to consume alcohol may be that it protects or enhances positive self-evaluations.

It has been suggested that one reason that individuals may drink is to create attributional ambiguity regarding their performance. That is, Berglas and Jones (1978; also Jones & Berglas, 1978) proposed that people may be motivated to drink as a self-handicapping strategy. When people fail at an important task, their self-esteem is threatened. However, if they can attribute failure to some other non-self-relevant factor (such as lack of practice) then self-esteem is protected (Tice, 1991). Thus, individuals may consume alcohol before an important performance task because if they failed they would be able to blame the failure on the alcohol rather than on themselves. Indeed, at least one study has shown that men use alcohol as a self-handicapping strategy (Tucker, Vuchinich, Sobell, & Maisto, 1980).

Alcohol also may help people to forget negative information about themselves. Because alcohol has been shown to lead to a reduction in self-awareness (Hull, Levenson, Young, & Sher, 1983), people may drink to forget about specific threats to their self-esteem. Indeed, Hull and Young (1983) found that after receiving false negative feedback, social drinkers who were high in public self-consciousness consumed more alcohol than did subjects who received success feedback.[1] Thus, it may be that people do not drink in response to any types of stress, but only those that have negative implications about the self. Research has shown that individuals consume alcohol in response to self-image threats (Higgins & Marlatt, 1975; Miller et al., 1974), but not in response to such things as threat of electric shock (Higgins & Marlatt, 1973). Thus, alcohol may assist people in dealing with potential threats to their self-esteem.

It is also possible that alcohol will directly influence feelings of self-evaluation. For instance, McClelland (1987) noted that alcohol often leads to a sense of increased power for men. McClelland, Davis, Kalin, and Wanner (1972) found that moderate doses of alcohol led to increases in feelings of personal power (such as being big and strong, or otherwise important), whereas large doses led to thoughts of personal dominance "of beating other people in competition or perhaps even beating them up" (McClelland, 1987, p. 299).

There is also impressive evidence showing that alcohol may lead to an inflated ego. When most people think about themselves, they compare their current standings on important traits to their ideal standings on those traits. To the extent that people are cognizant of their self-ideal discrepancies, they will tend to show some modesty. Many people, however, turn into braggarts when they are drinking, going on about their special skills and talents. Banaji and Steele (1989) found that for those who had large discrepancies between their ideal and current selves (i.e., some inhibitory conflict between their versions of the self), alcohol consumption was followed by describing oneself in increasingly ideal terms. In other words, no longer plagued by awareness of their real selves, subjects were free to describe themselves in their ideal terms. Intoxicated subjects lost their ability to inhibit or temper their optimistic views of the self based on a realistic assessment of their weaknesses. Thus, cognitive impairment produced by consumption of alcohol will, for those who have discrepancies between their current and ideal selves, tend to lead them to selectively focus on their ideal characteristics. For individuals whose self-esteem is threatened by large discrepancies between current and ideal standards, alcohol may serve an important tool for increasing positive self-regard.

---

[1]Subjects low in dispositional self-consciousness did not display this effect, perhaps because they are less worried about public evaluations.

For women, the relation between drinking and self-esteem is more complicated. Indeed, a study by Konovsky and Wilsnack (1982) found that intoxication led to decreased self-esteem in women. Moreover, although men may use alcohol as a self-handicapping strategy, apparently women do not (Bordini, Tucker, Vuchinich, & Rudd, 1986). Moreover, women report an increase in social anxiety when they believe they have consumed alcohol (Polivy, Schueneman, & Carlson, 1976). However, a recent study suggests that women who drink heavily report drinking to deal with feelings of anxiety, depression, and worthlessness (Thombs et al., 1993). Heavy drinking in women is fairly rare and not well understood. It might be that women generally drink less than men because they find it distressing. However, for women who are chronically distressed or depressed, alcohol may be a convenient and legal way to escape from their problems. In any case, women do not drink to increase self-esteem, but they may drink because of very low self-esteem.

DRINKING A GREAT DEAL

Thus far, we have focused on factors that prompt people to drink. To some extent, the same things that lead to the first drink also lead to the second and third and so forth. Yet there is considerable evidence that once people have begun drinking or become habitual drinkers, they become subject to additional forces and pressures that promote further drinking.

The following sections will focus on factors that roll the snowball—that is, factors that induce people to continue drinking once they have started. It must be emphasized that true self-regulation failure really only occurs at this stage. Apart from people with moral or religious prohibitions against consuming alcohol (and these people are relatively rare in Western societies, although there are some), having an occasional drink or two is not a matter of self-regulation failure. Serious intoxication—and particularly habitual, serious intoxication—is indisputably harmful. People who drink too much, too often, suffer from one of the most dangerous and destructive forms of self-regulation failure that we shall cover.

Zero-Tolerance Beliefs

We begin with the all too familiar case of the person who oscillates between heavy drinking and total abstinence from all alcohol. At first it might seem that hardly anyone would move between such extremes. But as we shall see later in this chapter, many treatment programs for alcoholics emphasize total abstinence as the only acceptable lifestyle for the recovering alcoholic. More generally, people who recognize that they have lost control of their drinking or who have had occasion to regret things they did (such as causing a traffic accident or engaging in spouse or child abuse) under the influence of severe intoxication may resolve never to drink again. Unfortunately, few people manage to live up to these resolutions to perfection, and the result is often a life in which periods of strict abstinence are punctuated by episodes of intense drunkenness.

Although Alcoholics Anonymous (AA) is the best-known treatment for alcoholism, the available evidence does not suggest that it is superior to other lesser known treatments (Walsh et al., 1991). One potential self-regulatory problem that is created by AA is the belief that the only viable outcome for alcoholism is complete abstinence. Although the evidence reviewed above does not support this proposition, most North Americans believe that total abstinence is a prerequisite for recovery from alcoholism (although note that the recovery process is perpetual: according to AA, you never stop being an alcoholic). Viewing abstinence as the desirable state of affairs may lead to a number of problems. In this section we consider the effects of zero-tolerance beliefs on the ability to control alcohol intake.

We have contended that "zero-tolerance" beliefs are an important contributor to lapse-activated snowballing patterns. Zero-tolerance beliefs hold up an ideal of complete abstinence, and such a strong attitude seems well calculated to discourage any initial indulgence. If an initial indulgence occurs, however, zero-tolerance beliefs tend to have the opposite effect, because they signify that self-control has already failed. The assumption that the cause is already hopelessly lost after a single drink may make it much easier for the person to continue drinking until a major binge is underway. Thus, at different stages, zero-tolerance beliefs both support and undermine self-regulation.

Of course, zero-tolerance beliefs may be necessary, despite their drawbacks, if they are objectively true. Thus, it is necessary to ask whether any usage of alcohol (or, by extension, other drugs) leads inexorably to complete self-regulatory breakdown.

If drugs and alcohol are bad for some people, perhaps they are bad for everyone. In Nancy Reagan's famous slogan, everyone should "just say no." However, the notion that everyone is at risk for development of problems with drugs and alcohol seems patently false (Peele, 1989). Indeed, some evidence indicates that experimentation with alcohol and common drugs such marijuana is part of the natural experience of growing up. Shedler and Block (1990) followed up over 100 boys and girls from age 3 to 18 and measured drug use at age 18. These researchers found that adolescents who had engaged in some limited degree of experimentation with drugs (usually marijuana) were psychologically well adjusted. In contrast, children who were either frequent drug users or total abstainers had a higher number of emotional and behavioral problems. Shedler and Block found that adolescents who never experimented with drugs were socially anxious, tended to be emotionally constricted, and had poor social skills. Parents of such children tended to be cold and unresponsive, and they tended to try to have great influence over their children's performance. Other studies have obtained largely the same findings (Kandel, Davies, Karus, & Yamaguchi, 1986; Newcomb & Bentler, 1988).

We are not trying to imply that parents should encourage their children to experiment with drugs and alcohol. However, a moderate amount of experimentation seems to be an acceptable adolescent activity with relatively few consequences. In contrast, forcing children to abstain completely and saying that anyone who experiments must be a drug addict or alcoholic may be counterproductive.

Peele (1989) noted that a major problem with labeling occasional users as addicts is that the label implies that they have developed a lack of control over the behavior. This is the exact opposite of what experimentation usually reaps, which is full knowledge that personal control *is* possible. The vast majority of those who try drugs such as alcohol, cocaine, or marijuana do not develop subsequent problems, and this may be due to the fact that such individuals learn that they can use the drugs in moderate amounts. They learn that they can self-regulate and it helps to develop self-regulatory strength. Not allowing children to experiment may be analogous to not allowing them to exercise because they may risk injury. Despite the good, protective intentions, one will end up creating anxious children who are weak in important ways.

The notion that a single use of any substance will inevitably lead to addiction appears to be false, although it is still quite widespread throughout popular culture. Many people believe that trying heroin or cocaine (especially via injection) will eventually lead to continued use and ultimately to addiction (Miller & Brown, 1991). Yet there have been many examples of individuals who have tried these drugs without becoming hooked (Peele, 1989). Moreover, even individuals who have extended exposure to these drugs may be able to walk away from them if they change environments. Robins, Helzer, and Davis (1975) found that many soldiers who used heroin in Vietnam (and even those who became addicted) simply quit using the substances on return to the United States.

Relapse and the Abstinence Violation Effect

One major problem with the goal of abstinence is that it is extremely difficult. After all, abstinence implies perfection, and it is the rare individual who manages to control behavior perfectly. For treatment programs that emphasize abstinence, the most common outcome is complete relapse and failure, with abstinence and controlled drinking vying for second place among probable outcomes (Rosenberg, 1993). Moreover, the likelihood of returning to moderate or controlled drinking is much less following treatments that emphasize an abstinence-only policy as compared to those that allow for moderate drinking outcomes (Armor, Polich, & Stambul, 1978). It is possible, therefore, that the goal of abstinence is counterproductive. It sets such a high standard for self-regulatory success that it may in the end increase the likelihood of failure.

Paradoxically, individuals who chronically try to restrict their intake of alcohol may be more likely to experience excessive drinking in the future

(Curry, Southwick, & Steele, 1987). The mechanism for such effects has often been described in terms of the *abstinence violation effect* (Marlatt, 1985). In Marlatt's view, the goal of abstinence may lead the alcoholic to view minor transgressions as catastrophic: "From this all-or-none perspective, a single drink or cigarette is sufficient to violate the rule of abstinence: once committed, the deed cannot be undone" (1985, p. 41). This is of course precisely the danger inherent in zero-tolerance beliefs in general: They become counterproductive and undermine any efforts to restore self-control after an initial misstep. Marlatt's theory of the relapse process has been extremely influential, and relapse prevention programs have become commonplace in the treatment of a variety of addictions (Rawson, Obert, McCann, & Marinelli-Casey, 1993).

Marlatt (1985) speculated that the goal of abstinence creates all-or-none thinking in those trying to give up addictions. People perceive themselves as either in control (abstinent) or out of control (indulgent). Threats to control occur during high-risk situations (such as social pressure, emotional distress, or interpersonal conflict). If the person is unable to cope with the situation, a lapse is likely to occur. However, a lapse does not necessarily lead to full-blown relapse. It is the attributions that are made for future control that are decisive. If the person attributes the failure to internal and stable failings, such as having a disease, then full relapse is likely to occur. If, however, the lapse is attributed to the situation or to a momentary weakness, and the person is able to cope with the mental consequences of the lapse, then full relapse is not inevitable. Thus, abstinence as a valued state promotes the snowball effects that were described in earlier chapters. The high-risk situation and inadequate coping lead to a minor transgression (lapse), but out-of-control behavior follows only when the alcoholic views the lapse as catastrophic and attributes the lapse to personal weakness.

Reduction of Monitoring

Throughout this work, we have emphasized that monitoring the self is an essential feature of effective self-regulation (Carver & Scheier, 1981). Self-regulation is difficult or even impossible if the person neglects to monitor his or her own behavior. As with other behaviors, self-regulation failures with drinking are often marked by a cessation of monitoring. If people had to specify each morning precisely how many drinks they would consume throughout that day, there would probably be much less drunkenness than there is. Indeed, most people would probably acknowledge that their most severe experiences of intoxication occurred when they lost track of how much alcohol they had consumed.

One effect of alcohol is to reduce self-awareness (Hull, 1981; Hull et al., 1983). Therefore, as people consume alcohol, they become less aware of their behavior. The result can be a vicious cycle that will contribute to snowballing effects of self-regulation failure: The drunker you get, the harder it is to keep track of how much you are drinking.

Another problem for heavy drinkers is they seem to become insensitive to the effects of alcohol, in that they lose track of their physiological state of impairment. Researchers have described a phenomenon called blood alcohol concentration (BAC) discrimination (Nathan, 1982). BAC refers to the amount of alcohol that is in the bloodstream, and these levels are tested for such things as drunken driving (usually, a BAC over .08 or .10 is regarded as intoxicated). People can be taught to estimate their own BAC through training, in which objective feedback (for BAC) is provided and the person introspects about his or her physiological state (Nathan, 1982). Most individuals can learn to estimate BAC accurately even when objective feedback is removed, and they can do so even when the number of drinks they have consumed is concealed (Huber, Karlin, & Nathan, 1976). Unlike most people, however, clinical alcoholics appear to be unable to learn BAC discrimination when they do not have access to the external cues (e.g., the amount consumed) (Nathan, 1982; Silverstein, Nathan, & Taylor, 1974). Thus, alcoholics appear to be relatively insensitive to their internal states, and if they fail to use other strategies for monitoring consumption (such as counting drinks and noting the passage of time), they will be unlikely to have any clear idea of how much they have drunk (Lansky, Nathan, & Lawson, 1978).

A final problem in terms of self-monitoring is that heavy drinking is associated with poor recall and therefore potential negative consequences associated with excessive drinking may not be properly encoded (Miller & Brown, 1991; Sayette, 1993). People may fail to attend to the negative consequences of their behavior because they do not remember the negative consequences! For instance, moderate amounts of alcohol are typically associated with positive moods, whereas large amounts of alcohol are linked to negative moods (Wilson, 1988). Because of the memory-impairing properties of alcohol, it may be that heavy drinkers mistakenly remember more positive than negative aspects of consumption.

The gradual cessation of monitoring is almost certainly a powerful cause of problem drinking. Heavy drinkers appear to lose the ability to keep track of their own alcohol consumption, and without reliable monitoring, the chances for effective self-regulation are greatly reduced.

Inertia

Although there is some controversy over whether alcoholics lose complete control of their drinking after they begin drinking (Heather, 1991; Stockwell, 1991), there is a tendency for alcohol to disinhibit all behaviors, including drinking. Drinking thus develops what we have called inertia, in which it becomes progressively harder to stop.

An intriguing experimental method of assessing desire to drink as a function of prior consumption of alcohol has been developed by Poulos (1987, cited in Heather, 1991). Poulos had a group of heavy drinkers and a group of light drinkers consume a small alcoholic beverage every 5 min for 90 min. (These were relatively small drinks so that 18 drinks barely rendered subjects illegally impaired.) Poulos asked subjects to rate how much they desired to take the next drink prior to each drink. In this forced drinking paradigm he found that both heavy and light drinkers increased in their ratings of desirability for the first four drinks. However, for the subsequent 14 drinks, light drinkers rated each drink less and less desirable, whereas heavy drinkers rated each drink as more and more desirable. Thus, although light and heavy drinkers did not initially differ in the extent to which they desired a drink, by the eighteenth drink there were large differences with only the heavy drinkers desiring to drink more.

Indeed, in a review of published studies, Stockwell (1991) noted that there is substantial evidence that priming doses of alcohol lead to increased desires to drink, especially when the priming dose is very large, when the priming dose is the preferred beverage, and when further alcohol is readily available (i.e., in sight). Stockwell also concluded that this priming effect varies as a function of the degree of dependence on alcohol.

Thus, problem drinkers may be particularly prone to the snowballing effect in which the more they drink, the more they want to drink. As the inertia for drinking builds up, self-stopping may become harder and harder. Inertia is a prototype for lapse-induced causal effects, because its causal power changes (i.e., increases) once the self-regulation breakdown is underway.

Loss of Control of Attention

Alcohol's specific pharmacological effects include an impairment of cognitive resources and a particular tendency to remain narrowly focused on immediate cues and circumstances. Steele and Josephs (1990) have termed this phenomenon *alcohol myopia*. As a result of this narrowed focus, alcoholics and problem drinkers may be especially vulnerable to cues that encourage alcohol consumption.

The circumstances that typically surround drinkers seem (and indeed are) designed to interact with alcohol myopia so as to facilitate maximal consumption of alcohol. For most people drinking is done socially, at parties or celebrations, in bars and taverns, at sporting events, or during meals. In each of these cases the primary focus is usually on the event rather than on drinking. Drinking situations tend to be situations in which there are several prodrinking cues but in which little attention is paid to rate or amount of consumption. Specific features of the situation may also promote inattention to amount consumed. For instance, bars are noisy and smoky places, with low lighting and often cheerful and attentive (if not pushy) service. McClelland et al. (1972) noted that after a few drinks people seem to lose track of time. All of these situational factors will focus attention away from self, and away from the normal inhibitory channels.

It is also worth noting that these situations interact with alcohol myopia to promote failure of transcendence. People would need to transcend the immediate forces, such as prodrinking cues, in order to moderate their intake of alcohol. But stimulus-rich settings such as cocktail parties and sport events make transcendence rare and difficult.

Consistent with the alcohol myopia hypothesis (and also with the cessation of personal monitoring caused by the loss of self-awareness), research has demonstrated that alcoholic subjects who are exposed to drinking cues (and who have been given a small priming dose of alcohol) report a greater desire to drink more than when not exposed to drinking cues (Kaplan, Meyer, & Stroebel, 1983; Laberg & Ellertsen, 1987). In situations in which others are drinking, people who have consumed alcohol may fail to attend to personal consumption; instead, they simply match their consumption to those around them (Collins & Marlatt, 1981). Lied and Marlatt (1979) found that heavy drinkers were most susceptible to social cues, drinking much more with heavy drinking models than did light drinkers.

Alcohol cues also lead to increased autonomic reactivity among heavy drinkers and alcoholics. For instance, Pomerleau, Fertig, Baker, and Cooney (1983) found that alcoholics showed increased reactivity to the sight and smell of alcohol. Laberg, Hugdahl, Stormark, Nordby, and Aas (1992) found that even pictures of alcoholic beverages may lead to increased autonomic arousal in alcoholics. Pictures of hard liquor produced stronger effects than did pictures of beer, which is consistent with the view that it is the desire for alcohol itself, rather than thirst, that is behind such effects. Thus, the smell or sight of alcohol or even images of alcohol produces an autonomic reaction among heavy drinkers. This autonomic reaction is also related to increased cravings for alcohol or desires to drink.

That cues influence the desire to drink has not been lost on AA. Their meetings are held in churches or schools, which are places not previously associated with drinking. In this way, AA helps self-regulation by keeping people away from the cues that might trigger impulses to drink. Thus, as we have previously suggested, one way for heavy drinkers to control consumption is to avoid the cues that trigger impulses to drink.

Overgeneralization

Individuals may begin drinking alcohol because of social norms and peer pressure, but over time the pharmacological and psychological effects of consumption will start to control intake. Thus, individuals may start out by having a drink at the end of each day to relax and unwind. For some individuals, the reasons for consuming alcohol will begin to multiply, so that they eventually become preoccupied with drinking (Reinert, 1968). For instance, Miller and

Rollnick (1991) noted that over time alcohol becomes an accustomed way to deal with emotional distress. They refer to this as *psychological dependence*. In Miller and Rollnick's words, "They [habitual drinkers] come to rely upon a drink (or sweets, or smoking, etc.) to help them deal with difficult or unpleasant states. It helps them relax, get to sleep, feel comfortable, forget, talk to people, feel powerful, be sexually disinhibited, or feel better. Over time, it becomes difficult to cope without the addictive behavior" (p. 40).

Orford (1985) hypothesized that the process of overgeneralization follows from an increasing misattribution of negative internal states to a lack of alcohol. He suggested that "internal cues that might otherwise be interpreted as fatigue, tension, or confusion, or else not labelled at all, may be interpreted as indicating a need" (p. 191). Thus, any form of negative distress, or any unpleasant internal sensations (such as those associated with common colds or occasional headaches) become labeled as the effects of the absence of alcohol, and the person may begin to drink in response to any negative feelings.

It might not be surprising that heavy drinkers view alcohol consumption as less harmful than light drinkers or nondrinkers. However, a recent study by Fabricius, Nagoshi, and MacKinnon (1993) found that heavy drinkers believed other drugs (even those that they had never tried) were less harmful than did nondrinkers or light drinkers. Thus, their experience with alcohol may lead them to ignore the potentially harmful aspects of other addictive substances, as a form of overgeneralization of their personal conclusion that alcohol is not harmful. These beliefs could conceivably promote an escalation in drug use which entails a progression from cigarettes and alcohol to the use of illicit drugs such as marijuana, cocaine, and heroin (Kandel & Faust, 1975). Further research will be needed to verify that these overgeneralization patterns do indeed contribute to escalating patterns of substance abuse, however.

In general, then, there are multiple indications that overgeneralized beliefs, particularly including flawed analyses of one's own inner states and one's reactions to alcohol, contribute to escalating patterns of alcohol abuse. This would be quite consistent with the role of mistaken beliefs about the self in contributing to many of the misregulation patterns already covered in previous chapters.

Spiraling Distress

For the alcoholic, a primary reason to drink is to relieve the negative symptoms associated with withdrawal, such as severe cravings. One drink may seem like the answer to all of the problems facing the drinker. Often, however, actually drinking will only make things worse. Indeed, some research indicates that heavy drinkers are more likely than light drinkers to consume alcohol as an attempt to escape negative emotions. We saw in Chapter 6 on affect regulation that alcohol is often a counterproductive strategy for mood control. This holds true even for heavy drinkers: Research has demonstrated that continued consumption actually worsens mood among alcoholics (Stockwell, 1985; Wilson, 1988). The logical or rational response would therefore be to avoid drinking when one is feeling bad; but if people have acquired the belief that alcohol will make them feel better, they may conclude that they feel bad simply because they have not drunk enough. The result may be a vicious cycle in which bad moods prompt alcohol consumption, which is followed by a worsening of mood, which leads to further drinking.

Even when alcohol does effectively alter mood, its effect may be reduced for heavy drinkers. Wilson, Abrams, and Lipscomb (1980) found that male social drinkers who were high in tolerance for alcohol showed less anxiety reduction than less tolerant males. They concluded that to the extent that alcohol does reduce anxiety, it does so better for those who are less familiar with alcohol (in the sense of being less accustomed and hence less habituated to its effects). Hence, the habitual drinker may try to compensate by drinking even more alcohol, which will ultimately increase tolerance and thereby keep increasing the amount of alcohol necessary to reduce anxiety (Wilson, 1988). Thus, tolerance and anxiety-reduction may interact to promote greater drinking in the future.

Physiologically, continued drinking will only exacerbate future withdrawal symptoms, as perhaps opponent-processes become more efficient (Solomon, 1980). More importantly, all of the negative consequences associated with drinking become more likely to occur as drinking escalates. For instance, one's career may suffer, one's social relationships may be damaged, and one's health problems will increase. Stockwell (1985) noted that several studies have found increasing mental health problems over time among heavy drinkers compared to light drinkers. These negative consequences, in turn, increase generalized distress, which also promotes further drinking. Thus, heavy drinkers who start to experience negative consequences of their drinking will increase their intake of alcohol in order to cope with or escape from the dysphoria and distress that accompany those consequences.

Alcoholism as a Disease

Popular psychology volumes present alcoholism as something that is beyond the person's normal control, and drinking is said to be something the alcoholic has no control over (Milam & Ketcham, 1981). In the disease or medical model, addicts are considered to have physiological differences from normal people, based in a genetic source or created through the chemical effects of drugs (Peele, 1989).

Miller (1993) has outlined four basic principles of the popular view of alcoholism as a disease. First, alcoholism is believed to be a unitary disease, such that people are either alcoholics or not alcoholics. Second, the alcoholism is supposedly caused by physiological factors that are largely genetically determined. Third, a key symptom is loss of control over drinking such that alcoholics are powerless over alcohol. Fourth, the disease of alcoholism is assumed to be irreversible. People who are abstinent from alcohol are considered to be in recovery, but they are never cured: "once an alcoholic, always an alcoholic."

The disease model of alcoholism has been widely influential (Peele, 1989). The popularity of the disease model is due, in part, to the publicity efforts undertaken by AA, an organization that was founded in 1935 by two recovered drinkers. AA currently has 30,000 chapters and a membership numbering more than a million people. Although one would assume that AA must be doing something right in order to attract so many members, well-controlled studies assessing the efficacy of AA are rare. A recent large study conducted by researchers at the Harvard School of Public Health found that AA was quite ineffective when compared to in-patient hospitalization (Walsh et al., 1991).

More generally, the view of alcoholism as a disease has come under repeated criticism from scientific researchers and social critics (e.g., Akers, 1991; Fingarette, 1988; Heather & Robertson, 1983; Kaminer, 1993; Peele, 1989; Shaffer, 1985). Miller (1993) has recently concluded that it is not necessary to completely abandon a disease model of alcoholism, but a biopsychosocial influence model will be needed to encompass all the findings (see also Zucker & Gomberg, 1986). We turn now to examine some of the problems that the classic disease model engenders for the successful self-regulation of alcohol consumption.

One of the central tenets of the disease model of alcohol is loss of control. From the earliest descriptions of the disease model, the inability to control alcohol intake has been taken as the cardinal indication of alcoholism. For instance, Jellinek (1960) argued that loss of control was "pathognomic" of the disease of alcoholism. The notion of loss of control has come under considerable criticism over the past thirty years, with the general arguments being that loss of control does not happen, that the concept is tautological, and that loss of control is a culture-bound phenomenon, appearing only in those cultures which emphasize personal control (Room, 1985). Nonetheless, as pointed out by Heather (1991), a feeling of being out of control is a central issue for those who have problems drinking. The subjective experience of alcoholism involves some lack of ability to gain control over alcohol intake. Moreover, the failure to stop drinking can be taken as evidence that at least some people are unable to control alcohol intake (Heather, 1991).

However, a variety of evidence contradicts any simple hypothesis of lack of control. For instance, alcoholics also appear to be able to control intake on any given occasion. Given free access to alcohol, alcoholics sometimes drink a lot, but they also sometimes choose not to drink anything at all, often depending on situational contingencies (Mello & Mendelson, 1972; Miller & Brown, 1991). An important study by British psychiatrist Julius Merry (1966) found that alcoholics who were unaware they were drinking alcohol did not develop an uncontrollable desire to drink more, contrary to the assertion by supporters of the disease model that a small amount of alcohol triggers uncontrollable craving. If alcoholics truly experience loss of control, then the subjects of the study should have reported higher craving whether they believed their beverages contained alcohol or not.

Similarly, a classic study conducted by Marlatt, Demming, and Reid (1973) used a balanced-placebo study in which subjects were administered either alcohol or placebo with an orthogonal expectancy manipulation such that half of the subjects expected alcohol and half expected placebo. Thus, there were four groups: given alcohol-told alcohol; given alcohol-told placebo; given placebo-told alcohol; and given placebo-told placebo. This study also included a "control group" of normal, social drinkers. After being given the priming dose of alcohol or placebo, and the expectational message, subjects were given a 20-min taste test, in which they had free access to alcohol.

Marlatt et al. (1973) found that both social drinkers and alcoholics consumed more subsequent alcohol when given the expectancy that the preload contained alcohol; but actual alcohol content did not affect subsequent drinking. This study is usually taken to indicate that loss of control may happen only because of the drinker's beliefs and not because of the pharmacological properties of alcohol. Thus, this experiment suggests that loss of control is a self-regulatory failure rather than an inevitable component of the disease of alcoholism. Later studies demonstrated that if the priming dose is large enough or if enough time transpires subsequent to the priming dose, that alcohol-told placebo may lead to increased drinking, especially increases in the rate of drinking (Stockwell, 1991). In summary, it appears that alcoholics do not inevitably lose control over their drinking when given small priming doses of alcohol, which contradicts one of the central tenets of the disease model and its AA proponents.

A recent longitudinal study of drinking among heavy drinkers and alcoholics found substantial variability in drinking patterns, such that there were few signs of progressive deterioration in drinking (Skog & Duckert, 1991). Both alcoholics and heavy drinkers went through periods of heavy drinking and moderation, but these varied on an individual basis, often due to social and economic pressures. They also found very little evidence for any loss of control by their subjects. Alcoholics who began moderate or light drinking did not inevitably lose control and move into a heavy drinking category. Skog and Duckert believe that these findings raise serious concerns about the theory that alcoholics are bound to follow an out-of-control progression of drinking behavior.

Thus, the hypothesis that alcohol directly causes loss of control of drinking (among alcoholics) does not appear to be correct. Another tenet of the disease model (and one that is aggressively touted by AA) is that the only successful treatment for alcoholism is complete abstinence. AA does not believe that abstinence cures the alcoholic; instead, their beliefs conform to the view that "once an alcoholic, always an alcoholic." From the perspective of the disease model, each sober alcoholic is only one drink away from reinstating his or her active alcoholism. Thus, the only possible successful resolution of alcoholism is complete abstinence.

The effectiveness of brief therapies poses a serious challenge to the disease concept. If people can improve after only one or two therapy sessions, then one has to question the notion that once people are alcoholics that they cannot return to moderate drinking. Bien, Miller, and Tonigan (1993) reviewed 32 controlled studies of brief interventions for problem drinking, which covered more than 6000 problem drinkers from 14 nations. Although many of the subjects were not alcoholics, all had been identified as having serious drinking problems. Bien et al. found substantial support for the idea that brief treatments are effective for reducing problems with alcohol, even among alcoholics. The components of the brief therapy that seemed to be most important for success included specific feedback about personal risk or impairment, an emphasis on personality responsibility for change, clear advice to try to change, a menu of possible change options, empathy, and an encouragement of the client's self-efficacy. Miller and Brown (1991) have proposed that behavior change might be best induced by pointing out the discrepancies between the person's current standings and desired goals. In this way, Miller and Brown suggest that the subsequent perceived discrepancy may increase the person's motives toward effective self-regulation.

A study by Davies (1962) provided an initial challenge to the notion that alcoholism is a progressive disease that can only be treated with abstinence. Davies examined the effectiveness of an alcoholism treatment program at the Maudsely Hospital in London. He reported a follow-up study of some 93 male alcoholics. Over a 7 to 11-year period, 11 of the 93 had returned to moderate and controlled drinking.

The debate that followed has been heated and occasionally vicious. For instance, Mark and Linda Sobell conducted a controlled-drinking study in the early 1970s in which operant techniques were used to teach alcoholics to control their drinking behavior. The Sobells concluded that, at least for some individuals, a return to moderate drinking was a viable outcome (Sobell & Sobell, 1973). An article in *Science* by Pendery, Maltzman, and West (1982) criticized the Sobells' research on a number of grounds, including charges that the Sobells misrepresented their findings. These charges of scientific misconduct were evaluated by no less than five international panels of inquiry, including the United States Congress and the American Psychological Association. In a nutshell, the Sobells received some criticisms for minor experimental sloppiness, but there were no indications that any fraud or misrepresentation had occurred (Sobell & Sobell, 1989). Marlatt has summed up the controversy in this way: "Anyone who suggests controlled drinking is branded as an agent of the devil, tempting the naive alcoholic back into the sin of drinking. If drinking is a sin, the only solution is salvation, a surrendering of personal control to a higher power" (1983, p. 1107).

In spite of the controversy over whether controlled drinking is a recommended treatment for alcoholism, there is considerable evidence that a return to moderate drinking does occur for some alcoholics (Miller, 1993; Rosenberg, 1993). Even when the treatment goal is abstinence, some 10–30% of alcoholics return to controlled drinking, which is comparable to the number who manage to obtain abstinence (Rosenberg, 1993). Heather and Robertson (1983) noted that controlled drinking was more likely to occur with less dependent drinkers, especially those who were younger, had regular employment, and who had not attended AA. A belief that abstinence is the only viable and desirable outcome is predictive of less likelihood of returning to controlled or moderate drinking (Armor et al., 1978).

The issue of controlled drinking is an important one for any self-regulatory model of alcohol intake. If alcoholism is a disease over which individuals do not have control, then efforts at self-control are for naught. However, considerable evidence indicates that some alcoholics may be able to develop self-control over their drinking behavior (Miller & Brown, 1991; Rosenberg, 1993). Understanding how people lose control over their drinking behavior will provide important information for individuals who are trying to control alcohol intake.

Yet another problem with a disease model is that it labels people as unable to control their behavior. By telling someone that he or she has no control over his or her ability to regulate alcohol intake, one undermines any degree of self-regulation (Peele, 1989). For instance, a study by Fisher and Farina (1979) found that giving individuals a genetic explanation for addiction leads people to feel they lack personal control, and this conclusion makes them more likely to use alcohol or other drugs in order to relieve distress, as compared with individuals given a social learning explanation.

Labeling may be especially problematic for children of alcoholics. Labeling someone the child of an alcoholic has a number of negative consequences (Burk & Sher, 1990). For instance, mental health professionals and peers rate putative children of alcoholics as likely to be suffering from psychopathology and to be psychologically unhealthy. Moreover, to the extent that such children are told that they are likely to develop drinking problems, this might undermine their self-regulatory strength (since they may never try to use or flex their self-regulatory muscles).

SUMMARY AND CONCLUSION

Alcohol abuse is one of the most dangerous and destructive forms of self-regulation failure, in terms of the annual cost to our society in human suffering, violence, health problems, and lost productivity. It therefore deserves careful consideration by researchers interested in self-regulation.

Failures to self-regulate alcohol consumption conform to the now familiar pattern in which self-regulatory failures are driven by two separate sets of causes. That is, one set of causes may prompt people to start drinking, and then other (lapse-activated) factors enter in to lead to excessive consumption. Properly speaking, self-regulation failure is mainly associated with the serious binge, but binges do begin with a first drink, so it is necessary to examine both the causes of initial consumption and the factors that promote snowballing.

People drink for multiple reasons, including the wish to be sociable and to go along with others, the expectation that drinking will bring pleasure, the wish to escape from bad moods, and occasionally some desire to rebel against established patterns of expected behavior. It is clear that alcohol does often bring pleasure, and so its consumption will tend to be reinforcing. Negative reinforcement is also apparent under some circumstances, insofar as drinking enables people to escape from some bad feelings. Both the positive and the negative reinforcement effects will strengthen the response of getting oneself a drink now and then.

Beliefs about the effects of alcohol have a strong and clear impact on drinking and on the effects of drinking. Some are well founded in the actual, physiological effects of alcohol, while others reflect cultural myths (although they may come to function as self-fulfilling prophecies). Beliefs are acquired from parents, from the mass media, and from peers. Alcohol consumption is increased by beliefs that alcohol is a reliable source of pleasure, that it is safe and harmless, that it is appropriate to drink under many different circumstances, and that most other people drink too. The belief that alcohol promotes disinhibition may increase people's tendency to ignore their normal morals and guidelines when they have been drinking, and further drinking may be one of the results of this disinhibition.

Drinking is marked by ambivalence, particularly among heavy drinkers, and (as usual) self-regulation is hampered when the person has conflicting standards or goals. Heavy drinkers often want to control their drinking and refrain from the excesses and problems that attend drunkenness, but they also want to enjoy the positive, desirable effects of alcohol.

We have explained many underregulation patterns with respect to a strength model, and patterns of alcohol abuse conform to this model. Excessive drinking and its problems are most likely to occur when people are tired or under stress (or both). Emotional turmoil is a major cause of alcohol abuse. Alcohol use also increases when people are not coping well with demands and stresses.

Part of the influence of emotional distress on alcohol abuse may be due to misregulation rather than underregulation, however. People sometimes turn to alcohol in the belief that it will cure their bad moods and unpleasant emotions. Of course, getting drunk will rarely solve the problem that is leading to the emotional distress, but sometimes people prefer to focus on the emotions rather than on the problem. Alcohol is not uniformly or reliably effective as a mood medication, however. Alcohol abuse is promoted by several patterns of overgeneralization, including unfounded beliefs that it will work for all bad emotions and will work under a broad variety of circumstances.

Lastly, some people (especially men) turn to drink following threats to their self-esteem. Multiple processes may be responsible for this pattern. Alcohol appears to reduce one's sensitivity to unpleasant implications of misfortune. It may also directly foster more positive feelings about the self, such as exaggerated feelings of power, control, attractiveness, and self-worth.

Once the person has had a drink or two, additional factors begin to operate to promote wholesale self-regulation failure. Foremost among these are attention effects of alcohol. As people drink, they lose their capacity to monitor their own behavior and to transcend the immediate situation. They become increasingly susceptible to situational cues that favor further drinking, just as they lose track of how much they have already consumed. Heavy drinkers also seem to find alcohol more and more appealing as they continue to drink, although most people lose some of their desire for alcohol after they have had several drinks. And heavy drinkers seem to lose their sensitivity to their own inner state of intoxication, with the result that they cease to be strongly affected by one of the most prominent and effective cues that can make people stop drinking. These cognitive and motivational patterns increase the inertia of drinking, making it more and more difficult for the person to bring his or her drinking under control.

Several beliefs about alcohol seem to promote the snowballing effect once drinking has started, particularly for people who have had alcohol problems. Zero-tolerance beliefs, such as promoted by some alcohol treatment regimens, insist that alcoholics must aspire to complete abstinence and that even a single drink constitutes a calamity. These beliefs may help people avoid taking that first drink, but they undermine efforts to stop drinking after that first drink. In the so-called abstinence violation effect, people learn to see themselves as either wholly abstinent and in control, or as wholly out of control, and so the first drink causes the person to perceive himself or herself as out of control and as already involved in uncontrolled drinking. Belief that alcoholism is a disease that cannot be controlled strengthens this pattern of response, because it encourages people to think that once they have had a drink they cannot possibly be held responsible for their actions and for their subsequent drinking.

Self-regulation failures in alcohol consumption may also snowball because of patterns of spiraling distress. Alcohol often makes bad moods worse, but as long as people sustain the belief that drinking will improve their mood they may consume more. The result may be a vicious cycle of emotional distress leading to drinking, which intensifies the distress and in turn prompts more drinking. Among heavy drinkers, overgeneralization effects may compound the problem: The person begins to interpret all bad moods as indicating the need for a drink.

The evidence is mixed regarding the extent to which people acquiesce in their failure to control their drinking. It is clear that people do acquiesce to the extent that the actions of preparing (or ordering) and consuming drinks is under their conscious control. On the other hand, people who are addicted to alcohol cannot simply refuse to drink without severe and even life-threatening suffering, because the withdrawal symptoms for alcoholism are quite powerful and occasionally fatal. Still, many alcoholics consume more than is required by their addiction. Among nonaddicted people, bouts of excessive drinking would seemingly reflect acquiescence in self-regulatory failure. The issue is further complicated by lapse-activated patterns, particularly the fact that the more one drinks, the harder it becomes to monitor how much one is drinking, and so people may lose track of how much they consume—which may reflect a thoroughgoing inability to keep track or may reflect some degree of acquiescence. (One could, after all, keep a written record of one's consumption, although we have never seen drinkers do this.) Another lapse-activated pattern is that consuming some alcohol increases the desire for further consumption among many people (especially heavy drinkers), so that it becomes harder to resist.

A loss of self-control when drinking alcohol thus seems to be affected by both physiological, genetic components (making some people more susceptible to alcohol abuse and addiction) and the equally important influence of beliefs and expectancies. Adherence to models of alcohol abuse that neglect these cognitive components may lead to self-control failures and alcoholic binges.

9

Eating Too Much

One of life's greatest pleasures is eating. Ingesting food is something everyone needs to do for survival, but the process of eating is also something that most people enjoy very much. Rituals and special occasions often involve elaborate feasts, and much of the social world revolves around food and eating. Common sense suggests that most eating is controlled by hunger and satiety: People eat when they feel hungry and they quit eating when they become full. Unfortunately, many people have difficulties controlling the amount of food they consume, either on some occasions or more generally. This chapter is concerned with the difficulties that people have controlling their food intake.

Occasional indulgences, such as splurging at Thanksgiving or at Christmas, are normal and should not be regarded as failures of self-control (Klesges, Klem, & Bene, 1989). Chronic overeating, however, can be a major health problem with devastating physical and psychological effects. For instance, overeating may contribute to obesity, which is associated with a significant number of medical complications, such as cardiac problems, hypertension, and gastric impairments (VanItallie & Lew, 1992), especially for those who become obese during childhood (Bray, 1985). Obesity also carries a variety of psychological problems, mainly because of the extreme negative stigma associated with being overweight. The obese are viewed as less attractive, less socially adept, less intelligent, and less productive than are their slimmer peers (Allon, 1982). Not surprisingly, perceiving oneself as overweight is related to lower self-esteem, depression, and heightened anxiety (Heatherton, 1993a). Thus, many individuals are motivated to achieve or maintain a slim figure (Brownell, 1991). Unfortunately, most individuals are unsuccessful at achieving their ideal figure; some 30% of North Americans are more than 15% above ideal body weights, and this figure has increased over the last few decades (Foreyt, 1987).

Not all obesity results from overeating, however. In fact, the evidence is quite clear that most obese people eat no more than most normal-weight people (Klesges, Klem, & Bene, 1989; Logue, 1991; O'Neil & Jarrell, 1992; Polivy & Herman, 1983). Although a few individuals do become obese because of over-eating (especially high-fat and high-calorie foods), many people are overweight because of a genetically determined natural weight or set-point (Polivy & Herman, 1983). A recent review of the research literature by Meyer and Stunkard (1993) revealed that approximately half the variability of body weight can be accounted for by genetic inheritance, and body weight shows greater genetic influence than does alcoholism, hypertension, breast cancer, schizophrenia, or heart disease. Thus, it is wrong to assume that all overweight people have difficulties controlling their intake of food. As will be made clear, it may be that some overweight people have difficulties controlling food intake because of their propensities to diet, which, in turn, promote self-regulation failure.

In response to fears of becoming overweight, many individuals undertake dieting. More than 75% of young women start dieting before age 13, and at any one time more than half of college age women are on a diet to lose weight (Heatherton & Polivy, 1992). Data from the National Health Interview Survey found that 46% of women and 24% of men were currently dieting (National Center for Health Statistics, 1985). Although dieting is less common among young men, by age 30 an increasing number of men begin dieting to lose weight, largely because almost one in two men gain at least 10 pounds in the 10 years following graduation from college (T.F. Heatherton, 1993b).

Dieting is a notoriously ineffective means of losing weight. Of those individuals who lose weight through dieting, some 95% will eventually regain the weight, and in many cases these people will gain more weight than they initially lost (Garner & Wooley, 1991; Stunkard & Pennick, 1979; Wilson & Brownell, 1980). A recent review of all published studies on the efficacy of weight-loss treatments revealed that almost no one managed to maintain weight loss for more than five years (NIH Technology Assessment Conference Panel, 1993). Yet dieting is big business, and some $30 billion are spent each year by people trying to lose weight (Brownell, 1991). Thus, failure to control food intake is one of our society's most common self-regulatory difficulties.

For some people, the inability to regulate food intake reaches clinical proportions. For instance, bulimia nervosa is a fairly common clinical syndrome which involves consuming large quantities of food followed by self-induced vomiting or other purgatives. Binge eating without concomitant purging is even more common, and it is estimated that up to 30% of some groups (i.e., the obese) engage in binge eating. A large study at Harvard University found one in five women engages in binge eating that is perceived as troublesome and out of control (T.F. Heatherton, 1993b). Anorexia nervosa is associated with excessively controlled intake, so much so that sufferers are at risk for death from starvation. As noted in Chapter 2, we consider this misregulation rather than overregulation. As we shall discuss, it is the standards that are inappropriate rather than the amount of self-control that is exerted to attain those standards.

UNDERREGULATION

Conflicting Standards

For most people, there is a conflict between indulgence in desired foods and worries about developing weight problems. Rare is the individual who can eat all he or she wants without paying the price in terms of weight gain. But nearly everyone periodically finds it hard to resist delicious food, because ingestion can be such a pleasurable and rewarding experience (Bennett, 1988; Capaldi & Powley, 1990). Moreover, as a general rule, the hungrier someone is, the better food tastes to him (Cabanac, 1971). Thus, especially when people have not eaten in a while, they may find it hard to resist indulgence in their favorite foods. Most people worry that if they overeat they might become fat, and therefore most individuals need to control or restrain their intake of food, at least to some extent (or they need to engage in compensatory behaviors such as exercise). This is the prototypical delay of gratification problem: needing to resist momentary pleasure in the service of long-term dietary goals.

One factor that makes controlling eating difficult is that many of the foods that bring the most pleasure are the worst for health. High-fat foods (for instance, American staples such as pizza, burgers, fries, potato chips) and sweets (chocolate, doughnuts, and ice cream) are found to be tastier for most people than vegetables, legumes, and liver. Indeed, people (especially children) are generally suspicious of foods that are described as "good for you." Unfortunately, most nutritionists note that the typical American diet is extremely unhealthy, and the average person consumes much more fat than is desirable for health maintenance (Sarafino, 1990). Some authors have noted that groups known for having especially poor nutritional habits (such as those lower in socioeconomic status) are especially likely to develop weight problems (Sobal & Stunkard, 1989). Thus, the basic conflict is between the ingestion of highly desirable and pleasurable foods and long-term fitness and health. People want to enjoy themselves, but they want to avoid becoming overweight by overeating.

Inertia

"No one can eat just one," or so the saying goes from a popular advertisement for potato chips. Everyone knows how difficult it is to eat just one peanut, just one potato chip, or just one candy bar. An appetizer means just that: something that whets one's appetite for further intake. Some people report that when they begin eating they just can't stop—they continue to eat until the refrigerator (or kitchen, or house) is empty. Such people are often called binge eaters, which is a hallmark of those suffering from *bulimia nervosa*. It may be that those who normally try to restrict or restrain intake are most vulnerable to excessive eating once they have started. These individuals are chronic dieters, who alternate between eating very little and eating a great deal. With every intention of not eating very much, they occasionally break their diets and eat much more than planned. Such alternations between famine and feast are a classic example of self-regulatory failure.

Herman and Mack (1975) examined eating behavior among college-age women who anecdotally reported dieting during the week and then overeating during weekends. In their study, chronic dieters (called restrained eaters) and nondieters were invited to the laboratory to engage in a supposed taste test, which was described as a test of perception (because the researchers did not want subjects to know that eating was being monitored). Participants were assigned to one of three conditions: no milkshake preload, one milkshake preload, or two milkshake preloads. Herman and Mack found that nondieters ate most when deprived of food, ate somewhat more after preloaded with one milkshake, and ate least when preloaded with two milkshakes (which makes sense if we consider the effects of drinking two large milkshakes on hunger level). Chronic dieters, however, showed the opposite pattern of eating most after the preloads. This has been called the "what the hell effect"; it's as if they say "I've blown my diet so I may as well continue eating," with abandon. Technically, this paradoxical eating behavior is known as *counterregulation*, in that chronic dieters seem to do the opposite of what would be expected if they were regulating their eating according to hunger and satiety signals (as were nondieters). Since the original Herman and Mack study, dozens of studies have replicated and extended the basic counterregulatory findings (see Herman & Polivy, 1980). For instance, McCann, Perri, Nezu, and Lowe (1992) found that obese dieters who also reported problems with binge eating showed a much more dramatic counterregulatory effect than obese dieters who did not report problems with binge eating (although these subjects also ate more following a preload than without one). Thus, there is substantial evidence that high-calorie preloads lead to excessive—disinhibited—eating among chronic dieters.

The key to this disinhibition of dietary restraints is the subjective perception of whether the diet is broken or intact—it is the subjective belief that the diet is broken that leads to counterregulation. A number of studies have demonstrated that the eating of chronic dieters is disinhibited only if they believed that the preload was high in calories; the actual caloric content is largely irrelevant (Knight & Boland, 1989; Spencer & Fremouw, 1979). For instance, if pudding is described as high calorie (even if it is actually very low in calories), dieters will become disinhibited, but if it is described as low calorie (even if it is actually high calorie), then restraints will remain intact. Similarly, certain classes of foods are more likely to lead to disinhibition than are others (Knight & Boland, 1989). For instance, a piece of cake with 200 calories is more likely to disinhibit a dieter than a salad that has 800 calories. Thus, continued eating (inertia) is more likely to occur when dieters perceive that they have broken their diets.

This pattern is parallel to what we reported regarding alcohol in the preceding chapter: People's beliefs, perceptions, and expectancies have a strong effect on self-regulatory failure, independent of what people have actually consumed. Certain beliefs support the view that some eating or drinking will lead to more of the same, and it is these beliefs that guide behavior, regardless of whether the drink actually contained alcohol or whether the food actually was high in calories.

Some researchers have contended that prolonged eating occurs because of impaired satiety mechanisms—in other words, people overeat because their body fails to send out the "full" signal that ordinarily stops people from eating more. Because dieters need to ignore hunger sensations, they develop an unresponsiveness to all internal signals (Heatherton, Polivy, & Herman, 1989). Thus, those who chronically diet (such as the majority of the obese) may not respond appropriately to internal satiety cues. For instance, Spiegel, Shrager, and Stellar (1989) found that obese subjects ate more following a sandwich preload than did lean subjects (see also Meyer & Pudel, 1972). Moreover, although normal weight individuals rated food as less palatable after a substantial amount of food has been consumed, obese people did not. They continued to rate food as good tasting even after they had eaten a lot of it. Thus, the normal mechanisms that put the brakes on eating seem to be malfunctioning in some obese individuals, especially those who are dieting.

A recent study of relapse episodes among those trying to lose weight revealed a number of findings relevant to the inertia of eating. Grilo, Shiffman, and Wing (1989) found that relapses tended to occur in the presence of other people (three-fourths of all relapse episodes) and that around half of all relapse episodes occurred while the subjects were already eating a meal. Indeed, subjects reported the food cues that were present as being the single most important determinant of their relapse to excessive eating. Again, once people have already started to eat it is extremely difficult to self-regulate intake. This may be especially true for those who have been restricting their intake, since food now tastes better and the body seems to be demanding additional intake.

A familiar example of eating inertia is the free samples that are offered in grocery stores. People often line up to try a small bite of cheese, a nibble of sausage, or to drink a thimble of soup. The notion is that once a person has had a small sample (effectively an appetizer), he will want to purchase the sampled product. Some research has demonstrated that this might be an effective selling strategy—but only for obese shoppers. Steinberg and Yalch (1978) found differential sensitivity by obese and nonobese shoppers to an in-store free food sample. Obese subjects exceeded their planned expenditures by a larger amount if they tasted a sample than if they did not; normal weight subjects were less affected by the free sample. Moreover, Nisbett and Kanouse (1969) showed that overweight shoppers actually purchased less food if they were hungry than if they had recently eaten. In contrast, they found that normal weight subjects tended to purchase more food when they were hungry than when they had just eaten. Tom (1983) analyzed the purchases of obese and normal weight subjects who were food-deprived or not food-deprived (the researcher also had access to the shopping lists which indicated planned purchases). Tom found that obese shoppers made more unplanned purchases when they had recently eaten than when they were food-deprived. The majority of these unplanned purchases were food items located at the end of aisles or as part of point-of-purchase displays, which supports the view that they were driven by spontaneous impulses activated by external cues.

These findings contradict common sense suggestions for dieters, who are often told not to shop when they are hungry (McNulty, 1992). It is the normal weight nondieters who should avoid shopping when hungry (and note that many nutritionists fit this category). Obese subjects (especially dieters) may be better able to resist tempting purchases when their eating restraints are intact, that is, when they are hungry. The feeling of hunger, for dieters, paradoxically gives them solace, since it tells them they are being successful at avoiding calories. Once their eating restraints are disinhibited, however, their shopping restraints quickly dissolve as well.

Reduction of Monitoring

One apparently common reason for overeating is a failure to monitor food intake. Many people have difficulty regulating intake in situations where there are ample food and many distractions (e.g., smorgasbords), and especially when the food is served in small portions (snack foods at a party). In these situations overeating is likely to result unless one pays specific attention to the amount he is eating. Some people seem to be less good at monitoring intake than others. For instance, Stuart (1967) noted that eating can become automatic for some individuals, such that people may eat without any real awareness of what they are doing.

Certain situations, such as parties, are especially likely to produce overeating (Logue, 1991). Similarly, many people are prone to overeat while watching television. In fact, eating in front of the television has been linked to failure at weight loss treatment (Leon & Chamberlain, 1973). Most human eating occurs in social settings, and it is precisely these settings that are associated with overeating. Studies have consistently shown that people eat more when eating socially than when eating alone (Conger, Conger, Costanzo, Wright, & Matter, 1980; Edelman, Engell, Bronstein, & Hirsch, 1986). Indeed, some have even noted that binge eating behaviors often occur in group settings, such as college dormitories (Crandall, 1988).

In Chapter 2, we noted that the attempt to escape from self-awareness often contributes to a reduction of inhibitions (see Baumeister, 1991a). People who have a painful awareness of themselves are motivated to escape from these feelings by narrowing attention away from long-term goals and standards, in favor of concrete stimuli in the here and now. In other words, people seek to avoid dysphoria by stopping self-reflection. This reduction in self-awareness is implicated in the disinhibition of behaviors that are normally inhibited, which for dieters implies that a lack of self-awareness will be related to overeating. In a review of the literature on binge eating, Heatherton and Baumeister (1991) found considerable support for an escape from self-awareness interpretation, in that binge eating was often associated with a reduction in self-awareness. A major part of the process is that self-awareness involves monitoring oneself (by definition), and so when people cease to be self-aware they also often cease to monitor what they are doing. And when monitoring is impaired, self-regulation tends to fail.

Polivy (1976) measured eating of sandwich quarters in nondieters, dieters whose diets were intact, and dieters whose diets had just been broken during the experiment (i.e., in dieters who were engaged in overeating). She subsequently asked subjects to recall how many they had eaten. Dieters who had broken their diets were much less accurate in their recall than nondieters or dieters whose diets remained intact—indeed, their mean error was almost fifty times as large as that of dieters who had not broken their diets! Similarly, Nisbett and Storms (1974) found that obese subjects underestimated intake of sandwiches cut into sixteenths more than did lean subjects; increased intake was associated with decreased accuracy. Likewise, Collins (1978) had dieters and nondieters eat M&M candies under conditions of high and low self-monitoring. Not only did dieters eat more M&Ms when they were in the low self-monitoring condition, but there were much more inaccurate in recalling how many they had consumed. All these results show a reduction or failure of monitoring—a powerful cause of failing to regulate eating.

Moreover, experimental manipulations that alter self-awareness have been shown to influence eating behavior. Heatherton, Polivy, Herman, and Baumeister (1993) gave dieters and nondieters either failure or neutral performance feedback on a problem-solving task. Failure subjects were then assigned to one of three self-awareness conditions; one group was forced to watch a video clip of themselves failing on the problem-solving task (high self-awareness), one group was asked to watch a distracting video clip on bighorn sheep (low self-awareness), and the final group was asked to sit quietly for 10 min. Subjects were then allowed to eat as much ice cream as they wanted, following the standard taste-test methodology. Only in those conditions that allowed low self-awareness did dieters show disinhibited eating. In the failure-plus-videotape condition, which enforced high levels of self-awareness, eating in dieters remained inhibited. Escaping from unpleasant self-awareness led to high levels of eating.

A variety of other studies have also demonstrated an important link between self-awareness and disinhibited eating. One study of women who had recently taken up dieting found that they ate three times as much while watching an engaging film as compared to activities that allowed for a higher level of self-awareness (Wardle & Beales, 1988). Similarly, Schotte, Cools, and McNally (1990) found chronic dieters ate much more popcorn when watching an intensely absorbing film (a clip from the horror movie, *Halloween*) than when watching a more neutral film (a travelogue on Australia). A follow-up study found that both horror films and comedies (outtakes from *Candid Camera*) led to increased popcorn intake for dieters than the more neutral travelogue (Cools, Schotte, & McNally, 1992). As mentioned, television watching has been identified as a particularly troublesome time for dieters. They become immersed in the action and may neglect to notice that they ingested an entire bag of potato chips or an entire box of chocolates.

As we discussed in the previous chapter, alcohol is known to reduce self-focus and has also been implicated in the disinhibition of a number of behaviors. Polivy and Herman (1976a, 1976b) gave moderate amounts of alcohol to chronic dieters and nondieters and found that alcohol disinhibited the eating restraints of the dieters. They also found that subjects who were falsely led to believe they were drinking alcohol (and whose self-awareness was therefore not reduced) failed to show the pattern of disinhibited eating. The link between alcohol and binge eating is most clearly established among those who have bulimia nervosa (Heatherton & Baumeister, 1991). For example, Williamson (1990) has noted that bulimics are more likely to binge and purge after a few drinks, and Abraham and Beumont (1982) found that 44% of their bulimic sample reported that drinking alcohol precipitated eating binges. Thus, for those who try to restrict food intake (such as dieters or bulimics), drinking alcohol not only brings about the ingestion of unwanted calories, but also unleashes further eating. Why? Again, alcohol reduces self-awareness, and so people gradually cease to monitor what they are doing.

If a reduction in self-awareness is related to overeating, then there should be evidence that heightened self-awareness is related to successful self-regulation of eating. Indeed, attending to one's eating appears to prevent disinhibition of eating restraints, both among dieters (Collins, 1978; Herman, Polivy, & Silver, 1979; Kirschenbaum & Tomarken, 1982; Pecsok & Fremouw, 1988; Polivy, Herman, Hackett, & Kuleshnyk, 1986), and among obese subjects (Pliner, 1976; Pliner & Iuppa, 1978). For example, when people think that someone is watching them eat, their behavior conforms to societal standards and norms of self-control (Herman et al., 1979). Likewise, if dieters are told to monitor their eating (i.e., if they have to count each cookie or measure portions), their restraints become stronger and they become relatively immune to disinhibited eating (Pecsok & Fremouw, 1988; Polivy et al., 1986). Similarly, if subjects are asked to speak about their thoughts during an eating task, chronic dieters do not eat more following a preload than without one; thus, requiring subjects to monitor their cognitive processes seems to wipe out the "what the hell effect" described previously (Jansen, Merckelbach, Oosterlaan, Tuiten, & van den Hout, 1988).

Self-monitoring of food intake appears to be perhaps the most important element of successful weight loss, with some referring to it as the "cornerstone" of behavioral treatment (Wadden, 1993, p. 201). A study by Fisher, Lowe, Jeffrey, Levenkron, and Newman (1982, cited in Baker & Kirschenbaum, 1993) found that weight loss clients who failed to self-monitor food intake over a three-week holiday period gained 57 times as much weight as those who continued self-monitoring! A recent study by Baker and Kirschenbaum (1993) found that those who regularly engaged in self-monitoring lost more weight than those who failed to self-monitor. Moreover, subjects lost more weight in the weeks that they self-monitored than the weeks in which they self-monitored less.

Thus, the first key to successful self-regulation of eating is to self-monitor food intake. Most nutritionists recommend that dieters follow specific meal plans that include elements of behavioral self-control: "Serving foods properly provides a pleasant dining experience, increases awareness of foods consumed, and fosters greater feelings of self-control" (McNulty, 1992, p. 346). Specific suggestions include eating only when seated, eating all foods from a plate, taking medium-sized portions, leaving some food on the plate, and eating in the same place for all meals and not in front of the television. All of these strategies help the dieter to be conscious of the process of eating so that he can control the amount of food that he consumes.

Loss of Control over Attention

One of us has an office located near to where people seem obliged to make popcorn five times per day. There are few things in this world as distracting as the smell of freshly made popcorn. In their study of relapse situations, Grilo et al. (1989) found that the most common reason given for diet failure (i.e., relapse) was the presence of food cues (such as the sight or smell of food) or having food be explicitly offered (such as by a host at a party). Food stimuli are particularly potent cues; they include sights, smells, and tastes that lead to immediate physiological events (i.e., salivation) and cravings. Who has not walked past the counter of a bakery and nearly been sucked out of his shoes by the wonderful smell of freshly baked bread? Smells are potent triggers of memories of fond times and happy circumstances. Thus, food cues are especially potent for capturing attention.

An influential theory of obesity proposed by Stanley Schachter (1971) suggested that some individuals (i.e., the obese) were extremely susceptible to external cues. Schachter's theory was based, in part, on work by Stunkard and Koch (1964), who demonstrated that the obese appeared to be insensitive to internal hunger cues. Stunkard and Koch found that stomach contractions were unrelated to people's verbal self-reports of hunger among obese people—unlike normal weight people, for whom stomach contractions are closely correlated with reports of feeling hungry. Schachter (1971) proposed that because the obese were insensitive to internal cues, their control over eating was based on external cues, such as the time of day, the sensory qualities of food, and social cues. Thus, salient external cues trigger eating among obese individuals.

An impressive variety of studies examined the susceptibility of obese individuals to salient external cues (Schachter & Rodin, 1974; Rodin, 1978). For instance, in a now classic study (Schachter & Gross, 1968), obese and nonobese individuals participated in a supposed study of the relationship between physiological reactions and psychological characteristics. The researchers left the subject to perform a simple task in the presence of a rigged clock. For half of the subjects the clock ran slowly (losing 15 min over a 50-min period), whereas for the remaining subjects the clock ran fast (gaining 30 min). Thus, some subjects were led to believe the time was 5:20 P.M., whereas other subjects were led to believe it was 6:05 P.M.: dinner time for those students. An experimenter returned to greet the subject with a box of crackers from which he was snacking. At this point, the experimenter offered some crackers to the subjects. The obese ate much more in the fast-clock condition than in the slow-clock condition, presumably because the clock indicated it was time to eat. Nonobese subjects actually ate less in the fast-clock condition, reporting that they didn't want to spoil their dinner.

Nisbett (1968) exposed obese and nonobese subjects to good and bad tasting ice cream (bad taste was manipulated by adding quinine). He found that the eating of obese subjects was affected to a much greater extent than nonobese subjects; they ate more good tasting ice cream and less bad tasting ice cream. A study by Herman, Olmsted, and Polivy (1983) found that overweight restaurant patrons were more likely than average weight patrons to order a dessert when the waitress visually displayed the dessert and described it as appetizing. Wooley, Wooley, and Woods (1975) found that obese individuals had elevated salivation to the presentation of palatable food cues, suggesting that the external cue is a much more potent trigger of eating for obese individuals. A study by Ross (1974) directly examined the effects of salience of cue and thinking about food on intake of highly desirable cashew nuts. He found that obese subjects told to think about the nuts ate more cashews than those not told to think about the nuts. However, this was especially true when the nuts were salient (when bright lights were shining on the nuts). Normal weight subjects were not influenced by these manipulations. Thus, when external cues to eat are particularly salient, obese individuals may be especially likely to overeat.

Although Schachter's externality theory was supported by a large number of studies, by the late 1970s evidence had mounted that externality might not be limited to obese individuals (Rodin, 1978). Herman and Polivy (1975) speculated that it was dieting, rather than obesity per se, that led to an external eating style. Because many obese individuals diet (roughly 85% of obese individuals regularly diet), it is possible that effects thought to be due to obesity were actually a consequence of dieting behavior. This would predict that individuals who diet, independent of whether they were obese, normal weight, or even underweight (and yes, there are people who are underweight who diet), are more susceptible to external cues than are nondieters.

Research has indicated that chronic dieters may be more prone to food cues than are nondieters. For example, following a highly caloric preload dieters display disinhibition only when the food is good tasting (Woody, Costanzo, Leifer, & Conger, 1981). Herman, Polivy, Klajner, and Esses (1981) described evidence suggesting that chronic dieters have elevated salivary response to food cues. For instance, Klajner, Herman, Polivy, and Chabra (1981) had subjects anticipate eating some pizza (which was displayed to them) and measured their saliva output. They found that dietary restraint was more important in predicting increased salivation than body weight; obese individuals salivated more than normals only if the obese subjects were also dieters. These researchers concluded that increased salivation to highly palatable food occurs because of chronic dieting rather than because of body weight. Although contradictory results have been noted (Herman et al., 1981), the general pattern seems to indicate that palatable food cues seem to trigger increased salivary responses in those who usually try to control food intake. One study exposed dieters and nondieters to the sight and smell of food and then measured subsequent eating (Rogers & Hill, 1989). Compared to a group that did not receive an exposure preload, dieters who were exposed to the sight and smell of food ate a great deal more during a taste test. Rogers and Hill (1989) argue that this demonstrates that mere exposure to food cues may disinhibit chronic dieters.

Bulimics and binge eaters have also been shown to be especially susceptible to external food cues (Heatherton & Baumeister, 1991). Bulimics tend to choose "fattening" or "forbidden" foods during the binge (Abraham & Beumont, 1982; APA, 1987; Johnson & Connors, 1987; Rosen, Leitenberg, Fisher, & Khazam, 1986), including pastries, breads, cookies, and other junk foods such as potato chips and chocolate bars (Mitchell & Pyle, 1988; Rodin & Reed, 1988). Steamed vegetables are rarely the focus of an eating binge!

Thus, considerable evidence demonstrates that food cues are potent stimuli for excessive eating. Such cues capture attention and trigger desires to eat. Although Schachter proposed that the obese were affected by such cues to a greater extent than normal weight individuals, evidence collected over the last decade indicates that it may be dieting behavior that leads to heightened external responsiveness. The process of dieting requires individuals to ignore their hunger sensations (after all, by definition the dieter is hungry most of the time) and to regulate their eating by external means. Thus, control over eating is given over to external rather than internal control, and situational cues and triggers may have an undue influence on food intake, promoting self-regulatory failure. It is therefore not surprising that many dietary regimens include specific training in dealing with food cues.

Many common treatments for obesity involve some degree of stimulus control (Agras, 1987; Stuart, 1967; Stunkard, 1992), which again points to the importance of attentional control in determining the success or failure of self-regulation. For example, as a behavioral supplement to very low-calorie diets, Wadden and Foster (1992) suggested that patients "clean house" to make the home and work environment conducive to diet efforts: "This is accomplished by removing candy dishes from end tables, banishing troublesome foods from the home, purchasing noncaloric beverages, and similar behaviors" (p. 311). Wadden and Foster described some preparatory behavior as critically important to ensuring successful weight loss. A recent study showed that for some individuals (obese individuals who are prone to compulsive eating), stimulus control with the addition of relapse prevention therapy is superior to only stimulus control training in terms of maintenance of weight loss (Mount, Neziroglu, & Taylor, 1990).

Trying Not to Think about Food

One possible method of controlling food intake is to suppress thoughts about eating or food in general. In some ways, this would appear to be the major challenge of dieting, since the dieter is trying to avoid thinking about how hungry she feels or about how pleasurable eating would be. Of course, a distinction needs to be made about being mindful of consumption (i.e., being aware of eating in order to control intake) versus focusing on the sensory allures of eating. The former is associated with increased control whereas the latter is associated with self-regulatory difficulties (Herman & Polivy, 1993). As discussed in Chapter 5, attempting to suppress thoughts is a difficult task and may actually lead to increased thinking about the object that one is trying to suppress (Wegner, 1992, 1994). Thus, it might be expected that individuals who try to suppress thoughts of food (i.e., dieters) will have difficulty doing so.

Considerable research has indicated that binge eaters and chronic dieters have difficulties suppressing thoughts of food and in fact are often quite preoccupied with such thoughts (Herman & Polivy, 1993). For example, Williamson reported one binge eater's claim that "the more he tried to 'think himself out of bingeing,' the greater his urges to binge grew" (1990, p. 137). Similarly, the Minnesota conscientious objectors study (Keys, Brozek, Henschel, Mickelson, & Taylor, 1950) found that individuals attempting to lose 25% of their body weight became obsessed with food; the men constantly talked about food, planned recipes, and imagined meal possibilities. It appears that dieting status may be the important determinant of obsessions about food, because it is not the case that obese individuals think about food any more than do normal weight individuals (Hunt & Rosen, 1981). Wegner (himself an admitted dieter) noted that failures to suppress thoughts are common among dieters: "Trying not to think about food works at first as a diet strategy, for example, and may even get us thin enough that we can allow ourselves once more to think about food. But in no time, a series of these cycles of indulgence can leave us totally obsessed and fat enough to scare the dog" (1989, p. 170).

Whether difficulties suppressing thoughts about food inevitably lead to eating is not entirely clear (Herman & Polivy, 1993). On the one hand, sensory cues such as sight and smell may lead to thoughts of eating, which might then promote eating (or overeating). On the other hand, for those trying to control food intake (such as dieters) food thoughts also signal danger, in that consuming the food would sabotage the diet. Thus, food cues may force dieters to concentrate on their dietary goals, which would subsequently strengthen self-control over eating. It does seem clear that attempting to suppress thoughts of food or eating is a particularly difficult challenge, especially for those who are food deprived. However, the effect that this has on subsequent eating is not entirely clear.

Strength Failure: Fatigue

From a strength perspective, it might be expected that individuals who are prone to overeating will be most likely to do so when they are fatigued or when their coping resources are otherwise exhausted. That does seem to be true. Dieters are most likely to overeat late in the day, when people are most likely to be tired (Grilo et al., 1989). Stunkard (1959) described a "night bingeing" pattern in which obese individuals would eat enormous quantities of food late in the evening. Johnson and Larson (1982) noted that few bulimic episodes occur early in the day, whereas most occur in the late afternoon or early evening.

These results seem to indicate that dieting is hard work—and it becomes harder as the day goes on. Although it may be easy to skip breakfast, for most people hunger sets in by lunch time. For those who skimp on lunch and dinner, physiological hunger signals may become especially profound in the evening.

Moreover, eating properly involves a great deal of physical expenditure. It is much easier to pick up the phone and order pizza, or stop off at Burger King on the way home, than it is to make a nutritionally balanced meal. Few people look forward to cooking a large meal following a hard day at work. Thus, one major challenge to successful self-control of eating is that eating properly is hard work (McNulty, 1992).

Strength Failure: Distress

We noted in the alcohol chapter that excessive drinking often follows from bad moods or emotional distress. The same may apply to excessive eating. If people are asked why they overeat, they often report doing so because they are sad, bored, or otherwise in a bad mood. One dieter who was in the midst of an extreme low-calorie diet wrote: "I was missing what probably had been my best friend over the past few years. Food as friend. Food as tranquilizer. Food to assuage loneliness. Food that enabled me to eat myself into the oblivion of sleep. Food the comforter" (Jasper, 1992, p. 422). A recent study of bulimia nervosa patients revealed that a sad mood was related to increased cravings for food (Laberg, Wilson, Eldredge, & Nordby, 1991). Wadden and Letizia (1992) noted that people who are experiencing a great deal of life stress (such as financial difficulties) are typically not able to follow a weight loss program, and these authors suggested that such individuals "wait for a more propitious time to lose weight" (p. 385). These comments seem quite consistent with the strength model of self-regulation failure: People can only succeed at some new self-regulatory effort when their strength is not being depleted by other demands. More generally, aversive emotions have been shown to be potent triggers for relapse among those trying to lose weight (Grilo et al., 1989; Rosenthal & Marx, 1981), and they have also been shown to trigger eating in those who chronically restrict or control their food intake (i.e., chronic dieters).

The earliest psychological accounts of eating in response to anxiety were developed from a psychoanalytical perspective, with the traditional explanation emphasizing a fixation at—or regression to—the oral stage of development (see Leon & Roth, 1977). In that view, the experience of anxiety or fear would create a desire to return to the primary source of security and comfort experienced during one's childhood, namely food. For example, Hamburger (1951) proposed that overeating in the obese occurred as a result of nonspecific tensions, as a substitute gratification when other aspects of life seem lacking, as a response to physical illness, and as a form of comfort at times of stress owing to previous associations between food and well-being or security.

In 1957, Kaplan and Kaplan reviewed the psychosomatic theory of obesity. They concluded that the relation between anxiety and eating results from temporal associations between aversive psychological states and hunger (such as might have occurred if a mother habitually frightened and neglected to feed her child). Such an association might be triggered when the child later encountered frightening situations (i.e., the child would feel hungry). They also argued that food could serve as a potent reinforcer for any drive or behavior, and that it was possible to learn that food could diminish fear or anxiety. This learned association between eating and a reduction of distress was proposed to motivate eating whenever the person experienced fear or anxiety.

Schachter (1971) agreed that the obese were likely to be insensitive to internal states, although he questioned the likelihood of their eating in response to distress. Schachter's externality theory suggests that the obese eat largely in accordance with environmental stimuli—eating more when faced with salient, good-tasting food and less when the food is less salient or less palatable. Schachter's theory dictated that the effect of stress on normal individuals would be to decrease eating (owing to their sensitivity to the autonomic correlates of stress, which are similar to those associated with satiety). However, as discussed earlier, Schachter believed that the obese were unresponsive to internal cues. For obese individuals, the effects of distress should be irrelevant because one cannot react to stimuli that cannot be perceived.

Considerable research has been conducted contrasting the externality theory with the psychosomatic theory. The first laboratory study conducted to examine distress-induced eating by the obese was by Schachter, Goldman, and Gordon in 1968. They manipulated subjects' internal states in two ways: first through a preload manipulation and second through a fear manipulation. High fear was created by telling subjects that they would receive a painful electrical shocks following the eating task (while other subjects in a low-fear condition were told that they would experience a mild tingling sensation). Obese and normal weight subjects were then presented with crackers to taste and rate for a 15 minute period. Normal weight subjects, as predicted, ate fewer crackers following both preloading and fear of electrical shock. Obese subjects ate slightly, although nonsignificantly, more crackers following preloading or fear. Schachter et al. (1968) therefore argued that their results refuted the psychosomatic hypothesis, because obese subjects did not eat more following the fear manipulation.

A series of subsequent studies have attempted to replicate or refute Schachter's major findings. Abramson and Wunderlich (1972) proposed that Schachter et al.'s null results for obese subjects were due to the inappropriate use of objective fear. They argued that, according to psychosomatic theorizing, neurotic anxiety (emotional upset) was a more appropriate stimulus than was objective fear for eliciting overeating in the obese. Accordingly, Abramson and Wunderlich used two different sorts of manipulations: a fear manipulation (shock threat) and an "interpersonal anxiety" manipulation. Interpersonal anxiety was manipulated by feedback on responses to a bogus Interpersonal Stability Questionnaire indicating that these individuals would experience serious "problems" in the future. In refutation of the psychosomatic hypothesis, Abramson and Wunderlich found that obese subjects did not significantly increase their eating following either of the stress manipulations.

The best support for the psychosomatic theory of obesity was obtained in a series of studies by Slochower and her colleagues (Slochower, 1976, 1983; Slochower & Kaplan, 1980, 1983; Slochower, Kaplan, & Mann, 1981). Slochower proposed the general notion that it was not the type of anxiety, per se, that caused overeating by the obese, but rather whether the anxiety was clearly identifiable (or more vague) and whether the anxiety was controllable (or not). In the first study (Slochower, 1976), anxiety was manipulated by providing false heart rate feedback that was either very fast (high arousal) or was slightly low (low arousal). In addition, some subjects were given a cause (noise; label condition) for the likely increase in heart rate, whereas other subjects were not provided with a cause (no-label condition). Slochower found that obese subjects in the high-arousal–no-label condition ate significantly more than obese subjects in other conditions. Slochower and Kaplan (1980) replicated these findings and showed that the ability to control the source of emotional arousal (using a breathing technique) prevented the overeating in the no-label arousal condition.

Slochower and Kaplan (1983) examined the interactive effects of stress and stimulus salience by offering subjects candies in either a clear (high salience) or opaque (low salience) box. Distress was produced by having subjects in the high-anxiety condition take a personality test designed to uncover hidden pathology; subjects in the low-anxiety condition completed a test to reveal one's artistic preferences. Obese subjects ate significantly more only when anxious and when the candies were salient, whereas normal weight subjects ate slightly less when anxious.

In the mid-1970s, Herman and Polivy (1975, 1980) proposed that dieting status—rather than body weight—predicted individual differences in eating. Thus, the eating behavior seen in some obese individuals was explained by their greater likelihood of dieting. Much research has indicated that dieting status is indeed important in explaining individual differences in eating (see Herman & Polivy, 1980). More specifically, studies have demonstrated that dieters show increased eating in response to a variety of experimental manipulations, such as caloric preloading, social influence, and anxiety (see Ruderman, 1986).

The first study to examine the response of dieters and nondieters to distress was modeled explicitly after Schachter et al. (1968). Restrained (i.e., dieting) and unrestrained subjects were presented with either a high-fear threat (painful electric shock) or low-fear threat (slight tingling). The effect of distress on nondieters was to suppress eating, whereas dieters ate slightly—but nonsignificantly—more (Herman & Polivy, 1975). Baucom and Aiken (1981) set out to test whether it was dieting or obesity which best predicted eating following distress. They manipulated distress by means of a concept formation task that subjects could either solve easily (success condition) or, because of bogus feedback, could not solve at all (failure condition). Baucom and Aiken found that when dieting status was held constant, no obese or normal differences were observed. However, dieters (whether obese or normal weight) ate significantly more following failure than success. Nondieters ate marginally less following failure than success. Ruderman (1985) conducted an exact replication of the Baucom and Aiken procedure but used a slightly different method of classifying dieters (i.e., she used the Restraint Scale [Herman & Polivy, 1980] rather than current dieting status). Ruderman found, as had Baucom and Aiken, that dieters ate significantly more and nondieters slightly less in response to being told that they had failed on the concept formation task.

A study by Frost et al. (1982) used self-referent statements to induce a positive, neutral, or negative mood (Velten, 1968). Dieters and nondieters were invited to help themselves to M&M candies while they read the sentences. Dieters ate significantly more in the negative condition than in the neutral or positive conditions (which did not differ from one another). Nondieters ate slightly less in the failure condition. Herman, Polivy, Lank, and Heatherton (1987) examined the effect of distress by leading some subjects to believe that they would have to compose and perform an advertising jingle extolling the virtues of a new "yuppie" ice cream (high anxiety), whereas other subjects were told that they would be asked to think about aspects of the ice cream which would be useful in advertising. An orthogonal preloading manipulation (i.e., a milkshake) resulted in a significant three-way interaction between dieting, anxiety, and preloading status. Restrained eaters ate more following stress only when they did not receive a milkshake preload. Two recent studies have demonstrated that anxiety-provoking film clips can lead to disinhibited eating among restrained eaters (Cools et al., 1992; Schotte et al., 1990). Considered together, these studies indicate that a variety of emotional experiences disinhibit chronic dieters, leading to extensive and possibly excessive eating.

These findings support the view that under emotional distress, strength is depleted, and so self-regulation failures will increase. They also fit a pattern we have often seen in this book, in which people's preoccupation with regulating their emotional states takes precedence over other spheres of self-regulation, leading to self-regulation failure in some areas. When people feel bad, they may channel their self-regulatory efforts into making themselves feel better. Eating something may be a means of accomplishing that goal. Meanwhile, the preoccupation with controlling emotions may leave the person unable to summon up the self-regulatory strength necessary to prevent an innocent snack from deteriorating into a binge.

The Role of Self

A review of the eating and emotionality literature by Herman, Polivy, and Heatherton (1990) found that the *type* of distress—in addition to dieting and obesity—is an important moderator of subsequent eating behavior. As reviewed above, experimental manipulations of physical fear (i.e., threat of electrical shock or blood sampling) have been found to reduce the eating of nondieting normal weight individuals significantly while not increasing significantly the eating of obese or dieting individuals (Herman & Polivy, 1975; McKenna, 1972; Schachter et al., 1968). On the other hand, experimental manipulations that threaten subjects' egos or emotional tranquility (i.e., failure or mood manipulations) have been found to increase eating by obese or dieting individuals significantly, but they do not significantly suppress eating by normal weight nondieters (Baucom & Aiken, 1981; Cools et al., 1992; Frost et al., 1982; Herman et al., 1987; Ruderman, 1985; Schotte et al., 1990; Slochower, 1976, 1983; Slochower & Kaplan, 1980, 1983; Slochower et al., 1981).

On the basis of this review, Herman et al. (1990) proposed that physical fear differs from more general dysphoria in its effects on eating. Physical fear manipulations suppress hunger sensations, probably because of their primary effects on the autonomic nervous system (as described above) whereas ego-disruptive manipulations lead to increased eating—by obese and dieting individuals—mainly because of their powerful disinhibiting properties. This proposition was tested by Heatherton, Herman, and Polivy (1991). They exposed chronic dieters and nondieters to three types of distress experience: fear of electrical shock, fear of having to give a speech in front of peers, or failure at a supposedly important task. Subjects were then given free access to ice cream in a putative taste task. Compared to a control group that did not experience distress, Heatherton et al. found that speech threat and task failure led to increased eating for dieters; the physical fear threat led to only a slight, nonsignificant increase. In contrast, only the physical fear threat led to significantly decreased eating among nondieters; both the speech threat and task failure led to slight, nonsignificant trends toward decreased eating.

The pattern demonstrated by Heatherton et al. (1991) implicates the role of self in the disinhibition of eating by dieting and obese individuals. Only those experiences that could be considered threatening to the self produced significant increases in eating for obese or dieting subjects; physical fear, which does not have any implications for the self, did not lead to overeating. Two recent studies conducted by Heatherton, Striepe, and Nichols (1994) provide further evidence of the role of self in distress-induced eating. Dieters and nondieters were exposed to self-referent (task failure) or non-self-referent (musical) mood induction procedures and food intake was subsequently recorded. In the first study, both types of distress experiences led to significantly increased eating among dieters and decreased eating among nondieters. Now, it might not be immediately clear how listening to sad music (a seemingly non-self-involving situation) might promote excessive food intake. However, Heatherton et al. (1994) found that listening to sad music led to specific decreases in satisfaction with physical appearance for dieters. That is, listening to sad music apparently led dieters to dwell on their displeasure with their bodies. In study two, dieters and nondieters were once again exposed to sad or neutral music, but half of the subjects were told that music might make them feel momentarily sad. The addition of this attributional label to the mood induction procedure eliminated the disinhibited eating that was observed in the unlabeled condition (for dieters).

How does such a pattern fit in with the proposal that only those experiences that threaten the self lead to disinhibited eating? When no obvious explanation is available for a current mood, people are motivated to seek out possible explanations (Salovey & Rodin, 1985; Schachter & Singer, 1962; Sedikides, 1992; Wegner & Giuliano, 1980). The subsequent behavioral consequences of the mood states subsequently depends upon the interpretation of the mood source (Martin, Ward, Achee, & Wyer, 1993). Attributing a bad mood to some temporary situational reason (e.g., being afraid of something) carries no implications about the self (Schwarz, 1990), and apparently when dieters can attribute their bad mood to a specific source they are not likely to overeat. However, when situational explanations are lacking, ambiguous mood states lead people to look inward in order to try to understand the source of the mood. Hence, ambiguous sad moods lead to increased self-focused attention (Ingram, 1990; Salovey, 1992; Sedikides, 1992; Wegner & Giuliano, 1980; Wood, Saltzberg, & Goldsamt, 1990). People in sad moods become more introspective and they may look to characteristic self-feelings to explain their mood state. Given the considerable evidence for mood-congruency effects (see the review by Singer &

Salovey, 1988), it seems likely that dysphoric moods would guide self-attention to negative rather than positive aspects of the self.

Brown and Mankowski (1993) have shown that people with low self-esteem are especially prone to negative self-evaluation following mood induction procedures. Chronic dieters, who are well known for having low self-esteem (Polivy, Heatherton, & Herman, 1988), tend to have an aversive sense of self-awareness, often focusing on their dissatisfaction with their body weight (see Heatherton, 1993a). Taylor and Cooper (1992) reported evidence that negative mood states led those concerned with body shape (such as chronic dieters) to overestimate body size to a greater extent than did those who did not have body-shape concerns. Hence, it appears that for dieters the general dysphoria that results from listening to sad music increases self-attention to physical appearance. Heatherton and Baumeister (1991) proposed that disinhibited eating results because dieters are motivated to shut out such painful awareness of self. Thus, it appears that any negative mood that has direct negative implications about the self, or any mood that is ambiguous so that dieters may misattribute their unhappiness to personal shortcomings, may lead to disinhibited eating. Obviously this implies that there are many different circumstances that will remove dieters' inhibitions against eatings. Indeed, this may be why dieters are better known for their failures to control eating than for their successes.

To summarize: Distressing emotional experiences appear to overwhelm the coping capacity of chronic dieters. Challenges to the self produce a state that is unpleasant and people will wish to escape these feelings in order to improve mood. Escaping from negative self-feelings can be accomplished by a reduction in self-awareness or self-reflection. However, since low self-awareness is related to overeating, such an escape may set the stage for disinhibited eating.

Spiraling Distress

Dieting seldom results in significant or lasting weight loss, and the majority of individuals who begin dieting will experience dietary failure. A common reaction to diet failure is to blame the failure on not having had enough willpower, with a simultaneous commitment to starting the diet again, but this time promising to try harder. Indeed, the weight loss industry is a profitable industry because most customers are return customers. However, these repeated failures may eventually wreak havoc with the self-regulation of eating.

Over time, successive dietary failures lead to increased negative affect. Striegel-Moore, Silberstein, Frensch, and Rodin (1989) examined changes in affect and in disordered eating patterns for 947 college students over their freshman year at college. They found that feeling stressed was associated with a worsening of eating problems for women students. This worsening of eating disorders was also related to increased feelings of dysphoria about weight, decreased self-ratings of attractiveness, and decreased feelings of self-efficacy. In a related vein, Rosen and Gross (1987) found that dieting was predictive of increased anxiety over a four-month period. Thus, being on a diet often leads people to experience increased anxiety, which may in turn exacerbate eating problems.

In order to create the motivation to diet, the dieter must feel convinced that he or she is unattractive, incompetent, or unworthy. The dieter hopes that losing weight will turn all of these negatives into positives—that it will transform him or her into someone who is more attractive, competent, and worthy. Thus, dieters help motivate themselves to diet by focusing on their least liked characteristics. Constantly thinking about how ugly or fat you are will challenge even the most robust sense of self-esteem, and it is therefore not surprising that dieters generally have a very low sense of self-esteem (Polivy et al., 1988).

Low self-esteem may not only be important to determining which individuals undertake dieting, but it may also be important in determining how successful they are at dieting. Low self-esteem dieters are more susceptible to dietary disinhibitors than are high self-esteem dieters (who are relatively few in number). Polivy et al. (1988) compared low to high self-esteem restrained eaters in a calorie preload paradigm. In the absence of a preload, low self-esteem restrained subjects ate very little, but they ate a great deal following a disinhibiting preload. In contrast, high self-esteem restrained subjects ate at an intermediate level and were unaffected by the preload manipulation (they ate the same amount whether preloaded or not). Unrestrained subjects, whether high or low in self-esteem, showed appropriate regulation to the preload by eating less when preloaded than when not preloaded. Similarly, Heatherton et al. (1991) found that low self-esteem restrained subjects were more likely to become disinhibited by ego threats than were high self-esteem restrained subjects. Once again, high self-esteem restrained subjects were less affected by the ego threats. Thus, low self-esteem individuals are not only more likely to try dieting, but they are also more likely to fail. Common sense dictates that people feel better about themselves when they succeed at important tasks. Conversely, when people fail, they feel worse about themselves, especially if they fail at something that is important to them. For the dieter, failing to lose weight will undoubtedly lead to decreased self-esteem.

When individuals begin this cycle of dieting and overeating, they have entered the *diet spiral*, where each dietary failure increases the need for additional dieting but reduces the likelihood of future success (Heatherton & Polivy, 1992). That is, negative affect and low self-esteem make diet failure more likely, and each failure increases negative affect and lowers self-esteem. The deeper into the diet spiral individuals are, the more likely they are to experience severe dysphoria and low self-esteem as a result of dietary failure. Thus, over time, dieting produces greater psychopathology and forces the dieter to engage in more extreme efforts to lose weight, such as by increasing restriction, increasing exercise, or by beginning some form of purging (Heatherton & Polivy, 1992).

As should be clear from the preceding analysis, it is difficult to break out of this diet spiral. People have low self-esteem partially because they don't like their physical appearance. Their efforts to improve self-esteem (through dieting) almost inevitably fail, with a resulting blow to their already fragile sense of self. Because the odds of successfully losing weight are so slim, the only viable solution may be to give up dieting. In this way, the individual no longer experiences the constant consequences of dietary failure. There is evidence that therapeutic interventions designed to stop dieting behaviors lead to increased self-esteem (Ciliska, 1990). For example, a ten-week program that stressed the importance of accepting one's body produced increases in self-esteem among a group of obese women. Thus, giving up dieting may help people gain control over their eating. Clearly, however, it will be very difficult for individuals to give up dieting in cultures where the stigma against obesity is so pervasive, as is the case in our society.

MISREGULATION

Inadequate or Wrong Knowledge

Because nourishing the body is basically a physiological process, it makes sense to regulate eating around how hungry or full one feels. However, it turns out that many individuals choose to base their eating decisions on cognitive rather than physiological factors. To be successful at dieting, individuals need to ignore the internal sensations of hunger that might otherwise promote (over)eating. Over time, cognitive cues (such as dietary quotas) may take on greater importance than physiological cues, and the eating of dieters may be especially vulnerable to external and cognitive influences (Knight & Boland, 1989). Heatherton, Polivy, and Herman (1989) reasoned that if cognitive cues were important to restrained eating largely because of relative insensitivity (or nonresponsiveness) to internal sensations, then a cognitive manipulation of hunger state should have a particularly strong effect on dieter's eating. Heatherton et al. (1989) gave restrained and unrestrained eaters a "vitamin" (actually a placebo) which was supposed to produce side effects that were similar to the sensations typically associated with hunger or satiety. Compared to a control group who were not led to expect any side effects, dieters (restrained subjects)—in two separate studies—ate more when they were led to expect sensations of hunger and ate less when they expected sensations of satiety. Thus, chronic dieters are poor self-regulators of eating partially because they are unresponsive to internal cues.

A variety of studies have also demonstrated that chronic dieters may use bizarre and irrational criteria for evaluating whether their diets are intact or broken. Polivy (1976) gave dieters and nondieters pudding that was described as high or low in calories, and for some subjects the pudding was actually high in calories, whereas for others it was low in calories. This balanced design revealed that dieters were disinhibited only when they believed that they had consumed a high-calorie preload. The actual caloric content of the food did not influence eating. This same pattern was later replicated by Spencer and Fremouw (1979), with restrained eaters becoming disinhibited only when they believed that they had surpassed some dietary quota.

A series of recent studies has expanded upon Polivy's (1976) finding. Knight and Boland (1989) found that it was the "type" of food rather than the perception of calories that disinhibited eating. That is, they found that the type of food (milkshake vs. cottage cheese) was more important than perceived caloric content in disinhibiting eating among dieters, such that milkshakes were more likely than cottage cheese to disinhibit dieters. Similarly, dieters became disinhibited when they expected to consume a forbidden food whether it was high or low in calories. The anticipation of nonforbidden foods did not disinhibit dieters. Thus, the subjective perception of food types is important to the maintenance of dietary restraints (see King, Herman, & Polivy, 1987).

Not only do chronic dieters appear to use inappropriate criteria for deciding whether their diets are intact, but they also may also be quite biased in their perceptions of the ideal body weight and shape. Although it is easy to understand why a very overweight person might feel compelled to diet, it does not make sense that so many women who are objectively average or underweight feel the need to lose weight. Some research has indicated that four out of five women would like to lose at least 10 pounds (T.F. Heatherton, 1993b), and as Rosen (1992) has stated: "The most remarkable finding in body-dissatisfaction research is that currently most women and girls report dissatisfaction with their appearance, believe that they weigh too much, and are trying to lose weight" (p. 161). Fallon and Rozin (1985) found that women prefer body shapes that are well below their current body shape and even smaller than what they acknowledge is admired by the average male. Such extreme standards for thinness are especially prevalent among those who express symptoms of eating psychopathology (Zellner, Harner, & Adler, 1989). Thus, there is a conflict in standards between what type of body most people are born with, and the type of body most individuals would like to have: "Many, if not most, individuals in our culture are in an all-out search for the perfect body" (Brownell, 1991, p. 1).

Trying to Control the Uncontrollable

Given that millions of Americans diet each year in order to lose weight— spending some $30 billion on treatment—common sense would suggest that there would be considerable evidence for the success of dietary interventions. In fact, recent reviews of the hundreds of studies that have examined weight loss have generally reached the same conclusion: Diets don't work (Garner & Wooley, 1991; Polivy & Herman, 1983). A recent review by the National Institutes of Health found that nearly two-thirds of those who lose weight regain that weight within one year and that by five years almost no one has managed to maintain weight loss (NIH Technology Assessment Conference Panel, 1993). Even very low-calorie diets (such as liquid diets) only lead to temporary weight loss; individuals regain the weight as soon as they begin eating solid foods (National Task Force on the Prevention and Treatment of Obesity, 1993). Dieters, then, may be trying to do the impossible (see Seligman, 1994).

Why do people have such great difficulty losing weight and/or maintaining the weight loss? One immediate answer is that there are biological limits to the mutability of body weight. Meyer and Stunkard (1993) reviewed the literature on the genetics of body weight and concluded that both weight and fat distribution are under strong genetic control. For instance, Bouchard et al. (1990) overfed identical twins for 84 days. There was a wide degree of variability in the amount of weight gained, but the correlation for abdominal fat gain was extremely high (0.72), suggesting that there is a large genetic role for how people put on weight. Moreover, there is considerable evidence that biological mechanisms limit the extent to which people have control over their body weight. For instance, in a study of WW II conscientious objectors, Ancel Keys and colleagues (Keys et al., 1950) asked men to attempt to lose 25% of their body weight. Although these men were able to lose weight in the short term, most men had great difficulty obtaining the goal of 25% loss. As was discussed earlier, these men became obsessed with food and eating and many had difficulty regulating their intake following the study. Other research indicates that for many people it is just as difficult to gain large amounts of weight (see Polivy & Herman, 1983). In general, there appears to be some form of biological setpoint around which only minor fluctuations are likely to occur (Bennett & Gurin, 1982; Keesey, 1986).

What is even more alarming is that considerable evidence indicates that repeated dietary failures may actually lead to increased weight: Drenick and Johnson noted that "a sizable number of patients who had maintained stable weight for years prior to treatment eventually ended up considerably more obese than before weight reduction" (1980, p. 33). Recent physiological work supports the notion that repeated dieting is counterproductive to successful weight loss. That is, weight loss and weight gain become progressively more difficult because of metabolic changes that lead to more or less efficient processing of food intake (see Bennett, 1984). There is considerable animal evidence showing that weight gain occurs much faster in previously starved animals than would be expected by caloric intake alone (Levitsky, Faust, & Glassman, 1976). Repeated alterations between caloric deprivation and overfeeding have also been shown to have cumulative metabolic effects, so that weight loss and metabolic functioning are slowed progressively more each time the animal is placed on caloric deprivation and weight gain occurs more rapidly with each occurrence of refeeding (Brownell, Greenwood, Stellar, & Shrager, 1986). This pattern has implications for the observation that so-called yo-yo dieting in humans can lead to less efficient weight loss and increased weight gain (Brownell, Greenwood, Stellar, & Shrayer, 1986).

Of course, if people managed to gain complete control over their eating they would eventually manage to lose weight. Individuals who go on hunger strikes for political causes continue to lose weight until they finally succumb to the physiological effects of starvation. However, most individuals who undertake dieting fail to lose substantial amounts of weight because they occasionally eat enough to cancel out the effects of caloric restriction. Food is not the same as alcohol, because people cannot avoid it entirely. Thus, it is not possible to completely abstain from eating. For some people, consuming even small amounts of food is enough to trigger a full-blown bout of binge eating. Dieters who constantly battle against consumption set themselves up for constant failure. Thus, people who diet in order to lose weight often end up having difficulties controlling their eating behavior, and these self-regulatory difficulties are an important component of dietary collapse.

SUMMARY AND CONCLUSION

The self-regulation of eating is a deceptively simple task: eat when hungry, quit eating when full. Most people manage to control their eating within reasonable boundaries, with the occasional splurge presenting no major challenge to overall self-control. However, many people who explicitly try to control their eating (i.e., through dieting) develop self-regulatory problems. These individuals exert a great amount of effort ignoring physiological cues to eat, but they then respond with abandon when they perceive their diet is broken or when they are emotionally upset. Moreover, by ignoring the physiological cues that might otherwise regulate intake, dieters allow themselves to be overwhelmed by situational cues and momentary impulses. Especially when self-awareness is low, or when they fail to monitor food intake, dieters often lose control over their eating, with the resulting binge leaving them worse off than if they had not dieted at all.

Failures in the self-regulation of eating conform to many patterns that were seen with failure to control alcohol consumption. Conflicting standards make self-regulation difficult. Circumstances that impair or reduce people's ability to monitor their food intake tend to promote excessive eating. Attentional control is vital to successful dieting; this presents special problems for regulating eating, because nature has programmed people to respond readily to the sight and smell of food.

When self-regulatory strength is depleted, because of fatigue or emotional distress, people are more likely to overeat. Some of these patterns may reflect a tendency to focus on regulating emotion, which results in a neglect of the regulation of eating.

Moreover, secondary causal patterns were abundantly apparent. It is not the first potato chip that constitutes the dietary failure, but after one has finished the entire bag one's diet is indeed ruined. Dieters show abundant and multiple patterns in which some initial eating snowballs into a destructive binge. Eating has considerable inertia, apparently, and it is much harder to interrupt oneself in the midst of an eating binge than to prevent it from starting. Moreover, failures at dieting produce emotional distress and lower self-esteem, which in turn can lead to further failures at self-regulation in a destructive spiral.

Eating resembles drinking in that people must cooperate to the extent of obtaining what they will consume, putting it into their mouth, and swallowing it. To that extent, people seem to acquiesce in self-regulation failures in both the eating and drinking spheres. The individual's acquiescence in failure to self-regulate eating seems clearer than in the failure to self-regulate drinking, however, for two reasons. First, food does not have the addictive properties that alcohol does. Second, food does not have the physiological effects of alcohol, particularly the reduction of self-awareness that impairs the capacity to monitor oneself, that accounts for some of the lapse-activated patterns with alcohol. On the other hand, food is harder to avoid than alcohol, because it is necessary to eat in order to survive. And binge eaters do suffer from one of the lapse-activated problems that also afflicts problem drinkers, namely the fact that initial consumption makes further consumption more appealing.

Misregulation of eating is often based on various false beliefs. These include beliefs about various foods and beliefs about the self. Indeed, a growing body of research indicates that almost all dieting is inherently futile, and so one could suggest that all dieting involves misregulation based on false beliefs, because in essence one is trying to control something (one's weight) that is not fundamentally controllable.

10

Smoking

In spite of overwhelming evidence that smoking cigarettes leads to premature death, some 50 million Americans continue to light up (Carmody, 1993). Although smoking has declined over the past 30 years, some 32% of men and 27% of American adults continue to smoke (Pierce, 1989). Smoking is linked to a number of health problems such as heart disease, respiratory problems, and a variety of cancers, and is blamed for over 400,000 deaths per year in the United States (McGinnis, Shopland, & Brown, 1987; United States Department of Health and Human Services, 1988). Cigarette smoke also causes health problems for nonsmoking bystanders, which may contribute to the alienation and rejection that smokers face in public. It is not uncommon to see smokers huddled outside of office towers or hospitals, braving both the elements and hostile looks from nonsmokers as they satisfy their cravings for nicotine. Smokers encounter difficulties taking airplanes for great distances since going hours without a cigarette may lead to unpleasant withdrawal sensations. They endure scoldings from physicians and loved ones who are concerned for their health and welfare, and they may be denied life insurance, housing, or even overnight accommodations. The monetary costs of smoking can be quite extraordinary. Not only does the pack-a-day smoker spend more than one thousand dollars per year on cigarettes, but he or she also pays more for life and house insurance. Why in the world would anyone wish to smoke?

In terms of self-regulation there are three issues that need to be addressed. First is the issue of why anyone would take up smoking. Cigarettes differ from the other behaviors that have been discussed in that they are neither necessary for survival (such as eating) nor socially acceptable in moderation (such as drinking). Relatively few people have the occasional social cigarette, and generally being a smoker is an all-or-none phenomenon; people are either smokers or nonsmokers (especially in the United States; see Peele, 1989). At issue is the decision process to begin smoking.

Once individuals become regular smokers, the self-regulatory issue is controlling the amount smoked, and this is the second issue. Individuals need to smoke enough to satisfy cravings and suppress withdrawal, but many smokers consciously try to reduce the number of cigarettes they smoke to minimize health consequences. Thus, some consideration of how people regulate their smoking intake needs to be considered.

Third, many smokers are in the process of trying to become ex-smokers. These individuals who are attempting to abstain completely from cigarettes face an extremely difficult self-regulatory task of trying to override a physically ingrained addiction.

BEGINNING TO SMOKE

It is hard to imagine any good reasons to start smoking. The first cigarette is seldom pleasant, and first attempts at smoking often involve a great deal of coughing, watering eyes, a terrible taste in the mouth, and feelings of nausea. Moreover, even the youngest would-be smoker cannot be totally ignorant of the potential health consequences associated with inhaling tobacco smoke. Nonetheless, a considerable number of adolescents take up smoking each year. Indeed, a recent study showed that after years of decline, smoking is increasing in popularity among adolescents (*Boston Globe*, January 1994). Most researchers point to powerful social influences as the leading cause of adolescent smoking (for a review, see Chassin, Presson, & Sherman, 1990; Kozlowski, 1979). Research has demonstrated that adolescents are more likely to smoke if their parents or friends are smokers (Biglan & Lichtenstein, 1984; Hansen et al., 1987; Russell, 1971), and the first cigarette is often smoked in the company of other smokers, or at least with the encouragement of their peer group (Sarafino, 1990). Moreover, many adolescent smokers appear to show a false consensus effect, in that they overestimate the number of adolescent and adult smokers (Sherman, Presson, Chassin, Corty, & Olshavsky, 1983). Thus, adolescents who incorrectly believe that smoking is normative may be especially vulnerable to experimenting with cigarettes.

Others have pointed to the potential meaning of "being a smoker" as having a powerful influence (Leventhal & Cleary, 1980). For instance, research has shown that smokers are viewed as having a number of positive qualities, such as being tough, sociable, and good with members of the opposite sex (Barton, Chassin, Presson, & Sherman, 1982). Children take up smoking partially to look "tough, cool, and independent of authority" (Leventhal & Cleary, 1980, p. 384). Thus, smoking may be one manner by which adolescents enhance their self-image as well as their public image (Chassin et al., 1990).

Of course, it is hard to look tough while gasping and retching, and so while most adolescents try one or two cigarettes, the majority do not go on to become regular smokers. Leventhal and Cleary (1980) have suggested, however, that any adolescent who manages to smoke four cigarettes is likely to become a regular smoker—in fact, Russell (1990) stated boldly that smoking four cigarettes seems to condemn adolescents to a 40-year sentence of cigarette smoking.

Why do some adolescents go on to become habitual smokers? There are two major categories of reasons for continuing to smoke. First, all the social pressures to have the fourth and fifth cigarette are often in force following the first cigarette. Adolescents who hang out with smokers will continue to face encouragement to smoke, and parental modeling will continue to have an influence. A longitudinal study by Murray, Swan, Johnson, and Bewley (1983) found that smoking became habitual when adolescents perceived their parents as unconcerned about or encouraging of smoking, or if they had siblings or peers who were smokers, or if they felt peer pressure to smoke (such as by dares or taunts), or if they held positive images of smokers. The effect of social pressures is augmented by the fact that over the course of a year or so individuals will become physically dependent on nicotine (Ashton & Stepney, 1982). It is now widely acknowledged that nicotine is of primary importance in motivating and maintaining smoking behavior (Fagerström & Schneider, 1989; Henningfield, 1984a; United States Department of Health and Human Services, 1988). Once the smoker becomes "hooked" on the drug nicotine, attempts to go without cigarettes will be very difficult because of unpleasant withdrawal symptoms, including heightened anxiety and distress (Jarvik, 1979; Russell, 1990).

Some adolescents appear to be at greater risk for becoming regular smokers. Self-regulatory weakness may be one central factor: Adolescents who have the greatest problems of general impulse control are the ones who go on to become regular smokers (Ashton & Stepney, 1982; Kozlowski, 1979; Russell, 1971). Although we hasten to note that the search for an addictive personality has been largely unsuccessful (Nathan, 1988), there is considerable evidence that adolescents who become smokers differ in substantial ways from those who do not become smokers (Ashton & Stepney, 1982; Jessor & Jessor, 1977). Thus, adolescents who tend to be rebellious and antisocial are more likely to smoke than their more conforming peers. This constellation of personality traits may also predispose adolescents to develop other impulse-control problems, such as excessive alcohol intake (Cox, 1985). It is therefore possible that individuals with poor self-regulatory skills are less able to resist peer pressure and temptations to smoke. They may have general problems with underregulation that surface in their increased risk-taking and antisocial behaviors. Proposed interventions to prevent adolescent smoking often include components that specifically address issues of self-control and resistance to temptation, and such programs have been shown to be more effective than standard public education interventions (Botvin, Eng, & Williams, 1980).

One final reason that some adolescents begin smoking deserves mention. It has been noted that cigarette smoking has increased more for women than for men over the past few decades (Ashton & Stepney, 1982). Historically, men were much more likely to be smokers than were women, but the gap has been closing over the past two decades (McGinnis et al., 1987), largely because men have quit smoking at a much greater rate than women (Pierce, 1989). A recent study of high school students by Pirie, Murray, and Luepker (1991) found that a greater proportion of females smoked (26.5%) than did males (22.6%).

Why are young women taking to cigarettes? One answer is that the media target them with messages, such as, "You've come a long way, baby," thus implying that liberated women should smoke. A more likely answer, however, is that many young women may be smoking in order to try to lose weight. Nicotine has well-known anorectic qualities and considerable research has shown that smokers weigh less than do nonsmokers (Grunberg, 1982; Klesges, Meyers, Klesges, & LaVasque, 1989; Wack & Rodin, 1982). Some large-scale surveys have found that young women are taking up smoking as a dieting strategy. For instance, Klesges and Klesges (1988) found that nearly 40% of women smokers reported that they used smoking as a weight loss strategy. Overweight women were especially likely to report starting smoking in an attempt to lose weight. From a health perspective, this is obviously a poor decision, because the long-term harm caused by smoking far outweighs any health benefit coming from a temporary loss of five pounds. Moreover, smoking as a means of weight loss might be an especially counterproductive practice, because smoking affects body fat distribution such that it promotes increased waist to hip ratio, which is itself a health risk (Shimokata, Muller, & Andres, 1989). It is important to remember, however, that the reasons that women want to lose weight seldom have anything to do with health effects; they have everything to do with wanting to improve personal appearance.

Yet smoking is also a strikingly ineffective means of improving physical attractiveness. Although smoking may help a person lose five pounds or so, most observers will not even notice such a small change. Moreover, smoking cigarettes interferes with blood circulation and contributes to premature aging of the skin—smokers have premature wrinkles and tough-looking skin. Even the very act of smoking may reduce attractiveness. A study by Polivy, Hackett, and Bycio (1979) also found that smoking targets (college aged) were rated as less attractive than nonsmoking targets. Thus, if anything, smoking makes people less attractive, not more.

THE REGULATION OF SMOKING

Some have claimed that nicotine is among the most addictive of the addictive substances (Russell & Feyerabend, 1978). Proponents of this view argue that each puff of a cigarette is a potent reinforcing event. Given that the average smoker has some 70,000 to 80,000 puffs per year (Kozlowski, 1982), there is considerable opportunity for reinforcement. Although the pharmacological effects of nicotine (such as tolerance and accumulation effects) probably render some puffs more influential than others (Kozlowski, 1982), smokers do differ from alcoholics and other addicts in that their consumption often starts within minutes after waking (Kozlowski, Director, & Harford, 1981; Heatherton, Kozlowski, Frecker, Rickert, & Robinson, 1989) and lasts until moments before retiring at night. Indeed, very dependent smokers sometimes have the first cigarette of the day before getting out of bed. Evidence that nicotine is particularly addictive is supported by research that asked approximately 1000 alcohol and drug abuse (i.e., heroin or cocaine) patients to say whether it would be harder to give up smoking or their "hard" addiction. Over half (57%) the addicts said that it would be more difficult to give up cigarettes! This response was especially true among alcoholics (Kozlowski, Wilkinson, et al., 1989). Thus, the dependent smoker is firmly hooked on cigarettes.

Considerable evidence over the last few years has led to the conclusion that nicotine is the major addictive substance in cigarettes (Ashton & Stepney, 1982; United States Department of Health and Human Services, 1988). This is not to say that sensory aspects of smoking (such as the feelings in the throat, taste, and smell) or the physical mechanics (such as doing something with the hands) are unimportant (see Rose, 1991), but it does seem that nicotine is the main active ingredient in cigarettes that promotes habitual or dependent use. The plasma half-life of nicotine is relatively short (approximately two hours, according to Benowitz, 1983) and therefore the smoker needs to replenish the supply at fairly regular intervals. The average smoker consumes around a pack a day, which in the United States is 20 cigarettes. In countries that sell packages of multiple size (e.g., Canada), smokers who buy their cigarettes in larger packages smoke more cigarettes per day and are generally heavier smokers (Kozlowski, Heatherton, & Ferrence, 1989), which suggests that smokers increase intake as a function of availability or convenience. Thus, smokers generally smoke within an hour of waking and continue to smoke one cigarette approximately every 45 min (Heatherton, Kozlowski, Frecker, Rickert, & Robinson, 1989), depending, of course, on situational constraints.

In response to mounting evidence that smoking leads to serious health consequences, many smokers are motivated to regulate intake so that they are smoking in the least harmful manner as possible. The most common of these methods is cutting down the number of cigarettes (Shapiro, Schwartz, Tursky, & Schnidman, 1971) and switching to cigarettes that supply a lower yield of tar and nicotine (McMorrow & Foxx, 1985; Russell, Jarvis, Iyer, & Feyerabend, 1980).

It is clear that smokers are able to cut down on the number of cigarettes that they smoke, usually in an attempt to achieve abstinence (Shapiro et al., 1971). Although gradually reducing the number of cigarettes smoked has not typically been found to be a successful method of cessation (Jarvik, 1979), research has demonstrated that smokers can cut down from over 60 cigarettes per day to an apparent minimum of approximately 10–12 (Shapiro et al., 1971). It is likely, however, that the effective dose of chemicals consumed is not practically reduced when smokers simply cut down on the number of cigarettes smoked because smokers compensate for the decreased number of cigarettes by altering the "topography" of the habit (Frederickson, 1976). For example, Benowitz, Jacob, Kozlowski, and Yu (1986) found that smokers were able to cut down from an average of 37 to an average of 5 cigarettes per day, but intake of toxins per cigarette increased threefold and so the net yield of tar and carbon monoxide decreased by only 50%. In other words, smokers consumed the fewer number of cigarettes more intensely, by taking more smoke per puff, by taking more puffs, and by smoking more of each cigarette (cf. Ashton & Watson, 1970).

A model of regulation proposed by Herman and Kozlowski (1979) provided a cogent explanation for the regulatory behavior of the addicted smoker. The *Boundary Model* proposed an integration between physiological models of nicotine addiction and psychosocial influences on smoking behavior (Herman & Kozlowski, 1979; Kozlowski & Herman, 1984). According to the Boundary Model, there is a range in which the smoker does not experience the aversive state of withdrawal nor the noxious condition of nicotine satiation, a so-called zone of biological indifference where smoking behavior can be affected by nonphysiological cues. For example, in the experienced smoker, when nicotine plasma levels fall below some critical value (i.e., a lower boundary), the smoker experiences physiological symptoms of withdrawal such as cravings, irritability, and the like, and is compelled to smoke in response to immediate physiological cues.

Conversely, when the smoker has overindulged (i.e., is smoked out), unpleasant physiological cues signal the individual to stop smoking. For example, Pomerleau, Fertig, and Shanahan (1983) found that smokers became satiated after a 1-hr smoking session in which they smoked five cigarettes. This satiation effect occurred only when the cigarettes contained a high level of nicotine; smokers continued to increase smoking of low-nicotine cigarettes over the 1-hr period.

Much of the time, however, the smoker is neither induced to smoke nor compelled to avoid smoking; this is the zone of indifference where nonphysiological cues have their impact on smoking. For example, Herman (1974) found that smokers were affected by cue salience mainly when they were in an indifferent state. During cigarette deprivation, when presumably physiological cues to smoke would increase, salience had less influence on smoking behavior. Herskovic, Rose, and Jarvik (1986) found that nicotine seeking varied as a direct function of cigarette deprivation. Nicotine preference (assessed by subjects' selection of nicotine content using a smoker mixer) was greatest after overnight deprivation (when smokers were presumably below their lower boundary), least after smoking satiation (when subjects were at their upper boundary), and intermediate after a short period of deprivation (when smokers were in the zone of indifference). These various studies provide considerable support for the boundary model.

Although it clearly appears that smokers compensate for reduced cigarette intake by increased intensity in smoking topography (Kozlowski, 1983), less is known about the regulatory processes underlying the other common method of minimizing the harmful effects of cigarettes: smoking low-yield cigarettes. McMorrow and Foxx (1985) noted that production and sales of low-yield cigarettes have been increasing at a dramatic rate. These so-called light cigarettes hold the promise of reducing the health consequences of smoking. Although common sense suggests that this would be a propitious strategy, some researchers suggested that the health advantages of switching to low-yield cigarettes have been largely offset by the tendency of smokers to compensate by increased inhalation or increased number of cigarettes (Maron & Fortmann, 1987; Russell et al., 1980). Schachter et al. (1977) had smokers smoke low-nicotine cigarettes during one week and high-nicotine cigarettes during another week. They found that subjects smoked more low-nicotine cigarettes, and this was especially true of heavier smokers.

Kozlowski (1983) noted an apparent paradox in the smoking behaviors of individuals attempting to minimize health risks by smoking low-yield, ventilated cigarettes. One of the most practical methods of reducing the noxious effects of tobacco is to ventilate the filter on the end of the cigarette, so that each puff can be diluted by up to 80% with ambient air (Kozlowski, 1981). However, up to 40% of smokers of vented filters have been found to negate the benefits of ventilation by blocking the air holes, either by their lips or fingers (Kozlowski, 1983). It is interesting to note that most of these smokers appeared to believe that their actions served only to make the cigarette easier to smoke and more flavorful, apparently unaware of the potentially powerful effect that this action had on the nicotine, tar, and carbon monoxide levels, and 40% were totally unaware of their hole-blocking (Kozlowski, 1983). Kozlowski, Heatherton, Frecker, and Nolte (1989) found that those who blocked the holes on their low-yield cigarettes often had levels of tobacco toxins that rivaled those smoking regular-yield cigarettes. They concluded that heavily dependent smokers who switched to low-yield cigarettes were especially likely to practice hole-blocking, thereby inadvertently defeating their efforts to minimize the health risks of smoking.

Thus, smokers often seem to thwart their own efforts to regulate their smoking. Some switch to cigarettes that are advertised as low in tar and nicotine—but then they smoke more of them. Others use cigarettes that are manufactured with ventilating mechanisms that dilute the smoke with air—but they block these air holes so as to prevent the ventilation effect from working. Such individuals may be deluding themselves by believing that their smoking is within safe levels when they are actually obtaining a potent dose of carcinogens. More to the point, they may be complacent in the belief that they have taken steps to regulate their smoking, unmindful of the fact that their subtle or even seemingly inadvertent behaviors systematically undermine their self-regulatory efforts.

Environmental and Situational Influences

Smoking is different from the other behaviors that have been considered because of its regularity of intake. As discussed, because the regulation of nicotine is the primary force underlying nicotine intake, most smokers smoke at regular intervals to replenish depleted nicotine levels. Of course, this is not always the case, as a growing number of social settings do not allow smokers to light up. For instance, during the last decade many businesses have banned smoking in the workplace; smokers now rush outside during breaks to grab a quick puff or two, and they may smoke more heavily during nonworking hours in order to compensate for limited intake. Similarly, smoking is becoming a rarity in many public locations—it is becoming hard to remember that people used to smoke in banks, movie theaters, classrooms, and airplanes. The city of Brookline in Massachusetts has enacted one of the most sweeping public smoking bans, which includes all restaurants, motel rooms, and workplaces. Thus, smokers are free to practice their habit only in the privacy of their homes and cars (unless, of course, they are forbidden by family or friends) or in the few public locations that remain havens for tobacco, notably taverns and casinos (note, however, that nonsmoking gaming tables are becoming commonplace in Las Vegas).

It may well be that our society's current intolerance of smoking makes the self-regulation of cigarette consumption an easier task. By effectively eliminating cues to smoke (including advertisements and television portrayals: no one smokes on television), society may reduce the cues that influence smokers to have a cigarette. Throughout this book, we have seen that controlling attention is often a powerful first step toward successful self-regulation, and the anti-smoking policies in contemporary U.S. society may be an effective application of this principle.

Given the power of the nicotine addiction, of course, serious addicts may be relatively unaffected by environmental cues. Light smokers, who are less driven by powerful, internally generated cues, may be more susceptible to the effects of environmental cues. Under the guise of an experiment on the effects of urban living on human behavior, Herman (1974) exposed smokers to six cigarettes that were either illuminated (high-salience condition) or in a shadow (low-salience condition). Although light smokers were strongly influenced by the salience manipulation (smoking more when the cigarettes were illuminated), heavy smokers had the same latency to smoke and smoked a similar number of cigarettes in both conditions. Herman argued that the smoking behavior of heavy smokers was under greater internal control than was that of nonsmokers, who presumably were trying to restrain their intake of cigarettes. These restrained smokers, then, responded in an analogous fashion as do restrained eaters (i.e., obese subjects) to cues associated with eating.

The greater effect of social cues on light smokers than on heavy smokers has been confirmed in other research. Glad and Adesso (1976) observed smoking behavior among a group of subjects waiting to be in an experiment. Subjects were in the company of a confederate who either smoked or did not smoke. All subjects smoked more when the confederate was smoking, but this effect was particularly prominent among light smokers. Thus, individuals who may be trying to restrain their intake of cigarettes are more susceptible to visual and social cues to smoke. Even if these light smokers were not purposefully restraining intake, it still makes sense that such cues influence their smoking to a greater extent than heavy smokers, who are smoking largely because of withdrawal sensations rather than because of cognitive control.

One situation that is closely related to cigarette smoking is the tavern. The relationship between alcohol intake and cigarette smoking is complex and not currently well understood (Sobell, Sobell, Kozlowski, & Toneatto, 1990). What is clear is that individuals who abuse alcohol are almost invariably smokers; some 80–95% of alcoholics are also smokers (Sobell et al., 1990). Drinking establishments are one of the last safe havens for smokers, but they are very dangerous places for those trying to stop smoking—research has shown that drinking alcohol is one of the most important triggers of smoking relapse episodes (Brandon, Tiffany, & Baker, 1986; Shiffman, 1982). Research studies have demonstrated that the normal effect of alcohol is to increase cigarette consumption among smokers (Griffiths, Bigelow, & Liebson, 1976; Mintz, Boyd, Rose, Charuvasta, & Jarvik, 1985). Thus, taverns not only serve as cues for smoking (the sight and smell of tobacco smoke), but alcohol also appears to increase smoking frequency. Research has not clarified whether this increased smoking is a result of alcohol's disinhibitory properties (since it is not known whether the smokers were trying to inhibit intake) or whether some other aspect of alcohol is responsible for increased intake (i.e., the interactive pharmacological effects of nicotine and alcohol or the effects of alcohol on taste and sensory aspects of smoking).

There have been virtually no studies on the effects of cognitive processes on cigarette smoking, which may be due to the simple-minded tendency of many researchers to consider nicotine regulation as the sole basis of smoking. The paucity of studies on this topic has been noted by a number of researchers (Ashton & Stepney, 1982; Pomerleau, 1979). Some smoking cessation programs include instructions to self-monitor cigarette intake, but it is not known whether a loss of self-awareness is implicated in the normal self-regulation of smoking. Some automatic aspects of smoking are commonly described, such as the fact that smokers say that they often light up cigarettes without really thinking about it (and sometimes they already have another cigarette burning). But there are few studies that specifically address the role of self-awareness in smoking. Wicklund (1975) contended that people may smoke as an attempt to reduce self-awareness by distracting themselves. If his view is correct, it would suggest that there may be a cyclic pattern of self-regulatory breakdown similar to what we saw with alcohol and possibly eating, in which people indulge in smoking in order to escape from self-awareness, and then the loss of self-awareness facilitates further indulgence (see also Baumeister, 1991a).

Wegner (1994) has noted an apparent ironic effect in the effects of self-monitoring of smoking on cigarette consumption. McFall (1970) had some smokers monitor the number of cigarettes that they had smoked, whereas other smokers monitored the number of times they thought about smoking but did not. McFall found that conscious monitoring of smoking led to increased smoking, whereas monitoring thoughts of not smoking led to decreased smoking. Thus, apparently, increased monitoring seemed to lead to less self-regulation, at least to the extent that people smoked more. These subjects were smokers who were not actively engaged in trying to curtail cigarette smoking. As will be discussed, when people are purposefully trying to reduce intake, self-monitoring may be an effective strategy for limiting cigarette intake (Sarafino, 1990). Wegner argued that this occurred because of an ironic mental process, such that focusing attention on smoking intensified the urge to smoke. In any case, it is clear that the control over attention is a powerful factor in determining impulsive behavior.

Distress and Smoking

When asked why they smoke, many smokers report that they find cigarettes relaxing and that smoking helps them cope with anxious situations. Apparently, just as dieters report being comforted by food, smokers report being comforted by cigarettes. From a self-regulatory strength perspective, it might be argued that people actually smoke when distressed because they are unable to cope with both the stressors and their desires to smoke. This would be consistent with the strength model, which contends that self-control is a limited resource.

A large body of literature supports the propositions that emotional distress leads to increased smoking (Ashton & Stepney, 1982) and that smoking is associated with reports of decreased emotionality (Gilbert, 1979). For instance, Schachter et al. (1977) found that smokers smoked more following laboratory inductions of anxiety (see also Ashton & Stepney, 1982, p. 111). Moreover, smoking does seem to relax smokers in stressful situations. For instance, Gilbert and Spielberger (1987) placed smokers in a stressful social situation while they smoked or did not smoke. When allowed to smoke they reported less anxiety and greater effectiveness in expressing themselves in the interaction.

These reports that smoking is relaxing contradicts the well-known physiological effects of nicotine, which are typically thought to lead to cortical and physiological arousal (Ashton & Stepney, 1982; Gilbert, 1979; Shiffman & Jarvik, 1984). This contradiction has come to be known as Nesbitt's (1973) paradox. Nesbitt found that smokers allowed to smoke during a distressing experience were calmer than smokers not allowed to smoke. A study by Silverstein (1982) clarified the possible underlying mechanism behind Nesbitt's paradox. Silverstein exposed nonsmokers and smokers to a distressing experience (electric shock) and assigned the smokers to one of three conditions: nonsmoking, smoking low-nicotine cigarettes, and smoking high-nicotine cigarettes. Smokers who were deprived of cigarettes and those smoking low-nicotine cigarettes were much more anxious than smokers of high-nicotine cigarettes and nonsmokers, who did not differ from each other. Silverstein concluded that cigarettes act to reduce withdrawal sensations rather than to reduce anxiety, and that it is the removal of the withdrawal sensations that smokers interpret as a reduction in anxiety. That is, "Deprived smokers appear to experience withdrawal symptoms that they may interpret as anxiety, particularly during periods of stress. After smoking a cigarette, smokers replenish their supply of nicotine, end withdrawal symptoms, and feel relaxed" (p. 949). Thus, smoking relaxes smokers because it reduces withdrawal rather than—or in spite of—having any direct effect on level of arousal.

Smoking not only relieves unpleasant withdrawal sensations, but it also provides some enhancement of cognitive functioning, such as attention, memory, motor skills, and problem solving (Ashton & Stepney, 1982; Henningfield, 1984b). Thus, when they need to perform complex tasks, smokers may receive some benefit from having a cigarette. Ashton and Stepney (1982) argued that smokers may use cigarettes to regulate their level of arousal. It is currently unclear whether the enhancement of cognitive performance is a function of the direct effects of nicotine or whether it is due to alleviation of withdrawal (Carmody, 1993). Nonetheless, for smokers, nicotine may help the self-regulation of attention and performance.

Continued Smoking as Self-Regulation Failure

With all of the evidence that smoking leads to early death, it is informative to examine the processes people use to rationalize and justify their continued smoking. In many ways, the decision to smoke conforms to the standard delay of gratification pattern. Smokers face the choice between obtaining immediate gratification of their addictive cravings and living for a longer period of time. In order to choose smoking over health and longevity, smokers must ignore or rationalize the long-term consequences of smoking. Thus, for instance, they claim that the evidence linking smoking to cancer is weak, or they fall prey to thoughts that they are personally invulnerable and that it will always be somebody else who develops cancer, heart disease, or lung disease. Indeed, Weinstein (1987) has found that most people feel that they are less likely to develop such diseases as diabetes, cardiac problems, obesity, cancer, and venereal disease than are other adults of their own age and sex. Weinstein speculated that four factors appeared to increase people's Pollyanic cognitions about susceptibility to disease. First, because people have not yet developed the disease, there is no reason to assume that they will in the future (e.g., "I've smoked for ten years and I am perfectly healthy"). Second, people believe that some individual action will protect them from the long-term consequences (e.g., "I will take lots of beta-carotene and not smoke very much"). Third, they tend to downplay the frequency of negative outcomes (e.g., "only some people die from smoking"). Finally, they have a lack of personal experience with the negative outcome (e.g., "I know many people who smoke and have lived for a long time"). Indeed, people who do not practice health-protective behaviors are less likely to believe that they are susceptible to development of illness (Becker & Rosenstock, 1984)—which seems perfectly rational, except if that belief is unfounded.

Of course, most of the time smokers (or other addicts) do not even think about the long-term consequences of their behavior. Indeed, being confronted with the inescapable truth about the hazards of smoking (such as watching a friend die of cancer or watching a peer struggle with emphysema) can be a potent trigger to stopping smoking (Heatherton & Nichols, in press). Research has demonstrated that confronting people with the cold hard facts about health problems (i.e., a fear-based appeal) is among the most successful means of motivating health behaviors and increasing control over impulses to smoke. Leventhal et al. (1967) showed smokers a movie of an actual operation to remove a diseased lung. The experience was so powerful that some smokers were so upset that they had to leave the room. When such vivid consequences were shown to them, smokers became much more likely to feel personally susceptible to developing cancer and reported being much more eager to stop smoking.

One form of misregulation that promotes continued smoking occurs when individuals decide that they do not want to quit smoking because they are afraid that they will gain weight. Concerns about weight gain have been identified as a major deterrent to efforts at stopping smoking (Gross, Stitzer, & Maldanado, 1989; Hall, McGee, Tunstall, Duffy, & Benowitz, 1989; Klesges & Klesges, 1988). Indeed, those who successfully quit smoking are likely to gain from five to twelve pounds (Blitzer, Rimm, & Giefer, 1977; Hall, Ginsberg, & Jones, 1986; Hall et al., 1989). It appears that nicotine is the chief culprit responsible for weight gain, because nicotine replacement (i.e., through nicotine gum) appears to prevent weight gain (Fagerström, 1987; Gross et al., 1989). Avoiding smoking cessation because of the fears of weight gain makes little sense from a health perspective, because the health risks associated with a small weight gain are minimal, whereas the health risks associated with continued smoking are quite severe. However, as noted repeatedly, weight gain and loss are largely matters of physical appearance concerns rather than health concerns. Smokers who resist quitting because of fears of weight gain need to be informed about the actual amount of weight they may gain and the possibility that nicotine replacement will minimize this effect.

SMOKING CESSATION AND RELAPSE

Most smokers, especially experienced smokers, want to quit smoking. Smoking is not only associated with health problems (such as sore throat and cougher's hack) and premature death, but it is also associated with societal stigma and rejection. Many smokers feel guilty smoking around others and they face a constant barrage of media, family, and physician pressures to quit their habit. Largely in response to growing knowledge of the health risks associated with smoking, and to social pressure, many millions of Americans have quit smoking over the past 30 years (Carmody, 1993; Pierce, 1989; Sarafino, 1990; United States Department of Health and Human Services, 1988). This section reviews evidence on how people quit smoking as well as the problems and setbacks that they have in their attempts at cessation.

Self Quitting

Of the more than 30 million Americans who have quit smoking, it is estimated that 70–80% have done so on their own, without any formal treatment (Perri, 1985; Sarafino, 1990). In a seminal study, Schachter (1982) interviewed 83 members of the Columbia University Psychology Department and 78 shopkeepers from Amagansett, New York. Schachter found that more than half of the smokers who had reported trying to quit smoking had done so successfully on their own, without any formal treatment. What was impressive was that the average length of abstinence was close to seven years. In contrast, the success rates associated with formal treatment are much more pessimistic, with long-term follow-up showing that only around 20% of smokers in formal treatment will be successful at quitting (Cohen et al., 1989). Why might those who quit on their own be more successful than those who quit in treatment?

Schachter (1982) offered three possible explanations for the superiority of quitting on one's own. First, it is possible that therapies simply do not work, or worse yet, that they impede success. There is little evidence to support such an assertion. Second, it is possible that smokers differ in the ease with which they are able to give up smoking. Indeed, considerable research has documented differences between those who are only slightly dependent on cigarettes and those who are highly dependent on cigarettes: The former group is much more likely to be successful in quitting smoking than the latter group (Cohen et al., 1989; Fagerström & Schneider, 1989; Kozlowski, Porter, Orleans, Pope, & Heatherton, in press). Carmody (1993) noted that those who have been unable to quit on their own are a particularly hard-core group of smokers who are very dependent on nicotine. Thus, those smokers who are not heavily addicted to nicotine may find it quite easy to quit on their own; they will experience minimal withdrawal and smoking does not play a central role in their lives. Heavily dependent smokers, however, will find quitting extremely difficult because of constant cravings and other negative physiological sensations (Jarvik, 1979).

Thus, the self-regulatory challenge is greater for heavy smokers trying to quit than it is for light smokers.

Schachter (1982) also proposed a third possibility for the finding that cessation rates are higher for those who try it on their own. Self-reports of success in Schachter's study were based on all attempts that a person had made. In contrast, success rates from treatment studies are based on single trials of attempting to quit smoking. Thus, it is possible that those who had quit in Schachter's study managed to do so only after repeated efforts at abstinence. This possibility is supported by a recent examination of 10 large longitudinal studies of smokers trying to quit on their own (Cohen et al., 1989). These researchers found that success rates on a single trial of trying to quit without treatment were no different than success rates associated with single treatment trials. Thus, on any given attempt, some 10–20% of smokers will successfully quit smoking. It may take multiple attempts for a smoker to manage to be successful, so that the old adage "try and try again" makes for an excellent suggestion.

From a self-regulatory perspective it makes sense that successful cessation is associated with multiple attempts. Self-regulation is viewed as a strength that develops through practice and the acquisition of new skills and strategies. Thus, just as the learning to become an Olympic athlete involves practice and the development of new skills, quitting smoking may require considerable effort over the long term. From this perspective, cessation is better viewed as a process than as an all-or-none phenomenon (DiClemente & Prochaska, 1982; Prochaska, Velicer, Guadagnoli, Rossi, & DiClemente, 1991).

Prochaska and DiClemente (1982, 1984, 1986) developed a transtheoretical model of change with four stages of change (precontemplation, contemplation, action, and maintenance) and ten processes of change (consciousness raising, self-liberation, social liberation, self-reevaluation, environmental reevaluation, counter conditioning, stimulus control, reinforcement management, dramatic relief, and helping relationships). In their model, the interaction of stages of change and processes of change with self-efficacy and decisional balance affect a person's decision to take action, to maintain change, or to relapse. This model has been used to predict behavioral change in a variety of domains, such as smoking cessation, recovery from alcoholism, and alleviation of emotional distress. DiClemente (1994) notes that individuals go through the cycle many times before successfully quitting smoking: "Individuals who have successfully changed an addictive behavior make at least three to five unsuccessful attempts before being successful" (pp. 188–189).

How do smokers quit on their own? Glasgow, Klesges, Mizes, and Pechacek (1985) studied smokers who agreed to stop smoking in order to win a trip to Disney World. They found that the smokers who were successful quit "cold turkey" rather than slowly withdrawing. Moreover, they found that successful abstainers rewarded themselves for their abstinence and used positive cognitive self-statements to reinforce their quitting behavior. In general, those who are successful at quitting on their own make comprehensive prior plans and use a greater number of strategies in dealing with temptation (Perri, 1985). Successful individuals are more committed to the process of change and have a specific course of action in mind (DiClemente, 1994). Successful ex-smokers are also motivated by intrinsic rather than extrinsic motivation (Curry, Wagner, & Grothaus, 1990; Harackiewicz, Sansone, Blair, Epstein, & Manderlink, 1987). Curry, Wagner, and Grothaus (1991) assigned smokers to either an intrinsic (personal confidence) or extrinsic (prize-drawing) incentive for abstinence. They found that those quitting for intrinsic reasons were twice as successful in quitting smoking.

Relapse and Failures

"To cease smoking is the easiest thing I ever did; I ought to know because I've done it a thousand times" (cited in Grunberg & Bowen, 1985) is the well-known phrase expressed by Mark Twain that best describes the typical success that smokers have in maintaining cessation. Almost all smokers try to stop occasionally. Some last for months, some last for weeks, some for days, and some for a mere few hours. Indeed, some 80% of smokers relapse within six months of abstinence (Carmody, 1993).

Smoking relapse is commonly assumed to be due to the withdrawal sensations associated with abstinence, which include tension, depression, irritability, restlessness, insomnia, inability to concentrate, and increased hunger (Shiffman & Jarvik, 1976). Cravings to smoke and other withdrawal symptoms are strongest in the two weeks following cessation, after which they gradually diminish. However, some ex-smokers report cravings for as long as nine years following abstinence (Jarvik, 1979). Of course, cravings and discomfort do not by themselves necessarily lead to relapse. Rather, it appears that certain situations and temptations are likely to promote disinhibition (i.e., lapse) among those trying to abstain.

From a learning theory perspective, certain situations and conditions become associated (through classical conditioning processes) with smoking (Poulos, Hinson, & Siegel, 1981). In the parlance of contemporary theories, these events and cues represent high-risk situations for those trying to maintain abstinence (Marlatt & Gordon, 1985). These high-risk situations often produce a minor lapse (i.e, the person has a cigarette). Lapse-activated processes may then come into play. If the person attributes the lapse to internal, stable, and global factors, then full-blown relapse is likely to occur (Marlatt, 1985). Curry, Marlatt, and Gordon (1987) found that people who feel personally responsible for having a cigarette often feel guilty for having done so. These individuals were especially likely to relapse to smoking following their single transgression.

The notion that situational cues interfere with cessation attempts has been widely influential to the understanding of smoking and alcohol relapse (for a review, see Niaura et al., 1988). There have been an impressive number of studies that have examined situational determinants that lead to lapse and relapse (e.g., Baer, Kamarck, Lichtenstein, & Ransom, 1989; Bliss, Garvey, Heinold, & Hitchcock, 1989; Carmody, 1993; Curry, Marlatt, & Gordon, 1987; Marlatt & Gordon, 1985; O'Connell, Cook, Gerkovich, Potocky, & Swan, 1990; O'Connell & Martin, 1987; Shiffman, Read, Maltese, Rapkin, & Jarvik, 1985). These studies have identified three situations that are predictive of smoking lapses: smoking cues, negative distress, and alcohol. The next sections will examine these.

Smoking Cues   One trigger of smoking lapses is the sight or smell of cigarettes or being in an environment that is strongly associated with smoking (Niaura et al., 1988). For instance, meals, social settings, and the sight of smoking paraphernalia (matches, cigarettes, ashtrays) may trigger urges to smoke. The most powerful cue may be the sight of other people enjoying or smoking cigarettes (Bliss et al., 1989; O'Connell & Martin, 1987). Other smokers not only provide visual and olfactory cues, but they might actively encourage the putative ex-smoker to "try just one." It may be that continuing smokers have to justify their own behavior (i.e., smoking) and therefore make comments to the ex-smoker such as "one cigarette won't hurt," or "you've got to die from something." These individuals also might actively discourage cessation attempts by pointing out how unlikely the person is to successfully quit smoking (Sorensen, Pechacek, & Pallonen, 1986). Indeed, nonsupportive family and friends have been reported as major barriers to successful behavioral change (Cohen & Lichtenstein, 1990; Heatherton & Nichols, in press). Those trying to quit smoking should avoid other smokers, at least until they develop specific coping strategies to deal with them. Similarly, avoiding the cues typically associated with smoking (i.e., stimulus control procedures) is an important component of any effort to stop smoking (Ashton & Stepney, 1982; Pechacek, 1979).

Emotional Distress   The single most important trigger for smoking urges is negative emotional states (Ashton & Stepney, 1982; Brownell, Marlatt, Lichtenstein, & Wilson, 1986; Marlatt, 1985). Shiffman (1982) found that negative emotional states were responsible for more than half of all relapses in smoking cessation. These states include boredom, frustration, anger, anxiety, and depression. Marlatt (1985) noted that it is not uncommon to hear statements such as "Everything was going well [i.e., with my attempt to quit smoking] until I failed my statistics exam. I was feeling low and decided a cigarette would cheer me up" (p. 38). Marlatt observed that social conflict is one major source of emotional distress. For instance, having a fight with one's spouse or a problem with co-workers may be predictive of a return to smoking. The link between negative affective states and urges to smoke has not been fully elucidated. It may be that those trying to quit misattribute negative mood states to smoking withdrawal such that they interpret their mood state as being due to the absence of cigarettes. Conversely, it is possible that those trying to quit misattribute withdrawal sensations to other factors, such as situational factors, and interpret normal withdrawal sensations as being in a bad mood.

The key issue is the perceived ability to cope with the negative emotional state (Brownell, Marlatt, Lichtenstein, & Wilson, 1986; Marlatt, 1985). When individuals feel overwhelmed with the situation they may be less able to deal with temptations, such as having a cigarette. Coping resources play an important role in Marlatt's relapse prevention model (Marlatt, 1985; Shiffman et al., 1985). Some have argued that a variety of different coping strategies work well, and that it is not the specific strategy but the number of strategies used that predicts successful resistance to temptation (Bliss et al., 1989). However, others have argued that some coping strategies are less effective, with ineffective responses being of lower quality, more vague, and less appropriate in the specific situation (Shiffman et al., 1985). Stevens and Hollis (1989) have advocated using an individually tailored skills-training approach. They argue that those trying to quit need to develop and rehearse specific techniques for dealing with stressful situations. By learning to resist temptation, smokers develop increased self-efficacy for future abilities to cope (Garcia, Schmitz, & Doerfler, 1990), which is similar to our notion of enhancing self-regulatory strength by exercising control. Thus, specific strategies that are rehearsed and practiced appear to help those trying to quit smoking.

Alcohol   Situations that involve the ingestion of alcoholic beverages have been identified as triggers for smoking lapse and relapse (Ashton & Stepney, 1982; Brandon et al., 1986). Shiffman (1982) found that many relapse crises occurred when the person trying to quit smoking had been drinking. As discussed earlier, the relation between alcohol and smoking is quite complex. It may be that alcohol disinhibits smoking cessation attempts because of its generalized disinhibitory qualities (in the same way that it disinhibits aggression, eating, and sexual behaviors). However, the social correlates of alcohol consumption are also likely to promote smoking lapses. Alcohol is usually consumed in social settings, and many heavy drinkers are also smokers (Sobell et al., 1990). Hence, many taverns are known—much to the chagrin of nonsmokers—for the veil of smoke which lingers during normal operating hours. Thus, those trying not to smoke are confronted with all manner of smoking cues, including the sight and smell of easily available cigarettes, the social pressures from smoking peers, the easy-going ambience that is reflective of relaxing and enjoying oneself, and the tastes and physiological effects of alcohol. Alcohol may also interfere with remembering appropriate coping strategies (Shiffman et al., 1985) so that people who have a few drinks are less able to bring their practiced coping strategies to bear. Considered together, all of these cues may combine to overwhelm even the most resistent smoker.

SUMMARY AND CONCLUSION

Smoking is extremely addictive, indeed possibly more so than alcohol or heroin. The high costs of smoking induce many people to want to limit their smoking and many others to try to quit. Failure at these self-regulatory efforts are common, partly because of the physical craving for nicotine. Weakness, fatigue, distress, and other factors contribute to self-regulatory failures. Although underregulation is common, misregulation has also been noted. Some people, especially women, seem to take up smoking in the often false belief that it will significantly enhance their attractiveness (or in some cases, their health) by fostering weight loss.

The highly addictive nature of nicotine would suggest that smoking would be one phenomenon where the person is least implicated as acquiescing in self-regulatory failure. Yet the current social and legal sanctions against smoking have resulted in making it difficult for smokers to smoke, and so they often must go to considerable lengths to light up. As a result, their acquiescence is undeniable. Smoking offers one potentially compelling general model for how acquiescence works. The inner desire and impulse become very strong, and resisting or overriding it is difficult. Eventually the person decides to give in. After this decision is made, the person then may become an active participant in doing precisely what he or she had resisted and had resolved to avoid.

Contemporary research on smoking cessation has emphasized coping with high-risk temptations and situations (Carmody, 1993; Marlatt, 1985). Smokers who are trying to give up smoking are instructed to identify these high-risk situations and plan specific strategies for dealing with temptation (Shiffman et al., 1985). Practicing and rehearsing the specific coping strategies are an important component of successful self-regulation (Stevens & Hollis, 1989). Learning new ways of dealing with negative emotional states is one important goal of contemporary therapy (Carmody, 1993). Thus, learning how to regulate affect more appropriately may inoculate the smoker when he experiences interpersonal conflict or other negative affective states. This view seems to indicate once again that self-regulatory failures arise when people place too much emphasis on regulating their feelings first and go about managing their moods in ways that contribute to self-regulatory breakdowns in other areas. Generally, the person trying to quit smoking has to develop the necessary self-regulatory skills to control emotion and resist temptation.

11

A Sampler of Other Behavioral Control Problems: Gambling, Shopping, and Aggression

Pick almost any behavior, and it is likely that someone has trouble controlling that behavior. Indeed, some social critics have noted that almost all behaviors have at one time been considered to be addictions (Kaminer, 1993; Peele, 1989). Researchers have described behavioral control problems such as hair pulling (Christenson, Mackenzie, & Mitchell, 1991), house cleaning (Dillon & Brooks, 1992), and facial picking (Stout, 1990)—as well as more mundane behaviors such as stealing, gambling, exercising, and shopping. Extreme and self-destructive versions of these behaviors are grouped in the *DSM–III–R* (the diagnostic manual of the American Psychiatric Association) under the title "Impulse Control Disorders Not Otherwise Classified," with the defining characteristics including giving in to an impulse or temptation to perform the behavior, an increase in nonspecific tension before engaging in the behavior, and some sense of relief or gratification from performing the behavior (APA, 1987). The clinical manifestations of these behaviors probably share a common diathesis, in that they all seem to represent forms of an affective disorder (McElroy, Hudson, Pope, Keck, & Aizley, 1992). However, not all people who have self-regulatory difficulties with these behaviors meet criteria for a genuine clinical disorder. In this chapter, the self-regulation of a number of important behaviors (gambling, shopping, and aggression) is considered.

GAMBLING

Las Vegas strikes some people as a monument to all manner of disinhibited behavior (hence its nickname "Sin City"). Of course, Las Vegas is best known for gambling. Its infamous Strip is lined with dozens of casinos that cater to appetites and impulses 24 hours every day of the year. Thousands of tourists flock to these casinos each day, hoping that they will beat the odds and leave as winners. Gambling, like drinking alcohol, is considered by many to be a harmless recreational pursuit when practiced in moderation. Whether it be playing the local state lottery, betting on horse races, or the once-a-year wager on the Super Bowl, gambling is part of the fabric of contemporary American life. Indeed, 71% of Americans reported wagering nearly $250 billion during 1989 (Lesieur, 1992). Thus, gambling is a common and relatively benign pastime for many Americans.

For some individuals, gambling represents considerable problems with self-control. Gambling problems have been around since Roman times and much has been written about them over the centuries. For instance, Jean Barbeyrac, writing in 1737, stated "the passion of gambling gives no time for breathing; it is an enemy which gives neither quarter nor truce; furious and indefatigable" (cited in Orford, 1985, p. 31). Lesieur (1992) estimated that 1–2% of the adult population can be considered pathological gamblers with another 2–3% considered problem gamblers. Volberg and Steadman (1989) interviewed 1750 residents of New Jersey and Maryland. They found that between approximately 2.5 and 3.0% of the sample were problem gamblers and 1.4% were pathological gamblers. Most surveys of gambling problems suggest that men are more likely to develop problems than are women. For instance, Volberg and Steadman (1989) found that in their survey close to 70% of the problem gamblers were male. Because these individuals tend to gamble a lot, a large percentage of the total money gambled each year is probably wagered by this group (Lesieur, 1992).

Compulsive gamblers differ from recreational gamblers in a number of ways (Peck, 1986). Notably, recreational gamblers can quit gambling at any point in time, whether they are winning or losing. Moreover, gambling does not interfere with other aspects of their lives; they do not risk losing their jobs or ruining their marriages, nor do they tend to criminal behaviors to support their habit (Lesieur, 1992). Finally, their sense of self-esteem does not appear to be linked to winning as it does for compulsive gamblers (Peck, 1986).

Underregulation of Gambling

The major conflict for recreational gamblers is that they want to have fun but they do not want to lose too much money. Thus, when they set out for Las Vegas they may set daily limits for themselves on the amount they are willing to gamble. They may also set time limits on their gambling, such as that they will walk away from the tables after so many hours, whether they have won or not (Peck, 1986). Many recreational gamblers know in advance that they will probably lose money, and they consider the loss to be part of the cost of entertainment. Thus, it is not uncommon to hear gamblers make such claims as "I would have spent $40 on drinks at a bar, so why not lose $40 at gambling?" Similarly, people who buy a ticket or two on the lottery, or who make a once-a-year wager on the Super Bowl, do not appear to have self-control difficulties.

Another limiting factor that promotes self-regulation of gambling is access. Although almost all states have some legal form of gambling (notably lotteries; Lesieur, 1992), casinos are a different matter. Most people do not encounter casinos in their daily lives, and there are relatively few cues to initiate gambling. Thus, other than purchasing lottery tickets or playing cards with friends, most Americans do not have easy access to places in which to gamble. Someone who wants to gamble usually has to travel some distance to do so (unlike food, cigarettes, or alcohol, which are easily purchased). Marlatt (1985) described the case of a compulsive gambler driving from San Francisco to Seattle. Following a fight with his wife he purposefully altered his route from the safety of traveling through Placerville, California, to the high-risk route of driving through Reno. (He justified the change by saying he just wanted a more scenic route). Stopping in Reno, the man "happened" to wander into a casino to find change for a parking meter. He then decided he would just test his luck with one bet. One bet led to another, and eventually it took his wife three days to get him out of the casinos following his loss of self-control. Thus, this man had to go a considerable distance out of his way to set up his self-regulation failure: a remarkable illustration of acquiescence in one's own self-regulatory breakdown. Marlatt (1985) observed that people trying to get over their problematic self-control behaviors (i.e., alcohol, cigarettes, or gambling) often seem to set up high-risk situations, which they then use to justify their resultant lapse or relapse. It is hard to justify losing control of gambling in Seattle, but it is not so difficult in Reno.

It is not surprising that people who have easy access (such as those who live in Las Vegas) have higher rates of compulsive gambling than do those who live in areas without legalized casinos (Lesieur, 1992). After all, many people move to Las Vegas because of the appeal of gambling. However, places that have legal casinos (such as New Jersey or the province of Quebec) have rates of problem gambling that are nearly double the rates in places that restrict gambling (such as Iowa; Lesieur, 1992). It is hard to be in Las Vegas without some exposure to gambling: Indeed, every major grocery store, many gas stations and restaurants, and most taverns have on-site gambling, such as slot machines or poker machines. The bright lights of casinos are difficult to ignore, especially the new bright spotlight of the Luxor Hotel, which can be seen clearly from the upper stratosphere. Thus, easy access and constant reminders increase the odds that someone will become a problem gambler.

When problems do occur for recreational gamblers, they are often due to reduction of monitoring and transcendence failure. Attention is systematically directed to immediate cues and kept away from anything that would facilitate monitoring oneself. Casinos seem to be set up entirely to hinder self-monitoring cues. For instance, it is impossible to see outside from inside a casino (the few windows and doors are often blacked out), so that it is impossible to tell whether it is day or night. There are no clocks on the walls, and dealers are reluctant to tell patrons the time. There are no mirrors or other self-referencing cues. There is plenty of noise and confusion and the sound of slot machines paying off serves as a constant reminder that some people are winning money— a compelling cue that the next bet may be the one that brings a big payoff. The drinks are free and free-flowing, and as we saw alcohol impairs both self-monitoring and transcendence. Moreover, the drinks are brought forth by scantily dressed cocktail servers who seem to promote disinhibition of sexual impulses. In short, everything is set up to disinhibit the potential gambler, primarily in order to part him from his money. After all, the odds are in the casino's favor; if people stay long enough, the vast majority will eventually leave money behind. The trick, from the casino's standpoint, is to keep people around long enough so that they do lose money. The free drinks, food, and gifts are used not only to entice recreational gamblers, but to keep them happy so that they will not leave.

Of course, compulsive gamblers probably are less influenced by the casino atmosphere than casual ones. However, this does not mean that they do not get caught up in the gambling process. One of the hallmarks of the compulsive gambler is that he or she becomes completely immersed in the gambling situation: "The desire to remain in action is so intense that many gamblers will go for days without sleep, without eating, and even without going to the bathroom" (Lesieur, 1992, pp. 43–44). Transcendence utterly disappears, in other words. Such gamblers may be especially loathe to leave a machine that they expect will pay off at any moment. Barbeyrac, in describing a gambler in 1737, noted, "it seems that gambling had acquired the right to occupy all his thoughts" (cited in Orford, 1985, p. 31). Indeed, the selective appeal of gambling may be that it helps people escape from their problems. Dickerson (1991) found that gamblers reported starting a session of gambling in order to "forget troubles" (p. 326). The onset of a gambling session was associated with negative affective states, such as frustration, disappointment, and concerns about money problems (Dickerson, 1991; Peck, 1986). Thus, just as some may seek out alcohol or food to escape their problems, some individuals may use gambling to regulate their negative affective states. In any case, the inability to see beyond the immediate cues and stimuli seems to be a common feature of a binge or frenzy of gambling, consistent with general pattern of transcendence failure.

There is also a great deal of inertia to casino gambling. The rhythmic nature of putting money in a coin slot becomes automatic, and it is an amusing sight to see people putting in money so fast that they barely stop to notice whether they won or lost. Dickerson (1991) describes an ongoing research project comparing those who gambled infrequently (once or twice in their lives) with those who gambled more frequently (at least once a month). This research examined the rate of betting and persistence during a session of playing a poker machine. They found that low-frequency players did not play for very long (mean session = 17 min). These players played at an inconsistent rate, often speeding up after a win and slowing down after a big win. When losing, these players tended to speed up for a few minutes (expecting a big payout—see later discussion of the gambler's fallacy), but they quit as they realized they were losing more than they had intended to risk. In contrast, high-frequency players persisted for much longer during a session (mean session = 40 min). These players also tended to persist much longer after failure than after success. This was especially true if they started the session when they were in a bad mood. Rachlin (1990) described a similar pattern of behavior among gamblers. He noted that gamblers often make large bets following a string of losses, partially in an attempt to recoup past losses. Similarly, McGlothin (1956) observed that bets on long shots at the racetrack tend to occur more during the later races than during the early races. People appear to make riskier bets at the end in order to try to break even. In these situations people appear to literally "go for broke."

The process of gambling for compulsive gamblers can be viewed as following the standard pattern of spiraling distress. Compulsive gamblers often have money problems because of their gambling, and many also have problems at their jobs and in their families. They decide to go gambling partially because they expect that gambling will cheer them up (Dickerson, 1991), but also because they see the opportunity to solve all of their problems with a big win. Indeed, most compulsive gamblers have had at least one major win in the past (at least a few months' salary), which according to Peck (1986) is what convinces the gambler that such an event could happen again. Unfortunately, most individuals who gamble lose, and so gamblers exacerbate their bad moods with the frustration and disappointment that come from relinquishing their money. Rather than stopping when they are losing, compulsive gamblers begin a process known as *chasing* (Dickerson, 1991; Peck, 1986; Rachlin, 1990). They expect that their luck will turn and they will eventually win, and so they start to take greater risks and bet larger amounts of money. To gamblers, this seems like a rational strategy: After all, if they quit they have no chance to win back their losses. Of course, larger bets mean larger losses, and therefore many compulsive gamblers end up losing much more than they can afford. In many cases they will fall into financial ruin because of their gambling, leading many to engage in illegal activities (especially passing bad checks or embezzling from their employer) in order to obtain money to continue gambling (Lesieur, 1992). They may justify their stealing by promising to pay back all the money when they finally have their big win. Eventually, gamblers lose their jobs, alienate family members, and get in way over their heads. "At this time, compulsive gamblers entertain four options: imprisonment (others controlling), running, suicide, or seeking help. The compelling urge to gamble is still there!" (Peck, 1986, p. 464).

Misregulation of Gambling

The odds of winning at games of chance are usually not in the gambler's favor. The chances of winning a major lottery are less than one in a million, and all casino games favor the house rather than the bettor (Wagenaar, Keren, & Pleit-Kuiper, 1984). Thus, most people who gamble lose. The essential question was best summed up by Rachlin: "Why do people gamble and keep gambling despite heavy losses?" (1990, p. 294).

We noted in our coverage of excessive persistence that such patterns of misregulation are often mediated by irrational or faulty beliefs. Such beliefs appear to be very central and powerful in excessive gambling. Thus, a first answer to Rachlin's question seems to be that many gamblers view chance outcomes as being partially controllable. An influential series of studies by Ellen Langer and her colleagues showed that many individuals have an "illusion of control" over objectively chance-determined events (Langer, 1975). Generally, individuals attribute success at chance events to themselves, while they tend to blame failures on external factors such as bad luck or to random events. In some situations people act as if they had control over chance outcomes. For instance, Langer (1975) gave some subjects a lottery ticket (i.e., chosen by the experimenter), whereas others were allowed to pick their own lottery ticket. Those who chose their own ticket were much less willing to part with the ticket, even though objectively the chances of winning were independent of who actually chose the ticket. It appears that by allowing people to choose their own ticket it gave them a great sense of control over the outcome. Similarly, Langer (1975) found that allowing subjects to "practice" a game of chance led them to have higher expectations for future success. In another study, Langer and Roth (1975) found that an early pattern of winning led subjects to believe that they had an increased ability to predict future outcomes. Based on these early successes, subjects may have concluded that they were skilled at the task (when, in reality, success rates were manipulated by the experimenter and beyond subjects' control).

Likewise, Gilovich (1983) found that people had different explanations for wins and losses: "Subjects tended to undo their losses and bolster their wins" (p. 1115). That is, people tend to discount losses to factors that are uncontrollable, whereas wins are seen as confirming personal skill at predicting outcomes (see also Gilovich & Douglas, 1986). Moreover, sometimes people view losses as near-wins. In all-or-none lotteries (i.e., you either get all of the numbers or you lose), people who get five out of six numbers view losing as missing just slightly. Such near-wins (even though they are objectively losses) may inspire future gambling behavior (Gilovich, 1991). In general, these patterns of overconfidence in judgment lead people to persist at behaviors that appear doomed to failure (Janoff-Bulman & Brickman, 1982).

People also view luck as a personal attribute, and there are stable individual differences in the extent to which people feel that they are lucky and believe that they will continue to be lucky (Darke, 1993). For instance, even those who are well acquainted with the laws of probability sometimes have rituals or superstitions that indicate they believe luck is controllable (perhaps they knock on wood, or carry a lucky charm). Henslin (1967) observed that gamblers often have magical practices that they employ to increase their chances of winning. For instance, crap-shooters blow on the dice, and if they drop the dice they assume they "dropped their luck." (The magic trick to fixing dropped dice is to rub them on the table [Henslin, 1967].) Rubbing the dice on a lucky person is also considered to be a prudent course of action. These rituals are done presumably because they enhance the sense of personal control over chance events.

Wagenaar and Keren (1988) described considerable evidence that people view luck as partially due to chance—but also due to skill. Thus, some people seem to be lucky whereas others seem to be unlucky. Each of us may have lucky days or lucky numbers, and these lucky qualities are believed to offset the chance aspects of the situation. For instance, everyone knows that the chance of winning the lottery is small, but someone does win. The winner is seen as being a lucky person rather than as having won solely because of chance (Wagenaar & Keren, 1988). The notion of being a lucky person is clearly related to the illusion of control. Being lucky means picking good numbers or making a particularly astute bet. Thus, luck almost always refers to the actions of the player rather than to the mechanics of the game and personal involvement is necessary for luck. As mentioned, some people believe that they are generally lucky and others believe that they are unlucky (Darke, 1993). Such thoughts are probably the result of biased recollections of past success and failure experiences (Gilovich, 1991). People who believe that they are generally lucky show an illusion of control that contributes to persistence at gambling. Paradoxically, because continued gambling is typically associated with failure, it may be that "lucky" people end up bigger losers than are those who are "unlucky."

People view luck as having an influence on outcomes that is separate from that of chance. Chance is generally used to describe seemingly arbitrary or surprising outcomes, whereas luck is used to describe seemingly consistent patterns in outcomes (Wagenaar & Keren, 1988). Moreover, people often tend to see patterns emerge from truly random data (Gilovich, 1991). For instance, Gilovich, Vallone, and Tversky (1985) examined the perception of lucky streaks in basketball shooting (the so-called hot hand). Although the vast majority of basketball enthusiasts believe that players have shooting streaks, in reality, one shot appears to have no statistical relationhip to future shots, apart from overall ability.

One general and well-known form of the misperception of random events is called the *gambler's fallacy* (Wagenaar, 1988). The gambler's fallacy is the belief that one can predict future chance events from knowing the outcome of past ones, because future and past outcomes must add up to a definite score. For example, people assume that flipping a coin should result in an equal number of heads and tails, but they conclude falsely that if it was heads last time it is more likely to be tails the next time.

In keeping with the gambler's fallacy, many gamblers who have lost a number of bets in a row assume that their luck is due to change at any moment. Consider the situation where the roulette ball landed on red five times in a row. What is the probability that it will land on red the next time? It is, of course, the same, independent of whether it was red or black the previous time. Thus, even if the ball has landed on red 1000 times, this does not affect the odds that the ball will land on red during the next trial.

People generally fail to notice that streaks occur naturally, and so when they finally notice streaks they tend to attribute them to luck rather than to chance (Wagenaar & Keren, 1988). Thus, some gamblers will wager large amounts following an apparent streak of bad luck because of the mistaken belief that this string of bad luck makes future success more likely. The ball can't always land on red, they suppose, so it must eventually end up on black. Moreover, because they expect that one bet may help them recoup their losses, gamblers may make risky bets (Rachlin, 1990) or follow irrational strategies (such as betting on long shots; Wagenaar et al., 1984) especially when they think that a losing streak is due to end. Thus, the gambler's fallacy contributes significantly to the misregulation of gambling.

Because gamblers associate luck with skill and believe that personal abilities make winning more likely, gambling may be related to one's overall sense of self-esteem. For instance, low self-esteem is related to feeling that one is generally unlucky (Darke, 1993). Moreover, people with low self-esteem may be less likely to take risks in general because they have fewer psychological resources to deal with the consequences of failure (Josephs, Larrick, Steele, & Nisbett, 1992). Baumeister et al. (1993) found that high self-esteem subjects made riskier bets when their abilities were called into question. Their heightened (and in some cases misplaced) sense of self-confidence makes high self-esteem people likely to believe that they will be successful in their risky endeavors. Thus, in contrast to alcohol and eating (in which excess is linked to low self-esteem), it might be the case that compulsive gambling is linked to high self-esteem. Some support for this proposition is found in Peck's (1986) description of the typical compulsive gambler. Gamblers are described as "strongly competitive . . . They also seem to like and thrive on challenges and are attracted to situations that are highly stimulating" (p. 463).

Peck (1986) concluded that compulsive gamblers differ from recreational gamblers in that the former group invests self-value into winning or losing. Gamblers like to emphasize that they are skilled in what they are doing and that their big wins are due to personal efforts rather than to chance. Thus, gamblers are well known for bragging about large wins, which would be nothing to brag about if there were no skill involved. Of course, some so-called games of chance actually do involve some degree of skill. Poker, for example, requires knowing the statistical odds of obtaining different hands, and interpersonal skills (e.g., being a good bluffer) also affect outcomes. Similarly, the skill of card counting (which involves an amazing feat of memory) allows blackjack players to increase their odds of beating the house. Still, these are exceptions; most games of chance are really games of chance. Gamblers take pride in being lucky, as much as or more than they take pride in being skillful.

Even frequent gamblers make irrational and risky decisions largely based on their expectations of luck (Wagenaar et al., 1984). Thus, some gamblers take pride in their skill level and have great expectations for future winnings. However, because winners and losers are determined mainly by the luck of the draw (i.e., chance), compulsive gamblers may be investing their sense of self into something over which they have little control. Continued losses over time may lead to diminished self-esteem (Peck, 1986), which may promote further gambling behavior. "This sense of personal inadequacy and loss compels the gambler to return to the comfort of gambling. If winning occurs, the sense of loss is removed, and an euphoric sense of self-confidence returns" (Peck, 1986, p. 463). Of course, if they do win, the heightened confidence probably also increases the likelihood that the gambler will return to the table. If he loses, the resultant negative mood may make him more likely to seek gambling as a way to escape his mood. Thus, gambling is motivated by both wins and losses, and it is easy to see why it is so hard for the compulsive gambler to stop.

SHOPPING

Many millions of Americans love to shop. Although making the occasional purchase is a necessary part of human existence, many people consider shopping and buying to be pleasurable and they spend a great deal of time browsing, trying things on, and looking for specific items. As a society, we tend to spend much more than we can afford. Some 83% of U.S. households carry consumer debt (other than mortgages), usually on credit cards (Arthur, 1992). Of course, not all of these people are overextended, but more than half say that they spend more than they should or more than they have (Arthur, 1992). Most financial problems associated with shopping are due to occasional, or not so occasional, impulse purchases (Rook, 1987). One study found that up to 60% of all department store purchases fell into the impulse category, depending on the category of item purchased (Bellenger, Robertson, & Hirschman, 1978). Rook (1987) observed that the modern conveniences of shopping (credit cards, home shopping networks, cash machines, 24-hour retail stores) make it easy for people to make impulsive purchases. Buying something on the spur of the moment can be quite pleasurable, such as when you find an item you've been seeking for some time, or when you encounter an item that you think would be fun to have. For most people, the occasional impulsive purchase does not represent a self-regulatory problem. However, when people consistently spend more money than they have, or when they purchase items that they do not need, their shopping behavior represents a considerable problem with self-control.

For some people, buying becomes an all-encompassing part of their daily lives. These compulsive purchasers experience strong impulses to shop and buy (Faber, 1992) and they often experience financial problems as a result of their spending habits. Arthur (1992) estimated that 15 million Americans could be described as compulsive shoppers, and she proposed that they generally fall into three major categories: those who go on buying binges once in a while (usually following an upsetting event); those who must shop at least once a day and often many times per day; and those who appear compelled to buy several of the same item, whether they need that item or not. For example, one compulsive buyer commented that he felt compelled to purchase neckties, even though he seldom wore them.

Most studies have found that women are more likely than men to be compulsive shoppers (Faber, 1992; O'Guinn & Faber, 1989). However, few studies have examined the demographics of shopping compulsion and little is known about the true extent of self-regulatory problems with shopping. Similarly, there have been few systematic studies on compulsive buying, and therefore all findings must be considered with caution. Although problem buying was observed as early as 1915 (by Kraepelin, cited in Faber, 1992), there have been relatively few empirical studies of compulsive purchasers. There have been some clinical accounts of compulsive shopping; these usually consider compulsive shopping to reflect general impulse control problems produced as part of an affective disorder (McElroy, Satlin, Pope, Keck, & Hudson, 1991). The next section considers the situational and individual factors that promote self-regulatory problems with shopping.

Underregulation of Shopping

Impulsive buying is fundamentally a problem of failing to delay gratification (Rook, 1987). Although most theoretical models of consumer behavior paint the purchaser as someone making rational choices given situational constraints (Foxall, 1990), others have noted that many shoppers are not rational at all (Faber, 1992). Hoch and Loewenstein (1991) have referred to irrational purchases as time-inconsistent preferences. Essentially, their model is similar to delay of gratification in that immediate rewards and temptations outweigh long-term planning, and the person makes unintended purchases. They argue that the key issue is a changing reference point, such that situational contingencies make delaying or giving into temptation more or less likely. For instance, items that are in physical proximity increase the desire to purchase an item, which underscores the impression that transcendence failure is a central cause. Similarly, social comparison processes may lead the person to feel deprived if she does not purchase the item. Hoch and Loewenstein (1991) concluded that relative deprivation is an important determinant of desires to obtain a commodity and that consumers need to engage in a number of self-regulatory strategies (such as distraction or trying to increase willpower) in order to avoid temptation.

Compulsive shoppers report being overwhelmed by their desires to achieve immediate gratification through purchasing. It seems likely that these comments are a way of articulating the failure of transcendence (and possibly of rationalizing the purchase). Consistent with the notion of transcendence failure, Rook (1987) analyzed micronarrative reports of impulse buying and found that spontaneous desire and disregard for long-term consequences were an important component of impulse buying. For instance, samples of statements made by his subjects included "I saw the ice cream and immediately wanted some" (p. 193), "There is no stopping me. The urge just comes over me all at once and seems to take control. It is such an overwhelming feeling that I just have to go along with it" (p. 195), and "To hell with everything else. I want it and I'm going to get it" (p. 195). Thus, the prototypical impulsive buying episode occurs when people encounter something that is immediately tempting. Long-term consequences (such as potential poverty) seem relatively unimportant and the person makes the decision to go ahead and buy the item.

In one respect, however, these comments do differ from what we have generally seen, namely in their reference to the overwhelming, irresistible power of the impulse (as opposed to the weakness of the person to stop it). Such comments imply that the level of acquiescence is negligible; the person simply cannot stop himself or herself from making the purchase. But is that plausible?

It does not take much to see that considerable acquiescence is involved in self-regulation failure in shopping. Making a purchase in a store requires a series of acts which could almost certainly be resisted. The person must take the item to the checkout counter, notify the store personnel of the intention to purchase, and count out money. Sometimes even more is involved, such as furnishing forms of identification and signing documents in connection with the paying. In our view, the characterizing of an impulse to buy something as irresistible or overwhelming is preposterous and is presumably recognized as such by the people who say such things; they are speaking metaphorically. They may indeed choose to ignore their options for self-stopping and allow themselves to become entirely focused on the desirability of the item they are purchasing. But it is hard to believe that the wish to buy something can be so strong that the person could not possibly resist it. Shopping is almost certainly a central example of acquiescence in self-regulation failure.

Shoppers furnish some of the liveliest examples of the role of attention in self-regulation failure. The major determinant of the rising impulse to purchase is, not surprisingly, encountering the item. Seeing an advertisement on television or coming across the item in a store gives rise to the impulse to purchase it. Rook (1987) found that consumers often described fantastic forces that captured their attention. Subjects reported being hypnotized or mesmerized by the object. Some subjects described the object as having animate properties: "I was standing in the grocery store checkout line, and the candy bar was staring there at me," "The pants were shrieking 'buy me'," "I had gone to a different department, but the sweater was following me. I felt like it was pulling me back to the men's department, where I finally bought it" (p. 194).

That consumers are likely to make impulse purchases has not escaped the attention of marketers and shopkeepers. Impulse items are often kept near the cash registers so that people encounter them while they are making other purchases. Huge displays are set up to capture people's attention, and store layouts often require people to walk past impulse items. As was noted in the section on the regulation of eating, internal states may have a profound influence on whether people buy these point-of-purchase items. Nisbett and Kanouse (1969) found that overweight shoppers purchased less food if they were hungry than if they had recently eaten (such as having a small sample of food; Steinberg & Yalch, 1978). Normal weight subjects tended to do just the opposite: They purchased more food when they were hungry than when they had just eaten. Tom (1983) found that the majority of unplanned purchases by obese subjects were food items located at the end of aisles or as part of point-of-purchase displays. Thus, internal cues interact with external cues to trigger impulses for food purchases.

There are other situational determinants of impulsive purchasing. As was the case with alcohol, eating, gambling, and tobacco, people are more likely to make impulsive purchases when they fail to self-monitor or when they become immersed in the situation. For instance, purchases at auctions are often impulsive, and people who get caught up in the excitement of bidding can often spend a great deal more than they intended. Similarly, compulsive shoppers appear to become totally preoccupied with thoughts of shopping. For instance, one of Rook's (1987) subjects was a 68-year-old man who impulsively purchased a painting: "For me it was a total mind filling experience. I could only think of one thing, and that was where I was going to put it when I got home" (p. 193). For some compulsive spenders, they report purchasing items solely because they want to buy *something*, not because they want to buy the specific object. They are lost in the world of shopping and sometimes they do not even realize what they are purchasing. One subject reported to O'Guinn and Faber (1989), "I couldn't tell you what I bought or where I bought it. It was like I was on automatic"; another said "I really think it's the spending. It's not that I want it, because sometimes I'll just buy it and I'll think, 'Ugh, another sweatshirt'" (p. 154). Such comments seem to reflect a cessation of monitoring.

Distress and Shopping

A common slogan seen on bumper stickers and T-shirts reads, "When the going gets tough, the tough go shopping." This slogan (and others like it, such as "shop 'til you drop") link shopping with negative affective states (Faber, 1992). Many therapies (such as weight loss treatments) suggest that people buy themselves treats when they are feeling down, as a way of rewarding the self for hard work. Thus, the implicit message is to use shopping as a way to battle depression: You shop to escape your troubles and problems. Many of those who have conducted research on compulsive shopping note that mood regulation is an important determinant of impulsive purchases (Faber, 1992; Rook, 1987; O'Guinn & Faber, 1989). For many compulsive shoppers, purchasing items added excitement to their lives: "Respondents described feeling a 'tingling sensation,' a 'warm feeling,' or a 'surge of energy' when struck by the impulse to buy" (Rook, 1987, p. 194). Rook's subjects described the shopping experience as particularly exciting, even thrilling or wild! Many of the subjects reported that buying something cheered them up when they were feeling down. O'Guinn and Faber (1989) noted "Informants often spoke of their need to lead more exciting lives, 'feel alive,' and be stimulated by their surroundings" (p. 154). Thus, impulsive purchases appear to lead to an emotional uplift for compulsive shoppers. However, this high is often followed by regret and remorse, as compulsive shoppers realize that they spent more than intended.

The pattern of shopping as a way of regulating emotion fits another pattern that we have often seen in this book, namely the self-regulatory preoccupation with affect. When people concentrate on regulating their emotions, they often do things that violate other self-regulatory programs. Shopping is a good example, because one may cheer oneself by shopping—but then end up being sorry when the bills arrive.

Feelings of guilt and remorse following impulsive purchases do appear to be common among people who have self-control problems. For instance, O'Guinn and Faber (1989) found that "compulsive buyers typically were ashamed and embarrassed by their behavior and felt that others could not understand it" (p. 155). Rook's (1987) subjects also referred to guilt and tended to see impulsive buying as evil winning out over good.

These observations suggest that the familiar, lapse-activated pattern of spiraling distress may be a potent factor in compulsive shopping. People shop as a means of escape or in an effort to improve their mood. However, the temporary increase in positive mood is short-lived, and soon feelings of regret, shame, and remorse surface. In addition, acting in an impulsive manner has definite and specific consequences: Spending money you don't have causes financial problems, alienates or angers your spouse, and brings disappointment with the self for giving in to temptation. One compulsive shopper summed up the negative feelings: "I don't drink, I don't smoke, I don't do dope. But, I can't stop. I can't control it. I said I can't go on like this. . . . My husband hates me. My kids hate me. I've destroyed everything. I was ashamed and I just wanted to die." (O'Guinn & Faber, 1989, p. 155). To escape from these negative moods the person once again goes shopping, and the cycle starts all over.

Misregulation of Shopping

One of the primary characteristics of compulsive shoppers is that they spend a great deal of time fantasizing. In the same way that an obese person may fantasize about being thin, or a gambler may fantasize about the big win, shoppers like to fantasize about owning things. O'Guinn and Faber (1989) note that fantasy episodes played an important role in buying decisions. For instance, one subject wrote "I'm thinking, 'Gee, wouldn't it be nice to really be able to do this, to really be able to afford this,' knowing all along full well that I couldn't possibly" (p. 153). Given that this group is prone to make social comparisons, they also spend time imagining what it would be like to have more money and be able to purchase whatever they liked (Hoch & Loewenstein, 1991). This fantasy life may create a false reference point so that individuals feel that they are deprived in comparison to most people. Thus, compulsive buying can be misperceived as an attempt to buy only what is deserved.

The notion that compulsive shoppers feel relatively deprived fits in well with the finding that they typically have low self-esteem (Faber, 1992; Rook, 1987). Indeed, Faber (1992) argued that compulsive shopping may be one strategy employed by people to bolster a low sense of self-esteem. Faber (1992) proposed that shopping can increase self-esteem in a number of ways. First, some shoppers pride themselves on being "good shoppers," in that they often know the best place to get bargains and they shop only at sales. They can take pride in shopping as a skill and be recognized by their peers as someone who is knowledgeable about saving money. Similarly, compulsive shoppers often know a great deal about the products that they purchase, and so others may come to them for advice on purchases. Thus, they come to be recognized as experts.

Another important form of self-esteem bolstering comes from interactions with sales staff. "Shopping for clothes, cosmetics, and gifts creates an interaction in which the salesperson dotes, telling buyers how attractive they look, what a good parent they are, or how much someone will appreciate them for buying this gift" (O'Guinn & Faber, 1989, p. 154). In a famous scene from the movie *Pretty Woman*, Richard Gere takes Julia Roberts shopping to cheer her up. He tells the manager that "what we really need here is to be sucked up to." The Beverly Hills store manager assures him that he's come to the right store—and the right town for that matter—for that sort of treatment. Even though people might rationally know that salespeople are simply performing their duties, most people still get an uplift from the positive compliments paid to them.

Compulsive shoppers may even develop strong relationships with the salespeople. For instance, some people call into the Home Shopping Network simply to speak to the on-air personalities, who always tell them what wise and prudent shoppers they are. Some order so much merchandise that they get to be friends with the delivery drivers. "I know the UPS drivers in my neighborhood real well. They all wave and say hello by first name," said one of O'Guinn and Faber's (1989) respondents. Sometimes the person makes purchases simply to please the salesperson. They want to be liked, and they believe they will only be liked if they purchase something, preferably something big. Purchasing something big also allows them to appear as if they were rich and powerful. Thus, sometimes compulsive shoppers like to shop in very exclusive (and expensive) shops and to use elite credit cards to give the impression that they are important and to be respected. As mentioned earlier, this helps them lead a sort of fantasy life, one in which they are confident and rich, rather than besieged by feelings of low self-esteem (Faber, 1992).

AGGRESSION

A very different form of self-regulation problem concerns the control of aggressive or violent impulses. As we write this, American society is consumed with debate about the rising tide of violence in seemingly all walks of life—on the streets, in homes and families, at work. Although the focus of popular discussion is on external control, ranging from gun laws to prison terms, the notion of self-regulation failure is a neglected but powerful aspect of the issue.

One important work has broken ground for looking at aggression in terms of self-regulation failure. Gottfredson and Hirschi (1990) proposed in *A General Theory of Crime* that most criminality reflects low self-control.

To support and elaborate their theory, Gottfredson and Hirschi presented considerable evidence that the majority of crimes conform to the following pattern. First, crimes offer immediate gratification, rather than deferred rewards. We have already seen the capacity to delay gratification as a prototype of effective self-regulation; the lack of this capacity among criminals characterizes them as low in self-control.

Second, most crimes are very easy and simple to commit. Few skills need to be acquired or used. Criminals are often not very competent at other things, whereas people who are successful in other ways tend to avoid committing crimes. Most crimes are rather spontaneous, and the obvious lack of planning is consistent with the view of them as impulsive actions. Crime seems to offer a way to get money without working hard, to get sex without courtship or commitment, and the like. Gottfredson and Hirschi reported that the vast majority of crimes are committed near the residences of the offenders, consistent with the view that they merely act on an impulse. Most burglars, for example, walk from their homes to the places they rob. As for sticking up places of business, it is no coincidence that convenience stores are the places most commonly robbed, because of their very convenience.

Third, crime involves risk, which makes it seem like an adventure. Committing crimes tends to be exciting. Katz (1988) characterized the quest for "sneaky thrills" as one major reason that people commit minor crimes such as shoplifting, because the majority of shoplifters could afford to buy what they stole, and most shoplifted objects are soon lost or forgotten. Subjective accounts of shoplifting also emphasize the thrill. Committing such crimes amounts to a form of affect regulation: it is a way of injecting some excitement into an otherwise humdrum or boring life. Gottfredson and Hirschi contend that the impulsive quest for excitement through illicit activity is consistent with the general pattern of people who lack self-control.

An alternative explanation of crime might regard it as an instrumental, even rational activity, especially as a way of getting money or solving problems. In fact, however, the evidence indicates that the vast majority of crimes bring neither large nor lasting benefits. Most robberies and burglaries bring less than $100, and the money gained in them is soon spent or lost (Gottfredson & Hirschi, 1990; Katz, 1988). This too is consistent with the emphasis on short-term, proximal goals and immediate gratification.

Consistent with other patterns of self-regulation failure, and consistent with the strength model, crimes are more likely to occur late in the evening or night. Gottfredson and Hirschi found that crimes of personal violence in particular tend to occur disproportionately between 1:00 and 2:00 A.M. (One exception to this general pattern is burglary; about half of all burglaries occur during the day, mainly because many dwellings are left unoccupied when people are at work, thereby making daytime the best opportunity for burglars.)

The notion that crimes occur because of a weakness of inhibitory strength is also supported by the evidence about alcohol. Steele and Southwick (1985) concluded that alcohol does not increase violent impulses or motivations, but it reduces inhibitions against them, and so intoxicated people become more willing to do things that they would like to do anyway but would override if they were sober (see also Zillman, 1993). The pervasive involvement of alcohol in violent crime suggests that it facilitates aggression by weakening inhibitors.

One bit of evidence raises a challenge to the argument that aggression derives from weak self-control, however. In a study of a sample of incarcerated violent offenders at a men's prison, Berkowitz (1978) noted that "again and again, the offenders described their behavior as driven, almost compulsive, in nature" (p. 154). Although we have noted that obsessive and compulsive behavior is generally described in terms of one's own weakness rather than the power of the impulse, Berkowitz here seems to be suggesting that the angry impulse to aggress was overpoweringly strong. If one takes these men's comments at face value, violence arises because such men have unduly strong violent urges rather than from the fact that their self-control and inhibitory capacity are unduly weak.

But can one take them at face value? Men who have been imprisoned for violent assault seem an unlikely group from whom to expect self-reports of being weak and unable to control oneself. Assuming that the assault was done as a way of upholding the honor and prestige of the self in response to the insults or disrespect of strangers (the prototype scenario Berkowitz presented), one must regard the violence as an effort to prove one's strength and dominance, and to characterize it as giving in to personal weakness would seemingly contradict that meaning.

Another possibility is that the angry impulse to aggress was indeed extremely strong, but that the power of the impulse itself reflected a deficiency at self-control—specifically, at affect regulation. The weakness was thus in allowing oneself to become violently angry, even if once the man was sufficiently angry there was little he could have done to control his behavior even if he had had a great deal of self-regulatory strength at that point.

Berkowitz's (1978) own conclusion seemed to straddle this distinction. He characterized these men as lacking strong inhibitions against aggression, but he also characterized them as quick to become extremely angry (p. 155). He also found reason to question the self-reports of overwhelming anger making any control possible, however. In a revealing anecdote, he quoted one man who was imprisoned for beating up his wife's lover. During the beating, he had seized a wine bottle and broken it to make a very dangerous weapon. At this point, however, he had stopped himself with the thought that if he used the broken bottle, he would probably kill the other man, which was more than he wanted to do (and which obviously would have had highly negative long-term consequences for himself). He therefore set down the bottle and simply worked the wife's lover over with his fists. Thus, the man's violent impulses were subject to self-control when he chose to use it, whether because of conscience or of considerations of self-interest.

If one is skeptical of this example, similar instances can be observed in nearly any football game. The job of many of the defensive players is to tackle the opposing quarterback as quickly as possible, and the norms in today's professional game are also to do it as roughly as possible (which accounts for the remarkably high rate of serious injury among quarterbacks). These players typically motivate themselves by stoking up anger and other strong urges to aggress against this individual, and moreover their aggression is usually increased further by the frustration of having to battle past the quarterback's teammates who strive to thwart the progress of the defenders. The intense emotional satisfactions that attend successfully "sacking" the quarterback are also undeniable, and indeed the professional league had to make rules restricting the celebratory antics of defensive players who have successfully tackled the quarterback.

What is remarkable, however, is how effectively these powerful and violent men can abruptly override their aggressive actions when the rules require. At one moment, one has finally eluded the blockers and is closing in on the quarterback with the intention of knocking him violently to the ground; less than a second later, one has to stop oneself and run by him innocuously, either because he has thrown the ball or because he has stepped out of bounds, either of which makes tackling him illegal. It is not surprising that occasionally someone fails to override the aggressive impulse at the final split second and illegally hits the quarterback; what seems more impressive is the fact that most of the time self-stopping is successful under those circumstances. Given the immense sums of money that currently accompany success at the sport, it is generally agreed that people go all out, including using every emotional and other technique to become maximally aggressive against the foe; yet people can rein it in almost instantaneously. These very strong impulses are not irresistible, however. When the rules are set up to punish irresistible impulses, those impulses become much rarer.

Thus, several factors point toward acquiescence even if people seem to want to describe self-regulatory failure in terms of being overwhelmed by irresistible impulses. The tendency to speak in terms of strong impulses may have two causes. First, the perpetrators of violence may prefer to describe their aggressive impulses as strong than to describe themselves as weak (in the sense of not being able to control themselves). Second, the legal system encourages people to describe violent impulses as uncontrollable, because more lenient penalties are used, and in some cases (such as temporary insanity) people are declared not guilty if they perpetrated violence that stemmed from a supposedly irresistible impulse.

In that connection, the concept of a subculture of violence may be revived. That concept was introduced in the late 1960s to explain the higher crime rates among lower socioeconomic and minority populations; the implication was that some people grew up in subcultures where violence was valued and so perpetrating aggressive crimes was a means of achieving prestige and respect. A series of research studies (including Berkowitz's own) tested the subculture of violence hypothesis and either failed to find support for it or found contradictory evidence, and most experts seem to have discarded the concept by now (see Tedeschi & Felson, in press, for a review).

The relevance of self-regulatory failure, and particularly of acquiescence in self-regulatory failure, may show the way in which part of the concept of a subculture of violence can be salvaged. Perhaps the subculture does not place positive value on violence, as was originally hypothesized. But perhaps the subculture does support and reinforce the belief that violent impulses cannot be resisted or controlled. Just as certain cultures foster the view that sexual impulses cannot be resisted by young males or by females or by whatever group, there may be cultural groups that believe that certain provocations make people so angry that they cannot stop themselves from acting violently. If, as we have suggested, that belief is objectively false—in other words, if violence can indeed usually be controlled and overridden—then people must allow themselves to be carried away by such impulses in order to act on them. And a culture that supports the view of irresistible, violent impulses would foster violence by encouraging people to acquiesce in being carried away.

We noted that the strength model of self-regulatory failure depicts it as a personality resource, and so if violence does arise from weak self-control, it should do so in dispositional or chronic patterns. There is considerable evidence that this is the case. For one thing, most criminals tend to be repeat offenders; in Berkowitz's sample, for example, most were "persistent troublemakers," and in fact 83% had previous criminal convictions. (Indeed, over half of them had more than six previous convictions, despite the fact that the majority of crimes do not lead to convictions.) Similar findings are commonplace.

Even more to the point, Gottfredson and Hirschi (1990) cited considerable evidence that most crimes occur in the context of a lifestyle that is marked by a variety of self-control failures, both legal and illegal. As they put it, criminals do not generally specialize in one kind of crime but rather commit a variety of crimes. They also tend to show other patterns reflecting lack of self-control, including sexual misbehavior, substance abuse, unstable relationships, involvement in unplanned pregnancy, impulsive spending, proneness to accidents and similar misfortunes, gambling, and many more. They noted that criminals tend to come from neglecting families or broken homes, in which they did not receive consistent parental supervision of the sort that is likely to instill self-regulatory skills. Gottfredson and Hirschi's view of criminality thus makes a compelling case for dispositional weakness of self-regulation as a major cause.

In general, it appears that people have some inhibitions against violent or aggressive actions, and so escape from self-awareness appears to be an important facilitator of violence. Mullen (1986) analyzed a large sample of incidents involving lynch mobs, and he concluded that when loss of self-awareness was facilitated by the situation (particularly because the ratio of mob members to victims shifted attention away from the individuals in the mob), the lynchings tended to be especially violent and atrocious. At a much lower level of aggression, Beaman et al. (1979) found that Halloween costumes that fostered loss of self-awareness tended to make children more prone to steal extra candy.

The reduction of self-awareness is presumably a major reason that alcohol often figures so prominently in aggression and violence. Indeed, it appears that alcohol is sometimes used deliberately to make people more aggressive or to help people cope with their own inner struggles over performing destructive acts. Gelles (1974) suggested that, because drinking is a "socially approved excuse for violent behavior, individuals who wish to carry out a violent act become intoxicated *in order to carry out the violent act*" (p. 117). Throughout history, soldiers going into battle have often been given an advance dose of alcohol, despite the fact that alcohol impairs certain motor skills and might therefore reduce optimal performance. Keegan (1976) documented this general pattern and furnished several vivid examples of this policy, including the World War I battle of the Somme, in which the first wave of the British assault ended up heavily drunk because they were mistakenly given both their own and the second wave's grog ration. (Moreover, they did this heavy drinking prior to the 7 A.M. assault, and generally on an empty stomach, because soldiers tended to avoid eating before battle out of fear of infection from a stomach wound.) Later that morning, when they were running toward the German machine guns and trenches (and setting some records for casualties in the process) they were heavily intoxicated.

Participating in the large-scale murder of unarmed citizens, especially women and children, is presumably one of the most objectionable and hence aversive of violent tasks. Evidence suggests that many participants in such activities rely heavily on alcohol to enable them to overcome their inhibitions. Lifton (1986) noted that the physicians who performed the selections (for gassing) at the Nazi concentration camps were nearly always heavily drunk. Browning (1992) said that the police responsible for shooting Jews during the Holocaust were liberally supplied with liquor and made full use of it. In particular, he recorded one incident in which the firing squad was so drunk that the majority of them passed out for an hour or two during the operation, and the killing had to be suspended for a period of time during the afternoon because the shooters were sleeping off their drunken stupor. Likewise, Wyden (1983) described several similar incidents from the Spanish Civil War (in which mass executions of civilians were increasingly common). Firing squads in that war too received heavy doses of brandy starting very early in the morning. In one theatre of that war, the man in charge of executions did most of his work in a cafe, starting at 6 P.M., and was rarely seen in a sober state.

Transcendence failure may also be an important factor in aggression. It appears that many people who commit violent acts have become immersed in the immediate situation. Gottfredson and Hirschi (1990) described how many violent acts arise simply because one gets angry at a stranger who taunts or insults one, and so one attacks him; indeed, to consider the incident in a rational and long-range context, the violent rebuttal of a stranger's opinion is certainly not worth going to prison (see also Berkowitz, 1978). By the same token, domestic violence occurs because the spouse's derogatory comments or the child's crying create a narrow focus on the intolerable present, so that the person lashes out. Katz (1988) concluded from his sample of accounts of violent crimes that an important effect of rage is to impair the ability to transcend the immediate situation: "Rage focuses consciousness completely on the here-and-now situation with an unparalleled intensity" (p. 31).

According to Averill (1982), all cultures on earth that regulate violence by law allow or prescribe leniency for persons who committed their transgressions in extreme emotional states. This special legal consideration for crimes committed "in the heat of passion" indicates a widespread belief that intense emotional experience (especially anger) can lead to a failure of one's ability to transcend the immediate situation and see the long-range consequences of one's actions.

In connection with the concept of transcendence, it is also worth reconsidering the example from the Berkowitz study in which the man broke the bottle to use in the fight but then set it down and attacked his rival with only his fists. Obviously, such a response transcends the immediate situation, because his proximal goal of hurting his enemy would be best served by using the broken bottle. To override that impulse and realize that killing his enemy would be detrimental to his own long-term self-interest would therefore require some ability to transcend the immediate situation. It is thus noteworthy that in the middle of his angry and jealous rage, he *could* briefly reconsider his intended action from that long-term perspective—and then resume (with only his fists) his violent attack on the person anyway! His actions did land him in prison, indicating that he may not have optimally served his long-term self-interest, but he did avoid what would almost certainly have been a much worse prison term had he murdered his opponent.

Before concluding our consideration of the self-regulation of aggression, it is worth asking whether there are any lapse-activated, snowballing patterns. We have focused mainly on how people cross the line so as to begin violent behavior; are there any factors that enter into the picture after the person has begun aggressing?

Probably the most important cause of escalating violence is desensitization. It is fairly certain that people have the most difficulty and inhibition regarding their first criminal or violent act. After performing several such acts, the subjective difficulty is greatly reduced. Browning's (1992) account of the socialization of ordinary, middle-aged German reserve policemen into the task of killing Jews offers a stark contrast between the agonizing trauma many suffered from participating in their first massacre and the much more casual attitude with which they fulfilled their duties after several months of such work. Of particular relevance was his account of a later massacre in which the majority of the force, by now well accustomed to such actions, was supplemented by the arrival of a batch of new recruits who participated in such killings for the first time. In testifying about this massacre many years later, the old hands gave rather vague and indistinct accounts of it, consistent with the view that it was not a particularly salient memory to them; but the new arrivals provided clear and vivid recollections of the same event, presumably because it stood out in their memories as their first time.

A second lapse-activated pattern may well operate, however, although to do an adequate treatment of it would take the present discussion far afield. This is the cycle that develops when the victim of initial aggression responds violently. The escalation of violence through reciprocal provocation is probably the norm. One person mocks another; the second responds with an obscene insult; the first shoves; the second hits; and it escalates until one person lies on the floor with a knife wound. Such depictions of escalating aggression are common in research accounts of crime and violence (Berkowitz, 1978; Katz, 1988; Toch, 1992). The initial aggressive action is almost certainly not regarded at the time as the first step in a lethal attack, but it elicits a response from one's victim that seems to justify an even more violent subsequent move. In this way, aggression breeds subsequent aggression, consistent with many of the snowballing patterns we have seen in various self-regulation failures throughout this work.

Zillman's work on excitation transfer provides one physiological mechanism that could contribute to such a lapse-activated pattern (see Zillman, 1993, for a review). In his view, escalating conflict can be conceptualized as a series of provocations, each triggering an excitatory reaction that dissipates slowly. If a second aggressive action occurs before the physiological effects of the first aggressive action have fully dissipated (as frequently happens in interpersonal confrontations), the second physiological reaction combines with the tail end of the first, increasing the physiological arousal and readiness for aggressive action. If a third aggressive action occurs before the tail ends of the first two have dissipated, then excitation and proneness to aggression continue to build.

SUMMARY AND CONCLUSION

The research literature on gambling indicates that there are two important factors that interfere with self-regulation. First, casinos and other gambling establishments manipulate attention in systematic ways that impair ordinary self-regulation. They seek to prevent transcendence and self-monitoring, so that people become immersed in the immediate fascination of betting. Alcohol and other factors likewise help undermine ordinary inhibitions.

Second, faulty beliefs about luck and illusions of control promote seemingly irrational beliefs about games of chance, consistent with general patterns of misregulation and destructive persistence. Gamblers seem motivated to misperceive the causes of both success and failure in ways that will support further efforts at gambling. Lapse-activated patterns may intensify compulsive gambling patterns over time, such as when accumulating losses (which have been explained away) create a wish to recoup one's money by making a big score, so the person bets more and more.

Compulsive shopping and buying follow many of the same patterns as the other self-control problem behaviors and indeed can often be understood as a variation on delay of gratification patterns. People become tempted when confronted with appealing merchandise. Compulsive shopping is also in many cases another example of placing affect regulation ahead of other forms of self-regulation: People shop to cheer themselves up, and only later do they discover that their inability to afford what they have bought will land them in serious trouble. Transcendence failure is of central importance, to the extent that people become immersed in the immediate situation and in their desire to own the particular item (which in many cases they may later regard as trivial or undesirable).

The resulting negative consequences cause them to feel ashamed and embarrassed, but to escape those consequences they go shopping again. Self-perceived shopping skill, admiration from others, and interactions with salespersons contribute to a boost in self-esteem experienced by compulsive shoppers.

Violence seems to be a very different sort of behavior from shopping, yet self-regulation patterns are similar in some respects. Current evidence points toward self-regulatory failure as a powerful cause of both individual acts of violence and the criminal lifestyle in general.

Self-esteem was implicated in all these forms of self-regulatory failure. Gamblers tend to be highly confident that they can win, whereas shoppers are often trying to compensate for a deficient sense of self-esteem. Violence often results from a blow to self-esteem, particularly when someone holds a high opinion of self but feels that others do not share that favorable appraisal.

We also conclude that people acquiesce in all these forms of self-regulatory failure. Gamblers seem very cunning and strategic in arranging for themselves to lose control during a gambling binge. Shoppers speak of being carried away by a desire to buy, but they show considerable awareness of rules and procedures in carrying out their purchases. Likewise, violent individuals often present themselves as moved by irresistible impulses, but ample evidence suggests that violent impulses can be resisted when necessary and desirable. In all cases, people appear to seek out settings—casinos, large sales, or violent subgroups—that encourage the relinquishing of self-control.

Part IV

Conclusion

12

Self-Regulation: Prospects, Problems, and Promises

Keep the faculty of effort alive in you by a little gratuitous exercise every day. That is, be systematically heroic in little unnecessary points, do every day or two something for no other reason than its difficulty, so that, when the hour of dire need draws nigh, it may find you not unnerved or untrained to stand the test. Asceticism of this sort is like the insurance which a man pays on his house and goods. The tax does him no good at the time, and possibly may never bring him a return. But if the fire does come, his having paid it will be his salvation from ruin. So with the man who has daily inured himself to habits of concentrated attention, energetic volition, and self-denial in unnecessary things. He will stand like a tower when everything rocks around him, and his softer fellow-mortals are winnowed like chaff in the blast.

—William James, *The Principles of Psychology*

In this book we have taken close looks at a series of spheres of self-regulation failure, one at a time. The final chapter will therefore undertake to summarize some of the common patterns that occurred repeatedly in multiple spheres. This will allow us to reexamine some of the main ideas about self-regulation failure that we proposed at the beginning of the book. In addition, however, we wish to offer some more speculative reflections that these several years of researching self-regulation failure have stimulated. In the spirit of this concluding chapter, therefore, we shall minimize our use of references (quite unlike the rest of the book) and focus on our own general thoughts and impressions.

HOW SELF-CONTROL FAILS

We begin by reviewing the main patterns and issues we have covered with regard to self-regulation failure. In the opening chapters of this book, we noted that self-regulation consists of three components, and so a breakdown or problem with any of them could conceivably be responsible for self-regulation failure. The three components are standards, monitoring, and strength.

Standards

Standards are essential as the targets of self-regulation, and when they are lacking or inconsistent, self-regulation cannot be effective. Problems regarding standards surfaced particularly in two areas, self-management and impulse control.

Regarding self-management, the issue is often a lack of standards. We noted that having both short-term and long-term standards (also known as proximal and distal goals) appears to be necessary for successful self-management. People who lack either one show deficits in self-management.

Another problem arises when people have unrealistic or inappropriate standards. Certain circumstances seem to cause people to set inappropriate goals, with the result that self-regulation is seriously compromised. Thus, people with high self-esteem who are subjected to ego threats seem particularly prone to taking on unrealistic aspirations and doing other things that are destructive for self-management.

Regarding impulse control, the problem is often one of conflicting standards. People have severe approach–avoidance conflicts with many appetitive patterns, such as alcohol and overeating. They are attracted to the activity by the pleasure and satisfaction it offers, but they are held away by their own resolutions, often motivated by recognition of problems that attend overindulgence.

Monitoring

Effective self-regulation depends on monitoring oneself, that is, comparing oneself (and one's circumstances) to the standards. When people are unable to monitor themselves, or when they cease monitoring themselves, self-regulation tends to become ineffective.

Problems with monitoring tend to be associated with underregulation. In some cases people simply do not bother to watch what they are doing. Money problems reflected this pattern; some people simply do not keep track of how much they are spending, with the result that their bills and expenses outstrip their capacity to pay. More generally, an increase in monitoring is often an effective way to improve self-regulation, whether of eating or drinking or studying or exercising or performing a task. Conversely, when people reduce their monitoring of their own behavior, self-regulation is more likely to break down. We noted evidence, for example, that breaking a diet seems to be associated with a serious reduction in monitoring of one's eating behavior.

Some factors seem to interfere directly with the capacity to monitor oneself. When people are under stress, distracted, or preoccupied, it becomes more difficult to continue their ordinary monitoring practices. Alcohol in particular seems to interfere with monitoring. Alcohol may therefore contribute to a broad variety of self-regulation failures, from aggression to task performance—and to escalating abuse of alcohol itself.

Strength Failure

Self-regulation may still fail even if the person has clear goals or standards and monitors himself or herself effectively. This is because it is nonetheless necessary for the person to override whatever action or desire or thought or emotion needs to be changed. We noted that the capacity to bring about these changes in oneself seems to conform to a strength model.

Many of the patterns covered in this book conform to the strength model. Self-regulation failures of many types are most likely to occur late in the day, when people are tired; this is true for dieting failures, aggressive acts, alcohol, and other substance abuse patterns. It is common knowledge that task performance, endurance, and persistence decline with tiredness. Furthermore, there is evidence that coping with stress consumes some of people's strength, and so many forms of self-regulation break down when people are under stress. (Even the aftereffects of stress have been shown to decrease self-regulation in some ways, consistent with the view that once one's strength has been depleted, it takes some time to recoup.) People resume smoking, drink too much, eat too much, stop exercising, lose control of their emotions and moods, and more. Emotional distress was repeatedly implicated in self-regulation failure, and although there are several possible ways that emotional distress could produce those effects, it is very plausible that distress consumes or undermines the person's self-regulatory strength.

The concept of strength has long-term implications as well. A person's degree of self-regulatory strength should be generally consistent across time, although conceivably someone could build up his or her strength through exercise. There was some evidence consistent with those views, but more research is needed. At present, the most relevant findings show that people who are prone to self-regulation failures in one sphere are more likely to have them in other spheres too, which does seem to imply that they have some form of chronic, undifferentiated weakness at self-regulation.

Misregulation

Two main sources of misregulation emerged in this work. One concerns false or misleading beliefs about the self and the environment. Such faulty knowledge leads people to make unrealistic commitments, to make nonoptimal trade-offs between speed and accuracy, to use counterproductive strategies in the attempt to control their emotions, and to persist in doomed endeavors.

The other main source is trying to control things that cannot be directly or properly controlled. Focusing self-regulatory efforts on one of these areas is doomed to fail. Thus, people tend to fail when they try directly to alter their mood states. Choking under pressure is likewise a matter of trying to control the uncontrollable, in the sense that choking occurs when people try to override the automatic quality of their skills and consciously control the process of performance. Trying to suppress thoughts directly falls into this category, because efforts at thought suppression are at best partly successful. Trying to control impulses directly—in the literal sense of preventing oneself from having the desires—is far less likely to succeed than focusing on preventing oneself from acting on those impulses.

A variation on this second form of misregulation is that people focus their regulatory efforts on the wrong thing. One common problem we saw was that people focus on regulating their emotions rather than dealing with objective problems; for example, the procrastinator may put off working on a task because to work on it creates anxiety, but even though this strategy will often minimize anxiety, in the long run it is self-destructive. Likewise, people may overeat, abuse alcohol, smoke cigarettes, or quit jobs or tasks as a way of ducking unpleasant emotional states and demands, but in the long run such coping mechanisms may be worse than nothing. A standard finding in the coping literature is that emotion-focused coping is often less adaptive and helpful than problem-focused coping. One important reason may be that emotion-focused coping allows the objective problem to get worse by neglecting the objective causes while one focuses on one's subjective reaction.

Attention and Transcendence

When people lose control of their attention, self-regulation is in jeopardy. Many forms of self-regulation failure begin with a loss of control over attention. Thus, for example, when people fail to delay gratification, the failure is often preceded by a shift of attention onto the immediately available rewards. Control over thoughts is lost when attention runs wild. Emotional states spin out of control when people are not able to move their attention off of some distressing event or stimulus. Task performance deteriorates when people cannot concentrate on the relevant information. Dieting, abstaining from alcohol, and other forms of regulating appetitive behavior break down when the person's attention fixes on the forbidden activity or stimulus.

Transcendence failure was repeatedly found to be a particularly important form of attentional problem. Many forms of self-regulation failure arise when people lose the capacity to see beyond the immediate situation or salient stimuli. Self-regulation often requires one to adopt a long-range context or higher value or abstract frame of reference. When, instead, attention is narrowly focused in the here and now, the capacity to override impulses or delay gratification or calm unwanted feelings or persist at an unpleasant task is reduced.

The effects of emotion on self-regulation failure may well be mediated by transcendence failure. Emotion tends to keep attention focused on the immediate stimulus (which is why some effective ways of controlling emotion emphasize cultivating an attitude of transcendence). In the grip of powerful emotional state, the person may be unable to look past the availability of a bottle of whiskey or a gun or a cheesecake and may therefore succumb to such temptations.

Lapse-Activated Patterns

Our analyses frequently indicated the need to use two panels of causes in order to explain self-regulation failure; for convenience, we have labeled the second set of causes as *lapse-activated*. The first set of causes prompts the initial lapse or misstep, that is, the initial infraction of a self-regulatory regimen. Other causes then come into play, however, and transform the small misstep into a full-blown binge. The latter factors can be said to promote snowballing, and serious self-regulation failure only occurs when such snowballing produces a large breakdown, but there must already be some lapse before snowballing can happen.

The best example of snowballing resulting from lapse-activated causes was alcohol abuse. Initial drinking can occur for a variety of reasons, including false beliefs about the effects of alcohol or the assumption that one is entitled to a small drink as a celebration or as relief from stress. Initial drinks impair the capacity to monitor oneself, however, so that one soon loses track of one's drinking (and with monitoring goes the capacity to control one's drinking). Drinking also seems to enhance the salience and appeal of alcohol and of cues that promote further drinking. Moreover, various beliefs promote the view that an alcoholic loses all control after a single drink, and so such zero-tolerance views may cause the person to believe that it is too late to stop.

The most common form of lapse-activated snowballing, however, was spiraling distress. After an initial breakdown or lapse occurs, people may feel bad, and their response to feeling bad may lead them to do things that compound the problem. This response resembles the pattern we have seen in which people place undue emphasis on regulating their emotions, at the expense of other self-regulatory efforts. The short-term efforts to overcome distress cause them to neglect other self-regulatory efforts, and this neglect in turn leads to more distress as self-control breaks down more and more.

Thus, for example, eating binges or problems occur because dieters feel bad when they eat too much and they eat too much when they feel bad. Shoppers buy things to cheer themselves up, but the realization of having spent money they could not afford causes them to feel worse, and the resulting distress

prompts them to shop again. Gamblers feel bad after losing and become determined to recoup their losses by making a big score, so they make further bets.
Likewise, in procrastination, once the person has fallen behind schedule, working on the task may bring up so much anxiety and worry that the person has to
stop working on the task in order to calm down. Such a pattern will obviously
contribute to further procrastination.

ISSUES, REFLECTIONS, AND SPECULATIONS

The concepts we have reviewed thus far seem adequate to furnish a basic
understanding of self-regulation failure. Although there are certainly enough
areas of ambiguity and unanswered questions to keep researchers occupied for
years to come, there is presently enough knowledge to support the view that the
basic dimensions of self-regulation failure involve standards, monitoring,
strength, lapse-activated causes, misregulation fueled by misconceptions, and
so forth.

At this point we wish to turn to some of the issues that are not so well
resolved. The ideas in this section represent tentative conclusions that we have
reached from these past five years of reading about self-regulation. That is, we
do not consider the evidence conclusive; rather, these are in the nature of our
best guesses based on preliminary evidence. These may therefore be considered
issues for further research.

Sequence of Control

One of the classic articles in social psychology in the 1980s was the analysis of control furnished by Rothbaum et al. (1982). They made the fundamental distinction between primary control, which is the attempt to change the
environment in order to suit the self, and secondary control, which involves
changing the self to fit in to the environment.

Although we have suggested that self-regulation can in many respects be
equated with secondary control, our review has suggested that the theoretical
issues may be deeper and more complex. After all, people do sometimes manipulate the environment in the service of dealing with their feelings or impulses.

When self-regulation is the issue, the theoretical relationship is perhaps
the reverse of the sequence proposed by Rothbaum et al. (1982) for controlling
the world. They assumed that people would always begin by trying to alter the
environment to suit the self, which is why they labeled that form of intervention
primary control; only if it failed, they reasoned, would people resort to changing the self (secondary control). Much of the control that people seek is control
over their environment or things external to themselves; people want control
over their career paths, over their interpersonal options, control over the things

that affect their lives. In these cases, seeking control over their environment is likely to be primary, and control by changing the self will remain secondary.

When self-regulation is the issue, however, the sequence is reversed. In self-regulation, one begins by trying to alter the self directly. Most people can succeed at this most of the time, and so nothing else is needed. That is, most people can exert sufficient control over their appetites, impulses, thoughts, and feelings. For those individuals who repeatedly fail at such control, however, the alternate response becomes one of changing the environment. These few people may have to remove all alcohol or fattening foods or cigarettes or dangerous weapons from their homes, because they find they cannot stop themselves from misusing them when available.

Thus, for self-regulation, the primary and most common strategy is to exert control directly on the self. Only when that fails do people resort to the secondary strategy of altering the environment.

Acquiescence

In this book we have repeatedly found that self-regulation failures involve active participation by the individual. This pattern applied mainly to under-regulation, rather than misregulation. The question of whether people ever acquiesce in misregulation remains an interesting issue for research on self-defeating behavior patterns, but in general misregulation does not seem to involve acquiescence. In underregulation, however, the person does accept and participate in the self-regulation failure.

Popular conceptions of self-regulation failure depict people becoming overwhelmed by irresistible impulses that they are powerless to control. Some of our own concepts may convey similar notions, such as the concept of strength, which when depleted presumably leaves the person a passive and helpless victim of inner and outer promptings. These are caricatures, however, not reality. A brief consideration of the active role people take in their own self-regulation failures should be enough to discredit them.

A more accurate view may be that people do feel that their strength is depleted and their capacity overwhelmed, and so they decide to give up trying to control themselves. Then they go on and take an active role in indulging their impulses.

Thus, a woman who goes on an eating binge continues to participate actively in that she finds the food, puts it in her mouth, and chews and swallows it. Possibly at the moment she abandoned self-control she felt weak and helpless, but afterward (while eating) she is far from helpless. A man who goes on a drinking binge shows the same pattern: He continues to order or prepare drinks and to raise the glass to his lips. Likewise, smokers must exert themselves substantially and creatively in order to indulge in uncontrolled smoking, because American society now places so many restrictions and obstacles in the way of smoking. A performer suffers from fatigue or boredom and allows the self to quit—and then actively withdraws from the performance and does other things instead.

Along the same lines, we cited evidence that people who suffer from obsessional thoughts experience the obsession as a weakness of their capacity for control rather than as some overwhelming power of the troubling thought. In their experience, it is more a matter of giving in to some constant inner nagging than being overcome by an irresistible thought. Likewise, emotions often cannot be directly controlled, but people can control whether they express their feelings and whether they act on them, and those choices do exert a potent effect on whether the emotion increases or dissipates. This particularly includes aggressive actions performed in the heat of anger. Once self-control is abandoned, the person may take a very active role in performing violent, aggressive actions.

Yet more examples can be found in self-management. In order to fail at delay of gratification, one must often make an active choice to take the immediate rewards, and the process of obtaining and enjoying them often involves active participation. Self-handicapping, meanwhile, is generally recognized as a strategic maneuver that the person performs with some degree of planning and insight (including the careful attention to how other people will perceive one's actions). Failing to set proper goals may sometimes be something the person acquiesces in doing, although it may often be merely passive. With procrastination, it seems likely that the person usually acquiesces to some degree, to the extent that the person knowingly puts off working on the task as the deadline approaches.

There are, certainly, some forms of self-regulation failure that do not (or do not always) entail acquiescence. With the self-regulation of inference processes and with self-deception, the degree of conscious acquiescence is difficult to establish (and is controversial among researchers). Choking under pressure is not usually a matter of acquiescing, nor is a failure to concentrate. There are some aspects to alcohol abuse that do not seem to involve acquiescence, such as the fact that once one has become somewhat inebriated, it becomes difficult to monitor one's behavior and regulate further drinking.

Still, there is plenty of evidence that most cases of underregulation involve the clear and active acquiescence by the individual. Self-regulation failure is not so much something that happens to you as something that you allow to happen. This analysis suggests that the crux of the matter is that a momentary loss of self-control is followed by a refusal to reinstate control. The person starts the eating or drinking binge but probably could stop after a few minutes. Yet the notion of stopping does not arise for a long time. The person postpones the issue of stopping, of reestablishing self-control, while indulging in the impulses.

The popular notion of the "irresistible impulse" must therefore be questioned. In recent years this notion has gained ever wider usage in the society, partly as defense lawyers in criminal trials have used it to argue that their clients should not be punished for performing violent actions (because they could not help what they did), and partly because addicts have used it to explain their destructive, pleasure-seeking behavior. The common thread is of course the excuse from responsibility. If an impulse is truly irresistible, one cannot be blamed for failing to resist it.

Undoubtedly there are some cases of truly irresistible impulses—but not very many. A truly irresistible impulse will be enacted regardless of perceived consequences and other rational calculations. Even if someone is holding a gun and threatening to shoot you, you will act on an irresistible impulse. For example, the urge to urinate or to lie down can eventually become irresistible, and under extreme conditions a person will do either of those things even when someone is threatening to shoot him or her for doing so. But overeating, or smoking a cigarette, or beating one's spouse would almost certainly not qualify as an irresistible impulse by that criterion. Self-regulation failure thus seems to involve a relinquishing of control because the exertion of controlling oneself is too unpleasant, and not because the impulse is too powerful.

Once the person has begun to indulge the impulse, it may become that much more difficult to control. We have cited ample evidence of inertia. Yet it is possible to reinstate control; eventually, after all, people do stop whatever "uncontrollable" behavior they are doing. The theoretical focus should perhaps be not on the initial impulse but on the failure to reinstate control. An angry person may have an impulse to kill someone who has provoked him. As we said, it may be impossible to prevent oneself from feeling the impulse, but it is possible to refrain from carrying out the action. Even if the anger becomes so intense that the person cannot stop himself from standing up to stomp out of the room, however, there would be ample opportunity to stop before one goes upstairs, fetches and loads the gun, and returns downstairs to shoot the person with whom one is angry. Yet sometimes people do not stop, just as they often fail to stop consumptive behavior after a few bites of ice cream or a single beer. In all of this, there would seem to be an element of passive self-deception. Having once decided to abandon control, the person refrains from reconsidering, even though in fact considerable self-control is necessary in carrying out the acts that accompany self-regulation failure.

The issue of acquiescence is thus an important one for further study. In our view, the direction that the incoming evidence points toward is greater recognition of acquiescence. We are less inclined now than we were when we started this book to regard people who fail at self-regulation as innocent, helpless victims; they look more like accomplices, or at least willing targets of seduction.

Yet it cannot be denied that there is still an important element of self-regulation failure, in the sense that at some level the person still wishes that he or she did not lose control. Seduction may indeed be a useful model, insofar as seduction involves manipulating consent—as opposed to rape, which simply overwhelms resistance. Although lawyers and other advocates of people who fail at self-regulation may sometimes wish to compare their clients' failures to being victims of rape, in the sense of being an innocent victim overpowered by irresistible forces, self-regulation failure is far more similar to being seduced than to being raped.

This is not to say that biological differences, genetic differences, or differences in past history and background are irrelevant to behavior. There is abundant evidence suggesting that some people are biologically prepared to become much more aroused than others in response to even a slight provocation, whereas others are more likely to seek out risky, thrilling events, others are much more genetically susceptible to becoming addicted to alcohol, and others to becoming obese. But these biological, genetic, or background differences that predispose people to anger, thrill seeking, alcoholism, obesity, and so forth do not lead directly to ruin. Rather, they suggest areas in which self-control is especially important. A person with a past history of alcohol abuse may need to exercise more self-control at a cocktail party than the person who has never wanted more than a couple of drinks at a time. A person with obese parents may need to exercise more control over dietary intake than a person who never gains weight no matter how many french fries or chocolate bars are eaten. These biological, genetic, or background differences merely predispose people to certain weaknesses where self-control will be particularly important—they do not necessarily condemn people to lives of alcoholism, violence, obesity, or danger.

The notion of transcendence failure may provide a valuable way to understand the complex problem that the person acquiesces in self-regulation failure while at the same time wishing that he or she could maintain control. The desire to maintain self-control exists at a high level of meaning, in a long-term context. You are unlikely to light up a cigarette as long as you are thinking about lung cancer and your promises to your spouse that you would quit. In that context, the tempting cigarette is merely an enemy of the self. What happens, however, is that the person ceases to transcend the immediate situation. Remote medical outcomes and spousal promises recede from awareness, and attention focuses on the immediate pleasure that a cigarette would offer. And once the person has allowed himself to limit awareness to the immediate situation, it presents little problem or conflict to *actively* go about lighting up and smoking.

Most of the evidence about acquiescence supports such a model, with one further provision: People often seem to arrange to lose control. They seek out settings or support groups that encourage them to give in to their impulses and even to regard them as irresistible. Whether the issue is a drinking binge, a shopping spree, a gambling frenzy, quitting early on a tedious task, or assaulting someone, people can find a place and a group where a consensus reigns that such actions cannot be prevented. Then and there, they can give up the wearisome inner struggle to maintain self-control by resisting those impulses. Once the decision is made to give up the struggle, people seem to find it easy to avoid raising the issue again, and they go about indulging themselves—sometimes to wild extremes. During this phase they often show considerable autonomy and active ingenuity in carrying out the behaviors they were previously trying to stop.

The issue of acquiescence may be of considerable importance to the future of our society. We suggested in Chapter 11 that the true meaning of a subculture of violence may be that it is a group of people who support each other's belief in the impossibility of resisting violent impulses. If that is correct, then America may be drifting toward being an increasingly violent culture, not because of any positive love of violence, but because of a growing consensus that human violent behavior is often caused by irresistible violent impulses. The parallel rise in addictive behaviors may be similarly fueled by the belief that people cannot control their desires for drugs or alcohol. Although there are powerful interest groups that advocate such views, it seems imperative that the contrary view be articulated and that people be exhorted to regard their behavior as controllable whenever possible. If the view prevails that self-regulation failure is something that happens to an individual and excuses his or her subsequent behavior, then gradually the culture itself will become a context that supports—and in a powerful sense encourages—such failures. Against this view, it seems essential to note the abundant evidence that self-regulatory failure is something that people actively acquiesce in, and that therefore should not excuse violent, addictive, delinquent, or other socially undesirable actions.

Self-Esteem

Although we did not place much emphasis on self-esteem in our initial exposition of self-regulation theory (in Chapter 2), the concern with self-esteem emerged repeatedly as a factor relevant to self-regulation failures. In particular, it appears that ego threats promote a broad variety of self-regulation failures.

Multiple performance patterns, involving both misregulation and underregulation, were related to ego threats. Drinking, quitting or persisting irrationally, and venting aggression all seem to involve breakdowns in self-regulation that occur following ego threats. Indeed, it may be that ego threats are involved in the process of acquiescence. For example, a person may decide that some humiliating experience or loss of dignity is too upsetting to make it worth the effort to exert oneself at maintaining self-control.

Self-management patterns were frequently undermined by ego threats or, in particular, by the wish to assert a highly favorable view of self in the face of some ego threat. Thus, self-handicapping reflects a destructive approach to managing one's affairs that is driven by the wish to protect and enhance favorable views of self. Overconfident, unrealistic, and hence destructive goal setting was also a common response (especially among people high in self-esteem) to ego threats. Procrastination was often motivated by the fear that one will not perform up to exalted expectations.

It must be noted that ego threats tend to produce emotional reactions too, and so some of the effects of ego threats may be due to the emotional distress that accompanies them. These include, for example, withdrawing effort and giving up after initial failure and consuming alcohol in response to ego threat.

We were somewhat surprised several years ago when ego threat emerged in preliminary laboratory pilot work as the most potent cause of self-regulation failure in the paradigm we were using (Baumeister et al., 1993). The literature review for this book has yielded plenty of additional evidence, although much of it has been indirect. Hence, we conclude that one priority for future research would be a systematic investigation of how and when ego threats contribute to self-regulation failure.

There do seem to be other ways in which self-esteem is tied in to self-regulation failure. As we have noted, evidence suggests that impulse-control problems are often linked to self-esteem, although not in consistent ways. Thus, gamblers tend to have high self-esteem, whereas alcoholics and binge eaters tend to suffer from low self-esteem. Many people who write about violent behavior claim that low self-esteem is a cause of violence, but our own reading of those studies suggests that high self-esteem—again, particularly high self-esteem combined with an ego threat—is more likely the major cause. The correlational nature of much of the data raises further conceptual problems, of course. Even if a link between low self-esteem and self-regulation failures were well established, it would not be clear whether poor self-regulation leads to lower self-esteem or vice versa.

Thus, although popular conceptions seem all too ready to identify low self-esteem as a uniform and central cause of self-regulation failure, we regard the relationship between self-esteem and self-regulation as very poorly understood. It is apparent that both high and low self-esteem can be linked to self-regulation failure, in different ways and under different circumstances (e.g., Heatherton & Ambady, 1993). Very possibly there are complex, reciprocal, and multifaceted relationships. In our view, most of the research on how self-esteem is related to self-regulation failure is yet to be done.

Generalized Disinhibition

In surveying the various literatures on self-regulation failure, we have repeatedly been led to conclude that failure is the product of intrapsychic changes that thwart or undermine all regulatory efforts. Such a conclusion is of course quite plausible and perhaps not in itself all that surprising. Yet it has a corollary that may have considerable theoretical interest. The factors that promote self-regulation failure in one sphere should tend to promote the roughly simultaneous failure in all spheres.

For example, if alcohol undermines people's ability to monitor their own behavior, then people who have consumed alcohol should show reduced inhibitions in all spheres. They should become more aggressive, more impulsive, more willing to engage in illicit sex or to break their diets, and so forth. Although alcohol is reasonably well recognized in the general culture as an all-purpose source of disinhibition, the important question is whether other states that reduce self-regulation in one sphere will simultaneously weaken inhibitions in other spheres.

It may also turn out that the matter is more complex. Possibly some factors promote generalized self-regulation failure while others are specific. Thus, a reduction in monitoring, a failure of transcendence, or a loss of strength may promote generalized failure. In contrast, acquiescence may be specific to certain spheres, as are particular beliefs that may foster misregulation or lapse-activated patterns.

Cultural Change

We began the book by noting that self-regulation failure is central to many problems that plague society. One may reasonably ask whether this is universally true or whether something particular about modern American society predisposes it to self-regulation problems.

A historical analysis of self-control is beyond the scope of this book, but several tentative answers can be suggested. It is obvious that self-regulation depends heavily on cultural factors. Among these are beliefs about self-control. For example, it is generally agreed that Europeans lack zero tolerance beliefs about alcohol, unlike Americans, and that—possibly as a result—they have fewer teetotalers *and* fewer alcoholics than America does (e.g., Peele, 1989). A second factor that varies among cultures is the nature and prevalence of temptations. Eating has been a problem for most societies in the history of the world, but the nature of the problem has been the opposite of what modern America faces. More precisely, most societies have faced famines, shortages, and other sources of inadequate food. Ancient Chinese peasants did not go on diets. Compounding the problem is that the material abundance in modern America is combined with advertising, which routinely seeks to encourage consumption (and often does so by trying to stimulate desire). In the view of many critics, the mass media have in general become a choir of voices shouting against self-regulation.

Given these cultural variations, it seems likely that the epidemic of self-regulation problems in modern America is a recent and unusual problem. To understand why it may have arisen, one will almost inevitably have to consider multiple sources. The ubiquitousness and power of the mass media are only one of these.

Much of twentieth-century American society has seen itself as reacting against what it saw as the destructive and possibly absurd excesses of the Victorian (i.e., late nineteenth century) era. Indeed, the term *Victorian* has become a synonym for sexual prudery, against which the twentieth century has waged a long sexual revolution. Middle-class Victorian society had not killed the sex drive, but it had certainly achieved a measure of control over sexual feelings that is now regarded as undesirable and excessive. As is typical for cultural changes in mass attitudes, however, the culture has moved from one extreme to another. Today, in the face of epidemics of AIDS, other venereal diseases, teen pregnancy, and child sexual abuse, some voices are arguing that America has gone too far toward relaxing the control over sexuality. Several newspaper columnists have even created a stir recently by proposing that sexual morality be reintroduced, at least in the form of stigmatizing unwed parenthood ("illegitimacy"). Our intent here is not to enter into this debate but simply to suggest that the general reaction against Victorian self-control may be a factor behind the rising tide of self-regulation problems.

Psychology itself probably bears some of the responsibility. Undoubtedly the most insightful critic of the Victorian mind was Sigmund Freud, and he argued very persuasively that stifling one's impulses and feelings and desires has psychologically harmful effects. We suspect that Freud would be aghast to find that his ideas have been taken as a justification for abandoning self-control on a large scale, but to some extent that is precisely what has happened. The general public's perception of the lesson of Freud does seem to be that one harms oneself whenever one fails to express or enact an emotion or desire (see Tavris, 1989).

A vicious cycle may have arisen. America is also a remarkably tolerant and compassionate society. Its efforts to offer systematic, enlightened help to the afflicted and downtrodden go far beyond what most societies in the past have done. To benefit from this largesse, one need only be a deserving victim. The wish to be free from responsibility for one's misdeeds has made notions of irresistible impulses very broadly appealing. As the number of alcoholics rises, there are more and more people who wish to believe that alcoholics should not be held responsible for their drinking. And as the culture accepts that view, more and more new individuals find that their own drinking is, sure enough, beyond their control. We have already suggested that America's acceptance of the notion of irresistible violent impulses may be an important factor that encourages people to give in to those impulses. What we are saying here is even more broad and general: As the culture believes in and accepts giving in to all sorts of impulses, self-regulation will be systematically undermined.

Still, the main place where self-regulation is instilled is in the parent–child interactions, and so it is to changes in parental socialization that one should look most carefully in order to find possible reasons for the spread of self-regulation problems. Two fundamental changes in parent–child relations dominate most analyses of the twentieth-century family, and both may have a hand in contributing to the decline of self-control.

The first change is the transformation of the family from an economic or work unit into a nexus of emotional relations. Burgess and Locke (1945) provided a classic analysis of this change. In their view, families in past eras operated largely as small corporations, in which each member had responsibilities to make a productive contribution and, indeed, most members tended to work together on joint tasks (especially in farming). Authority, discipline, and cooperation were necessarily well structured by the demands of joint work.

But the economic function of the family is largely obsolete. Instead, the family has become a locus of the search for emotional satisfaction. Intimacy, rather than economic production, is the goal of family relations. The need for self-regulation is clearly much lower in the modern family. The change may be especially marked if one accepts the view that instilling self-discipline in a child requires some harsh and firm treatment by the parent (e.g., insisting on firm rules, punishing infractions). In the old family, this would have been accepted as necessary, but modern parents may see it as likely to engender resentment by the child. People may seek intimacy with their children by trying to indulge their children's wishes, forgiving their infractions, and being maximally flexible and supportive. High school principals complain these days that parents want to be "pals" to their children and so shrink from disciplining them. Although such generalizations may have been made on the basis of the most salient examples and cannot be applied to all parents, they may also reflect a growing trend.

The second change in the family is the rise in single-parent households. By all measures and counts, the number and proportion of such households have risen sharply since 1960 and show no sign of letting up. Almost by definition, a single parent cannot spend as much time supervising a child as two parents can. Indeed, the difference may be especially dramatic when one considers that single parents are often chronically exhausted by the demands of supporting the family and providing the basic maintenance of food, shelter, and clothing, and so attending to matters of instilling delay of gratification and other rudiments of self-regulation may be too much to ask. In the last several years, research has continued to indicate that children of single parents are more likely than other children to show signs of self-regulation failure in many diverse spheres, ranging from achievement in school math class to juvenile delinquency and crime.

What can be done? There is little reason to think that single parenthood will decline any time soon. It seems ludicrous to expect day-care centers (which live under constant threats of lawsuits, investigations, and simple loss of business if children complain) to contribute much toward instilling self-regulation. Schools can be a partial substitute for parenting in instilling self-regulatory skills, but many factors, including budget cuts, emphases on noncoercive tolerance, and lack of parental support for school discipline, are weakening schools' ability to do this. (And as many educators complain, instilling self-discipline is not the main mission of the schools anyway and should not be their responsibility.)

Some changes could be made, at least at the level of federal policy. As we write this, the newspapers are full of a recent scandal based on a senatorial investigation (Associated Press, 1994). Some years ago the government began classifying drug and alcohol addiction as a disability, and this has allowed alcoholics and drug addicts to collect disability benefits from the Social Security Administration. In effect, the government mails monthly checks to a couple hundred thousand alcoholics and drug addicts. The investigating panel found that much of this money ends up being spent on alcohol and drugs, which is hardly surprising under the circumstances.

Of particular interest was the fact that the applicant's disability is treated as having begun when he or she first applied for benefits, even if the approval is initially denied and it takes a couple years for the appeals and approval process and the bureaucratic paperwork to finally start sending money. At that point, by the present policy, the person receives a lump sum payment for all the money that would have been sent in the intervening months. These payments, often amounting to $15,000 or even $20,000, have been used for major binges by some addicts and alcoholics. The Senate report documented cases of people who actually died from a drug overdose or alcohol-related tragedy that occurred right after the person received the large sum. In essence, the government financed a fatal binge for these individuals.

In general, it seems likely that American society should seek effective ways to get by under the circumstance that a large segment of the population will be prone to self-regulation failures. It therefore seems imperative that society look for ways to adapt to this likely outcome. Some sources of temptation can be removed, such as by restricting guns; those that cannot be removed can perhaps be managed and even perhaps used for the greater good of society, such as the way that gambling is now used as a source of revenue for many states.

DEVELOPING SELF-CONTROL THEORY

We have already concluded that the present state of the evidence is sufficient to furnish a broad understanding of self-regulation failure. A related but more far-reaching theoretical issue is the nature of self-regulation per se. Unfortunately, we do not think that the current state of available research evidence is ready to furnish a significant step forward in this basic understanding of self-regulation. The field seems to be in a transitional state, and the next generation of self-regulation theory may well be some years away (see Karoly, 1993). In this section, therefore, we offer only partial and fragmentary observations from our work that may be relevant to the next generation of self-regulation theory, whenever it arrives.

Self-regulation theory was greatly advanced by the introduction of feedback-loop models, especially as articulated by Carver and Scheier (1981; see also Miller et al., 1960; Powers, 1973). At present there is no reason to replace or even seriously revise that approach. Feedback-loop models are indeed clearly important and central in the process of self-regulation. The next generation of theory will probably not replace the feedback-loop approach so much as build on it. The task will therefore be to identify and remedy what is left out by feedback-loop analyses of self-regulation.

One issue concerns timing; that is, when does the feedback loop get activated at all? Carver and Scheier's analysis did begin to address this issue, such as in their explanation of the hierarchy of self-control levels and their discussion of how awareness can move from one level to another. Their contention that blockage or failure at one level initiates a shift to a lower level has been supported by research. Still, there are other factors relevant to the activation of a feedback loop. Sometimes people are motivated to turn off the feedback loop, to stop monitoring, to stop trying to improve. As we have already noted, in many cases people seem to acquiesce in self-regulation failure, and a full understanding of such acquiescence would be a powerful complement to feedback-loop models.

The "test" phase of the feedback loop—the monitoring process itself—is not very mysterious. One perceives oneself and current circumstances and compares against relevant standards. There are some issues to be explored there, including biased perception of self and selection of standards for comparison, but by and large this is not a complex problem at present.

On the other hand, the "operate" phase is much less well understood and must be considered a prime target for further work in theory and research. In other words, we suggest that a main focus of self-regulation should be *how* people change themselves, instead of focusing on how people decide whether to change or not. Our treatment of self-regulation as *process override* reflects this emphasis. What enables a person to succeed at overriding some impulse, resisting some motivation, or interrupting some activity that is in progress? When and why will such efforts fail?

In this connection, the distinction between automatic and controlled processes has to be incorporated into self-regulation theory. This distinction was only becoming a central concern of social psychologists when Carver and Scheier (1981) published their book, and so it is hardly surprising that they paid little attention to it. The next generation of self-regulation theory will undoubtedly place considerable emphasis on this distinction. Unfortunately, prevailing views about the nature of automatic and controlled processes and about the distinction between them are now changing, and so self-regulation theory may have to wait until those views have reached more of a consensus.

In any case, there is one aspect that will have to be effectively integrated into the next generation of self-regulation theory, and that is the distinction between two major kinds of automaticity. The old simple distinction gradually broke down because the term *automatic* was understood in two different ways, and so controversy raged. For self-regulation theory, however, both concepts are needed. The one concept was "true" automaticity, referring to processes that were not controlled and not controllable (Bargh, 1982). The other referred to processes that are not controlled but could potentially be controlled.

For self-regulation theory, the distinction is vital. True automatic processes, in the sense of processes that cannot be controlled, are by definition immune from self-regulation. Focusing self-regulatory efforts there will be futile—they fall into our category of trying to control the uncontrollable. We have suggested, for example, that impulses cannot be prevented when a latent motivation encounters an activating cue. If males are indeed biologically pro-grammed to respond to sexual novelty, then seeing a scantily clad woman on a beach or in a magazine may activate sexual desire for her, and that cannot be prevented; women who want their boyfriends or husbands not to notice other women are likely to be disappointed.

On the other hand, automatic processes in the looser sense—call them semiautomatic, for the moment—are perhaps the best place for self-regulation to intervene. These are habits or familiar responses or ways of doing things that are susceptible to control, and so self-regulatory processes can effectively over-ride them. Women can expect their boyfriends or husbands to refrain from making sexual advances toward these other women, even if preventing the interest or desire is unrealistic. That is because the link between desire and action is not automatic in the narrow sense. It is potentially controllable.

This issue complicates a great deal of the discussion of human social behavior and in particular many social problems. Does poverty cause crime? Does being a victim of abuse make one into an abuser? Do anger and jealousy cause violence? Such things create tendencies, but these are tendencies that can be overridden. Most poor people do not become criminals; many abuse victims do not become abusers themselves; many angry people refrain from inflicting violent harm. The causal process does increase the odds, but the potential for self-regulatory override may be the neglected factor in the moral equation (and in the moral judgment of responsibility).

The notion of overlearning raises another complication for the incorpo-ration of automaticity into self-regulation theory. Controlled processes involve self-regulation, in general, and perhaps by definition. But it is also well known that when some controlled process is repeated over and over, it gradually be-comes automatic (at least in the looser sense of the term automatic; this is the essence of overlearning). This logic presumably applies to self-regulation too, and so presumably there is some portion of self-regulation that is automatic. In an important sense, this is what many virtues (in the sense of positive character traits) are: ingrained habits of self-control. If you always do the right thing, it becomes easier to do. Physical exercise may be a good example. In order to exercise regularly, it is usually necessary to have a regular habit or routine, rather than having to face the struggle of making a decision about whether to exercise every day.

It is generally accepted that the reason for having automatic processes is that they conserve resources (Bargh, 1982). Controlled processes consume much more in the way of psychological resources than automatic processes do, by definition. These resources make up a great deal of what we have called self-regulatory strength, and indeed probably the biggest challenge facing further development of self-regulation theory is to explicate the nature of these resources.

Clearly, attention is one of these resources. Attention management emerged as a central factor in *all* self-regulation spheres we studied. Self-distraction was often effective as a means of self-regulation. Losing control of attention was associated with self-regulation failure in nearly every sphere—emotion, thought, task performance, impulse control.

Still, the resources involved in self-regulatory strength go beyond mere attention. Some motivational and dispositional factors probably need to be incorporated. Once researchers devise effective measures of strength, they may begin to investigate how it is depleted by fatigue or stress and whether it can be increased over time through exercise.

Transcendence is another issue that will deserve fuller treatment in future self-regulation theory. We have found that self-regulation failure is often marked by becoming immersed in the immediate situation, so that present, salient stimuli exert a powerful effect on behavior. The implication is that effective self-regulation depends on being able to be aware in a way that goes beyond the immediate situation and salient stimuli. The factors that contribute to the success or failure of transcendence deserve further study. Transcendence may involve a link between attention control and time perspectives, including distal goals and long-term interests.

Ultimately, self-regulation theory will need to draw on a clear understanding of how behavior happens ordinarily and how the individual can override these ordinary patterns to change them. As we said at the outset, self-stopping seems the simplest form of self-regulation, and it deserves emphasis by researchers who undertake to investigate how people override their thoughts, feelings, and actions.

IMPLICATIONS FOR CULTIVATING SELF-REGULATION

Given the widespread benefits of good self-regulation, and in view of the many undesirable outcomes that accompany self-regulation failure, one might well ask how good self-regulatory skills are to be instilled. What enables people to develop effective self-discipline? Although a systematic treatment of such questions is beyond the scope of this work, some speculative comments are in order.

Implications for Parenting

In our view, the weight of the evidence currently points to parental influence as the single most important determinant of self-regulatory capacity. Parents can thus accomplish a great deal in terms of instilling good self-control in their children. From our perspective, this may be the single most important and valuable goal of socializing children. We recommend that parents regard the inculcation of self-control as the premier goal in child-rearing (as opposed to cultivating self-esteem, creativity, obedience, sociability, love for parents, or other goals).

The importance of parental influence on self-regulation, however, also raises some cause for concern in the context of current societal trends. As we have already noted, the dramatic rise in single-parent households and dual-career families generally entails that parents have much less opportunity (as well as much less time and energy) to supervise their children than in previous eras. If the result is that children grow up with less supervision, or even with supervision that places less emphasis on instilling self-control, then society will likely see continuing increases in the problems of self-regulation failure, from impulsive crime to sexual misbehavior to problems with alcohol and eating and drugs.

The project of raising a child with high self-control must presumably involve both having a highly structured set of rules to which the child is held to conform and conferring a substantial and growing degree of autonomy on the child. Conventional wisdom among researchers tends to depict the *authoritative* parenting style (i.e., having firm rules with a rationality that is made clear to the child and that the child has some degree of participation in setting) as most effective for this, and there is no reason to dispute that at present. Consistency of rules and consistency of enforcement are probably of paramount importance, and that includes the notion that letting the child off the hook out of some lenient sentiment must be regarded as a potentially harmful neglect of parental duty. Severity of punishment is presumably much less important than consistency and foreseeability.

Given the importance of the capacity to delay gratification, instilling that capacity should probably be one of the key early emphases. It would be necessary to offer the child choices between immediate and delayed (but greater) rewards, as well as to improve the child's capacity to choose the delayed ones.

It is then of course extremely important that the delayed rewards are actually forthcoming. Indeed, the economic difficulties and other turbulence in lower-class households may often make it especially difficult to foster a capacity to delay gratification. Previous generations of researchers were fond of demonstrating that socioeconomic class was correlated with capacity to delay gratification, but this may simply reflect children's rational adaptation to the fact that promises of delayed rewards are often not kept because of unforeseen emergencies or other exigencies. The lesson one learns from such a chaotic environment is that only immediate and available rewards can be counted on, and so it is always best to choose them. Although that may be an optimal adaptation to such a home environment, it will of course be counterproductive in society at large. We suspect that it would not take very many broken promises to teach a child not to trust them, and the capacity to delay gratification may be seriously undermined in rather short order.

Training attentional skills must also be given high priority by parents, because of the pervasive importance of attention for self-regulation. Activities that require vigilance, concentration, or the genesis of multiple possibilities or multiple ideas should probably get high priority. Although it is now common for parents to complain about the influence of television, such as its high rate of sex and violence, we suspect that another (rarely mentioned) important problem with excessive television watching is that it fails to challenge or develop attentional skills. Watching television takes almost no mental effort, and programming is designed to seize and manipulate attention effectively. This can readily be seen by contrasting television with reading, because reading requires some degree of persistent concentration, and so it may be more effective in instilling the capacity to manage one's attention.

As already noted, a particularly important form of attentional control is transcendence. Teaching children to see beyond the immediate stimuli is probably quite helpful for the development of self-control. The ability to transcend the immediate situation helps overcome dangerous emotional reactions, helps hold impulses and appetites in check, increases long-range rationality, and has many other benefits. How one cultivates the ability to transcend the immediate situation is not easy to say. Possibly games such as chess, which require the player to imagine future outcomes beyond the immediate situation, may be helpful at some ages. Transcendence might also be taught as a method of dealing with emotional distress.

Perhaps the most important fundamental attitude should simply be to make a point of reinforcing behavior that shows good self-control. It is presumably easy to recognize (and punish) significant failures of self-control in one's children, because the failures create problems and attract attention. Positive feats of self-control, however, are less dramatic and might easily go unnoticed. If parents watch for such feats and are careful to reward them, they may be increased. Reinforcement has been shown to be more effective than punishment for producing desired behavior.

One final implication of these speculations is that effective socialization of self-control in children may demand considerable exercise of self-control on the part of parents. After all, the guidelines we have given require vigilant and consistent behavior on the part of parents. That contingency may have ominous implications about the future of our society, however. As children who grew up neglected by parents or raised with other goals (such as esteeming oneself regardless of one's actions) now become parents, their capacity for optimal parenting may be lacking. Moreover, and more unfortunately, lack of self-control makes it that much easier to become a parent, especially an unwed parent, simply by engaging in unprotected sexual behavior. The escalating patterns of parental neglect and abuse may reflect this "snowballing" of poor self-control from one generation to the next. If so, then this cycle may be extremely difficult to reverse, and society should brace itself for a rapid rise in all the problems that stem from self-regulation failure, as more and more children grow up with parents who themselves lack self-control.

Self-Improvement of Self-Control

For people who wish to increase their own capacity for self-regulation, our analysis offers several suggestions. The place to start would presumably be with the three main ingredients of self-regulation, that is, standards, monitoring, and strength.

Regarding standards, there is not much mystery. Setting appropriate goals and avoiding conflicts between one's goals or ideals is a necessary first step. There are of course two main approaches to setting standards. One is to set very high goals and try to come as close as possible. The other is to set relatively low goals and surpass them frequently (and substantially). The latter is likely to be more pleasant and to yield more in the way of satisfactions and other positive affect.

One should also be explicit about setting rewards and punishments in connection with these standards. Judicious use of self-reward is probably a good aid to self-regulation.

Monitoring of the self is vital to effective self-regulation. Probably most people who have difficulty with self-regulation might find it useful to try external forms of monitoring, such as recording one's progress on the calendar. (It may be easy to skip a day's exercise now and then, but if every glance at the calendar reveals how many days this month one has exercised one may be spurred on to do better than last month, or at least to consider whether one is in fact matching one's target.) Social relationships may also furnish a helpful context for external monitoring; many people find, for example, that involving a nonsmoking spouse is a helpful aid to one's own efforts to quit smoking, if only because the spouse is willing to keep an unbiased record of how much one smokes.

The third ingredient is strength. If our analysis is correct, self-regulatory strength should be able to be increased by effective exercise. In that case, setting oneself small but frequent challenges for self-improvement may be useful for building up a good capacity for self-discipline. Managing strength also suggests that one must sometimes be judicious in where to allocate it. When one is subjected to external demands or stresses, for example, it may be prudent to avoid making other demands on oneself, in order to conserve one's strength.

External sources of discipline may also be useful to some people. Religious and military organizations have always offered strong supports for personal self-control, and there may be other organizations that are also helpful.

Cultivating better control over attention in oneself, starting at adulthood, is not easy. Still, this is essentially what meditation involves (i.e., control over attention). Meditation is not easy and, indeed, making the time to meditate once or twice a day may itself be an undertaking that consumes self-regulatory strength, but if one can do it there may gradually be a substantial payoff in the capacity to control oneself. (At first, however, the effect may seem to be the opposite, because when one starts to meditate one typically realizes how little control one has over one's mind and attentional processes.)

Lastly, the careful pursuit of accurate self-knowledge can help prevent or minimize many forms of misregulation and of poor self-management. This is probably harder than it sounds, because most people believe that they do seek to learn about themselves. Evidence suggests, however, that people actually give a fairly low priority to finding out accurate information about themselves. Instead, they prefer first and foremost to hear positive things about themselves, and when that desire is satisfied they seek information that confirms what they already believe about themselves, leaving the quest for accurate self-knowledge a distant third (Sedikides, 1993). Making a fair list of one's virtues or abilities *and* one's faults and weaknesses is thus a rare and difficult undertaking, but to the extent that one can do this, self-management is likely to be facilitated.

FINAL REMARKS

The importance of self-regulation is only beginning to be appreciated, in social psychology as well as in Western society in general. One of the great misconceptions of modern times is that people have a true self hidden inside, needing only to be found. More likely, people have possibilities that need to be cultivated and realized. To do that requires a great deal of systematic effort to bring one's thoughts, feelings, and actions into agreement with one's ideals. Self-regulation is thus central to the essential nature of human selfhood. It is only by means of self-regulation that human beings can reach their potential and fulfill their ideals.

This book has taken us on a tour through many spheres of human failure and misery. We have examined people who give up too easily, quit their jobs, mismanage their task performances, suffer from unwanted thoughts, deceive themselves, are buffeted by uncontrolled emotions, eat too much, drink too much alcohol, smoke or gamble excessively, and in general ruin their lives. Self-regulation failure is indeed a pervasive source of human unhappiness. Indeed, people who fail at self-regulation often bring trouble and sadness not only on themselves but on people close to them and people who care about them.

Yet one should not despair. Self-regulation failure is the exception, not the rule. It is less remarkable that people sometimes fail at self-regulation than that they usually succeed. The capacity to alter and control oneself is one of the most powerfully adaptive and, indeed, miraculous aspects of the human psyche. Anything that science, therapy, public policy, or individual human beings can do to enhance it—and thereby reduce the painful and costly toll of self-regulation failures—holds the fair promise of being a contribution to the greater good of humanity.

References

Abraham, S.F., & Beumont, P.J.V. (1982). How patients describe bulimia or binge eating. *Psychological Medicine, 12,* 625–635.

Abrams, D.B., & Wilson, G.T. (1979). Effects of alcohol on social anxiety in women: Cognitive versus physiological arousal. *Journal of Abnormal Psychology, 88,* 161–173.

Abramson, E.E., & Wunderlich, R.A. (1972). Anxiety, fear and eating: A test of the psychosomatic concept of obesity. *Journal of Abnormal Psychology, 79,* 317–321.

Agras, W.S. (1987). *Eating disorders: Management of obesity, bulimia, and anorexia nervosa.* New York: Pergamon.

Ajzen, I., & Fishbein, M. (1977). Attitude–behavior relations: A theoretical analysis and review of empirical research. *Psychological Bulletin, 84,* 888–918.

Akers, R.L. (1991). Addiction: The troublesome concept. *The Journal of Drug Issues, 21,* 777–793.

Allon, N. (1982). The stigma of overweight in everyday life. In B.B. Wolman & S. DeBerry (Eds.), *Psychological aspects of obesity: A handbook* (pp. 130–174). New York: Van Nostrand Reinhold.

Allport, F.H. (1924). *Social psychology.* Boston: Houghton Mifflin.

Allsop, S., & Saunders, B. (1991). Reinforcing robust resolutions: Motivation in relapse prevention with severely dependent problem drinkers. In W.R. Miller & S. Rollnick (Eds.), *Motivational interviewing: Preparing people to change addictive behavior* (pp. 236–247). New York: Guilford.

American Psychiatric Association. (1987). *Diagnostic and statistical manual of mental disorders* (3rd rev. ed.). Washington, DC: Author.

Anderson, C.A., Lepper, M.R., & Ross, L. (1980). Perseverance of social theories: The role of explanation in the persistence of discredited information. *Journal of Personality and Social Psychology, 39,* 1037–1049.

Anderson, C.A., New, B.L., & Speer, J.R. (1985). Argument availability as a mediator of social theory perseverance. *Social Cognition, 3,* 235–249.

Aneshensel, C.S., & Huba, G.J. (1983). Depression, alcohol use, and smoking over one year: A four wave longitudinal causal model. *Journal of Abnormal Psychology, 92,* 119–133.

Armor, D.J., Polich, J.M., & Stambul, H. (1978). *Alcoholism and treatment*. New York: Wiley.

Arthur, C. (1992). Fifteen million Americans are shopping addicts. *American Demographics, 14*, 14–15.

Ashton, H., & Stepney, R. (1982). *Smoking: Psychology and pharmacology*. London: Tavistock.

Ashton, H., & Watson, D.W. (1970). Puffing frequency and nicotine intake in cigarette smokers. *British Medical Journal, 2*, 679–681.

Associated Press (1994, February 6). Benefits turn to drug money. *Daily Progress* (Charlottesville, VA), pp. A1, A12.

Averill, J.R. (1979). Anger. In H. Howe & R. Dienstbier (eds.), *Nebraska Symposium on Motivation, 1978* (p. 26). Lincoln: University of Nebraska Press.

Averill, J. (1980). A constructivist view of emotion. In R. Plutchik & H. Kellerman (Eds.), *Theories of emotion* (pp. 305–339). New York: Academic Press.

Averill, J. (1982). *Anger and aggression: An essay on emotion*. New York: Springer-Verlag.

Baer, J.S., Kamarck, T., Lichtenstein, E., & Ransom, C.C., Jr. (1989). Prediction of smoking relapse: Analyses of temptations and transgressions after initial cessation. *Journal of Consulting and Clinical Psychology, 57*, 623–627.

Baer, J., Marlatt, G.A., Kivlahan, D., Fromme, K., Larimer, M., & Williams, E. (1992). An experimental test of three methods of alcohol risk reduction with young adults. *Journal of Consulting and Clinical Psychology, 60*, 974–979.

Bahrke, M.S., & Morgan, W.P. (1978). Anxiety reduction following exercise and meditation. *Cognitive Therapy and Resarch, 2*, 323–333.

Baker, R.C., & Kirschenbaum, D.S. (1993). Self-monitoring may be necessary for successful weight control. *Behavior Therapy, 24*, 377–394.

Baldus, D.C., Woodworth, G., & Pulaski, C.A., Jr. (1990). *Equal justice and the death penalty*. Boston: Northeastern University Press.

Banaji, M.R., & Steele, C.M. (1989). Alcohol and self-evaluation: Is a social cognition approach beneficial? *Social Cognition, 7*, 137–151.

Bandura, A., & Schunk, D.H. (1981). Cultivating competence, self-efficacy, and intrinsic interest through proximal self-motivation. *Journal of Personality and Social Psychology, 41*, 586–598.

Bargh, J. (1982). Attention and automaticity in the processing of self-relevant information. *Journal of Personality and Social Psychology, 43*, 425–436.

Bar-On, D. (1989). *Legacy of silence: Encounters with children of the Third Reich*. Cambridge, MA: Harvard University Press.

Barton, J., Chassin, L., Presson, C.C., & Sherman, S.J. (1982). Social image factors as motivators of smoking initiation in early and middle adolescence. *Child Development, 53*, 1499–1511.

Baucom, D.H., & Aiken, P.A. (1981). Effect of depressed mood on eating among obese and nonobese dieting persons. *Journal of Personality and Social Psychology, 41*, 577–585.

Baumeister, R.F. (1982). Self-esteem, self-presentation, and future interaction: A dilemma of reputation. *Journal of Personality, 50*, 29–45.

Baumeister, R.F. (1984). Choking under pressure: Self-consciousness and paradoxical effects of incentives on skillful performance. *Journal of Personality and Social Psychology, 46*, 610–620.

Baumeister, R.F. (1985, April). The championship choke. *Psychology Today,* 19(4), 48–52.

Baumeister, R.F. (1989). *Masochism and the self.* Hillsdale, NJ: Erlbaum.

Baumeister, R.F. (1990). Suicide as escape from self. *Psychological Review,* 97, 90–113.

Baumeister, R.F. (1991a). *Escaping the self: Alcoholism, spirituality, masochism, and other flights from the burden of selfhood.* New York: Basic Books.

Baumeister, R.F. (1991b). *Meanings of life.* New York: Guilford.

Baumeister, R.F. (Ed.). (1993a) *Self-esteem: The puzzle of low self-regard.* New York: Plenum.

Baumeister, R.F., & Cairns, K.J. (1992). Repression and self-presentation: When audiences interfere with self-deceptive strategies. *Journal of Personality and Social Psychology, 62,* 851–862.

Baumeister, R.F. (1993b). Lying to yourself: The paradox of self-deception. In M. Lewis & C. Saarni (Eds.), *Lying and deception in everyday life* (pp. 166–183). New York: Guilford.

Baumeister, R.F., Hamilton, J.C., & Tice, D.M. (1985). Public versus private expectancy of success: Confidence booster or performance pressure? *Journal of Personality and Social Psychology, 48,* 1447–1457.

Baumeister, R.F., Heatherton, T.F., & Tice, D.M. (1993). When ego threats lead to self-regulation failure: Negative consequences of high self-esteem. *Journal of Personality and Social Psychology, 64,* 141–156.

Baumeister, R.F., Hutton, D.G., & Cairns, K.J. (1990). Negative effects of praise on skilled performance. *Basic and Applied Social Psychology, 11,* 131–148.

Baumeister, R.F., & Ilko, S.A. (1994). Shallow gratitude: Public and private acknowledgement of external help in accounts of success. *Basic and Applied Social Psychology.*

Baumeister, R.F., & Newman, L.S. (1994). Self-regulation of cognitive inference and decision processes. *Personality and Social Psychology Bulletin, 20,* 3–19.

Baumeister, R.F., Pelham, B., Krull, D., & Swinkels, A. (1987). Skill and effort as separate performance patterns. Unpublished research findings.

Baumeister, R.F., & Scher, S.J. (1988). Self-defeating behavior patterns among normal individuals: Review and analysis of common self-destructive tendencies. *Psychological Bulletin, 104,* 3–22.

Baumeister, R.F., & Showers, C.J. (1986). A review of paradoxical performance effects: Choking under pressure in sports and mental tests. *European Journal of Social Psychology, 16,* 361–383.

Baumeister, R.F., & Steinhilber, A. (1984). Paradoxical effects of supportive audiences on performance under pressure: The home field disadvantage in sports championships. *Journal of Personality and Social Psychology, 47,* 85–93.

Baumeister, R.F., & Stillwell, A.M. (1992, August). *Negative affect, risk appraisal, and self-defeating choices.* Paper presented to the annual convention of the American Psychological Association, Washington, DC.

Baumeister, R.F., Stillwell, A., & Wotman, S.R. (1990). Victim and perpetrator accounts of interpersonal conflict: Autobiographical narratives about anger. *Journal of Personality and Social Psychology, 59,* 994–1005.

Baumeister, R.F., Tice, D.M., & Hutton, D.G. (1989). Self-presentational motivations and personality differences in self-esteem. *Journal of Personality, 57,* 547–579.

Baumeister, R.F., & Wotman, S.R. (1992). *Breaking hearts: The two sides of unrequited love*. New York: Guilford.

Baumgardner, A.H. (1990). To know oneself is to like oneself: Self-certainty and self-affect. *Journal of Personality and Social Psychology, 58*, 1062–1072.

Bazerman, M.H., Giuliano, T., & Appelman, A. (1984). Escalation of commitment in individual and group decision making. *Organizational Behavior and Human Performance, 33*, 141–152.

Beaman, A.L., Klentz, B., Diener, E., & Svanum, S. (1979). Self-awareness and transgression in children: Two field studies. *Journal of Personality and Social Psychology, 37*, 1835–1846.

Becker, M.H., & Rosenstock, I.M. (1984). Compliance with medical advice. In A. Steptoe & A. Mathews (Eds.), *Health care and human behavior*. Orlando, FL: Academic Press.

Bellenger, D., Robertson, D.H., & Hirschman, E.C. (1978). Impulse buying varies by product. *Journal of Advertising Research, 18*, 15–18.

Belsky, G. (1993, March). Americans and their money. *Money, 22* (3), 114–117.

Bennett, G. (1988). *Eating matters: Why we eat what we eat*. London: Heinemann Kingswood.

Bennett, W.I. (1984). Dieting: Ideology versus physiology. *Psychiatric Clinics of North America, 7*, 321–334.

Bennett, W.I., & Gurin, G. (1982). *The dieter's dilemma*. New York: Basic Books.

Benowitz, N.L. (1983). The use of biologic fluid samples in assessing tobacco smoke consumption. In J. Grabowski & C.S. Bell (Eds.), *Measurement in the analysis and treatment of smoking behavior*. (NIDA Research Monograph No. 48, pp. 6–26). Washington, DC: US Government Printing Office.

Benowitz, N.L., Jacob, P., Kozlowski, L.T., & Yu, L. (1986). Influence of smoking fewer cigarettes on exposure to tar, nicotine, and carbon monoxide. *New England Journal of Medicine, 315*, 1310–1313.

Berglas, S., & Jones, E.E. (1978). Drug choice as a self-handicapping strategy in response to non-contingent success. *Journal of Personality and Social Psychology, 36*, 405–417.

Berkowitz, L. (1978). Is criminal violence normative behavior? Hostile and instrumental aggression in violent incidents. *Journal of Research in Crime and Delinquency, 15*, 148–161.

Berlyne, D.N. (1960). *Conflict, arousal, and curiosity*. New York: McGraw-Hill.

Bien, T.H., Miller, W.R., & Tonigan, J.S. (1993). Brief interventions for alcohol problems: A review. *Addiction, 88*, 315–336.

Biglan, A., & Lichtenstein, E. (1984). A behavior-analytic approach to smoking acquisition: Some recent findings. *Journal of Applied Social Psychology, 14*, 207–224.

Billings, A.G., & Moos, R.H. (1981). The role of coping responses and social resources in attenuating the impact of stressful life events. *Journal of Behavioral Medicine, 4*, 139–157.

Billings, A.G., & Moos, R.F. (1984). Coping, stress, and social resources among adults with unipolar depression. *Journal of Personality and Social Psychology, 46*, 877–891.

Blaine, B., & Crocker, J. (1993). Self-esteem and self-serving biases in reactions to positive and negative events: An integrative review. In R. Baumeister (Ed.), *Self-esteem: The puzzle of low self-regard* (pp. 55–85). New York: Plenum.

Bliss, R.E., Garvey, A.J., Heinold, J.W., & Hitchcock, J.L. (1989). The influence of situation and coping on relapse crisis outcomes after smoking cessation. *Journal of Consulting and Clinical Psychology, 57,* 443–449.

Blitzer, P.H., Rimm, A.S., & Giefer, E.E. (1977). The effects of cessation of smoking on body weight in 57,032 women: Cross-sectional and longitudinal analysis. *Journal of Chronic Disease, 30,* 415–429.

Bordini, E.J., Tucker, J., Vuchinich, R., & Rudd, E.J. (1986). Alcohol consumption as a self-handicapping strategy in women. *Journal of Abnormal Psychology, 95,* 346–349.

Botvin, G.J., Eng, A., & Williams, C. (1980). Preventing the onset of cigarette smoking through life skills training. *Preventive Medicine, 9,* 135–143.

Bouchard, C., Tremblay, A., Despres, J., Nadeau, A., Lupien, P.J., Theriault, G., Dussault, J., Moorjani, S., Pinault, S., & Fournier, G. (1990). The response to long-term overfeeding in identical twins. *New England Journal of Medicine, 322,* 1477–1482.

Brandon, T.H., Tiffany, S.T., & Baker, T.B. (1986). The process of smoking relapse. In F. Tims & C. Leukefeld (Eds.), *Relapse and recovery in drug abuse* (NIDA Research Monograph No. 72, pp. 104–117). Washington, DC: US Government Printing Office.

Bray, G.A. (1985). Complications of obesity. *Annals of Internal Medicine, 103,* 1052–1062.

Brehm, J.W. (1966). *A theory of psychological reactance.* New York: Academic Press.

Breuer, J., & Freud, S. (1982). *Studies on hysteria* (J. Strachey, Trans.). New York: Basic Books.

Brockner, J., Shaw, M.C., & Rubin, J.Z. (1979). Factors affecting withdrawal from an escalating conflict: Quitting before it's too late. *Journal of Experimental Social Psychology, 15,* 492–503.

Brown, J.D., & Mankowski, T.A. (1993). Self-esteem, mood, and self-evaluation: Changes in mood and the way you see you. *Journal of Personality and Social Psychology, 64,* 421–430.

Brown, S.A. (1985). Reinforcement expectancies and alcoholism treatment outcome after a one-year follow-up. *Journal of Studies on Alcohol, 46,* 304–308.

Brown, S.A., Creamer, V.A., & Stetson, B.A. (1987). Adolescent alcohol expectancies in relation to personal and parental drinking patterns. *Journal of Abnormal Psychology, 96,* 117–121.

Brown, S.A., Goldman, M.S., & Christiansen, B.A. (1985). Do alcohol expectancies mediate drinking patterns of adults? *Journal of Consulting and Clinical Psychology, 53,* 512–519.

Brownell, K.D. (1991). Dieting and the search for the perfect body: Where physiology and culture collide. *Behavior Therapy, 22,* 1–12.

Brownell, K.D., Greenwood, M.R.C., Stellar, E., & Shrager, E.E. (1986). The effects of repeated cycles of weight loss and regain in rats. *Physiology and Behavior, 38,* 459–464.

Brownell, K.D., Marlatt, G.A., Lichtenstein, E., & Wilson, G.T. (1986). Understanding and preventing relapse. *American Psychologist, 41,* 765–782.

Browning, C.R. (1992). *Ordinary men: Reserve Police Battalion 101 and the final solution in Poland.* New York: HarperCollins.

Bryant, J., & Zillman, D. (1984). Using television to alleviate boredom and stress:

Selective exposure as a function of induced emotional states. *Journal of Broadcasting, 28,* 1–20.

Bullough, V.L., & Brundage, J. (1982). *Sexual practices and the medieval church.* Buffalo, NY: Prometheus.

Burgess, E.W., & Locke, H.J. (1945). *The family: From institution to companionship.* New York: American Book Co.

Burk, J.P., & Sher, K.J. (1990). Labeling the child of an alcoholic: Negative stereotyping by mental health professionals and peers. *Journal of Studies on Alcohol, 51,* 156–163.

Cabanac, M. (1971). Physiological role of pleasure. *Science, 173,* 1103–1107.

Cacioppo, J.T., Petty, R.E., Losch, M.E., & Kim, H.S. (1986). Electromyographic activity over facial muscle regions can differentiate the valence and intensity of affective reactions. *Journal of Personality and Social Psychology, 50,* 260–268.

Campbell, J.D. (1990). Self-esteem and clarity of the self-concept. *Journal of Personality and Social Psychology, 59,* 538–549.

Campbell, J.D., & Lavallee, L.F. (1993). Who am I? The role of self-concept confusion in understanding the behavior of people with low self-esteem. In R. Baumeister (Ed.), *Self-esteem: The puzzle of low self-regard* (pp. 3–20). New York: Plenum.

Campos, J.J., Campos, R.G., & Barrett, K.C. (1989). Emergent themes in the study of emotional development and emotion regulation. *Developmental Psychology, 25,* 394–402.

Capaldi, E.D., & Powley, T.L. (1990). *Taste, experience, and feeding.* Washington, DC: American Psychological Association.

Cappell, H., & Greeley, J. (1987). Alcohol and tension reduction: An update on research and theory. In H.T. Blane & K.E. Leonard (Eds.), *Psychological theories of drinking and alcoholism* (pp. 15–54). New York: Guilford.

Cappell, H., & Herman, C.P. (1972). Alcohol and tension reduction: A review. *Quarterly Journal of Studies on Alcohol, 33,* 33–64.

Carey, K.B. (1993). Situational determinants of heavy drinking among college students. *Journal of Counseling Psychology, 40,* 217–220.

Carmody, T.P. (1993). Nicotine dependence: Psychological approaches to the prevention of smoking relapse. *Psychology of Addictive Behaviors, 7,* 96–102.

Carr, J.E., & Tan, E.K. (1976). In search of the true Amok: Amok as viewed within the Malay culture. *American Journal of Psychiatry, 133,* 1295–1299.

Carver, C.S., Ganellen, R.J., Froming, W.J., & Chambers, W. (1983). Modeling: An analysis in terms of category accessibility. *Journal of Experimental Social Psychology, 19,* 403–421.

Carver, C.S., & Scheier, M.F. (1981). *Attention and self-regulation: A control theory approach to human behavior.* New York: Springer-Verlag.

Carver, C.S., & Scheier, M.F. (1982). Control theory: A useful conceptual framework for personality—Social, clinical and health psychology. *Psychological Bulletin, 92,* 111–135.

Carver, C.S., Scheier, M.F., & Weintraub, J.K. (1989). Assessing coping strategies: A theoretically based approach. *Journal of Personality and Social Psychology, 56,* 267–283.

Catanzaro, S.J., & Mearns, J. (1990). Measuring generalized expectancies for negative mood regulation: Initial scale development and implications. *Journal of Personality Assessment, 54,* 546–563.

Chassin, L., Presson, C.C., & Sherman, S.J. (1990). Social psychological contributions to the understanding and prevention of adolescent cigarette smoking. *Personality and Social Psychology Bulletin, 16*, 133–151.

Christenson, G.A., Mackenzie, T.B., & Mitchell, J.E. (1991). Characteristics of 60 adult hair pullers. *American Journal of Psychiatry, 148*, 365–370.

Christiansen, B.A., Smith, G.T., Roehling, P.V., & Goldman, M.S. (1989). Using alcohol expectancies to predict adolescent drinking behavior after one year. *Journal of Consulting and Clinical Psychology, 57*, 93–99.

Cialdini, R.B., Darby, B., & Vincent, J. (1973). Transgression and altruism: A case for hedonism. *Journal of Experimental Social Psychology, 9*, 502–516.

Ciliska, D. (1990). *Beyond dieting—Psychoeducational interventions for chronically obese women: A non-dieting approach.* New York: Brunner/Mazel.

Clark, M.S., & Isen, A.M. (1982). Toward understanding the relationship between feeling states and social behavior. In A. Hastorf & A.M. Isen (Eds.), *Cognitive social psychology* (pp. 73–108). New York: Elsevier.

Cohen, S., & Lichtenstein, E. (1990). Partner behaviors that support quitting smoking. *Journal of Consulting and Clinical Psychology, 58*, 304–309.

Cohen, S., Lichtenstein, E., Prochaska, J.O., Rossi, J.S., Gritz, E.R., Carr, C.R., Orleans, C.T., Schoenbach, V.J., Biener, L., Abrams, D., DiClemente, C., Curry, S., Marlatt, G.A., Cummings, K.M., Emont, S.L., Giovino, G., and Ossip-Klein, D. (1989). Debunking myths about self-quitting: Evidence from 10 prospective studies of persons who attempt to quit smoking by themselves. *American Psychologist, 44*, 1355–1365.

Collins, J.E. (1978). Effects of restraint, monitoring, and stimulus salience on eating behavior. *Addictive Behaviors, 3*, 197–204.

Collins, R.L., & Marlatt, G.A. (1981). Social modeling as a determinant of drinking behavior: Implications for prevention and treatment. *Addictive Behaviors, 6*, 233–239.

Conger, J.C., Conger, A.J., Costanzo, P.R., Wright, K.L., & Matter, J.A. (1980). The effect of social cues on the eating behavior of obese and normal subjects. *Journal of Personality, 48*, 258–271.

Conger, J.J. (1956). Alcoholism: Theory, problem and challenge. II. Reinforcement theory and the dynamics of alcoholism. *Quarterly Journal of Alcoholism, 13*, 296–305.

Conlon, E.J., & Wolf, G. (1980). The moderating effects of strategy, visibility, and involvement on allocation behavior: An extension of Staw's escalation paradigm. *Organizational Behavior and Human Performance, 26*, 172–192.

Cools, J., Schotte, D.E., & McNally, R.J. (1992). Emotional arousal and overeating in restrained eaters. *Journal of Abnormal Psychology, 101*, 348–351.

Cooper, M.L., Russell, M., Skinner, J.B., Frone, M.R., & Mudar, P. (1992). Stress and alcohol use: Moderating effects of gender, coping, and alcohol expectancies. *Journal of Abnormal Psychology, 101*, 139–153.

Cox, W.M. (1985). Personality correlates of substance abuse. In M. Galizio & S.A. Maisto (Eds.), *Determinants of substance abuse: Biological, psychological, and environmental factors.* New York: Plenum.

Coyne, J.C., Kessler, R.C., Tal, M., Turnbull, J., Wortman, C.B., & Greden, J.F. (1987). Living with a depressed person. *Journal of Consulting and Clinical Psychology, 55*, 347–352.

Crandall, C.S. (1988). Social contagion of binge eating. *Journal of Personality and Social Psychology, 55*, 588–599.

Critchlow, B. (1986). The powers of John Barleycorn: Beliefs about the effects of alcohol on social behavior. *American Psychologist, 41*, 751–764.

Crocker, J., & Major, B. (1989). Social stigma and self-esteem: The self-protective properties of stigma. *Psychological Review, 96*, 608–630.

Csikszentmihalyi, M. (1990). *Flow: The psychology of optimal experience*. New York: Harper & Row.

Cunningham, J.C., Sobell, L.C., & Chow, V.M. (1992, November). *Beliefs about substance abuse and substance abusers: Implications for treatment*. Paper presented at the Association for the Advancement of Behavior Therapy, Boston.

Cupchick, G.C., & Leventhal, H. (1974). Consistency between expressive behavior and the evaluation of humorous stimuli: The role of sex and self-observation. *Journal of Personality and Social Psychology, 30*, 429–442.

Curry, S., Marlatt, G.A., & Gordon, J.R. (1987). Abstinence violation effect: Validation of an attributional construct with smoking cessation. *Journal of Consulting and Clinical Psychology, 55*, 145–149.

Curry, S., Southwick, L., & Steele, C. (1987). Restrained drinking: Risk factor for problems with alcohol? *Addictive Behaviors, 12*, 73–77.

Curry, S.J., Wagner, E.H., & Grothaus, L.C. (1990). Intrinsic and extrinsic motivation for smoking cessation. *Journal of Consulting and Clinical Psychology, 58*, 310–316.

Curry, S.J., Wagner, E.H., & Grothaus, L.C. (1991). Evaluation of intrinsic and extrinsic motivation interventions with a self-help smoking cessation program. *Journal of Consulting and Clinical Psychology, 59*, 318–324.

Darke, P.R. (1993). *The effect of a lucky event and belief in luck on confidence and risk-taking*. Unpublished doctoral dissertation. University of Toronto.

Darkes, J., & Goldman, M.S. (1993). Expectancy challenge and drinking reduction: Experimental evidence for a mediational process. *Journal of Consulting and Clinical Psychology, 61*, 344–353.

Darley, J.M., & Gross, P.H. (1983). A hypothesis-confirming bias in labeling effects. *Journal of Personality and Social Psychology, 44*, 20–33.

Davies, D.L. (1962). Normal drinking in recovered alcohol addicts. *Quarterly Journal of Studies on Alcohol, 23*, 94–104.

Dembroski, T.M., MacDougall, J.M., Shields, J.L., Petitto, J., & Lushene, R. (1978). Components of the Type A coronary-prone behavior pattern and cardiovascular responses to psychomotor performance challenge. *Journal of Behavioral Medicine, 1*, 159–176.

Devine, P.G. (1989). Stereotypes and prejudice: Their automatic and controlled components. *Journal of Personality and Social Psychology, 56*, 5–18.

Devine, P.G., Sedikides, C., & Fuhrman, R.W. (1989). Goals in social information processing: The case of anticipated interaction. *Journal of Personality and Social Psychology, 56*, 680–690.

De Volder, M.L., & Lens, W. (1982). Academic achievement and future time perspective as a cognitive–motivational concept. *Journal of Personality and Social Psychology, 42*, 566–571.

Diamond, E.L., Schneiderman, N., Schwartz, D., Smith, J.C., Vorp, R., & Pasin, R.D. (1984). Harassment, hostility, and Type A determinants of cardiovascular reactivity during competition. *Journal of Behavioral Medicine, 7,* 171–189.

Dickerson, M. (1991). Internal and external determinants of persistent gambling: Implications for treatment. In N. Heather, W.R. Miller, & J. Greeley (Eds.), *Self-control and the addictive behaviors* (pp. 317–338). Botany, Australia: Maxwell Macmillan.

Dickman, S. (1985). Impulsivity and perception: Individual differences in the processing of the local and global dimensions of stimuli. *Journal of Personality and Social Psychology, 48,* 133–149.

Dickman, S.J., & Meyer, D.E. (1988). Impulsivity and speed–accuracy tradeoffs in information processing. *Journal of Personality and Social Psychology, 54,* 274–290.

DiClemente, C.C. (1994). If behaviors change, can personality be far behind? In T.F. Heatherton & J.L. Weinberger (Eds.), *Can personality change?* (pp. 175–198). Washington, DC: American Psychological Association.

DiClemente, C.C., & Prochaska, J.O. (1982). Self-change and therapy change of smoking behavior: A comparison of processes of change in cessation and maintenance. *Addictive Behaviors, 7,* 133–142.

Diener, E. (1979). Deindividuation, self-awareness, and disinhibition. *Journal of Personality and Social Psychology, 37,* 1160–1171.

Diener, E., & Wallbom, M. (1976). Effects of self-awareness on antinormative behavior. *Journal of Research in Personality, 10,* 107–111.

Dillon, K.M., & Brooks, D. (1992). Unusual cleaning behavior in the luteal phase. *Psychological Reports, 70,* 35–39.

Dipboye, R.L. (1977). Alternative approaches to deindividuation. *Psychological Bulletin, 84,* 1057–1075.

Doweiko, H.E. (1990). *Concepts of chemical dependency.* Pacific Grove, CA: Brooks/ Cole.

Doyne, E.J., Chambless, D.L., & Beutler, L.E. (1983). Aerobic exercise as a treatment for depression in women. *Behavior Therapy, 14,* 434–440.

Drenick, E.J., & Johnson, D. (1980). Weight reduction by fasting and semistarvation in morbid obesity: Long-term follow-up. In G. Bray (Ed.), *Obesity: Comparative methods of weight control* (pp. 25–34). London: Libbey.

Duval, S., & Wicklund, R.A. (1972). *A theory of objective self-awareness.* New York: Academic Press.

Edelman, B., Engell, D., Bronstein, P., & Hirsch, E. (1986). Environmental effects on the intake of overweight and normal-weight men. *Appetite, 7,* 71–83.

Emmons, R.A., & King, L.A. (1988). Conflict among personal strivings: Immediate and long-term implications for psychological and physical well-being. *Journal of Personality and Social Psychology, 54,* 1040–1048.

Engebretson, T.O., Mathews, K.A., & Scheier, M.F. (1989). Relations between anger expression and cardiovascular reactivity: Reconciling inconsistent findings through a matching hypothesis. *Journal of Personality and Social Psychology, 57,* 513–521.

Erber, R., & Tesser, A. (1992). Task effort and mood regulation: The absorption hypothesis. *Journal of Experimental Social Psychology, 28,* 339–359.

Faber, R.J. (1992). Money changes everything: Compulsive buying from a biopsychosocial perspective. *American Behavioral Scientist, 35,* 809–819.

Fabricius, W.V., Nagoshi, C.T., & MacKinnon, D.P. (1993). Beliefs about the harmfulness of drug use in adults who use different drugs. *Psychology of Addictive Behaviors, 7,* 52–65.

Fagerström, K.O. (1987). Reducing the weight gain after stopping smoking. *Addictive Behaviors, 12,* 91–93.

Fagerström, K.O., & Schneider, N.G. (1989). Measuring nicotine dependence: A review of the Fagerström Tolerance Questionnaire. *Journal of Behavioral Medicine, 12,* 159–181.

Fallon, A.E., & Rozin, P. (1985). Sex differences in perceptions of desirable body shape. *Journal of Abnormal Psychology, 94,* 102–105.

Farha, J.G., & Sher, K.J. (1989). The effects of consent procedures on the psychophysiological assessment of anxiety: A methodological inquiry. *Psychophysiology, 26,* 185–191.

Fazio, R.H., Powell, M.C., & Herr, P.M. (1983). Toward a process model of the attitude–behavior relation: Accessing one's attitude upon mere observation of the attitude object. *Journal of Personality and Social Psychology, 44,* 723–735.

Feindler, E.L. (1989). Adolescent anger control: Review and critique. In M. Hersen, R.M. Eisler, & P.M. Miller (Eds.), *Progress in behavior modification.* Newbury Park, CA: Sage.

Feindler, E.L., & Ecton, R.B. (1986). *Adolescent anger control: Cognitive behavioral techniques.* Elmsford, NY: Pergamon.

Ferrari, J.R. (1991). Self-handicapping by procrastinators: Protecting self-esteem, social-esteem, or both? *Journal of Research in Personality, 25,* 245–261.

Ferrari, J.R. (1992). Procrastination and perfect behavior: An exploratory factor analysis of self-presentation, self-awareness, and self-handicapping components. *Journal of Research in Personality, 26,* 75–84.

Ferrari, J.R., & Olivette, M.J. (1994). Parental authoritarianism and development of dysfunctional procrastination. *Journal of Research in Personality, 28,* 87–100.

Fingarette, H. (1988). *Heavy drinking: The myth of alcoholism as a disease.* Berkeley, CA: University of California Press.

Fisher, J.D., & Farina, A. (1979). Consequences of beliefs about the nature of mental disorders. *Journal of Abnormal Psychology, 88,* 320–327.

Foreyt, J.P. (1987). Issues in the assessment and treatment of obesity. *Journal of Consulting and Clinical Psychology, 55,* 677–684.

Fox, F.V., & Staw, B.M. (1979). The trapped administrator: Effects of insecurity and policy resistance upon commitment to a course of action. *Administrative Sciences Quarterly, 24,* 449–471.

Foxall, G.R. (1990). *Consumer psychology in behavioural perspective.* London: Routledge.

Frank, S.J., Jacobson, S., & Tuer, M. (1990). Psychological predictors of young adults' drinking behaviors. *Journal of Personality and Social Psychology, 59,* 770–780.

Frankel, A., & Snyder, M.L. (1978). Poor performance following unsolvable problems: Learned helplessness or egotism? *Journal of Personality and Social Psychology, 36,* 1415–1423.

Frederickson, L.W. (1976). Single-case designs in the modification of smoking. *Addictive Behaviors, 1,* 311–319.

Freund, T., Kruglanski, A.W., & Shpitzajzen, A. (1985). The freezing and unfreezing of impressional primacy: Effects of the need for structure and the fear of invalidity. *Personality and Social Psychology Bulletin, 11,* 479–487.

Frost, R.O., Goolkasian, G.A., Ely, R.J., & Blanchard, F.A. (1982). Depression, restraint and eating behavior. *Behavior Research and Therapy, 20,* 113–121.

Funder, D.C., & Block, J. (1989). The role of ego-control, ego-resiliency, and IQ in delay of gratification in adolescence. *Journal of Personality and Social Psychology, 57,* 1041–1050.

Funder, D.C., Block, J.H., & Block, J. (1983). Delay of gratification: Some longitudinal personality correlates. *Journal of Personality and Social Psychology, 44,* 1198–1213.

Funkenstein, D.H., King, S.H., & Drolette, M. (1954). The direction of anger during a laboratory stress-inducing situation. *Psychosomatic Medicine, 16,* 404–413.

Fussell, P. (1989). *Wartime: Understanding and behavior in the Second World War.* New York: Oxford University Press.

Garcia, M.E., Schmitz, J.M., & Doerfler, L.A. (1990). A fine-grained analysis of the role of self-efficacy in self-initiated attempts to quit smoking. *Journal of Consulting and Clinical Psychology, 58,* 317–322.

Garner, D.M., & Wooley, S.C. (1991). Confronting the failure of behavioral and dietary treatments for obesity. *Clinical Psychology Review, 11,* 729–780.

Gelles, R.J. (1974). *The violent home.* Beverly Hills, CA: Sage.

Gelles, R.J. (1979). *Family violence.* Beverly Hills, CA: Sage.

Gellhorn, E. (1964). Motion and emotion: The role of proprioception in the physiology and pathology of emotions. *Psychological Review, 71,* 457–472.

Gilbert, D.G. (1979). Paradoxical tranquilizing and emotion-reducing effects of nicotine. *Psychological Bulletin, 86,* 643–661.

Gilbert, D.G., & Spielberger, C.D. (1987). Effects of smoking on heart rate, anxiety and feelings of success during social interaction. *Journal of Behavioral Medicine, 10,* 629–638.

Gilbert, D.T., Krull, D.S., & Pelham, B.W. (1988). Of thoughts unspoken: Social inference and the self-regulation of behavior. *Journal of Personality and Social Psychology, 55,* 685–694.

Gilbert, D.T., & Osborne, R.E. (1989). Thinking backward: Some curable and incurable consequences of cognitive busyness. *Journal of Personality and Social Psychology, 57,* 940–949.

Gilovich, T. (1983). Biased evaluation and persistence in gambling. *Journal of Personality and Social Psychology, 44,* 1110–1126.

Gilovich, T. (1991). *How we know what isn't so: The fallibility of human reason in everyday life.* New York: Free Press.

Gilovich, T., & Douglas, C. (1986). Biased evaluations of randomly determined gambling outcomes. *Journal of Experimental Social Psychology, 22,* 228–241.

Gilovich, T., Vallone, R., & Tversky, A. (1985). The hot hand in basketball: On the misperception of random sequences. *Cognitive Psychology, 17,* 295–314.

Glad, W., & Adesso, V.J. (1976). The relative importance of socially induced tension and behavioral contagion for smoking behavior. *Journal of Abnormal Psychology, 85,* 119–121.

Glasgow, R.E., Klesges, R.C., Mizes, J.S., & Pechacek, T.F. (1985). Quitting smoking: Strategies used and variables associated with success in a stop-smoking contest. *Journal of Consulting and Clinical Psychology, 53,* 905–912.

Glass, D.C., Singer, J.E., & Friedman, L.N. (1969). Psychic cost of adaptation to an environmental stressor. *Journal of Personality and Social Psychology, 12,* 200–210.

Golding, J.M., Burnam, M.A., Benjamin, B., & Wells, K.B. (1992). Reasons for drinking, alcohol use, and alcoholism among Mexican Americans and non-Hispanic whites. *Psychology of Addictive Behaviors, 6,* 155–167.

Goldstein, A.P., & Glick, B. (1987). *Aggression replacement training.* Champaign, IL: Research Press.

Gollwitzer, P.M., & Kinney, R.F. (1989). Effects of deliberative and implemental mindsets on illusion of control. *Journal of Personality and Social Psychology, 56,* 531–542.

Gondolf, E.W. (1985). *Men who batter: An integrated approach for stopping wife abuse.* Holmes Beach, FL: Learning Publications Inc.

Goodman, R.A., Istre, G.R., Jordan, F.B., Herndon, J.L., & Kelaghan, J. (1991). Alcohol and fatal injuries in Oklahoma. *Journal of Studies on Alcohol, 52,* 156–161.

Gottfredson, M.R., & Hirschi, T. (1990). *A general theory of crime.* Stanford, CA: Stanford University Press.

Grant, B.F., Harford, T.C., Chou, P., Pickering, R., Dawson, D.A., Stinson, F.S., & Noble, J. (1991). Epidemiologic Bulletin No. 27: Prevalence of DSM–III–R alcohol abuse and dependence: United States, 1988. *Alcohol Health Research World, 15,* 91–96.

Greist, J.H., Klein, M.H., Eischens, R.R., Faris, J., Gurman, A.S., & Morgan, W.P. (1979). Running as treatment for depression. *Comprehensive Psychiatry, 20,* 41–53.

Griffiths, R., Bigelow, G., & Liebson, I. (1976). Facilitation of human tobacco self-administration by ethanol: A behavioral analysis. *Journal of the Experimental Analysis of Behavior, 25,* 279–292.

Grilo, C.M., Shiffman, S., & Wing, R.R. (1989). Relapse crises and coping among dieters. *Journal of Consulting and Clinical Psychology, 57,* 488–495.

Gross, J., Stitzer, M.L., & Maldanado, J. (1989). Nicotine replacement: Effects on postcessation weight gain. *Journal of Consulting and Clinical Psychology, 57,* 87–92.

Grunberg, N.E. (1982). The effects of nicotine and cigarette smoking on food consumption and taste preferences. *Addictive Behaviors, 7,* 317–331.

Grunberg, N.E., & Bowen, D.J. (1985). Coping with sequelae of smoking cessation. *Journal of Cardiopulmonary Rehabilitation, 5,* 285–289.

Hackworth, D.H., & Sherman, J. (1989). *About face: The odyssey of an American warrior.* New York: Simon & Schuster.

Haight, M.R. (1980). *A study of self-deception.* Brighton, Sussex, England: Harvester Press.

Hall, S.M., Ginsberg, D., & Jones, R.T. (1986). Smoking cessation and weight gain. *Journal of Consulting and Clinical Psychology, 54,* 342–346.

Hall, S.M., McGee, R., Tunstall, C., Duffy, J., & Benowitz, N. (1989). Changes in food intake and activity after quitting smoking. *Journal of Consulting and Clinical Psychology, 57,* 81–86.

Hamburger, W.W. (1951). Emotional aspects of obesity. *Medical Clinics of North America, 35,* 483–499.

Hamilton, J.C., Aldarondo, F., Moss, M.M., & Clark, S.L. (1994). *Preliminary support for a self-regulation model of procrastination.* Manuscript in preparation.

Hansen, W.B., Graham, J.W., Sobel, J.L., Shelton, D.R., Flay, B.R., & Johnson, C.A. (1987). The consistency of peer and parental influences on tobacco, alcohol, and marijuana use among young adolescents. *Journal of Behavioral Medicine, 10,* 559–579.

Harackiewicz, J.M., Sansone, C., Blair, L., Epstein, J.A., & Manderlink, G. (1987). Attributional processes in behavior change and maintenance: Smoking cessation and continued abstinence. *Journal of Consulting and Clinical Psychology, 55,* 372–378.

Harburg, E., Erfurt, J.C., Hauenstien, L.S., Chape, C., Schull, W.J., & Schork, M.A. (1973). Socio-ecological stress, suppressed hostility, skin color, and black–white male blood pressure: Detroit. *Psychosomatic Medicine, 35,* 276–296.

Hatvany, N., & Strack, F. (1980). The impact of a discredited key witness. *Journal of Applied Social Psychology, 10,* 490–509.

Haynes, S.G., Feinleib, M., & Kannel, W.B. (1980). The relationship of psychosocial factors to coronary heart disease in the Framingham Study. III. Eight year incidence of coronary heart disease. *American Journal of Epidemiology, 111,* 37–58.

Heather, N. (1991). Impaired control over alcohol consumption. In N. Heather, W.R. Miller, & J. Greeley (Eds.), *Self-control and the addictive behaviors* (pp. 153–179). Botany, Australia: Maxwell Macmillan.

Heather, N., & Robertson, I. (1983). *Controlled drinking* (rev. ed.). London: Methuen.

Heatherton, T.F. (1993a). Body dissatisfaction, self-focus, and dieting status among women. *Psychology of Addictive Behaviors, 7,* 225–231.

Heatherton, T.F. (1993b, March). *Eating habits and practises 1982–1992.* Paper presented to the Society for Research in Child Development, New Orleans.

Heatherton, T.F., & Ambady, N. (1993). Self-esteem, self-prediction, and living up to commitments. In R. Baumeister (Ed.), *Self-esteem: The puzzle of low self-regard* (pp. 131–145). New York: Plenum.

Heatherton, T.F., & Baumeister, R.F. (1991). Binge eating as escape from self-awareness. *Psychological Bulletin, 110,* 86–108.

Heatherton, T.F., Herman, C.P., & Polivy, J. (1991). Effects of physical threat and ego threat on eating. *Journal of Personality and Social Psychology, 60,* 138–143.

Heatherton, T.F., Kozlowski, L.T., Frecker, R.C., Rickert, W., & Robinson, J. (1989). Measuring the heaviness of smoking: Using self-reported time to the first cigarette of the day and number of cigarettes smoked per day. *British Journal of Addiction, 84,* 791–800.

Heatherton, T.F., & Nichols, P.A. (in press). Personal accounts of successful versus failed attempts at life change. *Personality and Social Psychology Bulletin.*

Heatherton, T.F., & Polivy, J. (1992). Chronic dieting and eating disorders: A spiral model. In J. Crowther, S. Hobfall, M. Stephens, & D. Tennenbaum (Eds.), *The etiology of bulimia: The individual and familial context.* Washington, DC: Hemisphere.

Heatherton, T.F., Polivy, J., & Herman, C.P. (1989). Restraint and internal responsiveness: Effects of placebo manipulations of hunger state on eating. *Journal of Abnormal Psychology, 98,* 89–92.

Heatherton, T.F., Polivy, J., Herman, C.P., & Baumeister, R.F. (1993). Self-awareness, task failure, and disinhibition: How attentional focus affects eating. *Journal of Personality, 61,* 49–61.

Heatherton, T.F., Striepe, M., & Nichols, P. (1994). Effects of task failure and musical mood induction on coping behavior in dieters and nondieters. Manuscript submitted for publication.

Hecker, M.H.L., Chesney, M.A., Black, G.W., & Frautschi, N. (1988). Coronary prone behaviors in the Western Collaborative Group Study. *Psychosomatic Medicine, 50*, 153–164.

Heckhausen, H., & Strang, H. (1988). Efficiency under record performance demands: Exertion control—An individual difference variable? *Journal of Personality and Social Psychology, 55*, 489–498.

Henningfield, J.E. (1984a). Pharmacological basis and treatment of cigarette smoking. *Journal of Clinical Psychiatry, 45*, 24–34.

Henningfield, J.E. (1984b). Behavioral pharmacology of cigarette smoking. In T. Thompson, T.B. Dews, & J.E. Barrett (Eds.), *Advances in behavioral pharmacology* (Vol. 4, pp. 131–210). Orlando, FL: Academic Press.

Henslin, J.M. (1967). Craps and magic. *American Journal of Sociology, 73*, 316–330.

Herman, C.P. (1974). External and internal cues as determinants of the smoking behavior of light and heavy smokers. *Journal of Personality and Social Psychology, 30*, 664–672.

Herman, C.P., & Kozlowski, L.T. (1979). Indulgence, excess, and restraint: Perspectives on consummatory behavior in everyday life. *Journal of Drug Issues, 2*, 185–196.

Herman, C.P., & Mack, D. (1975). Restrained and unrestrained eating. *Journal of Personality, 43*, 647–660.

Herman, C.P., Olmsted, M.P., & Polivy, J. (1983). Obesity, externality, and susceptibility to social influence: An integrated analysis. *Journal of Personality and Social Psychology, 45*, 926–934.

Herman, C.P., & Polivy, J. (1975). Anxiety, restraint and eating behavior. *Journal of Abnormal Psychology, 84*, 666–672.

Herman, C.P., & Polivy, J. (1980). Restrained eating. In A.J. Stunkard (Ed.), *Obesity*. Philadelphia: Saunders.

Herman, C.P., & Polivy, J. (1993). Mental control of eating: Excitatory and inhibitory food thoughts. In D.M. Wegner & J.W. Pennebaker (Eds.), *Handbook of mental control* (pp. 491–505). Englewood Cliffs, NJ: Prentice Hall.

Herman, C.P., Polivy, J., & Heatherton, T.F. (1990). The effects of distress on eating: A review of the experimental literature. Submitted for publication.

Herman, C.P., Polivy, J., Klajner, F., & Esses, V. (1981). Salivation in dieters and nondieters. *Appetite, 2*, 356–361.

Herman, C.P., Polivy, J., Lank, C.L., & Heatherton, T.F. (1987). Anxiety, hunger and eating. *Journal of Abnormal Psychology, 96*, 264–269.

Herman, C.P., Polivy, J., & Silver, R. (1979). The effects of an observer on eating behavior: The induction of sensible eating. *Journal of Personality, 47*, 85–99.

Herskovic, J.E., Rose, J.E., & Jarvik, M.E. (1986). Cigarette desirability and nicotine preference in smokers. *Pharmacology Biochemistry and Behavior, 24*, 171–175.

Higgins, R.L., & Marlatt, G.A. (1973). Effect of anxiety arousal on the consumption of alcohol by alcoholics and social drinkers. *Journal of Consulting and Clinical Psychology, 41*, 426–433.

Higgins, R.L., & Marlatt, G.A. (1975). Fear of interpersonal evaluation as a determinant of alcohol consumption in male social drinkers. *Journal of Abnormal Psychology, 84*, 644–651.

Hoch, S.J., & Loewenstein, G.F. (1991). Time-inconsistent preferences and consumer self-control. *Journal of Consumer Research, 17*, 492–507.

Hodgson, R., Stockwell, T., & Rankin, H. (1979). Can alcohol reduce tension? *Behavior*

Research and Therapy, 17, 459–466.

Holroyd, K.A., & Gorkin, L. (1983). Young adults at risk for hypertension: Effects of family history and anger management in determining responses to interpersonal conflict. *Journal of Psychosomatic Research, 27,* 131–138.

Houghton, W.E. (1957). *The Victorian frame of mind, 1830–1879.* New Haven, CT: Yale University Press.

Huber, H., Karlin, R., & Nathan, P. (1976). Blood alcohol discrimination by nonalcoholics: The role of internal and external cues. *Journal of Studies on Alcohol, 37,* 27–39.

Huber, R.M. (1987). *The American idea of success.* New York: McGraw-Hill.

Hull, J.G. (1981). A self-awareness model of the causes and effects of alcohol consumption. *Journal of Abnormal Psychology, 90,* 586–600.

Hull, J.G., & Bond, C.F., Jr. (1986). Social and behavioral consequences of alcohol consumption and expectancy: A meta-analysis. *Psychological Bulletin, 99,* 347–360.

Hull, J.G., Levenson, R.W., Young, R.D., & Sher, K.J. (1983). Self-awareness-reducing effects of alcohol consumption. *Journal of Personality and Social Psychology, 44,* 461–473.

Hull, J.G., & Young, R.D. (1983). Self-consciousness, self-esteem, and success–failure as determinants of alcohol consumption in male social drinkers. *Journal of Personality and Social Psychology, 44,* 1097–1109.

Hunt, D.A., & Rosen, J.C. (1981). Thoughts about food by obese and nonobese individuals. *Cognitive Therapy and Research, 5,* 317–322.

Ingram, R.E. (1990). Self-focused attention in clinical disorders: Review and a conceptual model. *Psychological Bulletin, 107,* 156–176.

Izard, C.E. (1972). *Patterns of emotion: A new analysis of anxiety and depression.* New York: Academic Press.

Izard, C.E. (1977). *Human emotions.* New York: Plenum.

Izard, C.E. (1990). Facial expression and the regulation of emotions. *Journal of Personality and Social Psychology, 58,* 487–498.

Jacobson, E. (1929). *Progressive relaxation.* Chicago: University of Chicago Press.

James, W. (1890/1950). *The principles of psychology* (Vol. 2). New York: Dover.

Janoff-Bulman, R., & Brickman, P. (1982). Expectations and what people learn from failure. In N.T. Feather (Ed.), *Expectations and actions: Expectancy-value models in psychology.* Hillsdale, NJ: Erlbaum.

Jansen, A., Merckelbach, H., Oosterlaan, J., Tuiten, A., & van den Hout, M. (1988). Cognitions and self-talk during food intake of restrained and unrestrained eaters. *Behavior Research and Therapy, 26,* 393–398.

Jarvik, M.E. (1979). Biological influences on cigarette smoking. In N.A. Krasnegor (Ed.), *The behavioral aspects of smoking* (pp. 7–45). Washington, DC: Public Health Service, National Institute on Drug Abuse.

Jasper, J. (1992). The challenge of weight control: A personal view. In T.A. Wadden & T.B. VanItallie (Eds.), *Treatment of the seriously obese patient* (pp. 411–434). New York: Guilford.

Jellinek, E.M. (1960). *The disease concept of alcoholism.* New Brunswick, NJ: Hillhouse Press.

Jessor, R., & Jessor, S.L. (1977). *Problem behavior and psychosocial development: A longitudinal study of youth.* New York: Academic Press.

Johnson, C., & Connors, M.E. (1987). *The etiology and treatment of bulimia nervosa.* New York: Basic Books.

Johnson, C., & Larson, R. (1982). Bulimia: An analysis of moods and behavior. *Psychosomatic Medicine, 44,* 341–351.

Johnson, D.J., & Rusbult, C.E. (1989). Resisting temptation: Devaluation of alternative partners as a means of maintaining commitment in close relationships. *Journal of Personality and Social Psychology, 57,* 967–980.

Johnston, L.D., O'Malley, P.M., & Bachman, J.G. (1991). *Drug use among American high school seniors, college students, and young adults, 1975–1990. Volume 1: High school seniors.* Washington, DC: Department of Health and Human Services.

Jones, E.E., & Berglas, S.C. (1978). Control of attributions about the self through self-handicapping strategies: The appeal of alcohol and the role of underachievement. *Personality and Social Psychology Bulletin, 4,* 200–206.

Josephs, R.A., Larrick, R.P., Steele, C.M., & Nisbett, R.E. (1992). Protecting the self from the negative consequences of risky decisions. *Journal of Personality and Social Psychology, 62,* 26–37.

Kaminer, W. (1993). *I'm dysfunctional, you're dysfunctional: The recovery movement and other self-help fashions.* New York: Random House/Vintage.

Kandel, D.B., Davies, M., Karus, D., & Yamaguchi, K. (1986). The consequences in young adulthood of adolescent drug involvement. *Archives of General Psychiatry, 43,* 746–754.

Kandel, D., & Faust, R. (1975). Sequence and stages in patterns of adolescent drug use. *Archives of General Psychology, 32,* 923–932.

Kaplan, H.I., & Kaplan, H.S. (1957). The psychosomatic concept of obesity. *Journal of Nervous and Mental Disease, 125,* 181–201.

Kaplan, R.F., Meyer, R.W., & Stroebel, C.F. (1983). Alcohol dependence and responsivity to an ethanol stimulus as predictors of alcohol consumption. *British Journal of Addiction, 78,* 259–267.

Karniol, R., & Miller, D.T. (1983). Why not wait?: A cognitive model of self-imposed delay termination. *Journal of Personality and Social Psychology, 45,* 935–942.

Karoly, P. (1993). Mechanisms of self-regulation: An overview. *Annual Review of Psychology, 44,* 23–52.

Katz, J. (1988). *Seductions of crime: The moral and sensual attractions of doing evil.* New York: Basic Books.

Keegan, J. (1976). *The face of battle.* New York: Military Heritage Press.

Keesey, R.E. (1986). A set-point theory of obesity. In K. Brownell & J. Foreyt (Eds.), *Handbook of eating disorders: Physiology, psychology, and treatment of obesity, anorexia, and bulimia* (pp. 62–87). New York: Basic Books.

Keinan, G. (1987). Decision making under stress: Scanning of alternatives under controllable and uncontrollable threats. *Journal of Personality and Social Psychology, 52,* 639–644.

Kelly, E.L., & Conley, J.J. (1987). Personality and compatibility: A prospective analysis of marital stability and marital satisfaction. *Journal of Personality and Social Psychology, 52,* 27–40.

Keys, A., Brozek, J., Henschel, A., Mickelson, O., & Taylor, H.L. (1950). *The biology of human starvation* (Vol. 1). Minneapolis, MN: University of Minnesota Press.

Kimble, G., & Perlmuter, L. (1970). The problem of volition. *Psychological Review, 77,* 361–384.

King, G. A., Herman, C.P., & Polivy, J. (1987). Food perception in dieters and non-dieters. *Appetite, 8*, 147–158.

Kirsch, I., Mearns, J., & Catanzaro, S.J. (1990). Mood regulation expectancies as determinants of depression in college students. *Journal of Counseling Psychology, 37*, 306–312.

Kirschenbaum, D.S. (1987). Self-regulatory failure: A review with clinical implications. *Clinical Psychology Review, 7*, 77–104.

Kirschenbaum, D.S., Humphrey, L.L., & Malett, S.D. (1981). Specificity of planning in adult self-control: An applied investigation. *Journal of Personality and Social Psychology, 40*, 941–950.

Kirschenbaum, D.S., Malett, S., Humphrey, L.L., & Tomarken, A.J. (1982). Specificity of planning and the maintenance of self-control: 1 year follow-up of a study improvement program. *Behavior Therapy, 13*, 232–240.

Kirschenbaum, D.S., & Tomarken, A.J. (1982). Some antecedents of regulatory eating in restrained and unrestrained eaters. *Journal of Abnormal Psychology, 91*, 326–336.

Kirschenbaum, D.S., Tomarken, A.J., & Ordman, A.M. (1982). Specificity of planning and choice applied to adult self-control. *Journal of Personality and Social Psychology, 42*, 576–585.

Klajner, F., Herman, C.P., Polivy, J., & Chabra, R. (1981). Human obesity, dieting, and anticipatory salivation to food. *Physiology and Behavior, 27*, 195–198.

Kleinke, C.L., & Walton, G.H. (1982). Influence of reinforced smiling on the affective responses in an interview. *Journal of Personality and Social Psychology, 42*, 557–565.

Klesges, R.C., Klem, M.L., & Bene, C.R. (1989). Effects of dietary restraint, obesity, and gender on holiday eating behavior and weight gain. *Journal of Abnormal Psychology, 98*, 499–503.

Klesges, R.C., & Klesges, L.M. (1988). Cigarette smoking as a dieting strategy in a university population. *International Journal of Eating Disorders, 7*, 413–419.

Klesges, R.C., Meyers, A.W., Klesges, L.M., & LaVasque, M.E. (1989). Smoking, body weight, and their effects on smoking behavior: A comprehensive review of the literature. *Psychological Bulletin, 106*, 204–232.

Klinger, E. (1993). Clinical approaches to mood control. In D.M. Wegner & J.W. Pennebaker (Eds.), *Handbook of mental control* (pp. 344–369). Englewood Cliffs, NJ: Prentice Hall.

Knight, L., & Boland, F. (1989). Restrained eating: An experimental disentanglement of the disinhibiting variables of calories and food type. *Journal of Abnormal Psychology, 98*, 412–420.

Koch, H. (1978). *A history of Prussia*. New York: Dorset.

Konovsky, M., & Wilsnack, S. (1982). Social drinking and self-esteem in married couples. *Journal of Studies on Alcohol, 43*, 319–333.

Kopp, C.B. (1989). Regulation of distress and negative emotions: A developmental view. *Developmental Psychology, 25*, 343–354.

Koshland, D.E. (1989). Drunk driving and statistical mortality. *Science, 244*, 513.

Kouzis, A.C., & Labouvie, E.W. (1992). Use intensity, functional elaboration, and contextual constraints as facets of adolescent alcohol and marijuana use. *Psychology of Addictive Behaviors, 6*, 188–195.

Kozlowski, L.T. (1979). Psychosocial influences on cigarette smoking. In N.A. Krasnegor (Ed.), *The behavioral aspects of smoking* (pp. 97–125). Washington, DC: Public Health Service, National Institute on Drug Abuse.

Kozlowski, L.T. (1981). Smokers, non-smokers, and low tar smokers. *Lancet, 1,* 508.

Kozlowski, L.T. (1982). The determinants of tobacco use: Cigarette smoking in the context of other forms of tobacco use. *Canadian Journal of Public Health, 73,* 236–241.

Kozlowski, L.T. (1983). Physical indicators of actual tar and nicotine yields of cigarettes. In J. Grabowski & C.S. Bell (Eds.), *Measurement in the analysis of treatment of smoking behavior* (NIDA Research Monograph No. 48, pp. 50–61). Washington, DC: US Government Printing Office.

Kozlowski, L.T., Director, J., & Harford, M.A. (1981). Tobacco dependence, restraint and time to the first cigarette of the day. *Addictive Behaviors, 6,* 307–312.

Kozlowski, L.T., Heatherton, T.F., & Ferrence, R.G. (1989). Pack size, reported cigarette smoking rates and the heaviness of smoking. *Canadian Journal of Public Health, 80,* 266–270.

Kozlowski, L.T., Heatherton, T.F., Frecker, R.C., & Nolte, H.E. (1989). Self-selected behavioral blocking of vents on low-yield cigarettes. *Pharmacology, Biochemistry and Behavior, 33,* 815–819.

Kozlowski, L.T., & Herman, C.P. (1984). The interaction of psychosocial and biological determinants of tobacco use: More on the boundary model. *Journal of Applied Social Psychology, 14,* 244–256.

Kozlowski, L.T., Porter, C.Q., Orleans, C.T., Pope, M.A., & Heatherton, T.F. (in press). Predicting smoking cessation with self-reported measures of nicotine dependence: FTQ, FTND, and HSI. *Drug and Alcohol Dependence.*

Kozlowski, L.T., & Wilkinson, A.D. (1987). Use and misuse of the concept of craving by alcohol, tobacco, and drug researchers. *British Journal of Addiction, 82,* 31–36.

Kozlowski, L.T., Wilkinson, A., Skinner, W., Kent, C., Franklin, T., & Pope, M. (1989). Comparing tobacco cigarette dependence with other drug dependencies: Greater or equal 'difficulty quitting' and 'urges to use,' but less 'pleasure' from cigarettes. *Journal of the American Medical Association, 261,* 898–901.

Kraemer, D.L., & Hastrup, J.L. (1988). Crying in adults: Self-control and autonomic correlates. *Journal of Social and Clinical Psychology, 6,* 53–68.

Kraut, R.E. (1982). Social pressure, facial feedback, and emotion. *Journal of Personality and Social Psychology, 42,* 853–863.

Kruglanski, A.W. (1989). *Lay-epistemics and human knowledge: Cognitive and motivational bases.* New York: Plenum.

Kruglanski, A.W. (1990). Lay-epistemic theory in social–cognitive psychology. *Psychological Inquiry, 1,* 181–197.

Kruglanski, A.W., & Freund, T. (1983). The freezing and unfreezing of lay-inferences: Effects on impressional primacy, ethnic stereotyping, and numerical anchoring. *Journal of Experimental Social Psychology, 19,* 448–468.

Kunda, Z. (1990). The case for motivated reasoning. *Psychological Bulletin, 108,* 480–498.

Laberg, J.C., & Ellertsen, B. (1987). Psychophysiological indicators of craving in alcoholics. *British Journal of Addiction, 82,* 1341–1348.

Laberg, J.C., Hugdahl, K., Stormark, K.M., Nordby, H., & Aas, H. (1992). Effects of visual alcohol cues on alcoholics' autonomic arousal. *Psychology of Addictive Behaviors, 6*, 181–187.

Laberg, J.C., Wilson, G.T., Eldredge, K., & Nordby, H. (1991). Effects of mood on heart rate reactivity in bulimia nervosa. *International Journal of Eating Disorders, 10*, 169–178.

Laird, J.D. (1974). Self-attribution of emotion: The effects of expressive behavior on the quality of emotional experience. *Journal of Personality and Social Psychology, 29*, 475–486.

Laird, J.D. (1984). The real role of facial response in the experience of emotion: A reply to Tourangeau & Ellsworth, and others. *Journal of Personality and Social Psychology, 47*, 909–917.

Langer, E.J. (1975). The illusion of control. *Journal of Personality and Social Psychology, 32*, 191–198.

Langer, E.J., & Roth, J. (1975). Heads I win, tails it's chance: The illusion of control as a function of the sequence of outcomes in a purely chance task. *Journal of Personality and Social Psychology, 32*, 951–955.

Lansky, D., Nathan, P.E., & Lawson, D.M. (1978). Blood alcohol discrimination by alcoholics: The role of internal and external cues. *Journal of Consulting and Clinical Psychology, 46*, 953–960.

Lanzetta, J.T., Cartwright-Smith, J.E., & Kleck, R.E. (1976). Effects of nonverbal dissimulation of emotional experience and autonomic arousal. *Journal of Personality and Social Psychology, 33*, 354–370.

Larsen, R. (1993, August). *Mood regulation in everyday life.* Paper presented to the American Psychological Association, Toronto, Ontario, Canada.

Larsen, R.J. (1984). Theory and measurement of affect intensity as an individual difference characteristic. *Dissertation Abstracts International, 5*, 2297B. (University Microfilms No. 84-22112)

Larsen, R.J., Diener, E., & Emmons, R.A. (1986). Affect intensity and reactions to daily life. *Journal of Personality and Social Psychology, 51*, 803–814.

Larsen, R.J., & Ketelaar, T. (1989). Extraversion, neuroticism, and susceptibility to positive and negative mood induction procedures. *Personality and Individual Difference, 10*, 1221–1228.

Larsen, R.J., & Ketelaar, T. (1991). Personality and susceptibility to positive and negative emotional states. *Journal of Personality and Social Psychology, 61*, 132–140.

Lawson, A. (1988). *Adultery: An analysis of love and betrayal.* New York: Basic Books.

Lay, L.H. (1990). Working to schedule on personal projects: An assessment of person–project characteristics and trait procrastination. *Journal of Social Behavior & Personality, 5*, 91–104.

Lay, L.H., & Schouwenburg, H.C. (1993). Trait procrastination, time management, and academic behavior. *Journal of Social Behavior & Personality, 8*, 647–662.

Leigh, B.C., & Schafer, J.C. (1993). Heavy drinking occasions and the occurrence of sexual activity. *Psychology of Addictive Behaviors, 7*, 197–200.

Leon, G., & Chamberlain, K. (1973). Emotional arousal, eating patterns, and body image as differential factors associated with varying success in maintaining a weight loss. *Journal of Consulting and Clinical Psychology, 40*, 474.

Leon, G.R., & Roth, L. (1977). Obesity: Psychological causes, correlations, and speculations. *Psychological Bulletin, 84*, 117–139.

Leon, M.R., & Revelle, W. (1985). Effects of anxiety on analogical reasoning: A test of three theoretical models. *Journal of Personality and Social Psychology, 49*, 1302–1315.

Leonard, K.E. (1989). The impact of explicit aggressive and implicit nonaggressive cues on aggression in intoxicated and sober males. *Personality and Social Psychology Bulletin, 15*, 390–400.

Lesieur, H.R. (1992). Compulsive gambling. *Society, 29*, 43–50.

Levenson, R.W., Sher, K.J., Grossman, L.M., Newman, J., & Newlin, D.B. (1980). Alcohol and stress-response dampening: Pharmacological effects, expectancy, and tension reduction. *Journal of Abnormal Psychology, 89*, 528–538.

Leventhal, H., & Cleary, P.D. (1980). The smoking problem: A review of research and theory in behavioral risk modification. *Psychological Bulletin, 88*, 370–405.

Leventhal, H., & Mace, W. (1970). The effect of laughter on evaluation of a slapstick movie. *Journal of Personality, 38*, 16–30.

Leventhal, H., Watts, J., & Pagano, F. (1967). Effects of fear and instructions on how to cope with danger. *Journal of Personality and Social Psychology, 6*, 313–321.

Levine, H.G. (1978). The discovery of addiction: Changing conceptions of habitual drunkenness in America. *Journal of Studies on Alcohol, 39*, 143–174.

Levitsky, D.A., Faust, I., & Glassman, M. (1976). The ingestion of food and the recovery of body weight following fasting in the naive rat. *Physiology and Behavior, 17*, 575–580.

Lied, E.R., & Marlatt, G.A. (1979). Modelling as a determinant of alcohol consumption: Effect of subject sex and prior drinking history. *Addictive Behaviors, 4*, 47–54.

Lifton, R.J. (1986). *The Nazi doctors.* New York: Basic Books.

Lindemann, E. (1944). Symptomatology and management of acute grief. *American Journal of Psychiatry, 101*, 141–148.

Linder, D.E., Cooper, J., & Jones, E.E. (1967). Decision freedom as a determinant of the role of incentive magnitude in attitude change. *Journal of Personality and Social Psychology, 6*, 245–254.

Litt, M.D., Cooney, N.L., Kadden, R.M., & Gaupp, L. (1990). Reactivity to alcohol cues and induced moods in alcoholics. *Addictive Behaviors, 15*, 137–146.

Lochman, J.E. (1984). Psychological characteristics and assessment of aggressive adolescents. In C.R. Keith (Ed.), *The aggressive adolescent: Clinical perspectives.* New York: Free Press.

Logue, A.W. (1991). *The psychology of eating and drinking: An introduction* (2nd ed.). New York: Freeman.

Lyubomirsky, S., & Nolen-Hoeksema, S. (1993). Self-perpetuating properties of dysphoric rumination. *Journal of Personality and Social Psychology, 65*, 339–349.

MacDougall, J.M., Dembroski, T.M., Dimsdale, J.E., & Hackett, T.P. (1985). Components of Type A, hostility, and anger-in: Further relationships to angiographic findings. *Health Psychology, 4*, 137–152.

MacDougall, J.M., Dembroski, T.M., & Krantz, D.S. (1981). Effects of types of challenges on pressor and heart rate responses in Type A and B women. *Psychophysiology, 18*, 1–9.

Manderlink, G., & Harackiewicz, J.M. (1984). Proximal versus distal goal setting and intrinsic motivation. *Journal of Personality and Social Psychology, 47*, 918–928.

Maphet, H.W., & Miller, A.L. (1982). Compliance, temptation, and conflicting instructions. *Journal of Personality and Social Psychology, 42*, 137–144.

Marlatt, G.A. (1983). The controlled-drinking controversy: A commentary. *American Psychologist, 38,* 1097–1110.

Marlatt, G.A. (1985). Relapse prevention: Theoretical rationale and overview of the model. In G.A. Marlatt & J.R. Gordon (Eds.), *Relapse prevention* (pp. 3–70). New York: Guilford.

Marlatt, G.A. (1987). Alcohol, the magic elixir: Stress, expectancy, and the transformation of emotional states. In E. Gottheil, K. Druly, S. Pashko, & P. Weinstein (Eds.), *Stress and addiction* (pp. 302–322). New York: Brunner/Mazel.

Marlatt, G.A., Demming, B., & Reid, J.B. (1973). Loss of control drinking in alcoholics: An experimental analogue. *Journal of Abnormal Psychology, 82,* 223–241.

Marlatt, G.A., & Gordon, J.R. (Eds.). (1985). *Relapse prevention.* New York: Guilford.

Marlatt, G.A., Kosturn, C.F., & Lang, A.R. (1975). Provocation to anger and opportunity for retaliation as determinants of alcohol consumption in social drinkers. *Journal of Abnormal Psychology, 84,* 652–659.

Marlatt, G.A., & Rohsenow, D.J. (1980). Cognitive processes in alcohol use: Expectancy and the balanced placebo design. In N.K. Mello (Ed.), *Advances in substance abuse: Behavioral and biological research* (Vol. 1, pp. 159–199). Greenwich, CT: JAI Press.

Maron, D.J., & Fortmann, S.P. (1987). Nicotine yield and measures of cigarette smoke exposure in a large population: Are lower-yield cigarettes safer? *American Journal of Public Health, 77,* 546–549.

Martin, L.L., Ward, D.W., Achee, J.W., & Wyer, R.S., Jr. (1993). Mood as input: People have to interpret the motivational implications of their moods. *Journal of Personality and Social Psychology, 64,* 317–326.

Masters, W.H., & Johnson, V.E. (1970). *Human sexual inadequacy.* Boston: Little, Brown.

Mathews, K.A., Glass, D.C., Rosenman, R.H., & Bortner, R.W. (1977). Competitive drive, pattern A, and coronary heart disease: A further analysis of some data from the Western Collaborative Group Study. *Journal of Chronic Diseases, 30,* 489–498.

Mayer, J.D., & Gaschke, Y.N. (1988). The experience and meta-experience of mood. *Journal of Personality and Social Psychology, 55,* 102–111.

Mayer, J.D., Salovey, P., Gomberg-Kaufman, S., & Blainy, K. (1991). A broader conception of mood experience. *Journal of Personality and Social Psychology, 60,* 100–111.

McCann, I.L., & Holmes, D.S. (1984). Influence of aerobic exercise on depression. *Journal of Personality and Social Psychology, 46,* 1142–1147.

McCann, K.L., Perri, M.G., Nezu, A.M., & Lowe, M. (1992). An investigation of counterregulatory eating in obese clinic attenders. *International Journal of Eating Disorders, 12,* 161–169.

McClelland, D.C. (1987). *Human motivation.* Cambridge, England: Cambridge University Press.

McClelland, D.C., Davis, W.B., Kalin, R., & Wanner, E. (1972). *The drinking man: Alcohol and human motivation.* New York: Free Press.

McElroy, S.L., Hudson, J.I., Pope, H.G., Jr., Keck, P.E., Jr., & Aizley, H.G. (1992). The DSM–III–R impulse control disorders not elsewhere classified: Clinical characteristics and relationship to other psychiatric disorders. *American Journal of Psychiatry, 149,* 318–327.

McElroy, S.L., Satlin, A., Pope, H.G., Jr., Keck, P.E., & Hudson, J. I. (1991). Treatment of compulsive shopping with antidepressants: A report of three case studies. *Annals of Clinical Psychiatry, 3*, 199–204.

McFall, R.M. (1970). Effects of self-monitoring on normal smoking behavior. *Journal of Consulting and Clinical Psychology, 35*, 135–142.

McFarlin, D.B., & Blascovich, J. (1981). Effects of self-esteem and performance feedback on future affective preferences and cognitive expectations. *Journal of Personality and Social Psychology, 40*, 521–531.

McGinnis, J.M., Shopland, D., & Brown, C. (1987). Tobacco and health: Trends in smoking and smokeless tobacco consumption. In L. Breslow, J.E. Fielding, & L.B. Lave (Eds.), *Annual review of public health* (Vol. 8). Palo Alto, CA: Annual Reviews.

McGlothin, W.H. (1956). Stability of choices among uncertain alternatives. *American Journal of Psychology, 69*, 604–615.

McKenna, R.J. (1972). Some effects of anxiety level and food cues on the eating behavior of obese and normal subjects: A comparison of the Schachterian and psychosomatic conceptions. *Journal of Personality and Social Psychology, 22*, 311–319.

McMorrow, M.J., & Foxx, R.M. (1985). Cigarette brand switching: Relating assessment strategies to the critical issues. *Psychological Bulletin, 98*, 139–159.

McNeill, W.H. (1982). *The pursuit of power: Technology, armed force, and society since A.D. 1000*. Chicago: University of Chicago Press.

McNulty, S. (1992). Nutritional counseling during severe caloric restriction and weight maintenance. In T.A. Wadden & T.B. VanItallie (Eds.), *Treatment of the seriously obese patient* (pp. 331–353). New York: Guilford.

Mearns, J. (1991). Coping with a breakup: Negative mood regulation expectancies and depression following the end of a romantic relationship. *Journal of Personality and Social Psychology, 60*, 327–334.

Mello, N.K., & Mendelson, J.H. (1972). Drinking patterns during work-contingent and non-contingent alcohol acquisition. *Psychosomatic Medicine, 24*, 1116–1121.

Merry, J. (1966). The 'loss of control' myth. *Lancet, 1*, 1257–1258.

Meyer, D.H. (1976). American intellectuals and the Victorian crisis of faith. In D. Howe (Ed.), *Victorian America* (pp. 59–80). Philadelphia: University of Pennsylvania Press.

Meyer, J.E., & Pudel, V. (1972). Experimental studies on food-intake in obese and normal weight subjects. *Journal of Psychosomatic Research, 16*, 305–308.

Meyer, J.M., & Stunkard, A.J. (1993). Genetics and human obesity. In A.J. Stunkard & T. Wadden (Eds.), *Obesity therapy and treatment* (pp. 137–149). New York: Raven.

Mikulincer, M. (1989). Cognitive interference and learned helplessness: The effects of off-task cognitions on performance following unsolvable problems. *Journal of Personality and Social Psychology, 57*, 129–135.

Milam, J.R., & Ketcham, K. (1981). *Under the influence: A guide to myths and realities of alcoholism*. Seattle, WA: Madrona Publishers.

Milgram, N.A., Batori, G., & Mowrer, D. (1993). Correlates of acedemic procrastination. *Journal of School Psychology, 31*, 487–500.

Miller, G.A., Galanter, E., & Pribram, K.H. (1960). *Plans and the structure of behavior*. New York: Holt.

Miller, P.M., Hersen, M., Eisler, R.M., & Hilsman, G. (1974). Effects of social stress on operant drinking of alcoholics and social drinkers. *Behavioral Research Therapy,* *12,* 67–72.

Miller, S.M. (1987). Monitoring and blunting: Validation of a questionnaire to assess styles of information seeking under threat. *Journal of Personality and Social Psychology, 52,* 345–353.

Miller, W.R. (1993). Alcoholism: Toward a better disease model. *Psychology of Addictive Behaviors, 7,* 129–136.

Miller, W.R., & Brown, J.M. (1991). Self-regulation as a conceptual basis for the prevention and treatment of addictive behaviors. In N. Heather, W.R. Miller, & J. Greeley (Eds.), *Self-control and the addictive behaviors* (pp. 3–79). Botany, Australia: Maxwell Macmillan.

Miller, W.R., & Rollnick, S. (1991). *Motivational interviewing: Preparing people to change addictive behavior.* New York: Guilford.

Mintz, J., Boyd, G., Rose, J.E., Charuvastra, V.C., & Jarvik, M.E. (1985). Alcohol increased cigarette smoking: A laboratory demonstration. *Addictive Behaviors, 10,* 203–207.

Mischel, H.N., & Mischel, W. (1983). Development of children's knowledge of self-control strategies. *Child Development, 54,* 603–619.

Mischel, W. (1974). Processes in delay of gratification. In L. Berkowitz (Ed.), *Advances in experimental social psychology* (Vol. 7, pp. 249–292). New York: Academic Press.

Mischel, W., Shoda, Y., & Peake, P.K. (1988). The nature of adolescent competencies predicted by preschool delay of gratification. *Journal of Personality and Social Psychology, 54,* 687–696.

Mischel, W., Shoda, Y., & Rodriguez, M.L. (1989). Delay of gratification in children. *Science, 244,* 933–938.

Mitchell, J.E., & Pyle, R.L. (1988). The diagnosis and clinical characteristics of bulimia. In B.J. Blinder, B.F. Chaitin, & R. Goldstein (Eds.), *The eating disorders* (pp. 267–273). New York: PMA Publishing Co.

Monson, T.C., Keel, R., Stephens, D., & Genung, V. (1982). Trait attributions: Relative validity, covariation with behavior, and prospect of future interaction. *Journal of Personality and Social Psychology, 42,* 1014–1024.

Morgan, W.P. (1985). Affective beneficence of vigorous physical activity. *Medicine and Science in Sports and Exercise, 17,* 94–106.

Morris, W.N., & Reilly, N.P. (1987). Toward the self-regulation of mood: Theory and research. *Motivation and Emotion, 11,* 215–249.

Morrow, J., & Nolen-Hoeksema, S. (1990). Effects of responses to depression on the remediation of depressive affect. *Journal of Personality and Social Psychology, 585,* 519–527.

Mount, R., Neziroglu, F., & Taylor, C.J. (1990). An obsessive–compulsive view of obesity and its treatment. *Journal of Clinical Psychology, 46,* 68–79.

Mullen, B. (1986). Atrocity as a function of lynch mob composition. *Personality and Social Psychology Bulletin, 12,* 187–197.

Mullen, B. (1987). Self-attention theory: Effects of group composition on the individual. In B. Mullen & G.R. Goethels (Eds.), *Theories of group behavior* (pp. 125–146). New York: Springer-Verlag.

Murray, D.M., Swan, A.V., Johnson, M.R., & Bewley, B.R. (1983). Some factors associated with increased risk of smoking by children. *Journal of Child Psychology and Psychiatry, 24,* 223–232.

Nathan, P.E. (1982). Blood alcohol level discrimination and diagnosis. In E.M. Pattison & E. Kaufman (Eds.), *Encyclopedic handbook of alcoholism* (pp. 64–71). New York: Gardner Press.

Nathan, P.E. (1988). The addictive personality is the behavior of the addict. *Journal of Consulting and Clinical Psychology, 56,* 183–190.

Nathan, P.E., Titler, N.A., Lowenstein, L., Solomon, P., & Rossi, A. (1970). Behavioral analysis of chronic alcoholism. *Archives of General Psychiatry, 22,* 419–430.

National Center for Health Statistics. (1985). Provisional data from the Health Promotion and Disease Prevention Supplement to the National Health Interview Survey: United States, January–March, 1985. *Advancedata,* November 2–5.

National Council on Alcoholism. (1986). *Facts on alcoholism.* New York: Author.

National Task Force on the Prevention and Treatment of Obesity. (1993). Very low-calorie diets. *Journal of the American Medical Association, 270,* 967–974.

Nesbitt, P.D. (1973). Smoking, physiological arousal, and emotional response. *Journal of Personality and Social Psychology, 25,* 137–144.

Neuberg, S.L. (1989). The goal of forming accurate impressions during social interactions: Attenuating the impact of negative expectancies. *Journal of Personality and Social Psychology, 56,* 374–386.

Newcomb, M., & Bentler, P. (1988). *Consequences of adolescent drug use: Impact on the lives of young adults.* Newbury Park, CA: Sage.

Niaura, R.S., Rohsenow, D.J., Binkoff, J.A., Monti, P.M., Pedraza, M., & Abrams, D.B. (1988). Relevance of cue reactivity to understanding alcohol and smoking relapse. *Journal of Abnormal Psychology, 97,* 133–152.

Nichols, S.L., & Newman, J.P. (1986). Effects of punishment on response latency in extroverts. *Journal of Personality and Social Psychology, 50,* 624–630.

NIH Technology Assessment Conference Panel. (1993). Methods for voluntary weight loss and control. *Annals of Internal Medicine, 199,* 764–770.

Nisbett, R.E. (1968). Taste, deprivation, and weight determinants of eating behavior. *Journal of Personality and Social Psychology, 10,* 107–116.

Nisbett, R., & Kanouse, D.E. (1969). Obesity, food deprivation, and supermarket shopping behavior. *Journal of Personality and Social Psychology, 12,* 289–294.

Nisbett, R.E., & Storms, M.D. (1974). Cognitive and social determinants of food intake. In H. London & R.E. Nisbett (Eds.), *Thought and feeling: Cognitive alteration of feeling states* (pp. 190–208). Chicago: Aldine.

Nisbett, R.E., & Wilson, T.D. (1977). Telling more than we can know: Verbal reports on mental processes. *Psychological Review, 84,* 231–259.

Nolen-Hoeksema, S. (1990). *Sex differences in depression.* Stanford, CA: Stanford University Press.

Nolen-Hoeksema, S. (1993). Sex differences in control of depression. In D.M. Wegner & J.W. Pennebaker (Eds.), *Handbook of mental control* (pp. 306–324). Englewood Cliffs, NJ: Prentice Hall.

Nolen-Hoeksema, S., & Morrow, J. (1991). A prospective study of depression and posttraumatic stress symptoms after a natural disaster: The 1989 Loma Prieta Earthquake. *Journal of Personality and Social Psychology, 61,* 115–121.

Notarius, C.I., Wemple, C., Ingraham, L.J., Burns, T.J., & Kollar, E. (1982). Multichannel responses to an interpersonal stressor: Interrelationships among facial display, heart rate, self-report of emotion, and threat appraisal. *Journal of Personality and*

Social Psychology, 43, 400–408.

Novaco, R.W. (1975). *Anger control: The development and evaluation of an experimental treatment.* Lexington, MA: Heath, Lexington Books.

Novaco, R.W. (1979). The cognitive regulation of anger and stress. In P.C. Kendall & S.D. Hollon (Eds.), *Cognitive–behavioral interventions: Theory, research, and procedures.* New York: Academic Press.

O'Connell, K.A., Cook, M.R., Gerkovich, M.M., Potocky, M., & Swan, G.E. (1990). Reversal theory and smoking: A state-based approach to ex-smokers' highly tempting situations. *Journal of Consulting and Clinical Psychology, 58*, 489–494.

O'Connell, K.A., & Martin, E.J. (1987). Highly tempting situations associated with abstinence, temporary lapse, and relapse among participants in smoking cessation programs. *Journal of Consulting and Clinical Psychology, 55*, 367–371.

O'Guinn, T.C., & Faber, R.J. (1989). Compulsive buying: A phenomenological exploration. *Journal of Consumer Research, 16*, 147–157.

O'Neil, P.M., & Jarrell, M.P. (1992). Psychological aspects of obesity and dieting. In T.A. Wadden & T.B. VanItallie (Eds.), *Treatment of the seriously obese patient* (pp. 252–270). New York: Guilford.

Orford, J. (1985). *Excessive appetites: A psychological view of addictions.* New York: Wiley.

Overmier, J.B., & Seligman, M.E.P. (1967). Effects of inescapable shock upon subsequent escape and avoidance learning. *Journal of Comparative and Physiological Psychology, 63*, 23–33.

Parker, G. (1987). *The Thirty Years' War.* New York: Military Heritage Press.

Parker, G.B., & Brown, L.B. (1979). Repertoires of responses to potential precipitants of depression. *Australian and New Zealand Journal of Psychiatry, 13*, 327–333.

Parker, G.B., & Brown, L.B. (1982). Coping behaviors that mediate between life events and depression. *Archives of General Psychology, 39*, 1386–1391.

Parrott, W.G. (1993). Beyond hedonism: Motives for inhibiting good moods and for maintaining bad moods. In D.M. Wegner & J.W. Pennebaker (Eds.), *Handbook of mental control* (pp. 278–305). Englewood Cliffs, NJ: Prentice Hall.

Pearlin, L.I., & Radabaugh, C.W. (1976). Economic strains and the coping functions of alcohol. *American Journal of Sociology, 82*, 652–663.

Pechacek, T. (1979). Modification of smoking behavior. In J. Grabowski & C.S. Bell (Eds.), *Measurement in the analysis of treatment of smoking behavior* (NIDA Research Monograph No. 48, pp. 127–188). Washington, DC: US Government Printing Office.

Peck, C.P. (1986). Risk-taking behavior and compulsive gambling. *American Psychologist, 41*, 461–465.

Pecsok, E.H., & Fremouw, W.J. (1988). Controlling laboratory bingeing among restrained eaters through self-monitoring and cognitive restructuring procedures. *Addictive Behaviors, 13*, 37–44.

Peele, S. (1989). *The diseasing of America.* Boston, MA: Houghton Mifflin.

Pendery, M.L., Maltzman, I.M., & West, L.J. (1982). Controlled drinking by alcoholics? New findings and a reevaluation of a major affirmative study. *Science, 217*, 169–174.

Pennebaker, J.W. (1989). Stream of consciousness and stress: Levels of thinking. In J.S. Uleman & J.A. Bargh (Eds.), *The direction of thought: Limits of awareness, intention and control* (pp. 327–350). New York: Guilford.

Pennebaker, J.W. (1990). *Opening up: The healing powers of confiding in others*. New York: Morrow.

Pennebaker, J.W. (1993). Social mechanisms of constraint. In D.M. Wegner & J.W. Pennebaker (Eds.), *Handbook of mental control* (pp. 200–219). Englewood Cliffs, NJ: Prentice Hall.

Pennebaker, J.W., & Chew, C.H. (1985). Behavioral inhibition and electrodermal activity during deception. *Journal of Personality and Social Psychology, 49*, 1427–1433.

Pennebaker, J.W., & Lightner, J.L. (1980). Competition of internal and external information in an exercise setting. *Journal of Personality and Social Psychology, 39*, 165–174.

Perri, M.G. (1985). Self-change strategies for the control of smoking, obesity, and problem drinking. In S. Shiffman & T.A. Wills (Eds.), *Coping and substance use* (pp. 295–317). Orlando, FL: Academic Press.

Pierce, J.P. (1989). International comparisons of trends in cigarette smoking prevalence. *American Journal of Public Health, 79*, 152–157.

Pihl, R.O., & Peterson, J.B. (1992). Etiology. In J. Langenbucher, B. McCrady, W. Frankenstein, & P.E. Nathan (Eds.), *Annual review of addictions research and treatment* (pp. 153–175). New York: Pergamon.

Pirie, P.L., Murray, D.M., & Luepker, R.V. (1991). Gender differences in cigarette smoking and quitting in a cohort of young adults. *American Journal of Public Health, 81*, 324–328.

Pliner, P. (1976). External responsiveness in the obese. *Addictive Behaviors, 1*, 169–175.

Pliner, P., & Iuppa, G. (1978). Effects of increasing awareness on food intake consumption in obese and normal weight subjects. *Addictive Behaviors, 3*, 19–24.

Polivy, J. (1976). Perception of calories and regulation of intake in restrained and unrestrained subjects. *Addictive Behaviors, 1*, 237–243.

Polivy, J. (1981). On the induction of mood in the laboratory: Discrete moods or multiple affect states? *Journal of Personality and Social Psychology, 41*, 803–817.

Polivy, J., Hackett, R., & Bycio, P. (1979). The effect of perceived smoking status on attractiveness. *Personality and Social Psychology Bulletin, 5*, 401–404.

Polivy, J., Heatherton, T.F., & Herman, C.P. (1988). Self-esteem, restraint, and eating behavior. *Journal of Abnormal Psychology, 97*, 354–356.

Polivy, J., & Herman, C.P. (1976a). The effects of alcohol on eating behavior: Disinhibition or sedation? *Addictive Behaviors, 1*, 121–125.

Polivy, J., & Herman, C.P. (1976b). Effects of alcohol on eating behavior: Influence of mood and perceived intoxication. *Journal of Abnormal Psychology, 85*, 601–606.

Polivy, J., & Herman, C.P. (1983). *Breaking the diet habit: The natural weight alternative*. New York: Basic Books.

Polivy, J., & Herman, C.P. (1985). Dieting and bingeing: A causal analysis. *American Psychologist, 40*, 193–201.

Polivy, J., Herman, C.P., Hackett, R., & Kuleshnyk, I. (1986). The effects of self-attention and public attention on eating in restrained and unrestrained subjects. *Journal of Personality and Social Psychology, 50*, 1253–1260.

Polivy, J., Schueneman, A.L., & Carlson, K. (1976). Alcohol and tension reduction: Cognitive and physiological effects. *Journal of Abnormal Psychology, 85*, 595–600.

Pomerleau, O.F. (1979). Behavioral factors in the establishment, maintenance, and cessation of smoking. In N.A. Krasnegor (Ed.), *The behavioral aspects of smoking* (pp. 47–96). Washington, DC: Public Health Service, National Institute on Drug Abuse.

Pomerleau, O.F., Fertig, J., Baker, L., & Cooney, N. (1983). Reactivity to alcohol cues in alcoholics and nonalcoholics: Implications for a stimulus control analysis of drinking. *Addictive Behaviors, 8*, 1–10.

Pomerleau, O.F., Fertig, J.B., & Shanahan, S.O. (1983). Nicotine dependence in cigarette smoking: An empirically-based multivariate model. *Pharmacology, Biochemistry and Behavior, 19*, 291–299.

Poulos, C.X., Hinson, R.E., & Siegel, S. (1981). The role of Pavlovian processes in drug tolerance and dependence: Implications for treatment. *Addictive Behaviors, 6*, 205–211.

Powers, W.T. (1973). *Behavior: The control of perception.* Chicago: Aldine.

Prochaska, J.O., & DiClemente, C.C. (1982). Transtheoretical therapy: Toward a more integrative model of change. *Psychotherapy: Theory, Research and Practice, 19*, 275–288.

Prochaska, J.O., & DiClemente, C.C. (1984). *The transtheoretical approach: Crossing traditional boundaries of change.* Homewood, IL: Dow Jones/Irwin, Inc.

Prochaska, J.O., & DiClemente, C.C. (1986). Toward a comprehensive model of change. In W. Miller and N. Heather (Eds.), *Treating addictive behaviors: Processes of change* (pp. 3–27). New York: Plenum.

Prochaska, J.O., Velicer, W.F., Guadagnoli, E., Rossi, J.S., & DiClemente, C.C. (1991). Patterns of change: Dynamic typology applied to smoking cessation. *Multivariate Behavioral Research, 26*, 83–107.

Pyszczynski, T., & Greenberg, J. (1987). Self-regulatory perseveration and the depressive self-focusing style: A self-awareness theory of reactive depression. *Psychological Bulletin, 201*, 122–138.

Rachlin, H. (1990). Why do people gamble and keep gambling despite heavy losses? *Psychological Science, 1*, 294–297.

Rachman, S., & de Silva, P. (1978). Abnormal and normal obsessions. *Behaviour Research and Therapy, 16*, 233–248.

Rachman, S.J., & Hodgson, R.J. (1980). *Obsessions and compulsions.* Englewood Cliffs, NJ: Prentice Hall.

Rawson, R.A., Obert, J.L., McCann, M.J., & Marinelli-Casey, P. (1993). Relapse prevention strategies in outpatient substance abuse treatment. *Psychology of Addictive Behaviors, 7*, 85–95.

Reed, G.F. (1985). *Obsessional experience and compulsive behaviour: A cognitive–structural approach.* Orlando, FL: Academic Press.

Reinert, R. (1968). The concept of alcoholism as a bad habit. *Bulletin of the Menninger Clinic, 20*, 166–180.

Repetti, R.L. (1989). Effects of daily workload on subsequent behavior during marital interaction: The roles of social withdrawal and spouse support. *Journal of Personality and Social Psychology, 57*, 651–659.

Rippere, V. (1976). Antidepressive behaviour: A preliminary report. *Behaviour Research and Therapy, 14*, 289–299.

Rippere, V. (1977). "What's the thing to do when you're feeling depressed?" A pilot study. *Behavior Research and Therapy, 15*, 185–191.

Riskind, J.H. (1984). They stoop to conquer: Guiding and self-regulatory functions of physical posture after success and failure. *Journal of Personality and Social Psychology, 47*, 479–493.

Riskind, J.H., & Gotay, C.C. (1982). Physical posture: Could it have regulatory or feedback effects on motivation and emotion? *Motivation and Emotion, 6*, 273–298.

Robins, L.N., Helzer, J.E., & Davis, D.H. (1975). Narcotic use in Southeast Asia and afterward: An interview study of 898 Vietnam veterans. *Archives of General Psychiatry, 32*, 955–961.

Rodgers, D.T. (1978). *The work ethic in industrial America 1850–1920.* Chicago: University of Chicago Press.

Rodin, J. (1978). Has the distinction between internal versus external control of feeding outlived its usefulness? In G. A. Bray (Eds.), *Recent advances in obesity research* (pp. 75–85). London: Newman.

Rodin, J., & Reed, D. (1988). Sweetness and eating disorders. In J. Dobbing (Ed.), *Sweetness* (pp. 193–204). Berlin: Springer-Verlag.

Rodriguez, M.L., Mischel, W., & Shoda, Y. (1989). Cognitive person variables in the delay of gratification of older children at risk. *Journal of Personality and Social Psychology, 57*, 358–367.

Rogers, P.J., & Hill, A.J. (1989). Breakdown of dietary restraint following mere exposure to food stimuli: Interrelationships between restraint, hunger, and food intake. *Addictive Behaviors, 14*, 387–397.

Rohde, P., Lewinsohn, P.M., Tilson, M., & Seeley, J.R. (1990). Dimensionality of coping and its relation to depression. *Journal of Personality and Social Psychology, 58*, 499–511.

Rohsenow, D.J. (1983). Drinking habits and expectancies about alcohol's effects for self versus others. *Journal of Consulting and Clinical Psychology, 51*, 752–756.

Rook, D.W. (1987). The buying impulse. *Journal of Consumer Research, 14*, 189–199.

Room, R. (1985). Dependence and society. *British Journal of Addiction, 80*, 133–139.

Rose, J.E. (1991). Transdermal nicotine and nasal nicotine administration as smoking-cessation treatments. In J.A. Cocores (Ed.), *The clinical management of nicotine dependence* (pp. 196–207). New York: Springer-Verlag.

Rosen, J.C. (1992). Body-image disorder: Definition, development, and contribution to eating disorders. In J.H. Crowther, S.E. Hobfall, M.A.P. Stephens, & D.L. Tennenbaum (Eds.), *The etiology of bulimia nervosa: The individual and familial context* (pp. 157–177). Washington, DC: Hemisphere.

Rosen, J.C., & Gross, J. (1987). Prevalence of weight reducing and weight gaining in adolescent girls and boys. *Health Psychology, 6*, 131–147.

Rosen, J.C., Leitenberg, H., Fisher, C., & Khazam, C. (1986). Binge-eating episodes in bulimia nervosa: The amount and type of food consumed. *International Journal of Eating Disorders, 5*, 255–267.

Rosenberg, H. (1993). Prediction of controlled drinking by alcoholics and problem drinkers. *Psychological Bulletin, 113*, 129–139.

Rosenthal, B.S., & Marx, R.D. (1981). Determinants of initial relapse episodes among dieters. *Obesity/Bariatric Medicine, 10*, 94–97.

Ross, L.D. (1974). Effects of manipulating salience of food upon consumption by obese and normal eaters. In S. Schachter & J. Rodin (Eds.) *Obese humans and rats*, (pp. 3–51). Hillsdale, NJ: Erlbaum.

Ross, L., Greene, D., & House, P. (1977). The 'false consensus effect': An egocentric bias in social perception and attribution processes. *Journal of Experimental Social Psychology, 13*, 279–301.

Roth, S., & Bootzin, R.R. (1974). Effects of experimentally induced expectancies of external control: An investigation of learned helplessness. *Journal of Personality and Social Psychology, 29*, 253–264.

Roth, S., & Kubal, L. (1975). Effects of noncontingent reinforcement on tasks of differing importance: Facilitation and learned helplessness. *Journal of Personality and Social Psychology, 32*, 680–691.

Rothbaum, F., Weisz, J.R., & Snyder, S.S. (1982). Changing the world and changing the self: A two-process model of perceived control. *Journal of Personality and Social Psychology, 42*, 5–37.

Rubin, L.B. (1976). *Worlds of pain: Life in the working-class family.* New York: Basic Books.

Ruderman, A.J. (1985). Dysphoric mood and overeating: A test of restraint theory's disinhibition hypothesis. *Journal of Abnormal Psychology, 94*, 78–85.

Ruderman, A.J. (1986). Dietary restraint: A theoretical and empirical review. *Psychological Bulletin, 99*, 247–262.

Russell, J.B. (1988). *The Prince of Darkness: Radical evil and the power of good in history.* Ithaca, NY: Cornell University Press.

Russell, M.A.H. (1971). Cigarette smoking: Natural history of a dependence disorder. *British Journal of Medical Psychology, 44*, 1–16.

Russell, M.A.H. (1990). The nicotine trap: A 40-year sentence for four cigarettes. *British Journal of Addiction, 85*, 293–300.

Russell, M.A.H., & Feyerabend, C. (1978). Cigarette smoking: A dependence on high-nicotine boli. *Drug Metabolism Reviews, 8*, 29–57.

Russell, M.A.H., Jarvis, M., Iyer, R., & Feyerabend, C. (1980). Relation of nicotine yield of cigarettes to blood nicotine concentrations in smokers. *British Medical Journal, 280*, 972–976.

Salovey, P. (1992). Mood-induced self-focused attention. *Journal of Personality and Social Psychology, 62*, 699–707.

Salovey, P. (1994, August). *Where it hurts most: Social comparison, jealousy, envy, and self-concept.* Paper presented to the American Psychological Association, Los Angeles.

Salovey, P., Hsee, C.K., & Mayer, J.D. (1993). Emotional intelligence and the self-regulation of affect. In D.M. Wegner & J.W. Pennebaker (Eds.), *Handbook of mental control* (pp. 258–277). Englewood Cliffs, NJ: Prentice Hall.

Salovey, P., & Mayer, J.D. (1990). Emotional intelligence. *Imagination, Cognition, & Personality, 9*, 185–212.

Salovey, P., & Rodin, J. (1985). Cognitions about the self: Connecting feelings states and social behavior. In P. Shaver (Ed.), *Self, situations, and social behavior: Review of personality and social psychology* (Vol. 6, pp. 143–166). Beverly Hills, CA: Sage.

Sangiacomo, M. (1990, September 9). Phone sex: What you don't know about 900 lines could hurt you (and your wallet). *Plain Dealer Magazine*, pp. 18–22.

Sansone, C., & Harackiewicz, J.M. (in press). "I don't feel like it": The function of interest in self-regulation. In L. Martin & A. Tesser (Eds.), *Goals and affect.* Hillsdale, NJ: Erlbaum.

Sansone, C., Weir, C., Harpster, L., & Morgan, C. (1992). Once a boring task, always a boring task? Interest as a self-regulatory mechanism. *Journal of Personality and*

Social Psychology, 63, 379–390.

Sarafino, E.P. (1990). *Health psychology: Biopsychosocial interactions.* New York: Wiley.

Sarason, I. (1981). Test anxiety, stress, and social support. *Journal of Personality, 49*, 101–114.

Sartre, J.P. (1953). *The existential psychoanalysis* (H.E. Barnes, Trans.). New York: Philosophical Library.

Sayette, M.A. (1993). An appraisal-disruption model of alcohol's effectiveness on stress responses in social drinkers. *Psychological Bulletin, 114*, 459–476.

Schachter, S. (1971). Some extraordinary facts about obese humans and rats. *American Psychologist, 26*, 129–144.

Schachter, S. (1982). Recidivism and self-cure of smoking and obesity. *American Psychologist, 37*, 436–444.

Schachter, S., Goldman, R., & Gordon, A. (1968). Effects of fear, food deprivation, and obesity on eating. *Journal of Personality and Social Psychology, 10*, 91–97.

Schachter, S., & Gross, L.P. (1968). Manipulated time and eating behavior. *Journal of Personality and Social Psychology, 20*, 98–106.

Schachter, S., & Rodin, J. (1974). *Obese humans and rats.* Hillsdale, NJ: Erlbaum.

Schachter, S., Silverstein, B., Kozlowski, L.T., Perlick, D., Herman, C.P., & Liebling, B. (1977). Studies of the interaction of psychological and pharmacological determinants of smoking. *Journal of Experimental Psychology: General, 106*, 3–40.

Schachter, S., & Singer, J.E. (1962). Cognitive, social and physiological determinants of emotional state. *Psychological Review, 69*, 379–399.

Schalling, D. (1985). Personality correlates of elevated blood pressure: Anxiety, unexpressed anger, and lack of assertiveness. In C. Spielberger, I. Sarason, & P. Defares (Eds.), *Stress and anxiety* (pp. 241–251). Washington, DC: Hemisphere.

Schotte, D.E., Cools, J., & McNally, R.J. (1990). Film-induced negative affect triggers overeating in restrained eaters. *Journal of Abnormal Psychology, 99*, 317–320.

Schwarz, N. (1990). Feelings as information: Informational and motivational function of affective states. In E.T. Higgins & R.M. Sorrentino (Eds.), *Handbook of motivation and cognition* (Vol. 2, pp. 527–561). New York: Guilford Press.

Sedikides, C. (1992). Changes in the valence of the self as a function of mood. In M. Clark (Ed.), *Emotion and social behavior: Review of personality and social psychology* (pp. 271–311). Newbury Park, CA: Sage.

Sedikides, C. (1993). Assessment, enhancement, and verification determinants of the self-evaluation process. *Journal of Personality and Social Psychology, 65*, 317–338.

Seligman, M.E.P. (1975). *Helplessness: On depression, development, and death.* San Francisco: Freeman.

Seligman, M.E.P. (1994). *What you can change and what you can't: The ultimate guide to self-improvement.* New York: Knopf.

Shaffer, D.R., & Case, T. (1982). On the decision to testify in one's own behalf: Effects of withheld evidence, defendant's sexual preferences, and juror dogmatism on juridic decisions. *Journal of Personality and Social Psychology, 42*, 335–346.

Shaffer, H.J. (1985). The disease controversy: Of metaphors, maps and menus. *Journal of Psychoactive Drugs, 17*, 65–76.

Shapiro, D., Schwartz, G.E., Tursky, B., & Schnidman, S.R. (1971). Smoking on cue: A behavioral approach to smoking reduction. *Journal of Health and Social Behavior, 12*, 108–113.

Shedler, J., & Block, J. (1990). Adolescent drug use and psychological health. *American Psychologist, 45*, 612–630.

Sherman, S.J., Presson, C., Chassin, L., Corty, E., & Olshavsky, R. (1983). The false consensus effect in estimates of smoking prevalence: Underlying mechanisms. *Personality and Social Psychology Bulletin, 9*, 197–207.

Shiffman, S.M. (1982). Relapse following smoking cessation: A situational analysis. *Journal of Consulting and Clinical Psychology, 50*, 71–86.

Shiffman, S.M., & Jarvik, M.E. (1976). Smoking withdrawal symptoms in two weeks of abstinence. *Psychopharmacology, 50*, 35–39.

Shiffman, S., & Jarvik, M.E. (1984). Cigarette smoking, physiological arousal, and emotional response: Nesbitt's paradox re-examined. *Addictive Behaviors, 9*, 95–98.

Shiffman, S., Read, L., Maltese, J., Rapkin, D., & Jarvik, M.E. (1985). Preventing relapse in ex-smokers: A self-management approach. in G.A. Marlatt & J.R. Gordon (Eds.), *Relapse prevention: Maintenance strategies in the treatment of addictive behaviors* (pp. 472–520). New York: Guilford.

Shimokata, H., Muller, D.C., & Andres, R. (1989). Studies in the distribution of body fat: III. Effects of cigarette smoking. *Journal of the American Medical Association, 261*, 1169–1175.

Shoda, Y., Mischel, W., & Peake, P.K. (1990). Predicting adolescent cognitive and self-regulatory competencies from preschool delay of gratification: Identifying diagnostic conditions. *Developmental Psychology, 26*, 978–986.

Sichrovsky, P. (1988). *Born guilty: Children of Nazi families* (J. Steinberg, Trans.). New York: Basic Books.

Silver, R.L., Boon, C., & Stones, M.H. (1983). Searching for meaning in misfortune: Making sense of incest. *Journal of Social Issues, 39*, 81–102.

Silverstein, B. (1982). Cigarette smoking, nicotine addiction, and relaxation. *Journal of Personality and Social Psychology, 42*, 946–950.

Silverstein, S.J., Nathan, P.E., & Taylor, H. (1974). Blood alcohol level estimation and controlled drinking by alcoholics. *Behavior Therapy, 5*, 1–15.

Singer, J.A., & Salovey, P. (1988). Mood and memory: Evaluating the network theory of affect. *Clinical Psychology Review, 8*, 211–251.

Skog, O., & Duckert, F. (1991). The development of alcoholics' and heavy drinkers' consumption: A longitudinal study. *Journal of Studies on Alcohol, 54*, 178–188.

Slochower, J. (1976). Emotional labelling and overeating in obese and normal weight individuals. *Psychosomatic Medicine, 38*, 131–139.

Slochower, J. (1983). Life stress, weight, and cue salience. In J. Slochower (Ed.), *Excessive eating* (pp. 75–87). New York: Human Sciences Press.

Slochower, J., & Kaplan, S.P. (1980). Anxiety, perceived control and eating in obese and normal weight persons. *Appetite, 1*, 75–83.

Slochower, J., & Kaplan, S.P. (1983). Effects of cue salience and weight on responsiveness to uncontrollable anxiety. In J. Slochower (Ed.), *Excessive eating* (pp. 68–74). New York: Human Sciences Press.

Slochower, J., Kaplan, S.P., & Mann, L. (1981). The effects of life stress and weight on mood and eating. *Appetite, 2*, 115–125.

Smith, S.M., Goodman, R., Thacker, S., Burton, A., Parsons, J., & Hudson, P. (1989). Alcohol and fatal injuries: Temporal patterns. *American Journal of Preventive Medicine, 5*, 296–302.

Sobal, J., & Stunkard, A.J. (1989). Socioeconomic status and obesity: A review of the literature. *Psychological Bulletin, 105*, 260–275.

Sobell, L.C., Sobell, M.B., Kozlowski, L.T., & Toneatto, T. (1990). Alcohol or tobacco research versus alcohol and tobacco research. *British Journal of Addiction, 85*, 263–269.

Sobell, L.C., Sobell, M.B., & Toneatto, T. (1991). Recovery from alcohol problems without treatment. In N. Heather, W.R. Miller, & J. Greeley (Eds.), *Self-control and the addictive behaviors* (pp. 198–242). Botany, Australia: Maxwell Macmillan.

Sobell, M.B., & Sobell, L.C. (1973). Individualized behavior therapy for alcoholics. *Behavior Therapy, 4*, 49–72.

Sobell, M.B., & Sobell, L.C. (1989). Moratorium on Maltzman: An appeal to reason. *Journal of Studies on Alcohol, 50*, 473–480.

Soloman, L.J., & Rothblum, E.D. (1984). Academic procrastination: Frequency and cognitive–behavioral correlates. *Journal of Counseling Psychology, 31*, 503–509.

Solomon, R.L. (1980). The opponent-process theory of acquired motivations: The costs of pleasure and the benefits of pain. *American Psychologist, 35*, 691–712.

Solomon, R.L., & Corbit, J.D. (1974). An opponent-process theory of motivation: I. Temporal dynamics of affect. *Psychological Review, 81*, 119–145.

Sorensen, G., Pechacek, T., & Pallonen, U. (1986). Occupational and worksite norms and attitudes about smoking cessation. *American Journal of Public Health, 76*, 544–549.

Spence, J.T., Helmreich, R.L., & Pred, R.S. (1987). Impatience versus achievement strivings in the type A pattern: Differential effects on students' health and academic achievement. *Journal of Applied Psychology, 72*, 522–528.

Spencer, J.A., & Fremouw, W.J. (1979). Binge eating as a function of restraint and weight classification. *Journal of Abnormal Psychology, 88*, 262–267.

Spiegel, T.A., Shrager, E.E., & Stellar, E. (1989). Responses of lean and obese subjects to preloads, deprivation, and palatability. *Appetite, 13*, 45–69.

Staw, B.M. (1976). Knee-deep in the big muddy: A study of escalating commitment to a chosen course of action. *Organizational Behavior and Human Performance, 16*, 27–44.

Steele, C.M. (1992, April). Race and the schooling of black Americans. *Atlantic, 269*(4), 68–77.

Steele, C.M., & Josephs, R.A. (1990). Alcohol myopia: Its prized and dangerous effects. *American Psychologist, 45*, 921–933.

Steele, C.M., & Southwick, L. (1985). Alcohol and social behavior I: The psychology of drunken excess. *Journal of Personality and Social Psychology, 48*, 18–34.

Steinberg, S.A., & Yalch, R.F. (1978). When eating begets buying: The effects of food samples on obese and nonobese shoppers. *Journal of Consumer Research, 4*, 243–246.

Steinmetz, S.K. (1977). *The cycle of violence*. New York: Praeger.

Stekel, W. (1949). *Compulsion and doubt*. New York: Grosset & Dunlap.

Stevens, V.J., & Hollis, J.F. (1989). Preventing smoking relapse, using an individually tailored skills-training technique. *Journal of Consulting and Clinical Psychology, 57*, 420–424.

Stockwell, T. (1985). Stress and alcohol. *Stress Medicine, 1*, 209–215.

Stockwell, T. (1991). Experimental analogues of loss of control: A review of human drinking studies. In N. Heather, W.R. Miller, & J. Greeley (Eds.), *Self-control and the addictive behaviors* (pp. 180–197). Botany, Australia: Maxwell Macmillan.

Stout, R.J. (1990). Fluoxetine for the treatment of compulsive face picking [letter]. *American Journal of Psychiatry, 147,* 370.

Strack, F., Martin, L., & Stepper, S. (1988). Inhibiting and facilitating conditions of the human smile: A nonobtrusive test of the facial feedback hypothesis. *Journal of Personality and Social Psychology, 54,* 768–777.

Strack, S., & Coyne, J.W. (1983). Social confirmation of dysphoria: Shared and private reactions to depression. *Journal of Personality and Social Psychology, 44,* 798–806.

Straus, M. (1974). Leveling, civility, and violence in the family. *Journal of Marriage and Family, 36,* 13–29.

Straus, M., Gelles, R., & Steinmetz, S. (1980). *Behind closed doors: Violence in the American family.* New York: Anchor/Doubleday.

Strickler, D.P., Tomaszewski, R., Maxwell, W., & Suib, M.R. (1979). The effects of relaxation instructions on drinking behaviours in the presence of stress. *Behaviour Research and Therapy, 17,* 45–51.

Striegel-Moore, R.H., Silberstein, L.R., Frensch, P., & Rodin, J. (1989). A prospective study of disordered eating among college students. *International Journal of Eating Disorders, 8,* 499–509.

Strube, M.J., Turner, C.W., Cerro, D., Stevens, J., & Hinchey, F. (1984). Interpersonal aggression and the Type-A coronary-prone behavior pattern: A theoretical distinction and practical implications. *Journal of Personality and Social Psychology, 47,* 839–847.

Stuart, R. (1967). Behavioural control of overeating. *Behaviour Research and Therapy, 5,* 357–365.

Stunkard, A.J. (1959). Obesity and the denial of hunger. *Psychosomatic Medicine, 21,* 281–289.

Stunkard, A.J. (1992). An overview of current treatments for obesity. In T.A. Wadden & T.B. VanItallie (Eds.), *Treatment of the seriously obese patient* (pp. 33–43). New York: Guilford.

Stunkard, A.J., & Koch, C. (1964). The interpretation of gastric motility I: Apparent bias in the reports of hunger by obese patients. *Archives of General Psychiatry, 11,* 74–82.

Stunkard, A.J., & Pennick, S.B. (1979). Behavior modification in the treatment of obesity: The problem of maintaining weight loss. *Archives of General Psychiatry, 36,* 801–806.

Sullivan, H.S. (1953). *The interpersonal theory of psychiatry.* New York: Norton.

Tavris, C. (1989). *Anger: The misunderstood emotion.* New York: Simon & Shuster (Touchstone).

Taylor, M.J., & Cooper, P.J. (1992). An experimental study of the effect of mood on body size perception. *Behaviour Research and Therapy, 30,* 53–58.

Taylor, S.E. (1989). *Positive illusions: Creative self-deception and the healthy mind.* New York: Basic Books.

Taylor, S.E., & Brown, J.D. (1988). Illusion and well-being: A social psychological perspective on mental health. *Psychological Bulletin, 103,* 193–210.

Taylor, S.P., & Leonard, K.E. (1983). Alcohol and human physical aggression. In R.G.

Geen & E.I. Donnnerstein (Eds.), *Aggression: Theoretical and empirical reviews: Vol 2. Issues in research* (pp. 77–101). New York: Academic Press.

Tedeschi, J.T., & Felson, R.B. (in press). *Aggression and coercive actions: A social interactionist perspective*. Washington, DC: American Psychological Association.

Tetlock, P.E. (1985). Accountability: A social check on the fundamental attribution error. *Social Psychology Quarterly, 48*, 227–236.

Tetlock, P.E., & Boettger, R. (1989). Accountability: A social magnifier of the dilution effect. *Journal of Personality and Social Psychology, 57*, 388–398.

Thayer, R.E. (1987). Energy, tiredness, and tension effects of a sugar snack versus moderate exercise. *Journal of Personality and Social Psychology, 52*, 119–125.

Thayer, R.E. (1989). *The biopsychology of mood and arousal*. New York: Oxford University Press.

Thombs, D.L., Beck, K.H., & Mahoney, C.A. (1993). Effects of social context and gender on drinking patterns of young adults. *Journal of Counseling Psychology, 40*, 115–119.

Tice, D.M. (1991). Esteem protection or enhancement? Self-handicapping motives and attributions differ by trait self-esteem. *Journal of Personality and Social Psychology, 60*, 711–725.

Tice, D.M. (1993). The social motivations of people with low self-esteem. In R. Baumeister (Ed.), *Self-esteem: The puzzle of low self-regard* (pp. 37–53). New York: Plenum.

Tice, D.M. (1994). *Staying angry: Health effects of suppressing versus venting anger*. Manuscript in preparation.

Tice, D.M., & Baumeister, R.F. (1990). Self-esteem, self-handicapping, and self-presentation: The strategy of inadequate practice. *Journal of Personality, 58*, 443–464.

Tice, D.M., & Baumeister, R.F. (1993). Controlling anger: Self-induced emotion change. In D.M. Wegner & J.W. Pennebaker (Eds.), *Handbook of mental control* (pp. 393–409). Englewood Cliffs, NJ: Prentice Hall.

Tice, D.M., Muraven, M., & Baumeister, R.F. (1994). *Techniques of affect regulation: Everyday methods of altering emotional states*. Manuscript in preparation.

Toch, H. (1992). *Violent men: An inquiry into the psychology of violence*. Washington, DC: American Psychological Association.

Tom, G. (1983). Effect of deprivation on the grocery shopping behavior of obese and nonobese consumers. *International Journal of Obesity, 7*, 307–311.

Tucker, J.A., Vuchinich, R.E., Sobell, M.B., & Maisto, S.A. (1980). Normal drinkers' alcohol consumption as a function of conflicting motives induced by intellectual performance stress. *Addictive Behaviors, 15*, 171–178.

Underwood, B., Moore, B.S., & Rosenhan, D.L. (1973). Affect and self-gratification. *Developmental Psychology, 8*, 209–214.

United States Department of Health and Human Services. (1988). *The health consequences of smoking: Nicotine addiction. A report of the Surgeon General*. Washington, DC: US Government Printing Office.

United States Department of Health and Human Services. (1993). *Alcohol and health* [Preprint]. Public Health Service, National Institute of Alcohol Abuse and Alcoholism. Washington, DC: US Government Printing Office

Vaillant, G.E. (1983). *The natural history of alcoholism*. Cambridge, MA: Harvard University Press.

Vallacher, R.R., & Wegner, D.M. (1985). *A theory of action identification*. Hillsdale, NJ: Erlbaum.

Vallacher, R.R., & Wegner, D.M. (1987). What do people think they're doing?: Action identification and human behavior. *Psychological Review, 94*, 3–15.

Vallone, R.P., Griffin, D.W., Lin, S., & Ross, L. (1990). Overconfident prediction of future actions and outcomes by self and others. *Journal of Personality and Social Psychology, 58*, 582–592.

VanEgern, L.F., Abelson, J.L., & Thornton, D.W. (1978). Cardiovascular consequences of expressing anger in a mutually dependent relationship. *Journal of Psychosomatic Research, 22*, 537–548.

Van Hook, E., & Higgins, E.T. (1988). Self-related problems beyond the self-concept: Motivational consequences of discrepant self-guides. *Journal of Personality and Social Psychology, 55*, 625–633.

VanItallie, T.B., & Lew, E.A. (1992). Assessment of morbidity and mortality risk in the overweight patient. In T.A. Wadden & T.B. VanItallie (Eds.), *Treatment of the seriously obese patient* (pp. 3–32). New York: Guilford.

Velten, E. (1968). A laboratory task for the induction of mood states. *Behavior Research and Therapy, 6*, 473–482.

Volberg, R.A., & Steadman, H.J. (1989). Prevalence estimates of pathological gambling in New Jersey and Maryland. *American Journal of Psychiatry, 146*, 1618–1620.

Wack, J.T., & Rodin, J. (1982). Smoking and its effects on body weight and the systems of caloric regulation. *American Journal of Clinical Nutrition, 35*, 366–380.

Wadden, T.A. (1993). The treatment of obesity: An overview. In A.J. Stunkard & T.A. Wadden (Eds.), *Obesity: Theory and Therapy* (2nd edition) (pp. 197–218). New York: Raven Press.

Wadden, T.A., & Foster, G.D. (1992). Behavioral assessment and treatment of markedly obese patients. In T.A. Wadden & T.B. VanItallie (Eds.), *Treatment of the seriously obese patient* (pp. 290–330). New York: Guilford.

Wadden, T.A., & Letizia, K.A. (1992). Predictors of attrition and weight loss in patients treated by moderate and caloric restriction. In T.A. Wadden & T.B. VanItallie (Eds.), *Treatment of the seriously obese patient* (pp. 383–410). New York: Guilford.

Wagenaar, W.A. (1988). *Paradoxes of gambling behaviour*. Hillsdale, NJ: Erlbaum.

Wagenaar, W.A., & Keren, G. (1988). Chance and luck are not the same thing. *Journal of Behavioral Decision Making, 1*, 65–75.

Wagenaar, W.A., Keren, G., & Pleit-Kuiper, A. (1984). The multiple objectives of gamblers. *Acta Psychologica, 56*, 167–178.

Wagner, R.K., & Sternberg, R.J. (1985). Practical intelligence in real-world pursuits: The role of tacit knowledge. *Journal of Personality and Social Psychology, 49*, 436–458.

Waid, W.M., & Orne, M.T. (1982). Reduced electrodermal response to conflict, failure to inhibit dominant behaviors, and delinquency proneness. *Journal of Personality and Social Psychology, 43*, 769–774.

Walsh, D.C., Hingson, R.W., Merrigan, D.M., Levenson, S.M., Cupples, L.A., Heeren, T., Coffman, G.A., Becker, C.A., Barker, T.A., Hamilton, S.K., McGuire, T.G., & Kelly, C.A. (1991). A randomized trial of treatment options for alcohol-abusing workers. *New England Journal of Medicine, 325*, 775–782.

Ward, C.H., & Eisler, R.M. (1987). Type A behavior, achievement striving, and a dysfunctional self-evaluation system. *Journal of Personality and Social Psychology, 53*, 318–326.

Wardle, J., & Beales, S. (1988). Control and loss of control over eating: An experimental investigation. *Journal of Abnormal Psychology, 97*, 35–40.

Wegner, D.M. (1989). *White bears and other unwanted thoughts.* New York: Vintage.

Wegner, D.M. (1992). You can't always think what you want: Problems in the suppression of unwanted thoughts. In M. Zanna (Ed.), *Advances in experimental social psychology* (Vol. 25). San Diego: Academic Press.

Wegner, D.M. (1994). Ironic processes of mental control. *Psychological Review, 101*, 34–52.

Wegner, D.M., & Erber, R. (1992). The hyperaccessibility of suppressed thoughts. *Journal of Personality and Social Psychology, 63*, 903–912.

Wegner, D.M., & Erber, R. (1993). Social foundations of mental control. In D.M. Wegner & J.W. Pennebaker (Eds.), *Handbook of mental control* (pp. 36–56). Englewood Cliffs, NJ: Prentice Hall.

Wegner, D.M., Erber, R., & Zanakos, S. (1993). Ironic processes in the mental control of mood and mood related thought. *Journal of Personality and Social Psychology, 65*, 1093–1107.

Wegner, D.M., & Giuliano, T. (1980). Arousal-induced attention to self. *Journal of Personality and Social Psychology, 38*, 719–726.

Wegner, D.M., Schneider, D.J., Carter, S.R., & White, T.L. (1987). Paradoxical effects of thought suppression. *Journal of Personality and Social Psychology, 53*, 5–13.

Wegner, D.M., Shortt, J.W., Blake, A.W., & Page, M.S. (1990). The suppression of exciting thoughts. *Journal of Personality and Social Psychology, 58*, 409–418.

Wegner, D.M., Vallacher, R.R., & Dizadji, D. (1989). Do alcoholics know what they're doing? Identifications of the act of drinking. *Basic and Applied Social Psychology, 10*, 197–210.

Weinstein, N.D. (1987). Unrealistic optimism about susceptibility to health problems: Conclusions from a community-wide sample. *Journal of Behavioral Medicine, 10*, 481–500.

Weisfeld, G.E., & Beresford, J.M. (1982). Erectness of posture as an indicator of dominance or success in humans. *Motivation and Emotion, 6*, 113–131.

Wenzlaff, R.M., Wegner, D.M., & Klein, S.B. (1991). The role of thought suppression in the bonding of thought and mood. *Journal of Personality and Social Psychology, 60*, 500–508.

Wenzlaff, R.M., Wegner, D.M., & Roper, D.W. (1988). Depression and mental control: The resurgence of unwanted negative thoughts. *Journal of Personality and Social Psychology, 55*, 882–892.

Wertheim, E.H., & Schwartz, J.C. (1983). Depression, guilt, and self-management of pleasant and unpleasant events. *Journal of Personality and Social Psychology, 45*, 884–889.

Wicker, A.W. (1969). Attitudes versus actions: The relationship of verbal and overt behavioral responses to attitude objects. *Journal of Social Issues, 25*, 41–78.

Wicklund, R.A. (1975). Discrepancy reduction or attempted distraction? A reply to Liebling and Shaver. *Journal of Experimental Social Psychology, 11*, 78–81.

Wicklund, R.A. (1982). How society uses self-awareness. In J. Sulb (Ed.), *Psychological Perspectives on the Self* (Vol. 1, pp. 209–230). Hillsdale, NJ: Erlbaum.

Williamson, D.A. (1990). *Assessment of eating disorders: Obesity, anorexia, and bulimia nervosa.* New York: Pergamon.

Wilson, G.D. (1982). Feminism and marital dissatisfaction. *Individual Differences, 3,* 345–347.

Wilson, G.T. (1988). Alcohol and anxiety. *Behavior Research and Therapy, 26,* 369–381.

Wilson, G.T., Abrams, D.B., & Lipscomb, T. (1980). Effects of increasing levels of intoxication and drinking pattern on social anxiety. *Journal of Studies on Alcohol, 41,* 250–264.

Wilson, G.T., & Brownell, K.D. (1980). Behavior therapy for obesity: An evaluation of treatment outcome. *Advances in Behavior Research and Therapy, 3,* 49–86.

Wilson, T.D., Dunn, D.S., Bybee, J.A., Hyman, D.B., & Rotondo, J.A. (1984). Effects of analyzing reasons on attitude–behavior consistency. *Journal of Personality and Social Psychology, 44,* 5–16.

Wine, J. (1971). Test anxiety and direction of attention. *Psychological Bulletin, 76,* 92–104.

Wise, R.A., & Bozarth, M.A. (1987). A psychomotor stimulant theory of addictions. *Psychological Review, 94,* 469–492.

Wood, J.V., Saltzberg, J.A., & Goldsamt, L.A. (1990). Does affect induce self-focused attention? *Journal of Personality and Social Psychology, 58,* 899–908.

Woody, E.Z., Costanzo, P.R., Leifer, H., & Conger, J. (1981). The effects of taste and caloric perceptions on the eating of restrained and unrestrained subjects. *Cognitive Research and Therapy, 5,* 381–390.

Wooley, O.W., Wooley, S.C., & Woods, W. (1975). Appetite for palatable food as a function of the caloric density of previous meal. *Journal of Comparative and Physiological Psychology, 89,* 619–625.

Wright, J., & Mischel, W. (1982). Influence of affect on cognitive social learning person variables. *Journal of Personality and Social Psychology, 43,* 901–914.

Wyden, P. (1983). *The passionate war: The narrative history of the Spanish Civil War.* New York: Simon & Schuster (Touchstone).

Wyer, R.S., Jr., & Unverzagt, W.H. (1985). Effects of instructions to disregard information on its subsequent recall and use in making judgments. *Journal of Personality and Social Psychology, 48,* 533–549.

Zajonc, R. (1965). Social facilitation. *Science, 149,* 269–274.

Zeigarnik, B. (1927). Über das Behalten von erledigten und unerledigten Handlungen. *Psychologische Forschung, 9,* 1–85.

Zellner, D.A., Harner, D.E., & Adler, R.L. (1989). Effects of eating abnormalities and gender on perceptions of desirable body shapes. *Journal of Abnormal Psychology, 98,* 93–96.

Zillman, D. (1978). Attribution and misattribution of excitatory reactions. In J.H. Harvey, W.J. Ickes, & R.F. Kidd (Eds.), *New directions in attribution research* (Vol. 2, pp. 335–368). Hillsdale, NJ: Erlbaum.

Zillman, D. (1979). *Hostility and aggression.* Hillsdale, NJ: Erlbaum.

Zillman, D. (1988). Mood management: Using entertainment to full advantage. In L. Donohew, H.E. Sypher, & E.T. Higgins (Eds.), *Communication, social cognition, and affect* (pp. 147–171). Hillsdale, NJ: Erlbaum.

Zillman, D. (1993). The mental control of angry aggression. In D.M. Wegner & J.W. Pennebaker (Eds.), *Handbook of mental control* (pp. 370–392). Englewood Cliffs, NJ: Prentice Hall.

Zillman, D., Hezel, R.T., & Medoff, N.J. (1980). The effect of affective states on selective exposure to televised entertainment fare. *Journal of Applied Social Psychology, 10,* 323–339.

Zillman, D., Johnson, R.C., & Day, K. (1974). Attribution of apparent arousal and proficiency of recovery from sympathetic activation affecting excitation transfer to aggressive behavior. *Journal of Experimental Social Psychology, 10,* 503–515.

Zillman, D., Katcher, A.H., & Milavsky, B. (1972). Excitation transfer from physical exercise to subsequent aggressive behavior. *Journal of Experimental Social Psychology, 8,* 247–259.

Zucker, R.A., & Gomberg, E.S.L. (1986). Etiology of alcoholism reconsidered: The case for a biopsychosocial process. *American Psychologist, 41,* 783–793.

Index